Transboundary Risk Management

Saïd Business School
University of Oxford

Shelfmark: *JNE EER*
(lin)

The International Institute for Applied Systems Analysis

is an interdisciplinary, nongovernmental research institution founded in 1972 by leading scientific organizations in 12 countries. Situated near Vienna, in the center of Europe, IIASA has been producing valuable scientific research on economic, technological, and environmental issues for nearly three decades.

IIASA was one of the first international institutes to systematically study global issues of environment, technology, and development. IIASA's Governing Council states that the Institute's goal is: *to conduct international and interdisciplinary scientific studies to provide timely and relevant information and options, addressing critical issues of global environmental, economic, and social change, for the benefit of the public, the scientific community, and national and international institutions.* Research is organized around three central themes:

- Energy and Technology;
- Environment and Natural Resources;
- Population and Society.

The Institute now has National Member Organizations in the following countries:

Austria
The Austrian Academy of Sciences

Bulgaria*
Ministry of Environment and Waters

Czech Republic
The Academy of Sciences of the Czech Republic

Finland
The Finnish Committee for IIASA

Germany**
The Association for the Advancement of IIASA

Hungary
The Hungarian Committee for Applied Systems Analysis

Japan
The Japan Committee for IIASA

Republic of Kazakhstan*
The Ministry of Science –
The Academy of Sciences

Netherlands
The Netherlands Organization for Scientific Research (NWO)

Norway
The Research Council of Norway

Poland
The Polish Academy of Sciences

Russian Federation
The Russian Academy of Sciences

Slovak Republic*
The Executive Slovak National Committee for IIASA

Sweden
The Swedish Research Council for Environment, Agricultural Sciences and Spatial Planning (FORMAS)

Ukraine
The Ukrainian Academy of Sciences

United States of America
The American Academy of Arts and Sciences

*Associate member
**Affiliate

RISK, SOCIETY, AND POLICY SERIES
Edited by Ragnar E. Löfstedt

Transboundary Risk Management

Edited by

Joanne Linnerooth-Bayer, Ragnar E. Löfstedt,
and Gunnar Sjöstedt

IIASA

International Institute for Applied Systems Analysis
Laxenburg, Austria

Earthscan Publications Ltd
London and Sterling, VA

First published in the UK and USA in 2001
by Earthscan Publications Ltd

Copyright © International Institute for Applied Systems Analysis (IIASA), 2001

ISBN: 1 85383 537 4

Typesetting by IIASA
Printed and bound in the UK by Creative Print and Design Wales, Ebbw Vale
Cover design by Yvonne Booth

For a full list of publications please contact:

Earthscan Publications Ltd
120 Pentonville Road, London, N1 9JN, UK
Tel: +44 (0)20 7278 0433
Fax: +44 (0)20 7278 1142
Email: earthinfo@earthscan.co.uk
http://www.earthscan.co.uk

22883 Quicksilver Drive, Sterling, VA 20166-2012, USA

Earthscan is an editorially independent subsidiary of Kogan Page Ltd and publishes in
association with WWF-UK and the International Institute for Environment and
Development

A catalogue record for this book is available from the British Library

Library of Congress Cataloging-in-Publication Data

Transboundary risk management.
        p. cm.
    ISBN 1-85383-537-4 (pbk.)
    1. Environmental risk assessment–Europe.

GE160.E85 T73 2000
363.7'094–dc21

00-067274

This book is printed on elemental chlorine free paper

Contents

Preface

This book has its origins in the early 1990s at the International Institute for Applied Systems Analysis (IIASA), where we shared our concerns about the Chernobyl nuclear accident and other transboundary risk crises of that time. Representing the academic fields of geography, economics, and international negotiation, our perspectives on the issues were different in important ways, but were also complementary. Committed to an interdisciplinary and international perspective, we approached The Swedish Council for Planning and Coordination of Research (FRN) for funding for a workshop on Transboundary Risk Management. This workshop, which took place in Stockholm in 1995, brought together academics and practitioners to discuss problems of European East–West transboundary risks. Given the awareness in Sweden of both transboundary air pollutants and the risks posed by the Ignalina nuclear power plant in Lithuania, the conference attracted a great deal of attention from Swedish policymakers. Indeed, Birgitta Dahl, the speaker of the Swedish Parliament, gave an address at the public session of the conference, a transcript of which is presented at the end of this book. In addition, Uno Svedin, research director at FRN, contributed a foreword to this book highlighting the social and political dimensions of transborder risks. The interest in this conference prompted FRN to support us in organizing a second workshop in Poland, which took place in Warsaw in 1996. The chapters in this book largely developed from the papers presented at these conferences.

It is not surprising that the Swedes were keenly interested in our topic of transboundary risk. In the late 1960s, Swedish researchers reported that the destruction of freshwater ecosystems was due mainly to transboundary and not local air pollution. After the breakup of the Soviet Union, these transborder risks became especially apparent and topical in Sweden, and throughout Europe. The natural/physical dynamics of many transboundary environmental risk problems, such as the acid rain phenomenon, are now fairly well understood; however, the policy and social dimensions of these risk issues have been largely ignored by the interdisciplinary community of risk researchers. The purpose of this book is to address this imbalance by focusing on case studies of transboundary risk management and examining the social and policy issues they raise.

This book would not have been possible without the generous funding made available by FRN, and we are particularly thankful for the guidance and encouragement provided by Arne Jernelöv, Berit Örnevall, and Lars-Erik Svensson. We are also extremely grateful to Richard Andrews, who reviewed an earlier version of the book and gave us challenging suggestions for improvement. We are also indebted to Ellen Bergschneider, Diana Hargreaves, and Laura Kelly for their English-language editing skills. Joanne Linnerooth-Bayer thanks her IIASA colleagues for their support. Ragnar Löfstedt would like to thank Professor Roland Clift at the Centre for Environmental Strategy, University of Surrey, for allowing him to spend several weeks in Stockholm and in Vienna working on this book.

We are also grateful to IIASA, the Royal Society of Arts and Manufacturing, and the Swedish Institute for International Affairs for providing meeting space for our many editorial meetings. Finally, and as always, we would like to thank our respective other halves – Kurt for Joanne, Laura for Ragnar, and Renne for Gunnar – for encouraging us to complete this book even though it involved weekend traveling, late evenings, and weeks away from home.

Joanne Linnerooth-Bayer, Laxenburg
Ragnar E. Löfstedt, Guildford
Gunnar Sjöstedt, Stockholm

Foreword

Uno Svedin

This book is about more than managing risks that cross political borders; it is also about science, institutions, and governance in an increasingly global society. The transboundary risk problems discussed here highlight the importance of creating Europe-wide democratic institutions that promote openness, transparency, and trust. A study of transboundary risks also highlights considerations regarding the diversity of cultural settings within and between borders, as well as the dynamics of social change in a globalized world occupied by a large number of actors. The heterogeneous production of knowledge in such a system and the dynamics created by the use of scientific "facts" in the political arena are topics of particular interest for this book.

Issues associated with societal risks have been growing in importance on the international research agenda. The patterns of systemic risks to society, rather than the risks of accidents localized in time and space, are of particular interest. Such broader societal risks may occur, for example, in conjunction with a specific development of a technology, such as information technology; with regard to the control of complex technical systems, such as air traffic control; or with respect to national energy policies on fossil fuels, nuclear power, hydropower, and bioenergy. The risk panorama also extends to the economic and cultural realms, influencing trust or distrust in, for instance, financial institutions like the banking system, social security systems, or pension systems. Disruptions in these complex institutional structures by voluntary processes, or even involuntary processes inherent in the buildup of the institutions, are threats characterizing most modern societies.

These complex systemic issues also characterize transboundary environmental and public health risks. Many of the transboundary risk cases examined in this book are drawn from Central and Eastern Europe. One reason for this is the concern on the part of Western Europe about nuclear risks in the East, especially after the Chernobyl nuclear accident in 1986. But other risks in Central and Eastern Europe rival the nuclear threat. The long-range pollution from energy production, for instance in the Black Triangle region, with its effects on southern Poland, the Czech Republic, Germany, and much of Europe, is of particular concern.

The earlier political and economic differences between Western Europe and the former Soviet Union are still of interest today, a decade after the fall of the Iron Curtain. The capacity to cope with environmental dangers continues to be distinctly lower in the East than in the West, creating a situation that has strong implications for the European environment and for future investments and strategies for European economies. There are also implications for international cooperation in Europe. In some cases, countries have chosen to locate their source of environmental risk at national borders. This has enhanced or aggravated existing tensions in border regions – tensions that may have their roots in historical military or ethnic conflicts. Transboundary risks can reinforce historical tensions and therefore destabilize international efforts for cooperation.

Countries handle transboundary risk issues in many different ways, for example, in the way regulations are legislated and implemented, in the chosen risk-management philosophies, or even in the capacity to pay adequate salaries to professionals involved in managing the risks. These different management constraints, opportunities, and styles can lead to national conflicts as well as conflicts among the stakeholders on all sides of the borders. It is interesting to note, however, that tensions may be stronger at the political level than among the experts and the public.

A crucial issue in the management of transboundary risks concerns the erosion of trust in societal institutions. In some cases, disasters have revealed a society's inability to manage risks, even those on a grand scale such as the Chernobyl accident. Moreover, after disasters have occurred, the public has all too frequently been inadequately informed or misinformed. This has destabilized many institutions involved in the handling of risks, which in turn has created more intensely destructive tensions in the countries of the former Eastern bloc and throughout Europe.

Another complication in dealing with risks on the East–West borders of Europe has resulted from the abrupt changes in patterns of personal and institutional responsibility and accountability. Hazardous facilities built in Eastern Europe and the former Soviet Union were embedded in a responsibility structure unique to that system – and quite different from those of Western systems. After the dismantling of the Soviet Union, new and untested patterns of responsibilities only faintly resembling those of the past emerged, operated by a new set of accountable state and non-state actors.

The Chernobyl accident demonstrated how perverse the dynamics of this process could be. Radioactive fallout via airborne transmission to Belarus and the Baltic states was later "exported" from those republics through the river systems. The initial response on the part of the Ukrainian authorities tended not to acknowledge that the pollution originated in their country. Such problems with disrupted lines of responsibility are widespread. For example, who in the Baltic states or in former East Germany is now responsible for risks created during the Soviet era?

Transboundary risk issues can be viewed from a "sustainable development" perspective, exhibiting political, economic, technical, cultural, legal, and environmental dimensions. The management of transboundary risks can only be carried out by taking these facets of the problems into account. This is the intent of studies in this book, which includes examples from a broad spectrum of perspectives, including

- the way in which the transboundary issues are approached,
- the contexts in space and time within which the issues are addressed,
- the policy and communication frameworks within which the issues are dealt with,
- the underlying, perhaps even hidden, agendas and issues that permeate the problems.

There are *different types* of transboundary risks and different approaches to their assessment and management. One approach can be viewed as "science based." This paradigm stresses organizational aspects, risk reduction, and economic efficiency in the prioritization of risk problems. The emphasis is on the instrumental use of knowledge. A second paradigm, based in a social science setting, stresses the social circumstances: the social construction of risk, the perception of risk, and the possibility of alternative contexts. This paradigm emphasizes an "understanding of the risk context."

As the focus of this book is *transboundary* risks, an obvious starting point for the investigations is to ask what a border is. A border can lie between nations, thus highlighting national sovereignty and the definition of a nation-state. A border can also distinguish managerial domains or cultural domains with different styles of imagining, perceiving, and reacting to risks.

The "transboundary-ness" of the risk issues illuminates interesting geographical and spatial aspects of risk management. With regard to nation-states, there are examples of both deliberate *hazard internalization*, where the risk is handled or managed domestically, and *hazard export*, where high-risk activities are located close to the national border.

Transboundary risks exist in the context of time. Some risks may be confined within borders in the short term, but over a longer time frame may "leak" to become risks over wider geographical domains. There may, therefore, be a change of spatial arrangements and/or management practices over time. The Chernobyl case, for example, illuminates the change of institutional context over time, since the Soviet Union, the responsible authority at the time of the accident, no longer exists.

The political and scientific framings of transboundary risk issues are related to the selection, or even the "production," of "the facts" and are thus connected to the choice of the analytical "science-based" and "social science–based" paradigms discussed above. As a case in point, the early concerns about the risks of DDT (dichloro-diphenyl-trichloroethane) were not only about the identification of a biologically active metabolite and its environmental effects, but were also about how this "fact" would be incorporated into a larger regulatory and legal process within which the risk would be handled. On the transboundary scale, the issue can be framed quite differently by the authorities of different countries and by the experts. In this sense, transboundary conflicts may be battles of expertise more so than national conflicts.

The interplay between "science" and "politics" thus emerges as a major topic of this book, and the role and credibility of science in assessing and managing transboundary risks is an important focal issue. It may thus seem paradoxical that precisely this domain, which now shows increasing tensions, provided a depoliticized bridge of communication between the East and the West during the Cold War period.

The political domain also governs the forms of public communication. Differentiating between the goals of the communication process – that is, communication as education (one way) or as dialogue (two way) – is important in the management of risks and, as this book demonstrates, is becoming increasingly important in the transboundary context. Communication can even be a major tool for resolving transboundary risk conflicts and is closely related to trust in the risk-managing institutions on the part of the public and other stakeholders. This link was demonstrated by the communication failures – within and outside of borders – in the immediate aftermath of the Chernobyl disaster.

The issues of governance and institutional change, including transparency and trust in European and cross-border risk management institutions, are the fundaments of this analysis. In particular, this book addresses the following broad clusters of issues:

- The transboundary environmental risk challenges
- The political and cultural framing of present and future "realities"
- The role of nation-states in a situation of emerging European cooperation, including the various styles of governance
- The different interpretations of "the rule of law"
- The crucial issues of trust in and legitimacy of our societies as the basis of the different forms of participatory democracy that have evolved in Europe

The transboundary risk topics addressed in this book therefore highlight the key political, economic, social, and cultural issues of our times. The issues pertain to hopes in Central and Eastern Europe for quick paths to economic development, for "leap-frogging" over the problems encountered by countries in the West when they were in the same phase of economic development. They also pertain to the challenges envisaged within the broader European collaborative framework and thus to the future of the European Union.

The transboundary risk management cases discussed in this book ultimately demonstrate the importance of expanded European integration. At the same time, transboundary environmental and public health risks demonstrate structural, political, and cultural obstacles that must be overcome if such risks are to be managed successfully. Thus, the case studies and analyses in this book serve as a checklist of issues that must be addressed if the European Union is to build credible trans-national risk management procedures and institutions, and if the integrative process is to be expedited. These issues must be faced in the context of European *diversity* at the operational level, but with a *common* historical perspective gradually saturating the strategic frame of mind.

Chapter 1

Introduction

Joanne Linnerooth-Bayer

Since the 1986 Chernobyl nuclear accident and the Sandoz fire in Switzerland that same year, Europeans have become acutely aware that risks to their health and environment cross political borders. In many recent cases this awareness has turned to outrage as the public has attributed the risks from genetically modified (GM) crops or bovine spongiform encephalopathy (BSE) to the influence of multinational companies and possible negligence on the part of the controlling authorities. The recent disastrous cyanide spill that has polluted the Tisza and Danube Rivers in Central Europe illustrates the risks from industrial and economic globalization. In this case, the cyanide was released from a waste storage facility of a (partly) Australian-owned gold mine in Romania. The costs of this disaster will undoubtedly be borne mainly by fishermen and other victims in Hungary and other downstream countries, with few social or economic ramifications for the Romanian and Australian mine owners or their governments. Transboundary risks can also be global in their consequences, and problems of ozone depletion and climate change have featured prominently on European negotiating agendas.

To an important extent, how Europeans deal with their transboundary environmental and technological risks will shape the environmental

1

and political future of Europe. An especially worrying feature of past and ongoing European risk controversies has been their tendency to aggravate ethnic hostilities or otherwise prove divisive. The acid rain issue in the early 1960s, for instance, was interpreted by some Swedes as a form of involuntary foreign intervention by West Germany and Britain (Litfin, 1998). The construction of the Gabcikovo hydropower station on the Danube River has considerably worsened diplomatic relations between Slovakia and Hungary. And the BSE issue has rekindled historical conflicts between Britain and Germany and the rest of Europe.

Trade relations are also at issue. In its evolving role as a supranational risk management entity, the European Commission (EC), along with institutions such as the World Trade Organization (WTO), must reconcile the objective of unrestricted international trade with increasing national and local demands for more autonomy in assessing and regulating the risks from this trade. Solving this conflict may be one of the most formidable challenges to trade within the EU and around the globe.

The authors in this volume present case studies of environmental and technological risk issues in Europe as well as a contrasting study of transboundary processes in Asia. An important motivating issue raised by the case studies is how the emerging risk management processes and institutions at the EU level can avoid the crises in governance that have characterized local risk debates. In examining European acid rain negotiations, Swedish aid to the Ignalina nuclear power plant in Lithuania, the conflict on the Danube River over the Gabcikovo hydropower station, the BSE crisis, and the current furor over trade in GM foods, the authors of the case studies flag a rich set of issues that present formidable challenges to European integration and the EU. Three thematic chapters examine these issues and make suggestions for improving cross-border communication, public participatory and conflict resolution forums, and bi- and multilateral negotiating procedures.

1.1   Background

Unlike their domestic counterparts, transboundary risks pass beyond the limits of the nation-state into what students of international relations call "international anarchy": a realm within which the responsibilities and obligations that are enforced by sovereign states are largely absent. Many see the solution in strengthening transborder property rights and liabilities at the individual and corporate level, and relying to a large extent on the market and courts to self-regulate (Held, 1995; Arrow, 1996). Transboundary liability regimes are forming, for instance, with respect to oil pollution on the seas (Brubaker, 1993; Brans, 1996) and nuclear power in Western Europe (Faure, 1995). However, for the most part there is still a general lack of state, corporate, or private liability for agents producing transboundary risk (Zemanek, 1992; Bodansky, 1995).

Others view the market as the problem. Some social scientists speak of a "global risk society," where risks are becoming increasingly uncontrolled and uninsurable as they spread beyond political boundaries (Beck, 1992, 1997). These theorists speculate that the globalization of economies and the resultant "hollowing out" of the nation-state can only exacerbate transboundary risks. Still others suggest that, even without calling for a system of world government, transboundary risks can be brought under control through systems of regional and global governance. These systems or regimes can encompass the activities of governments and the United Nations (UN), as well as those of many other social systems and institutions, from enterprises to the microcosm of the family (Young, 1994; Rosenau, 1995).

International regime governance can be seen as a complement to the emerging forms of individualistic, market-based transborder regulation, and there is considerable evidence that this is indeed what is happening. There are now over 170 multilateral environmental agreements (UNEP, 1993), and the EU member states have relinquished some of their sovereignty in order to allow the regulation of risks at the supranational level (Majone, 1992, 1996). In Europe, important transboundary treaties have concerned the pollution of the Baltic Sea (Henttonen, 1996), the cross-border transport of hazardous wastes (Murphy, 1994), the management of the Danube River (Linnerooth-Bayer, 1990), and the control of sulfur emissions (see Chapter 4). Despite concerns about the effectiveness of these agreements, a recent study shows that most countries comply with their treaty obligations most of the time (Victor *et al.*, 1998; Victor and Skolnikoff, 1999). Compliance appears, however, to be an inevitable outcome of the fact that states generally sign agreements that are in their immediate interests and that they can easily carry out.

Market-based institutions and governance by regimes, however, are not the only forms that international organization can take in dealing with transboundary risks (Schwarz and Thompson, 1990; Thompson, *et al.*, 1990). One need only recollect the Brent Spar case (Löfstedt and Renn, 1997), in which Greenpeace's eleventh-hour intervention so dramatically transformed the outcome that had been agreed between Shell and the British government, to realize that non-state and non-market actors constitute a third organizing force that can either complement or compete with market-style institutions and national or international authority (Goldman, 1998). In implementing international agreements there is a remarkable convergence in national policy styles in including nongovernmental organizations (NGOs) more extensively through increasingly permissive access structures (Ausubel and Victor, 1992; Victor *et al.*, 1998).

With the realm beyond the nation-state now colonized by the very same actors – firms, governments, and NGOs – that have long been active within it, the national/international distinction begins to lose its primacy and transboundary anarchy no longer appears inevitable. Indeed, Litfin (1998) points out the fallacy of assuming that ecological issues are eroding national sovereignty; rather, sovereignty is "on the move" and must be understood as a socially constructed concept with multiple meanings and practices. In this light, national borders are not so dissimilar to other boundaries – between the provinces within a nation-state, between municipalities within the provinces, and all the way to the fenceless boundaries between neighboring family farmers. Environmental and technical risks cross all these boundaries, and the same types of organizing forces combine to manage them at these different scales.

The re-construction of national sovereignty will quite naturally lead to the demise of what Rayner (1994) describes as the realist model of transboundary risk management, where individual nation-states determine their negotiating positions according to national self-interest, and the respective governments and their networks of scientific experts negotiate transboundary agreements. To many, the end of the Cold War signaled the opening of previously closed government processes to the voices and ideas of the public. Stakeholders operating within and across borders are demanding more openness and participation with regard to issues transcending national political borders. Building institutions at the transborder level that foster citizen participation, and thus build democracy across borders, may be one of the greatest challenges to effective risk management in Europe.

Effective and democratic risk management in Europe is the challenge addressed in this book. Controversies over issues such as hazardous waste shipments, genetically modified organisms (GMOs), and BSE have revealed dramatically declining confidence in the experts and in the public institutions charged with managing risks. In Britain, where trust in scientists has plummeted with the BSE crisis and the furor over "Frankenstein foods," there is a consensus developing in the scientific community that public concerns should be included in the assessment of risk (Royal Commission on the Environment and Pollution, 1998). The same is true in several other European countries, particularly in the Netherlands, where this consensus has existed for some time (Klingemann and Fuchs, 1995).

In the United States, this decline in trust of risk management institutions has led to a study by the National Research Council (NRC), which has proposed that the risk assessment process be reconceived (Stern and Fineberg, 1996). In the past, the process of risk assessment was seen as a presentation of scientific findings on environmental and public health risks for the use of the public or private decision makers, with little or no involvement of the affected and interested parties, at least during the early "fact-finding" stages. This understanding of science and the role of the risk analyst has only served to aggravate risk controversies and to lessen the public's esteem of both the scientists and the policymakers. The authors of the NRC volume recommend an analytic–deliberative process, the success of which depends on "deliberations that formulate the decision problem, guide analysis to improve decision participants' understanding, seek the meaning of analytic findings and uncertainties, and improve the ability of interested and affected parties to participate effectively in the risk decision process" (Stern and Fineberg, 1996:3). This does not mean that scientific rigor and public participation can easily coexist, but environmental policy institutions at the local level are increasingly showing that they can remain attentive to multiple viewpoints without compromising analytic and scientific rigor (Jasanoff, 1996). By improving stakeholder participation in framing the problems, providing expertise, and participating in policy implementation, it is thought that trust in the risk managing institutions can be increased.

1.2   Purposes and Questions

The NRC recommendation builds on extensive experience and studies of the successes and failures of risk management at the national and local levels. In contrast, with some important exceptions, there have been few practical or theoretical studies of risk management processes across national political boundaries. This book addresses that gap with case studies of transboundary risk issues in Europe, with a contrasting study of transboundary processes in Asia. These studies include

- conflicts over Swedish aid to improve the safety of the Ignalina nuclear power plant in Lithuania,
- the conflict between Hungary and Slovakia over the Gabcikovo–Nagymaros hydropower station on the Danube River,
- the European negotiations to reduce acid rain on the continent,
- the European crisis over BSE,
- trade issues over GM crops and foods, and
- conflicts over large dam projects in the Himalayan region.

This volume has two main purposes. The first is to show how the social, political, and cultural complexities of risk management processes at the local and national levels manifest themselves across the political boundaries of Europe, and in particular how changing forms of democratic governance at the national levels are placing demands on risk policy-making at the European level. The authors raise issues of governance and democracy at the European level. A second purpose of this volume is to address these challenges with concrete suggestions for improving transboundary risk management, particularly with regard to introducing improved institutions and procedures for risk communication, public participation, conflict management, and negotiation. Three thematic chapters build on the case studies and address these procedural reforms.

In their descriptions of how transboundary risk issues have emerged on political and public agendas, and how they have been dealt with in these arenas, the authors of the case studies make a number of observations. Most generally, they document the European public's demands for more local authority and democratization of decisions affecting their health and environment, and the need to reconcile these demands with the expert-dominated processes that have characterized many transboundary risk management decisions. As these processes become more open and transparent, the public is witnessing large and seemingly irreconcilable differences in expert assessments of the same risks, not only by experts representing different groups within countries, but between official assessments by authoritative experts in neighboring countries as well.

Environmental NGOs are gaining greater access to international negotiating processes, yet channels for effective communication about health and safety risks, and forums for public participation across political borders are practically nonexistent. Most worrying, with some important exceptions, the cases demonstrate a general failure of current transboundary risk management processes to resolve environmental and technological risk issues in a way that promotes the legitimacy of European and EC institutions. In fact, the cases indicate that trust in European institutions for managing risks may be declining.

More specifically, the authors document the acute lack of accepted principles, procedures, and institutions – and the failure of those that do exist – to resolve European transboundary environmental risk conflicts. As a case in point, the International Court of Justice (ICJ) has failed to fully resolve the conflict between Hungary and Slovakia concerning the diversion of the Danube River to feed the Gabcikovo hydropower station. The case of the Ignalina nuclear power plant in Lithuania shows that even if all countries involved can reap substantial joint gains, action may be hampered by historical, economic, and cultural circumstances. Swedish efforts to donate aid for improving the safety of the Ignalina plant have not been fully accepted by the policymakers and members of the public of either country. Nor are matters going smoothly with regard to EU plans for harmonizing risk assessments across member countries to promote unrestricted trade in the Union. The case of GM crops shows clearly the problems of harmonizing EU policies based on scientific risk evaluations and the contradictions in separating values from science. Likewise, European national conflicts over the handling of the BSE issue have escalated, mainly because of culturally contingent differences in the interpretation of the underlying science.

These and other observations by the case study authors flag a set of issues that present formidable challenges to European integration and the EU. Many of these issues, particularly those concerning the effectiveness of international treaty making and the use of market instruments for managing risks, are addressed elsewhere in the literature (see Victor *et al.*, 1998). The thematic chapters of this volume examine the following questions:

- How are transboundary risks different from their national counterparts? What distinctive challenges do they raise? How are the signals that motivate management interventions amplified and attenuated across borders?

- What constitutes effective risk communication? How can transboundary risk communication be improved?
- How can differing scientific risk assessments within and between countries be reconciled? Or, more realistically, how can transborder risk handling processes be put in place in the face of often irreconcilable differences in the risk assessments?
- How can democratic risk management processes be established to reconcile competing perceptions and cultural constructions of risk problems across borders?
- What are the impediments to European integration imposed by East–West environmental risk issues? How might negotiation procedures be improved to reduce these impediments?

1.3   Characterizing Transboundary Risks

Natural hazards – storms, droughts, infectious diseases, agricultural blights – have never respected political boundaries. Recent concern, however, has centered on the expanding list of transboundary risks that arise from human activities. This list was once thought to include mainly the accidental and routine releases of hazardous substances and the risks these substances pose to human health and ecosystems, but it now encompasses such wide-ranging risks as those arising from decreased biodiversity and from the marketing of GM foods. The list also includes the human and environmental risks from age-old natural hazards and diseases as they are increasingly linked to human activities: the growing human and economic losses from storms, floods, and other extreme types of weather as a possible result of greenhouse gas emissions; the increased losses from all sorts of disasters because of the worldwide tendency of capital to move across jurisdictions and into vulnerable areas; and the spread of the human immunodeficiency virus (HIV) through international blood banks and sex tourism, to name a few examples.

In this volume, Roger Kasperson and Jeanne Kasperson define transboundary risks as risks that arise when *human activities* in one nation-state threaten current or future environmental quality, human health, or well-being in one or more other nation-states (see Chapter 8). As the cases in this volume show, these transborder risks can be distinguished by the ways in which they cross borders, the regions they affect, and how they are managed (Linnerooth-Bayer and Löfstedt, 1996). The damage from acid rain in Europe shows how the atmosphere can carry pollutants generated by human activities to regions far from their origin. Likewise, trade in GM foods and British beef means the transport of risks across borders via roads, railways, and airlines. Hazards to the environment or human health can originate in, and endanger, single or multiple regions. The risks from the Gabcikovo hydropower station have affected mainly two countries and thus have engaged bilateral discussions; the risks from sulfur emissions originating in the Black Triangle region of Central Europe affect several countries and have engaged multilateral discussions; and the release of greenhouse gases affects the entire globe, leading to global discussions. The damage might be to common property resources, for example, the ozone layer, or to private or public property, for example, damage to European forests from acid rain. Risks that originate in wealthy countries but affect poor countries may be viewed very differently from risks, such as those posed by the Ignalina plant, that originate in poor countries and affect wealthy ones.

1.3.1 The "risk" concept

The concept of "risk" usually encompasses the probability of a negative event or threat occurring and the possible consequences. One goal for public policy has been to manage environmental risks "rationally," or to place priority on reducing the most serious risks at the lowest cost (Zeckhauser and Viscusi, 1990). While basing risk management decisions on expert risk assessments with the aim of cost efficiency has been a laudable goal, it has inevitably become entangled with issues of risk perception and construction, as well as questions concerning the fairness of the risk distribution (Linnerooth-Bayer, 1996, 1999). Knowledge of the ways accidents, illnesses, and damage to ecosystems result from exposure to pollutants and technologies is often incomplete, and most risks are characterized by conflicting scientific expert evidence and opinion in their production and control.

Moreover, the concept of risk entails more than just expert assessments of the probability and harm of an activity. Indeed, the concerns on the part of the public, even the informed public, have rarely been based on expert assessments. Early work on risk perception showed that risks are multidimensional, and that public perceptions are related to, among other factors, whether the risk is voluntary, controllable, familiar, potentially catastrophic, and known to science, and whether it has the potential to affect future generations (Slovic, 1987). This early work, however, did not explain why perceptions about the same risk were so varied. Differences among individuals and groups might be linked to interests, but also, anthropologists claim, to different worldviews or ways of life (Douglas, 1992). Experts, policymakers, and individual citizens operate in a social context that influences how they construct their views of the seriousness of environmental and technological risks (Schwarz and Thompson, 1990; Thompson *et al.*, 1990; Wildavsky and Dake, 1991). Many also argue that public and expert values inevitably influence risk assessments, and therefore the notion of separating scientific risk assessment from risk management is questionable (Jasanoff, 1986, 1990; Wynne, 1991).

Because of these complexities in assessing risks, the NCR-sponsored book *Understanding Risk* calls for risk characterization as an important part of risk assessment (Stern and Fineberg, 1996). Risks should be "characterized" with analyses that are appropriate to the problem and that respond to the needs of the interested and affected parties. At a minimum, a risk characterization would include information on the scientific uncertainties of the estimates and the scientific controversies surrounding them, who bears the risks and who benefits, the perceptions and concerns of the interested and affected parties, and the different culturally linked views on the acceptability of the risks.

1.3.2   Characterizing the case-study risks

Without attempting to discuss all the factors relevant to characterizing the risk situations discussed in the case studies in this book, it may be useful to compare and contrast some of their more salient features. *Table 1.1* gives an overview of the nature of the transboundary risks, the processes in place for their management, and possible improvements in their management.

The Ignalina nuclear power plant in Lithuania imposes a relatively low probability of a major disaster affecting large regions. Especially since the Chernobyl accident, nuclear power plants are a source of a great deal of public and expert concern, which has led to a ban on nuclear power in many countries in Western Europe. Expert assessments of the Ignalina plant indicate that it poses a higher risk of an accident than Western-designed nuclear power stations, and public perception studies have shown that nuclear power ranks high on the dimensions of "dread" and "unfamiliarity." Risk perceptions about nuclear power, however, are by no means homogeneous in any country or between countries. Partly as a result of their differing views of nature and the environment, but also certainly because of their interest in economic development, many Lithuanians are less concerned than their Swedish counterparts about the risks from Ignalina (see Chapter 2).

Like the Ignalina nuclear power plant, the Arun-3 hydropower dam proposed for the Mahakali River (which forms the border between Nepal and India) can be characterized as a large-scale technological system that poses risks to the environment and population (see Chapter 7). This project has raised concerns about its possible catastrophic failure (even through deliberate sabotage by upstream countries) and about the effects of the dam on the surrounding villages and the ecology of the region.

Public and expert concerns about the construction of a hydropower dam at Gabcikovo in Slovakia centered less on the risk of a catastrophic dam break than on the ecological impacts on the surrounding region from the diversion of the river (see Chapter 6). In the face of greatly differing expert assessments of the risks, the acceptability or unacceptability of the Gabcikovo project appeared to depend largely on culturally determined and politically motivated views about large-scale interventions in nature.

A novel type of technological risk accompanies the introduction of GMOs. In many ways, the GMO risks are similar to the risks associated with nuclear power plants, at least as nuclear risks were perceived in the early years of nuclear plant operation: the risks are potentially catastrophic, unknown to science, unfamiliar, and have the potential to affect future generations. The two types of risk are also different in important ways: a nuclear power plant is centralized and easily identifiable, whereas fields of GM crops can be small and diverse, and the presence of modified genes can be difficult to detect in the chain of agricultural products. Like nuclear power, concerns over GMOs appear to be polarized, and the conflicts are escalating.

The BSE issue is historically quite different from other risk issues, since the risks from consuming British beef became public knowledge only after the public had been exposed to them. Yet, the risks are similarly regarded as unfamiliar and potentially catastrophic. Like the conflicts over the Ignalina nuclear power plant, the Gabcikovo and Arun-3 hydropower dams, and GM food crops, the conflict surrounding the BSE

Table 1.1. Characteristics of case study risks and their management.

	Involuntary		Voluntary			
	Ignalina nuclear power plant	Gabcikovo hydropower dam	Acid rain from air pollution	BSE from British beef	GM foods and crops	Arun-3 hydro-power dam
Countries involved	Lithuania, Sweden, and other European countries	Hungary, Slovakia, and Austria	All of Europe and elsewhere	All of Europe and elsewhere	All of Europe and elsewhere	India and Nepal
Nature of the risk	Human health, potentially catastrophic	Ecosystem, potentially irreversible	Mainly to forests and lakes, significant economic damage	Human health, potentially catastrophic	Ecosystem and human health, potentially irreversible	Ecosystem and human safety, potentially catastrophic
Nature of transboundary risk	Accidental nuclear release crossing borders	Long-term effects of dam on neighbor countries	Long-term effects of long-range pollution across borders	Trade in British beef exposing public in importing countries, crisis situation	Concerns about trade in GM foods affecting public health and ecosystems	Large-scale project may have risks of accident and effects on ecosystems
Scientific evidence of risk	Few rigorous probabilistic risk assessments, large uncertainties	Few quantitative assessments of ecosystem risks, recent international studies	Many studies of acidification effects, computer model showing impacts on soils	Scientific studies made public very late, risk estimates controversial	Many scientific risk assessments with different results	Risk assessments performed by academic institutions

Abbreviations: BSE = bovine spongiform encephalopathy; EU = European Union; GM = genetically modified; ICJ = International Court of Justice; IIASA = International Institute for Applied Systems Analysis.

Table 1.1. Continued.

	Involuntary			Voluntary		
	Ignalina nuclear power plant	Gabcikovo hydropower dam	Acid rain from air pollution	BSE from British beef	GM foods and crops	Arun-3 hydro-power dam
Risk management process	Bilateral negotiations on Swedish aid to improve plant safety, no public involvement	Bilateral negotiations to reach compromise on construction of plant, little public participation, decision made by ICJ	Multilateral, European negotiations aided by IIASA computer model, little public concern	Multilateral crisis management coordinated by EU	EU involved in setting conditions for trade, much public and interest group concern and protest	Bilateral negotiations complimented by great deal of public and interest group concern and involvement
Problems with present process	Swedish aid viewed as "selfish aid," decrease in international good will	Loss of trust in national authorities and in international court	Few problems, process apparently successful	Potential loss of trust in EU as risk management institution, increasing national hostilities	Potential loss of trust in EU as risk management institution	Potential increase in national hostilities, loss of trust in authorities on both sides of border
Suggestions for improved risk management process	Expand nuclear liability regimes, improve aid process with more input from interest groups	Develop deliberative, participatory process for resolving expert disputes and involving public	Improve monitoring and implementation of international agreements	Improve crisis management capability of EU	Develop deliberative, participatory process for resolving expert disputes and involving public	Develop deliberative, participatory process for resolving expert disputes and involving public

Abbreviations: BSE = bovine spongiform encephalopathy; EU = European Union; GM = genetically modified; ICJ = International Court of Justice; IIASA = International Institute for Applied Systems Analysis.

issue exposed large culturally contingent differences in the interpretation of the underlying science (see Chapter 5).

For our purposes, an important distinguishing feature of transboundary risks is whether or not they cross borders voluntarily or with the consent of the importing country. For instance, neither Sweden nor any country in Europe has consented to the risks they bear from the operation of nuclear power plants in neighboring or even distant countries. Nor is it legally or physically possible for a country to reduce nuclear risks that cross its border without the agreement of the country in which the plant operates. In contrast to such *involuntary* transboundary risks are those that can be prevented from crossing borders and thus require the implicit or explicit consent of the importer. The import of GM tomatoes and hormone-fed beef from the United States are examples of *voluntary* transboundary risks.

1.4   The Case Studies

1.4.1   Unauthorized transboundary risks

Unauthorized transboundary risks – those that cannot be detained at the borders and thus do not require consent – are pervasive. As Kasperson and Kasperson point out in Chapter 8, they can arise from industrial developments located on or close to borders, such as the Gabcikovo hydropower dam project in Slovakia, or from point source pollution in one country that can or does affect neighboring countries. The Chernobyl accident, the archetype of the latter risk situation, has sensitized Europeans to the very high stakes of involuntary nuclear risks in Europe. Although less dramatic, the international regime developing to deal with the pollution of the Danube River demonstrates the complexity of the international context. In this case, the upstream–downstream issues must be dealt with by seven riparian countries with very different economic and military circumstances (Linnerooth-Bayer, 1990). Unauthorized transboundary risks can also arise from less identifiable and more diffuse effects associated with the energy, transportation, and other structural developments of an economy, such as China's decision to burn high-sulfur coal. These risks can be global in nature or affect many countries in a large region, and many are ecological rather than human health risks.

National authorities often negotiate reductions in unauthorized risks by offering to pay for the risk reduction or linking the agreement to other issues of concern to the risk-imposing country. The cleanup of the Rhine River, for example, proceeded only after the Netherlands, the downstream riparian, agreed to compensate the upstream countries, especially France, for their expenditures (Linnerooth-Bayer and Löfstedt, 1996). However much they violate the established polluter-pays principle, deals that offer gains to both the risk-imposing and risk-bearing countries would appear to be a pragmatic solution to transboundary risks and perhaps an equitable solution where the risk-imposing country cannot afford to take mitigation measures. This route was taken after the disintegration of the Soviet Union, when Western countries, most notably Sweden, Finland, and Austria, as well as financial institutions such as the European Bank for Reconstruction and Development (EBRD), invested in measures to improve the safety of the nuclear stations in Eastern Europe and the Commonwealth of Independent States (CIS) countries.

Swedish policymakers are particularly concerned about the risks from the Ignalina nuclear power plant in nearby Lithuania, and Swedish aid to improve its safety would appear to be a mutually beneficial and acceptable solution. Yet, as Ragnar Löfstedt and Vidmantas Jankauskas show in Chapter 2, Swedish aid to the Ignalina plant has not been overwhelmingly accepted by the public and policymakers in either Lithuania or Sweden. The Lithuanians are concerned that conditional aid impinges on national sovereignty and often lands in the pockets of Swedish consultants. The Swedish authorities are critical of the aid insofar as it enables what many view to be an inherently unsafe plant to continue operating. The authorities are also becoming more cautious about safety investments as they contemplate the legal possibility of Swedish liability should an accident occur. Moreover, many Lithuanian policymakers and the Lithuanian public have expressed frustration that aid is not being given for what they view as more serious local environmental problems. While the Lithuanian public and policymakers still welcome Swedish aid, one has to ask if the longer-term relations between the two countries are served by what is increasingly viewed as "selfish aid."

Public views on a fair solution to another transboundary policy conflict are reported in the case study by Anna Vari and Joanne Linnerooth-Bayer on the Gabcikovo–Nagymaros hydropower dam project on the Danube River (see Chapter 6). This project began as an authorized border risk on the part of both Czechoslovakia and Hungary. However, it changed to an unauthorized environmental risk when Hungary withdrew from the project in 1992 and Slovakia diverted the river and constructed the Gabcikovo hydropower station fully on Slovak territory. The authors argue that, although the verdict on the environmental damage from the project is still out and the verdict of the ICJ has only prolonged the conflict, the project failed from the standpoint of building the credibility of the newly formed democratic governments in both countries.

The differences in the political cultures of Slovakia and Hungary and their current differing perceptions and constructions of the benefits and costs of the dam system underscore what Brian Wynne and Kerstin Dressel show with respect to the BSE issue (see Chapter 5): the difficulties in managing transboundary risk conflicts overlie more subtle cultural dislocations over knowledge and its social roles and limits. Many Slovaks still view the Gabcikovo project as a triumph of technological know-how and development. In contrast, many Hungarians see the project as belonging to a past era of gigantic developments pushed on the public by an expert elite, with little attention given to the ecological consequences. Throughout the debate, very different uses were made of expertise by the authorities on both sides of the river, with remarkably contrasting constructions of the environmental risks. Yet, looking closer, one finds that many of the groups that were active in the process had the same problem construction and concerns as their counterparts on the other side of the river. The local Slovak and Hungarian citizens showed a willingness to reach a constructive compromise to the conflict; however, from the beginning their views were excluded in the expert-driven, political negotiations.

1.4.2 Authorized transboundary risks

National authorities cannot erect barriers to stop nuclear risks or air pollutants from crossing their borders, but they can prevent trade in hazardous substances and the operation of hazardous activities within their borders. Perhaps the classic case of banning risks at the border is the Basel Convention, which has greatly restricted the export of hazardous wastes from Organisation for Economic Co-operation and Development (OECD) nations to developing nations (Hoppe and Olson, 1994). The politics of consent in the EU, however, has been complicated by the objective set out in the Treaty of Rome of "undistorted competition," which has been translated into privatization, market liberalization, and unrestricted international trade (Laudati, 1996; Majone, 1996). While the EC and other institutions such as the OECD and the WTO are promoting barrier-free global trade, local communities and national governments are at the same time demanding more autonomy in their risk assessment and management processes. This conflict of "globalization" versus "localization" motivated much of the recent protest in Seattle against the WTO's negotiations to further liberalize trade. Pursuit of the competitive market in the EU has thus been hindered by the tension between centralized regulation and uniformity, and the subsidiarity principle aimed at protecting the regulatory diversity of the member states (Majone, 1996).

Two case studies in this volume deal explicitly with this conflict between global trade and local or national autonomy in granting consent for importing risks: the harmonization of EU policies on GMOs and the multicountry ban on British beef during the crisis over BSE. In the first case, a 1990 EC Directive mandated formal and harmonized risk assessments for releases of GM crops at the national level. Since the risks of GM crops do not change as they cross borders, except as such crops are affected by natural geographic differences, harmonization should only be a matter of obtaining scientific information on these differences.

In reality, however, this is far from the case, a fact that Les Levidow attributes to the technocratic harmonization model (see Chapter 3). In practice, the environmental values brought into the licensing arena vary across EU member states, so scientific agreement cannot readily be reached on the possible measurable harm of GM crops. One such value difference has arisen through disparate national interpretations of "precaution" – for example, how to evaluate predictive uncertainties about the potential effects of GMO production and consumption. Another difference has arisen in defining "adverse effects." In the case of transgenic oilseed rape, for example, member states have evaluated differently the risk that the inserted herbicide-tolerant gene might spread to related plants, thus jeopardizing the efficacy of the herbicide. In the United Kingdom, this potential effect was initially classified as an "agricultural problem," not as environmental harm, whereas other national authorities regarded such an effect as a risk of jeopardizing future options for sustainable agriculture.

In their discussion of BSE in Europe, Wynne and Dressel show that, in addition to contending valuations and constructions of the risks involved, national conflicts concerning the risks of commercial products may have their roots in different constructions of the science involved (see Chapter 5). These constructions are based on underlying and unrecognized presuppositions about what counts as scientific knowledge and "non-knowledge" (including its social role and limits), and what warrants commitment in each national system.

BSE began as a case of an authorized transboundary risk, and the BSE issue manifested itself as a transboundary issue when the authorities in many European countries and throughout the world withdrew their consent by banning the import of British beef. The scientific uncertainty surrounding the BSE issue, and particularly the transmission of Creutzfeld-Jakob disease to humans, has made this transboundary risk issue immensely complex. Yet, the crisis was in many ways familiar, involving a trade-off of public health risk against economic benefits and interests in the face of highly uncertain knowledge of effects and processes, and demands by the public for the elimination of any risk, however remote.

With evidence mounting on the transmission of Creutzfeld-Jakob disease to humans, the issue for the EC was how to assess the risks. Again, the process was framed as analytical rather than deliberative. In this case, the "taken-for-granted" procedures in place in the United Kingdom turned out to be inadequate and unacceptable to Germany and many other countries in Europe. Subsequently, the British response to the EU ban was that it was a "German plot" or evidence of German hysteria in the face of risk. The BSE issue thus generated an international crisis of political trust and mutual loyalty among EU member states, which the authors attribute in part to the lack of cultural unity within the EU. The pragmatic and empiricist approach in the United Kingdom, in contrast to that in Germany, tends to exclude abstract uncertainties or ignorance and thus to underplay precautionary views. Although the authors acknowledge the importance of national interests and deliberate actions, they stress the cultural component of how risks are handled by "unreflexive elaboration of existing and familiar routines and culturally comforting behaviours, beliefs and assumptions."

To the extent that the shaping of the policy response and the construction of the knowledge in support of this response depend on national institutional cultures, risk conflicts at the international scale will not be resolved by promoting a consensus on the scientific bases of the risk assessments. Numerous research studies have demonstrated that different but logically equivalent ways of summarizing the same risk data and information can lead to different understandings of the risks. The important point is that the analytic results will quite legitimately be framed and interpreted in a manner consistent with the preferences, worldviews, or interests of the persons or organizations carrying out or commissioning the analyses. The analytical–deliberative process recommended by the NRC, and others, is an attempt to explicitly bring these different understandings into the risk characterization process.

The question raised by the GMO and BSE cases, as well as by the other cases discussed in this volume, is how or whether deliberation might have informed analysis had there been an attempt to make the process more broadly participatory at an early stage. Rather than basing transboundary policy on formal risk assessment, could the risks have been characterized in a process with broadly based, cross-national deliberation such that decision-relevant knowledge entered the process, that different views and risk constructs were considered, and that the parties' legitimate concerns about the inclusiveness and openness of the process were addressed?

Some important insights into this question can be found by looking to Asia. In Chapter 7, Michael Thompson and Dipak Gyawali show how transboundary conflicts in the Himalayan region are becoming increasingly democratic with the involvement of diverse groups with very different views of the problems and their solutions. The discourse over the construction of the Arun-3 hydropower dam in Nepal became "pluralized" – and the project was abandoned – with a shift in the distribution of power brought about by a dramatic expansion in the number and variety of interested and affected parties in the debate, including entrepreneurial academics and NGOs. This pressure to abandon the Arun-3 project, along with other pluralized debates concerning proposed treaties on the use of the water from the Mahakali River, are leading to increased transparency in public transboundary policies and, ultimately, to the democratization of decision making in the area.

1.4.3   Acid rain: A case of contrasts

The European negotiation process on transboundary air pollution leading to the 1994 Second Sulphur Protocol to the Convention on Long-Range Transboundary Air Pollution was unusual in many respects. First, it made use of a computer model developed at the International Institute for Applied Systems Analysis (IIASA), which proved instrumental in the eventual adoption of a cost-effective solution to meeting European targets based on the "critical load" concept.[1] Although the cost-effective approach was an important advancement for many environmental treaties, in Chapter 4 Anthony Patt examines the puzzle of why the negotiating community was not willing to weigh the costs and benefits of emission reduction. In doing so, an explicit decision could have been made on the value of reducing the risks of acid rain in view of possible alternative uses of the requisite funds. This trade-off is especially pertinent to East and Central European (ECE) countries, since these funds could be used to reduce the more serious risks of local pollution. Patt argues that, because cost–benefit analysis (CBA) explicitly incorporates the values of the public, a CBA may not be useful information in the international negotiation setting. To take a hypothetical example, if the Swedes value their lakes more than the Poles do, the Poles might end up paying more to reduce emissions headed for Sweden than to reduce those headed to their own lakes. These differential reductions *based on value judgements* may be far more difficult for the negotiators to justify back home than differential reductions based on a physical measure of the damage to soils. For this and other reasons, the negotiators focus on what Patt calls "bright lines," or easily quantifiable and justifiable emission goals. In contrast, the local policymakers in the Black Triangle region of Central Europe appear to make benefit and cost trade-offs in formulating their policies for reducing air pollution in the region.

This case describing the successful negotiation of major reductions in sulfur emissions in Europe contrasts sharply with the other cases discussed in this volume. Agreement was achieved by an uncontested expert-dominated process, and there was no duel of experts proclaiming different risk estimates. As Patt shows, the IIASA model was recognized, even by its developers, to have conceptual and data deficiencies, but its perceived impartiality combined with the need to have quantified estimates of emissions, damage, and costs of reduction added to its acceptability to the European negotiating community. Use of the model went virtually unchallenged, and by focusing on critical loads instead of risks and benefits, the process successfully bypassed any diverging values in the participating countries. This across-the-board acceptance of the underlying science and analysis contrasts markedly with European attempts to harmonize risk analyses of GM crops and with the attempts to settle the disagreement between Slovakia and Hungary on the environmental effects of the Gabcikovo dam.

What explains this contrast? First, the risks are different. Familiar and controllable risks, like air pollution, are usually less threatening than risks that are little known to science and potentially catastrophic (Slovic, 1987). Second, the problem at hand involved the reduction of an existing risk rather than the imposition of a new one, and, unlike in the BSE case, to varying degrees all European countries were and are responsible for the risk-imposing behavior. Third, any reduction in the damage from acid rain is seen as desirable, and in contrast to the cases involving the Ignalina nuclear power plant and the Gabcikovo hydropower dam project, here there were no expectations or demands for zero risk. Finally, the early negotiations on sulfur reductions took place at a time when there were fewer demands in Europe for openness and participation by NGOs and lobbying groups.

Still, it is remarkable that agreement was reached given the starkly higher and more costly obligations that the protocol placed on Poland and other Central European countries compared with their Western counterparts (since West European countries had already reduced their sulfur dioxide emissions considerably). This readiness of the polluting (poor) countries to pay for reductions stands in sharp contrast with, for example, the case of the Rhine River cleanup, where the Dutch, as victims, paid the (wealthy) upstream countries to reduce their emissions into the river. Another contrast is the ongoing, high-stake debate on reducing global greenhouse gas emissions. The 1997 Kyoto Protocol to the United Nations Framework Convention on Climate Change explicitly excluded poor countries from any obligations, even given that the most efficient global strategy is to reduce emissions in the "South" (Toth, 1999). But requiring the poor countries to reduce their greenhouse gas emissions appears unfair (unlike obligating the East European countries to reduce their sulfur emissions) given the "North's" historical contribution to the problem. Arguments of responsibility, along with considerations of endowment and need, have thus been a key feature of the discourse on how to allocate the costs of climate change abatement (Linnerooth-Bayer, 1999).

The concept of responsibility can also help explain conflicts over policies that entail net gains to *all* countries involved. For example, West European countries can often benefit more by investing in pollution reduction in Eastern Europe and reducing transborder pollutants than investing these same funds in reducing domestic sources of pollution. Yet, not everyone considers this efficient policy to be a fair one. In a survey of the Swedish public, many Swedes felt that it was the responsibility of the East European countries to deal with their own pollution, even if it meant more risks to the Swedish public (Löfstedt, 1994).

1.5 The Thematic Chapters: Risk Amplification and Attenuation, Trust, Communication, Participation, and Negotiation

Ideas of what is fair and trustworthy figure strongly in the case studies discussed in this volume. Unfortunately, the case material points to declining trust in many European institutions for transboundary risk management. After the Chernobyl accident, there was widespread skepticism that European governments would provide trustworthy information about the contamination risks. This lack of trust goes beyond the provision of information in a crisis situation. In both Slovakia and Hungary, the public expressed doubts that either of the governments or the International Court of Justice could successfully resolve the conflict over the Gabcikovo hydropower dam project. Moreover, only about a third of the public sampled thought their government experts were objective. A similar state of distrust is reported by Thompson and Gyawali in their account of the Arun-3 hydropower dam (see Chapter 7). The authors attribute the appalling state of distrust of the Nepalese authorities responsible for the development of Nepal's water resources, and the Nepalese and Indian authorities' distrust of one another, to the lack of institutional and cultural diversity in the decision-making processes.

Issues of institutional credibility and trust are not confined to involuntary, bilateral risk controversies. In Britain, the failure to inform the public of the possible human health risks of BSE at an early stage and the diverging assessments of the risk in the scientific community have led to a crucial loss of trust in scientific and government institutions. Moreover, the unreflective application of familiar risk management practices in the United Kingdom without taking into account the different cultures operating in Europe could, according to Wynne and Dressel, undermine the essentials of EU institutional viability – trust and mutual respect between the member states (see Chapter 5). The BSE issue raised for first time the

EU's role in responding to a risk crisis, and it was crucial for this response to build trust in the emerging EC institutions. Trust is also a core concern in the EU's attempts to harmonize legislation and regulatory criteria for GM crops and food. Basing the harmonization process on technical risk assessments has led to value collisions among the members, discrediting the Commission's harmonization policies and fueling risk conflicts among its members and with its trading partners.

A core concept in building trustworthy processes for risk management is recognizing and respecting the diverse values, interests, and worldviews of the interested and affected parties. As cultural theorists point out, there often are greater similarities in the views and interests of like-minded parties or groups across borders than in those of opposing groups within the same country (Thompson, *et al.*, 1999). Thus in the case studies we find Hungarian, Austrian, and Slovak groups organizing joint demonstrations against the Gabcikovo hydropower dam project, coalitions of national consumer groups lobbying against the trade of GMOs, Swedish and Lithuanian anti-nuclear groups protesting against continued operation of the Ignalina nuclear power plant, and groups as diverse as the Nepali Alliance for Energy and the International Rivers Network based in California forming coalitions against the Arun-3 hydropower plant in Nepal.

These cross-border coalitions are becoming more influential in transboundary risk issues, and Ortwin Renn and Andreas Klinke speak of them as an emerging "corporatist" risk management regime (see Chapter 9). This corporatist process, however, will inevitably run up against controversies of factual evidence and conflicts about institutional performance, values, and worldviews. Yet, continuing to rely on expert-based risk management without respecting the demands of stakeholders and the public for more information and access to regulatory processes will accelerate the decline in the legitimacy of social risk-managing institutions. This decline has been attributed to a loss of trust in governments, and an explicit motivation for improving risk communication and public participation has been to increase public trust (Kasperson *et al.*, 1992; Renn and Levine, 1991).

In Chapter 8, Kasperson and Kasperson argue that the most telling attribute of transboundary risks is their great potential for the social amplification or attenuation of risk, which can lead to increased distrust between citizens and policymakers across borders. If the countries involved have a history of conflict, cultural differences, or ongoing tensions, even minor potential "exports" of risk may generate widespread media coverage, societal attention, public concern, and protests. The public may be especially averse to even minor risks emanating from a country they regard as hostile or untrustworthy, especially if the public views the risk producers as receiving large benefits.

Using the social amplification of risk as a framework for analysis and drawing upon empirical evidence of transboundary risk conflicts in this book and elsewhere, Kasperson and Kasperson argue that transboundary risks cannot be viewed as a single problem or challenge, but in fact come in different forms and levels of complexity. Distinguishing among them can provide greater clarity about the resulting processes of the social amplification of risk and the feasibility and likely effectiveness of strategies of managerial intervention, including risk communication.

The authors distinguish four different types of transboundary risk, based on the nature of the risk, the relationships among the countries involved, and the social context:

- *Border-impact risks* involve activities, industrial plants, or developments in a border region that affect populations or ecosystems in the border region on both sides of the boundary.
- *Point-source transboundary risks* involve one or several clear point sources of potential pollution or accident that threaten an adjoining country or region (or several countries or regions).
- *Structural/policy transboundary risks* involve less identifiable and more subtle and diffuse effects associated with state policy, transportation or energy systems, or the structure of the economy.
- *Global environmental risks* involve human activities in any given country that affect many or all other countries through alterations of the global "systemic" environment.

For *border-impact risks*, political groups within each country may exploit the risk issues for political reasons. This was the case in the Gabcikovo controversy, and the difficult communication between Slovakia and Hungary illustrates what Kasperson and Kasperson view as important determinants of the risk communication process: the nature of relations between the two adjoining states and the nature of relations among groups or interests within the boundary area itself. The authors suggest that, in contrast to border-impact risks, *point-source risks* may have fewer impediments to effective communication across borders. However, lack of trust in the safety management at the risk source may intensify public concerns over hazards and generate significant social amplification of the risks.

Structural/policy transboundary risks, according to Kasperson and Kasperson, may be the most difficult to communicate to policymakers and members of the public across borders. Linking environmental and human health effects from these risks entails a level of assessment and communication beyond the capability of most current approaches to risk analysis. Yet, as the authors note, this may be the most important of the transboundary risk problems.

Finally, the authors discuss the impediments and obstacles to communicating about *global environmental risks*: the risk sources are widely distributed, the links between human activities and changes in global atmospheric and other systems are uncertain, the links between risk sources and affected populations are often remote, and management options lie embedded in larger problems of growing global inequalities and conflicting views of responsibility and values.

Communication alone, of course, cannot resolve transborder conflicts about risks, particularly if the benefits and risks are distributed unequally across the respective borders. Moving beyond communication, in Chapter 9 Renn and Klinke discuss two main types of conflict resolution between sovereign states. The first is the application of conflict mediation involving a neutral facilitator, which works best for disputes over goods or "bads" that are not the exclusive use of either country. Conflicts about values such as security, power, or worldviews concerning technology and development, however, are least likely to be resolved through mediation. A second form of conflict resolution and joint problem solving is brought about through long-term cooperation set up by international organizations, international conventions, and above all international regimes.

The planned accession of ECE countries to the EU has increased the urgency of instituting improved risk conflict resolution mechanisms. In Chapter 10, Gunnar Sjöstedt discusses the difficulty of expanding the environmental risk politics of Western Europe to ECE countries, with their differences in public attitudes and economic resources. He suggests that a combination of negotiating strategies may prove useful, including incentives for complying with Western standards, external assistance from the EU, and a process of collective learning.

Collective learning will entail greater transparency, openness, and participation by all interested and affected parties. A great deal of attention has been given to involving NGOs in a kind of corporatist international regime, but involving the general public as a nongovernmental actor in foreign policy-making has been rather neglected. This neglect is apparent in the case studies in this volume, where the single and unsuccessful effort at involving the public was in the case of the Gabcikovo–Nagymaros conflict. In Chapter 9, Renn and Klinke argue that more successful participatory regimes are quite feasible, both in expanding the corporatist forms of NGO interaction and in providing a close-to-home forum for resolving transboundary, single-issue disputes. However, involving citizens in policy-making processes is difficult and requires careful planning, thoughtful preparation, and the flexibility to change procedures on the demand of the affected constituencies. As Renn and Klinke ask, if citizen involvement is so difficult, why should any national agency bother to promote transborder participation? To the authors, the answer is clear. The acceptance, and ultimately the implementation, of any transnational policy affecting the health and safety of the public or the integrity of the environment are closely tied to the perception of a transparent and fair procedure in making the decision. The possibility of halting and reversing the decline in trust in the EU's risk management institutions is a persuasive argument for moving beyond international corporatist risk management by involving the public more directly in the transboundary decision-making process. But is it possible to involve citizens in a decision-making process that spans national boundaries?

Renn and Klinke suggest how their three-stage "cooperative discourse" procedure might be adapted to public participation in a transboundary setting (see Renn *et al.*, 1993). The first part of the discourse to define values and concerns would take place within each participating country. Questions regarding factual knowledge would be resolved in the second stage at a workshop with experts from all involved countries. The third and final step – combining the values with the expert evidence on the "facts" – would proceed via randomly selected citizen panels in each country so as to avoid problems of language and cultural value differences. Reaching scientific consensus across borders is, of course, a difficult task. Could a Delphi process have helped, for instance, in reaching a consensus between Hungarian and Slovak experts on the effects of the Gabcikovo hydropower dam, or could such a process have led to a consensus between

German and British scientists on the value of precautionary practices with regard to the BSE issue? As difficult as it appears, the authors feel there is no rational alternative to such a procedure.

Putting transboundary participatory procedures into place requires more than just a replica of relevant domestic experience. Transboundary participation models can only be implemented if the requisite institutional arrangements are in place and, as Jasanoff (1996) has emphasized, if there is a sense of community and trust.

1.6 Conclusions

The consequences of transboundary risk management will have wide effects on the crucial conditions for international institutional viability and democracy in Europe: trust and mutual respect. This is the important message for the EC with regard to its evolving role in harmonizing risk regulatory regimes and responding to risk crises. This message will become increasingly important to European policymakers with the expansion of the EU to include the ECE countries.

The solution is not simply to improve the efficiency of transboundary risk outcomes, the processes of transborder risk management must be improved as well. The acceptance and ultimately the implementation of transnational policies affecting the health and safety of the public and the integrity of the environment are crucially tied to developing transparent and participatory procedures in setting these policies. It is essential that the EU move beyond the corporatist risk management style to involve the public more directly in transborder decision-making processes. As shown in this volume, this is feasible. Numerous models now exist for involving the affected and interested parties, ranging from regional referenda to focus groups and including the cooperative discourse procedure described in Chapter 9. Of course, any move toward more directly democratic processes requires openness and transparency on the part of governments and experts, and many models now exist in North America and Europe for open disclosure of risk information and for communicating this information to the public.

The challenges for transboundary risk management are formidable. National cultural styles, languages, and the plurality of risk constructions and interests complicate the practical and conceptual aspects of such a process considerably. Yet, the alternative – perpetuating an expert-dominated style characteristic of the traditional realist model of transborder risk management – will almost inevitably discredit efforts by the EC and other international bodies to build processes and institutions that command broad public support and build democracy within and across the borders of Europe.

Note

[1] The critical load of a soil region is the amount of pollution that a given place can absorb before showing adverse effects.

References

Arrow, K.J., 1996, The theory of risk bearing: Small and great risks, *Journal of Risk and Uncertainty*, **12**:103–111.

Ausubel, J.H., and Victor, D.G., 1992, Verification of international environmental agreements, *Annual Review of Energy and the Environment*, **17**:1–43.

Beck, U., 1992, *Risk Society: Towards a New Modernity*, Sage, London, UK.

Beck, U., 1997, Global risk politics, *The Political Quarterly*, Blackwell Publishers, Oxford, UK.

Bodansky, D., 1995, Customary (and not so customary) international environmental law, *Indiana Journal of Global Legal Studies*, **3**(1):105–119 (Fall).

Brans, E.H.P., 1996, Liability and compensation for natural resource damage under the international oil pollution conventions, *Review of European Community & International Environmental Law*, **5**:260–268.

Brubaker, D., 1993, *Marine Pollution and International Law: Principles and Practice*, Belhaven, London, UK.

Douglas, M., 1992, Risk and blame, *Essays in Cultural Theory*, Routledge, London, UK.

Faure, M.G., 1995, Economic models of compensation for damage caused by nuclear accidents: Some lessons for the revision of the Paris and Vienna Conventions, *European Journal of Law and Economics*, **2**:21–43.

Goldman, M., ed., 1998, *Privatizing Nature's Political Struggles for the Global Commons*, Pluto, London, UK.

Held, D., 1995, Democracy and the new international order, in D. Archiburgi and D. Held, eds, *Cosmopolitan Democracy: An Agenda for a New World Order*, Polity Press, Cambridge, UK.

Henttonen, J., 1996, Co-operation for improvement of the environment in North-Eastern Europe: The Finnish concept, in R.E. Löfstedt and G. Sjöstedt, eds, *Environmental Aid Programmes to Eastern Europe*, Avebury Studies in Green Research, Aldershot, UK.

Hoppe, R., and Olson, K.J., 1994, The shrinking world of hazardous waste exports: A guide through the conundrum, *Journal of Environmental Regulation*, **4**:43–55.

Jasanoff, S., 1986, *Risk Management and Political Culture*, Russell Sage, New York, NY, USA.

Jasanoff, S., 1990, *The Fifth Branch: Science Advisers as Policymakers*, Harvard University Press, Cambridge, MA, USA.

Jasanoff, S., 1996, The dilemma of environmental democracy, *Issues in Science and Technology*, (Fall):63–70.

Kasperson, R.E., Golding, D., and Tuler, S., 1992, Siting hazardous facilities and communicating risks under conditions of high social distrust, *Journal of Social Issues*, **48**:161–187.

Klingemann, H.D., and Fuchs, D., eds, 1995, *Citizens and the State*, Oxford University Press, Oxford, UK.

Laudati, L., 1996, The European Commission as regulator: The uncertain pursuit of the competitive market, in G. Majone, ed., *Regulating Europe*, Routledge, London, UK.

Linnerooth-Bayer, J., 1990, The Danube River basin: Negotiating settlements to transboundary environmental issues, *Natural Resources Journal*, **30**: 629–660.

Linnerooth-Bayer, J., 1996, Does society mismange risk?, in R. Zeckhauser, R. Keeney, and J. Sebenius, eds, *Wise Choices: Decisions, Games, and Negotiations*, Harvard Business School Press, Boston, MA, USA.

Linnerooth-Bayer, J., 1999, Climate change and multiple views of fairness, in F.L. Toth, ed., *Fair Weather? Equity Concerns in Climate Change*, Earthscan, London, UK.

Linnerooth-Bayer, J., and Löfstedt, R., 1996, Transboundary Environmental Risk Management: An Overview, Paper presented at the Conference on Transboundary Environmental Risk Management, 6–8 October, Warsaw, Poland.

Litfin, K., 1998, The greening of sovereignty: An introduction, in K. Litfin, ed., *The Greening of Sovereignty in World Politics*, MIT Press, Cambridge, MA, USA.

Löfstedt, R.E., 1994, Environmental aid to Eastern Europe: Swedish and Estonian perspectives, *Post Soviet Geography*, **35**:594–607.

Löfstedt, R., and Renn, O., 1997, The Brent Spar controversy: An example of risk communication gone wrong, *Risk Analysis*, **17**(2):131–136.

Majone, G., 1992, Market integration and regulation: Europe after 1992, *Metro-economica*, **43**:131–156.

Majone, G., 1996, *Regulating Europe*, Routledge, London, UK.

Murphy, S.D., 1994, Prospective liability regimes for the transboundary movement of hazardous wastes, *The American Journal of International Law*, **88**:24–75.

Rayner, S., 1994, Governance and the Global Commons, Discussion Paper 8, The Centre for the Study of Global Governance, London School of Economics, London, UK.

Renn O., and Levine, D., 1991, *Credibility and Trust in Risk Communication*, Springer-Verlag, Berlin, Germany.

Renn, O., Webler, T., Rakel, H., Dienel, P.C., and Johnson, B., 1993, Public participation in decision making: A three-step procedure, *Policy Sciences*, **26**:189–214.

Rosenau, J.N., 1995, Governance in the twenty-first century, *Global Governance*, **1**:13–43.

Royal Commission on the Environment and Pollution, 1998, *Setting Environmental Standards*, Her Majesty's Stationery Office, London, UK.

Schwarz, M., and Thompson, M., 1990, *Divided We Stand: Redefining Politics, Technology and Social Choice*, Harvester-Wheatsheaf, London, UK, and University of Pennsylvania Press, Philadelphia, PA, USA.

Slovic, P., 1987, Perception of risk, *Science*, **236**:280–285.

Stern, P.C., and Fineberg, H.V., 1996, *Understanding Risk: Informing Decisions in a Democratic Society*, National Academy Press, Washington, DC, USA.

Thompson, M., Ellis, R., and Wildavsky, A., 1990, *Cultural Theory*, Westview, Boulder, CO, USA.

Thompson, M., Grendstad, G., and Selle, P., 1999, *Cultural Theory as Political Science*, Routledge, London, UK.

Toth, F.L., 1999, *Fair Weather? Equity Concerns in Climate Change*, Earthscan, London, UK.

UNEP (United Nations Environment Programme), 1993, Register of International Treaties and other Agreements in the Field of the Environment, Nairobi, Kenya.

Victor, D.G., and Skolnikoff, E.B., 1999, Translating intent into action: Implementing environmental commitments, *Environment*, **42**:16–20, 39–44.

Victor, D.G., Raustiala, K., and Skolnikoff, E.B., eds, 1998, *The Implementation and Effectiveness of International Environmental Commitments: Theory and Practice*, MIT Press, Cambridge, MA, USA.

Wildavsky, A., and Dake, K., 1991, Theories of risk perception: Who fears what and why?, *Daedalus*, **119**:41–61.

Wynne, B., 1991, Misunderstood misunderstanding: Social identities and the public uptake of science, *Public Understanding of Science*, **1**(3):281–304.

Young, O.R., 1994, *International Governance: Protecting the Environment in a Stateless Society*, Cornell University Press, Ithaca, NY, USA.

Zemanek, K., 1992, State responsibility and liability, in W. Lang, H. Neuhold, and K. Zemanek, eds, *Environmental Protection and International Law*, Graham & Trotman, London, UK.

Zeckhauser, R., and Viscusi, K., 1990, Risk within reason, *Science*, **248**: 559–564.

Chapter 2

Swedish Aid and the Ignalina Nuclear Power Plant

Ragnar E. Löfstedt and Vidmantas Jankauskas

2.1 Introduction

The Ignalina nuclear power plant is located around 200 kilometers (km) from Vilnius, the capital of Lithuania, and only 600 km from the Swedish coast. After the Chernobyl accident in 1986, people in many countries became apprehensive of an accident at Ignalina, with the associated risk of far-reaching, transboundary consequences. After the fall of the Soviet Union in 1989, the Swedish government took steps to improve the safety of Ignalina at the cost of the Swedish taxpayers.

Environmental aid from Western Europe to the countries of Eastern and Central Europe (ECE) for the primary purpose of reducing transboundary risks – the risks to both the aid recipients and the donors – has become an important instrument for transboundary risk management in Europe (Löfstedt, 1996c). However, transboundary environmental aid is not problem free. Aid can be viewed as violating an important principle accepted in the West, the polluter pays principle, and thus as inadvertently subsidizing the activities producing the risks. Violating this principle can be justified if the aid corrects decisions of the past that involved unacceptable risk, but not if doing so encourages (as many argue) the continued operation of an inherently unsafe technology. Recognizing the dire economic circumstances of the newly independent states of Central Europe, a basic premise of this aid is that the taxpayers in Western Europe are willing to accept that they, the victims, must pay.

Transboundary environmental aid also raises concerns on the part of the aid recipients. The recipient population may not view the transboundary risk as their greatest environmental priority. Even in the event that both countries gain from bilateral aid, the recipient country may resent the motivation of the aid givers if the aid is given primarily to reduce the risks to the donor country. This resentment may be magnified if the local population feels that the funds could be used to reduce more serious risks within the recipient country.

Swedish aid to Ignalina raises issues of transborder perceptions and equitable solutions similar to those of the Hungarian–Slovak dispute over the Gabcikovo dam and hydropower station. Although the Hungarian and Slovak public negotiators inflexibly pursued perceived national interests, members of the public in both countries were more sensitive to the needs of those on the other side of the border. The Hungarians, who like the Swedes were the victims of the project, were prepared to pay more to realize a joint and mutually satisfactory solution to the problem.

In this chapter, we examine the views of Lithuanian and Swedish policymakers with respect to Swedish aid to improve the safety of the Ignalina nuclear power plant. We also investigate the public's perceptions of the risks from the Ignalina plant in both Sweden and Lithuania, as well as their views on the effectiveness and fairness of transboundary aid from Sweden. Specifically, we report on in-depth interviews with key policymakers, a study of the local and national media in Sweden, and a questionnaire given to members of the public in both countries.

The Ignalina plant contains two 1,500 megawatt (MW) reactors – among the largest in the world. The Russian-designed RBMK reactors are the same design as those at the Chernobyl plant. They consist of two parallel cooling loops, a direct cycle, fuel clusters loaded into individual channels, and, more importantly, a neutron spectrum that is thermalized by a massive graphite moderator block. In general, these reactors are not as well understood by Western nuclear experts as the Russian-designed

VVER reactors, which are similar to the pressurized water reactors widely used in the West.

Although many safety improvements have been made to the RBMK reactors since the Chernobyl accident, many nuclear experts hold that the safety of these reactors cannot be upgraded to acceptable levels for long-term operation. According to experts at the Nuclear Safety Account at the European Bank for Reconstruction and Development (EBRD), modern RBMK reactors, such as at Ignalina, have a number of safety faults (EBRD, 1994), including the following:

- Insufficient fire protection
- Poor redundancy and shortcomings in emergency power supply
- Lack of a containment structure
- Insufficient reactor core venting capacity
- Insufficient diversity of emergency shutdown systems
- Complicated system for controlling the power distribution in the reactor core
- Complicated operating procedures due to the large volume of the reactor core

In March 1997, a safety report was conducted on Ignalina for the EBRD. The report was critical in its conclusions, calling the plant's management "too old-fashioned" and recommending that it be replaced and that a backup, quick-stop system and a containment structure be installed (Selander, 1997). The Swedish government has pledged US$20 million for a management system and a backup quick-stop system. However, US$50 million are still required, and the director of the Swedish International Project (SIP) does not believe that the Lithuanian government can provide the additional funds. Consequently, the safety mechanisms are not likely to be implemented (Selander, 1997).

At the Ignalina plant, Reactors 1 and 2 are 14 and 11 years old, respectively. Currently, no one is certain about the lifetimes of the reactors. The main factor affecting reactor lifetime is the fuel channels, which are generally thought to last approximately 15 years. These fuel channels can be replaced, as was done at the nuclear power station at Sosnovyj Bor near St. Petersburg, extending the reactor lifetime up to an additional 15–20 years. Reactor 1 had its license renewed in September 1999. It was unable to complete the various safety requirements by the date originally set for the license review procedure (May) and as a result was closed down for a period of two months. Reactor 1 is now set to operate until 2005, at which time it will be permanently closed down. Reactor 2 will have a series of safety systems added to it in 2002, during which time it will be temporarily shut down. After the safety improvements have been made, the Lithuanian government will decide how long Reactor 2 will remain in operation. This decision will be based on a revised National Energy Strategy Plan. In September 1999 the Lithuanian government signed a contract stipulating that it will not replace the fuel channels for either Reactor 1 or 2, and the European Union (EU) has stated that Lithuania will not be allowed to accede to the EU if it breaks this contract (L.-G. Larsson, director of the Nuclear Safety Department, European Bank for Reconstruction and Development, personal communication, 27 June 2000).

The reactors have been a source of controversy since they were built in the 1980s. At that time, Lithuania was a part of the Soviet Union and the Politburo in Moscow had plans to make Ignalina the largest nuclear power plant in the world, with at least four 1,500 MW reactors that would provide electricity not only for Lithuania, but also for Latvia and Belarus. To build and run the nuclear reactors, a town, Visaginas, was built only 7 km from the plant to house the workers. The Lithuanians were not trusted to build and operate the facility, and the policymakers in Moscow brought in large numbers of Russians and Ukrainians to work on and at the plant. To the anger of the ethnic Lithuanians, Visaginas effectively became a Russian city. Following the Chernobyl accident in 1986, public concerns arose regarding the safety of the plant. Plans to finish Reactor 3 and start work on Reactor 4 were shelved until 1989 because of public protest. Following Lithuanian independence in 1991, there was a move to close Reactors 1 and 2, but policymakers argued that the electricity was needed and that the plant should stay in operation.

In the years following independence, Ignalina provided considerable revenue for the Lithuanian government through electricity exports to Latvia and Belarus. By late 1994, the export revenues had declined, primarily as a result of the faltering economies of these countries. Today, depending on the operation of the reactors, Ignalina generates from 70–90% of the country's electricity, making Lithuania the most nuclear-dependent nation in the world. At the present time, Lithuania has a generating surplus, since electricity demand has decreased by more than 40% (1995 final figures) compared with 1990–1991 (Paskevicius, 1995).

This is not to say that there are no other electricity-generating sources in Lithuania. According to the authorities at Ignalina, however, nuclear energy is cheaper than electricity generated by the main alternatives, hydropower and combined heat and power plants that use natural gas and heavy fuel oil. The costs of nuclear electricity are mainly for operation and maintenance, as the capital costs were incurred by the Soviet Union. However, this calculation ignores the amount needed to cover the costs of eventual decommissioning of the plant or storage of nuclear waste. Some Western experts feel that these costs should be included in electricity rates (Snihs, 1995). However, it would be difficult to increase electricity prices in Lithuania as they are heavily subsidized by the state.

Since the plant went into operation it has been beset by a series of safety problems, most of which have resulted in the accidental release of small amounts of radioactivity to the surrounding environment. Recently, however, Ignalina has been plagued by another problem – terrorism. In the summer of 1994, the son of Lithuania's mafia chief was arrested in connection with a series of murders. His father threatened to blow up Ignalina if his son was found guilty. His threats were taken seriously, and a defense in depth system to protect against unauthorized entry is being developed. The threat resulted in unwanted publicity for Ignalina and 10 million Swedish krona (SEK) in immediate security improvements (Nistad, 1995a, 1995b). In early 1995, the son was executed in secrecy, without the mafia chief carrying out his threat.

The long-term problem associated with the plant is the management of its nuclear waste. In the past, when Lithuania was a part of the Soviet Union, the waste was shipped to Siberia for final storage. Today, that possibility no longer exists, and the waste is temporarily stored in cooling tanks at the plant itself

2.2   Transboundary Risks and Swedish Aid to Ignalina

Ignalina became a major concern to Western policymakers after the Chernobyl nuclear accident. Before this accident, nuclear experts and policymakers did not associate nuclear power with transboundary risks. It was not envisaged that a nuclear accident in Ukraine could result in the contamination of reindeer in northern Sweden or of lambs in Cumbria in the United Kingdom. Policymakers now realize that if there is a nuclear accident in Eastern Europe, the West could be quite seriously affected.

With the exception of France, there is a trend in Europe away from nuclear toward natural gas–generated electricity. Nations with large nuclear programs, such as Sweden, are under considerable public pressure not to build any more nuclear power plants and to phase out those currently in use. An accident in Eastern Europe, albeit at a reactor of a totally different design, could accelerate this process, resulting in major economic problems in countries with a high proportion of nuclear power in their electricity mix. As a result, many stakeholders in Western nations have an interest in ensuring that another Chernobyl-type accident does not occur. This consideration has no doubt influenced aid programs to help East European nations to improve nuclear safety.

Eastern Europe's economic upheavals coupled with major environmental problems (some of which affect Sweden) have led the Swedish government to make overseas aid available to these nations. In 1992, the Swedish government established a special Economic Assistance Fund (SEK 3 billion) for its East European neighbors,[1] making Sweden a major donor of development aid to these countries. Funding has been given mainly for investigative research to determine potential solutions to energy and environmental problems, rather than for directly financing cleanup activities. Consequently, a large proportion of the funds have been given to Swedish consultants. However, money has also been made available for urgent repairs to unsafe nuclear reactors that pose potential environmental threats.

The accident at Chernobyl provides a useful reference point for the analysis of Sweden's policy concerning transboundary environmental hazards. Prior to the Chernobyl accident, only limited attention had been paid to environmental risk management in the East, mainly in the form of exchanges of information. There was little attempt by Sweden, or any other Western nation, to give advice on environmental management. Policymakers felt that the countries of Eastern Europe would be unable or unwilling to utilize such information (Salay, 1991). Following the Chernobyl accident, it became apparent that new ways of dealing with questions of transboundary regulation and responsibility were needed. The accident also brought about the realization for both policymakers and the public that acid rain was not the only transboundary hazard originating in Eastern Europe. However, it was not until 1989, when the political climate in the

Communist bloc changed, that Sweden began to give more environmental aid to Eastern Europe (Löfstedt, 1995).

The Ignalina plant is the largest recipient of Swedish environmental aid in Eastern Europe. As of 1999, it had received a total of SEK 320 million. However, rather than directing the money to the Lithuanian nuclear authorities, the Swedish government gives most of the money directly to the Swedish Nuclear Inspectorate (SKI) and the National Institute for Radiation Protection (SSI). These institutes distribute the funds to consulting firms, utility companies such as Sydkraft and Vattenfall, and multinational firms such as ABB to identify and carry out safety improvements.

There is a strong belief in Sweden that this aid is necessary. For over a decade the Ignalina plant, located just 600 km from the Swedish coast, has been the target of reports in the Swedish press concerning safety problems.[2] The Swedish King, Carl Gustav XVI, nearly refused to visit Lithuania in the autumn of 1992 because of the fear of radiation from the plant.

Sweden depends on nuclear power to meet 50% of its energy needs. There is concern within Sweden's energy industry that if a nuclear accident comparable with that at Chernobyl were to occur at Ignalina, there would not only be a large loss of life in Lithuania and in the surrounding region (including Sweden), but also a strong and permanent antinuclear backlash in Sweden, resulting in the demise of the country's own nuclear industry. Therefore, the industry has a vested interest in improving the safety of the Ignalina plant. In February 1994, the EBRD provided an ECU 33 million grant for Ignalina through its Nuclear Safety Account to carry out urgent and feasible safety upgrades (EBRD, 1994).

In late 1996, the Swedish Confederation of Industries announced that it would be willing to fund the closure of the existing reactors at Ignalina and the construction of a new plant at the site on the condition that the Swedish government would not phase out nuclear power in Sweden. Industry spokespersons emphasized the logic of phasing out and replacing one of Eastern Europe's least safe nuclear reactors as an alternative to phasing out a safer Swedish reactor (Selander, 1996). Swedish Prime Minister Goran Person, however, rejected this deal. In his parliamentary statement, Person emphasized that the "poor" Lithuanians should not be asked to phase out nuclear power before the "rich" Swedes did so.

Since 1991, aid for Ignalina, which is mainly channeled through the Swedish Nuclear Inspectorate's Swedish International Project (SIP), has amounted to SEK 320 million. This aid is targeted at three areas: cooperation between authorities, staff training, and technical projects. The safety improvements that Sweden has funded include installing fire doors at the plant, installing early warning radiation systems at the plant itself and at various locations throughout Lithuania, funding and setting up a Lithuanian nuclear inspectorate (VATESI) based on the Swedish model, examining the strength of the metal in the emergency cooling system, building an interim nuclear waste storage site, upgrading operating procedures, and improving maintenance of the plant (Nistad, 1993, 1994a, 1994b, 1995a, 1995b; Svenningsson, 1994).

The aid, however, has not been problem free. Initially, the Lithuanians were suspicious about the purpose of the aid and concerned about losing sovereignty and control of Ignalina. It took a great deal of convincing before the Lithuanians agreed to allow aid transfers to take place. For Sweden, there was a problem of liability. The Lithuanian Environmental Protection Department wanted Sweden to be financially liable for the safety features that had been installed at the plant by Swedish firms. This demand has been reversed since Lithuania joined the International Atomic Energy Agency (Crona, 1994) and signed the international Vienna Convention on Civil Liability for Nuclear Damage. Other nations – including neighboring Belarus – have not signed the convention. Thus, if an accident with transboundary ramifications were to occur at Ignalina, the government of Belarus could, in theory, sue Swedish firms for compensation. For this reason, the Swedish authorities have decided not to carry out some of the originally planned safety work (Svenningsson, 1994).

The use of aid funds to deal with nuclear waste is presenting additional problems. According to the head of the Ignalina plant, Sweden should pay for storing the nuclear waste at the Ignalina site, tantamount to asking Swedish taxpayers to subsidize Lithuanian electricity consumers. The Swedish authorities are in a difficult situation, as it is virtually impossible to raise electricity prices in Lithuania to fund the storage site. The Swedes are concerned that without the site, nuclear contamination from the wastes may affect Sweden (J.O. Snihs, personal communication, May 1995).

Although much of the aid channeled to Ignalina has been administered efficiently (Svenningsson, 1994), it is unclear whether the aid will be needed if Lithuania's energy strategy changes. It may be a waste of taxpayers' money to make safety improvements on Reactor 1 if it is closed down in the near future, as is currently being contemplated. Perhaps it would be better to use the aid money to improve the quality of drinking water in Lithuania by installing more wastewater cleaning plants and upgrading the sewage system. Policymakers at both the EBRD and the Swedish Nuclear Inspectorate argue, however, that safety improvements are needed now to stop an accident from occurring in the future (G. Grabia, personal communication, 1995).

2.3   The Importance of Ignalina to Lithuania

In recent years there has been a series of studies discussing the future of Ignalina and nuclear power in Lithuania. Overall, oil is the most important fuel in Lithuania's energy mix, representing almost 50% of the total. Nuclear power is the second most important fuel, with 25% of the total. However, Lithuania's gross domestic product (GDP) declined by approximately 50% after independence, and energy consumption is currently quite low, with a per capita consumption of 1.3 tons of oil equivalent compared with 2.6 tons of oil equivalent in 1989. Moreover, electricity consumption has decreased on a per capita basis from a high of 3.4 megawatt hours (MWh) in 1989 to a current level of 1.8 MWh, of which industry is the largest consumer. If consumption remains at these levels, a phaseout of the reactors at Ignalina might be feasible.

In a grant agreement between the Lithuanian government, the EBRD, and the Ignalina nuclear power station, it was decided that a least-cost program for power sector development should be established to determine if and when Ignalina could be closed down. The study, which was carried out by energy experts at the Lithuanian Energy Institute, members of the PHARE program, and foreign experts, came to the conclusion that early closure of the second reactor was the least-cost solution. Additional investments in both units at Ignalina would be economically inefficient, as the plant cannot be utilized at full capacity without large export volumes (Lithuanian Energy Institute, 1995). Closure would result in increased air pollution in the form of emissions of sulfur dioxide, nitrogen oxides, and particulates. This increase, however, could be offset by the installation of emission abatement technologies and greater use of natural gas imported from Russia.

Prior to the independence of the Baltic states, the most accepted way to protest against the Soviet Union was to do so on ecological issues. This was the case in Estonia, where there was public protest about the continued mining of phosphorite (Taagepera, 1993). In Lithuania, the public was concerned about both nuclear power and environmental degradation in general. After the Baltic states gained their independence, environmental issues often were quickly forgotten, and there was more concern about surviving the tough economic situation (Löfstedt, 1994). Studies have shown that the public is willing to accept the risks of Ignalina in return for affordable electricity rates.

2.4 Transboundary Risk Management Issues

Given the substantial amount of Swedish aid to improve the safety of the Ignalina plant, it is important to ask whether this is the best use of Swedish funds. How serious do policymakers and the general public in Sweden and Lithuania perceive the risks from Ignalina to be? This question must be asked in view of other risks that are competing for Swedish funds, both in Sweden and in Lithuania. Thus, it is important to ask how the public and policymakers in both the donor and recipient countries prioritize transboundary environmental aid. Furthermore, the Swedes are interested not only in reducing the transboundary risks from Lithuania, but also in improving their political relations with this Baltic neighbor. For this reason, it is important to explore whether environmental aid is promoting cooperation and building mutual respect between the two countries.

These issues were explored in an empirical study of the views of Swedish and Lithuanian policymakers concerning the risks of the Ignalina nuclear power plant and the efficiency and equity of Swedish aid to improve its safety. In-depth interviews with financiers (e.g., the EBRD and the World Bank), policymakers, and academics in the energy and environmental fields in Sweden and Lithuania were carried out to determine their views on transboundary risks, with specific reference to the Ignalina case. In addition, a random face-to-face survey of 100 residents in Kaunas, Lithuania, and a random telephone survey of 100 individuals in Malmö, Sweden, were conducted in the spring of 1995 to provide information on public perceptions of the risks from the Ignalina plant and Sweden's aid to it. In the Malmö sample, 154 telephone calls were required to achieve a sample size of 100, representing a response rate of 65%; in Kaunas,

140 people were approached to yield a sample size of 100, representing a response rate of 71%. Finally, a three-year mass media analysis of Sweden's largest daily newspaper (*Dagens Nyheter* with a circulation of 380,000) was conducted to assess the extent and content of media information available to the Swedish public and policymakers.

Malmö was chosen because it is the largest city in southern Sweden on the Baltic Sea and it has been severely affected by transboundary environmental problems such as acid rain and pollution of the Baltic. Kaunas is the second largest city in Lithuania, with a population of 430,000. As an important industrial center, Kaunas has severe environmental problems. The air is heavily polluted and there is, to date, no properly functioning municipal sewage system.

2.5   Views of Lithuanian and Swedish Policymakers

2.5.1   Lithuanian policymakers

Among the policymakers interviewed in Lithuania, there is a general belief that the public does not currently influence the policy-making process. Compared with when Lithuania was gaining its independence, the public appears to be uninterested in environmental issues. As a result, policymakers see little point in trying to involve them in the decision-making process. However, policymakers did try to involve the public when the attempted increase in electricity prices led to the resignation of the energy minister. The policymakers also expressed the view that the public has been experiencing information overload since Lithuania gained its independence; there is so much information available to the public that they do not know what to believe and whom to trust.

Discussions with Lithuanian policymakers focused on the role of the public, the seriousness of transboundary risks, and whether nuclear power should be prioritized over other environmental problems. Lithuanian policymakers were concerned about both the transboundary and local risks posed by Ignalina and were grateful for the aid that Sweden provided for it:

> I am concerned about the risks posed by Ignalina as I am antinuclear power, so I am grateful for all the aid that is made available.

Q: Would it be better for Swedish aid money to fund other environmental problems such as improving the quality of the drinking water?

No, not really. It is good to use Sweden's aid to make Ignalina better. We can use aid from other countries to build sewage plants and the like. [Lithuanian policymaker, May 1995]

These views were shared by another senior official in the Environment Ministry:

Lithuania is generally concerned about the risks posed by Ignalina. The plant is unsafe and an accident could occur there at any time, affecting Lithuania and the rest of Europe. However, we don't want to close the plant down as we need the electricity. [Lithuanian policymaker, May 1995]

This view was echoed by another senior policymaker in the Energy Ministry:

The problem is that we are so dependent on Ignalina. It is a difficult environmental issue compared to, say, sewage. Although I don't think that we will have a major accident at Ignalina, you never can be sure. We have to make sure that Ignalina is safe, as we can't afford to close it. Drinking water is also important, but Ignalina should be prioritized. [Lithuanian policymaker, April 1994]

Ignalina was seen by some to be more than just an environmental problem, since the plant was staffed by Russians:

In theory, it would be possible to close down Ignalina since we have a large generation surplus, but in practice it is not so easy. The plant has a workforce of 6,000, of which 90% are non-Lithuanians and of which Russians make up the biggest group. If the plant were closed down, there would be an uproar among the staff, and it could prompt some form of Russian intervention – something we do not need. [Lithuanian energy professor, May 1995]

These opinions suggest that Ignalina is viewed as an important environmental risk problem by the country's policymakers. However, there have been problems associated with aid, such as who determines how it is spent. Policymakers indicated that Sweden and other Western nations were making decisions about how the environmental aid was to be spent without adequately consulting them:

A great deal of the aid is decided by the Swedes and not by us. Sweden, for instance, decided to install 10 early warning radiation systems in Lithuania. We didn't ask for them, but they said it would be good for all parties. The situation is not much better with Germany. Germany's environmental aid mainly helps German industry.

Q: Are you concerned about the safety features on Ignalina?

Yes, I am, but the Swedes should be concerned about their plants as well. They built one plant (Barsebäck) only 20 kilometers away from Copenhagen. That was not smart. Additionally, we are not allowed to make safety inspections of their plants, but they do at ours, and that is not fair. [Lithuanian environmental policymaker, May 1995]

If Sweden is sending aid to Ignalina, it may be because the Swedes are more concerned about the plant than the Lithuanians. This was well illustrated by comments from the director of the plant:

Ignalina is as safe as a Western reactor. All this writing about us being 100 times less safe than Western plants is wrong. But I do not mind if the Swedes are concerned about safety. As long as the Swedes are concerned and pay for their concern, we will be concerned as well. [Head of the Ignalina nuclear power station, May 1995]

On the whole, Lithuanian policymakers are positive toward the environmental aid they receive from Sweden. However, it is not clear whether they support Ignalina's priority status for this aid. The Lithuanian Environmental Strategy Task Force, which selects environmental problems for priority funding, has prepared a report indicating that, because Ignalina generates such a substantial amount of Lithuania's electricity, it would be unrealistic to recommend its closure at this time. However, the task force also suggested implementing a long-term program of energy conservation and development of renewable energy sources so the plant can eventually be closed. This means that the Lithuanian government may increasingly view aid to the Ignalina plant as an unwise long-term investment (Williams, 1995).

2.5.2   Swedish policymakers

Discussions with Swedish policymakers focused on their views concerning transboundary environmental risks and, more specifically, their views on aid to improve the safety of the Ignalina plant. Most of the policymakers interviewed were more concerned about local environmental problems than about transboundary environmental risks. This was especially true for local government officials in southern Sweden:

> Of course, we are concerned about acid rain and such problems. Here in Skåne [the region where Malmö is located] many of these problems come from foreign sources. But we are even more worried about local environmental issues like car emissions, as they affect us so much more. [Local policymaker in a southern Swedish town, October, 1993]

This view is somewhat surprising. The respondent comes from a region in Sweden that is heavily exposed to acid rain originating from abroad, which has caused considerable damage to crops, forests, and lakes (Danish–Swedish Environmental Committee, 1994).

This policymaker's views were shared by a representative of a nongovernmental organization (NGO) in a southern Swedish town:

> Policymakers win votes by focusing on local environmental problems such as traffic. They do not win votes by discussing transboundary problems. Policymakers can do something about local problems where they have power – for example, they can set up traffic-free zones – but they have little influence on international environmental policies. [Swedish NGO representative, May 1995]

National policymakers were more concerned about transboundary environmental problems than were their local counterparts:

> In general it is fair to say that Swedish environmental standards are very high. There is not much more that we can do domestically to combat environmental problems. However, we are heavily affected by transboundary environmental problems. I am especially worried about unsafe nuclear power stations and acid rain. Look what happened with Chernobyl. I therefore support the government's efforts in aiding these nations in reducing the risks from their installations. This does not only help them but also us. [Conservative environmental spokesperson, May 1995]

This was also the view of another politician from the opposite end of the political spectrum, the former Swedish environment minister:

> I am very concerned about Eastern European nuclear reactors. Sweden does not want another Chernobyl. We were severely affected then. I am glad that Sweden is sending advisors to Eastern European nuclear reactors to help to make them safe.
>
> Q: Are you particularly concerned about Ignalina?
>
> Ignalina is quite often reported in the Swedish media. It is one of the nuclear power stations closest to Sweden, and it is known to have many safety problems. Of course, I am concerned about it. [Birgitta Dahl, June 1995]

High-level staff at the Swedish Nuclear Inspectorate and the Swedish National Institute for Radiation Protection, who administer the aid for Ignalina, were generally positive about the Ignalina aid program. They felt that the plant was unsafe and that its operation could have serious implications for Sweden:

> We have received a mandate from the Parliament to give aid to Ignalina and that is why we do it.
>
> Q: But why did you get this mandate?
>
> Senior Swedish politicians are obviously very concerned about the safety of Ignalina and the waste that it produces, as this could affect Sweden's environment and the rest of Europe. It is no more complicated than that. [Spokesperson for the Swedish Nuclear Inspectorate, June 1995]

This view was shared by a spokesperson for the Swedish Institute for Radiation Protection:

> We give aid to Ignalina because we can be affected by it. For instance, we are concerned about the waste as this may be smuggled into Sweden for terrorist purposes. Then it is better that the Lithuanians keep it. [Spokesperson for the Swedish Institute for Radiation Protection, June 1995]

2.6 Results of a Public Questionnaire

2.6.1 Lithuanian Public

In sharp contrast to Lithuanian policymakers' views that the public is indifferent to the environment, 96 of the 100 respondents in the Kaunas survey stated that they were concerned about environmental problems. As shown in open-ended Question 1 (for which the respondent can give multiple answers), among the problems mentioned most frequently were water pollution, air pollution, and trash.

Question 1. What types of environmental problems are you concerned about?

Groundwater pollution	46
Air pollution	37
Trash	16
Industrial wastes	16
Polluted lakes	14
Nuclear power	8
Lack of wastewater treatment	8
Traffic	7
Industry in general	6
Soil contamination	6
Power generation	3
Ozone hole	3
Effects on plants and animals	3
Contaminated food	2

$N=96$

Like those interviewed in Malmö, the Kaunas respondents were more concerned with local environmental problems than with transboundary ones such as acid rain. Lithuanian policymakers agreed that it is more important to concentrate on local rather than transboundary environmental issues. As one official said,

> We are somewhat concerned about transboundary environmental problems, but we have so many acute local ones that need to be dealt with as soon as possible. [Policymaker in the Lithuanian Environment Ministry, November 1993]

It is noteworthy that so few respondents mentioned the environmental risks posed by Ignalina. When questioned specifically about the plant later in the survey, respondents said that they were very concerned about the risks posed by it. The respondents were also aware that their environmental problems affected other countries. Sixty-seven percent of the respondents believed that pollution originating in Lithuania caused environmental damage elsewhere. As shown in the results of Question 2 (open-ended), among the environmental problems that the respondents thought that Lithuania exported were water and air pollution.

Question 2. What environmental problems does Lithuania cause in other countries?

River water pollution	30
Air pollution	30
Seawater pollution	22
Nuclear power risks	17
Radiation	16
Acid rain	6
Chemicals	4
Do not know	12

N=67

These results suggest that there has been some discussion of transboundary environmental problems in Lithuania. Thirty-three of the 67 respondents were aware that one of Lithuania's main transboundary environmental problems is the threat of a possible release of radiation due to an accident at the Ignalina plant. All 100 of the respondents had heard of the Ignalina nuclear power station, especially that the plant is unsafe, as shown in Question 3 (open-ended).

Question 3. What have you heard about Ignalina?

Unsafe power plant	24
Bad operators, bad organization	10
Many faults in operation	10
Bad reactor design	8
Could cause radioactive contamination	7
Produces cheap electricity	7
Fuel has disappeared	5
Threat to all of Europe	3
Operated by non-Lithuanians	3
Other	6
Do not know	21

N=100

It appears that most of what the respondents had heard about Ignalina was negative. The risks of Ignalina have been discussed a great deal in the media, especially since Lithuania's independence. Several factors have helped to put Ignalina firmly in the public eye. First, it is a Russian-designed reactor mainly operated by Russian staff and located in Lithuania on orders from Moscow. In other words, ethnic Lithuanians have had an involuntary risk imposed upon them, over which they may feel they currently have little control. Generally, Lithuanians are critical toward Russian products, which are synonymous with bad quality. Additionally, environmentalists, who were very strong in Lithuania and the other Baltic states around the time of independence, have brought attention to the risks of Ignalina. These risks have been amplified by Western concern. Local newspapers frequently carry coverage of various aid agencies visiting Lithuania to provide funding for safety improvements at the plant. Finally, in 1994 a member of the Lithuanian mafia threatened to bomb the plant. The terrorist threat was front-page news in Lithuania for more than a week. Another reason for local concern about Ignalina is mistrust of the responsible authorities. As shown in Question 4, 63 of the 100 respondents did not trust the authorities' handling of the discussions concerning Ignalina.

Question 4. Do you trust the Lithuanian authorities in handling the discussions concerning Ignalina?

Yes	7
No	63
Maybe	26
Do not know	4

$N=100$

As shown in Question 5 (open-ended), there were many different reasons why the respondents did not trust the authorities.

Question 5. Why do you not trust the authorities?

I don't trust them at all	12
They all lie	12
They are not trustworthy	11
Their thinking is outmoded	11
They don't care about people	11
Bad legislation system	5
Do not know	3

$N=63$

Many politicians in the Baltic states were active members of the Communist party during the Soviet occupation. The public is likely to be skeptical about any politician who appears to have changed his or her political views to remain in power. Another factor promoting distrust is that policymakers in the Baltic states are not well paid and therefore are seen as sometimes using devious methods to increase their income. In general, there is a high turnover of politicians in the Baltic states, partly due to infighting and bickering between party coalitions.

2.6.2 Swedish Public

The respondents in Malmö were aware of transboundary environmental problems and their effects on Sweden, but they were more concerned about local environmental problems, particularly emissions from cars. As shown by the open-ended responses to Question 1, environmental problems specifically associated with Eastern Europe, such as acid rain, pollution of the Öresund Strait of the Baltic Sea, and forest die-off, did not dominate. Most interestingly, the risks associated with East European nuclear reactors were not mentioned by any of the respondents.

Question 1. What are the environmental problems that this region is subject to?

Car emissions	37
Air pollution in general	17
Acid rain	14
Contamination of groundwater	11
Waste from chemical plants	7
Industry in general	7
Pollution of the Baltic	6
Other	26
Do not know	3

$N=100$

The level of concern about car emissions has several explanations. The urban environment of Malmö makes air pollution, particularly car emissions, very noticeable. The government's policy stance on the issue is also very distinctive: gasoline prices are among the highest in Europe (Löfstedt, 1993, 1997), partially to encourage the public to drive less.

The media have also concentrated on domestic environmental problems. In our analysis of more than 120 newspaper articles on domestic energy and environmental issues between September 1992 and February 1994, only eight articles discussed Eastern Europe's environmental problems and only four articles discussed how these problems affect Sweden. Despite this seeming indifference to transboundary environmental problems originating in Eastern Europe, nearly all the respondents in Malmö

(98%) felt that Sweden was affected by them. As shown in the open-ended responses to Question 2, acid rain, industrial waste, and nuclear power were the examples cited most often.

Question 2. How is Sweden affected by Eastern Europe's environmental problems?

Source of acid rain in Sweden	46
High level of industrial waste	44
Unsafe nuclear power plants	21
Air pollution	18
Pollution of the Baltic Sea	16
Swedes live so near to the area	4
Pollution from coal plants	2
Other	6
Do not know	2

N=98

It is not surprising that acid rain was mentioned by so many of the respondents. It is a very visible problem and has been a subject of national concern for over 25 years (Lundgren, 1991). Studies indicate that some 14,000 lakes in Sweden have been damaged by acid rain, and the government is spending SEK 200 million (US$25.5 million) a year to neutralize the lakes with lime (Swedish Parliament, 1994). There are also concerns that acid rain is affecting the nation's forest industry, a major source of Sweden's foreign exchange and a very important part of the country's economy (Danish–Swedish Environmental Committee, 1994).

The respondents' perception of industrial waste as an issue, however, is more difficult to explain. East European industries produce large quantities of industrial waste, but how the waste affects Sweden is less clear. A possible explanation is that, because of a lack of technology and expertise in waste treatment, the waste products could leach into rivers and other water bodies, thereby affecting Sweden via the Baltic Sea.

The safety of Eastern Europe's nuclear power plants has been widely discussed by both policymakers and journalists since the 1986 accident at Chernobyl, which resulted in radioactive fallout over large parts of Sweden (Sjöberg and Drottz, 1987; Holmberg, 1988; Löfstedt, 1993). One policymaker said,

> I am more concerned about the potential environmental consequences of an accident at an Eastern European nuclear reactor than

the everyday effects of acid rain. At least we can do something about acid rain.

Q: What do you mean?

We can lime lakes and forests, but look at Chernobyl and the effects that the radioactive fallout still has on certain groups of the Swedish population. [Policymaker in the Swedish Parliament, February 1994]

The pollution of the Baltic Sea has also been the subject of public debate. In recent years there has been rising concern in Sweden over the increasing quantities of heavy metals in Baltic fish. The Swedish government has recommended that the public limit their consumption of fish from the Baltic Sea (Karlsson, 1993).

As almost all of the Malmö respondents felt that East European environmental problems affected Sweden, self-interest would suggest that aid be targeted at transboundary problems. Our survey showed that 92% of the respondents supported environmental aid for Eastern Europe. As shown by the open-ended responses to Question 3, aid was viewed as a way for both the recipient and the donor nations to improve their environments.

Question 3. Reasons why Sweden should give environmental aid to Eastern Europe

To help save their environment	62
Save Sweden's environment	50
Good for Swedish industry	7
We have more money than they have	6
It is more effective there	2
Other	3

N=92

Policymakers and analysts alike have viewed environmental aid as an efficient measure for improving the environment of Europe (Westerberg, 1993). This view was also expressed by local officials:

Of course we should give environmental aid to Eastern Europe. It is much more efficient to spend a crown there than a crown on reducing further the already low levels of pollution at home.

Q: Can you think of any other reasons?

By giving environmental aid to Eastern Europe we are also helping Swedish industry. [Mayor of a southern Swedish town, April 1994]

In addition, when policymakers were asked whether they felt that the general public would be in favor of giving environmental aid, the transboundary nature of the problems was cited. For example,

> I think that the Swedish public are in favor of us giving environmental aid to Eastern Europe. We have received letters from school children saying how good it is that we are saving the Baltic Sea, and recent surveys echo this.
>
> Q: Why do you think that this is the case?
>
> There are probably several reasons, the most likely being that the public realizes that we are affected by their environmental problems and that something has to be done. [Policymaker in the Swedish Environmental Ministry, February 1993]

Many of the respondents were vague or unaware of what precisely Swedish environmental aid was being used for in Eastern Europe, as shown by the responses to Question 4 (open-ended).

Question 4. What is Swedish aid being used for in Eastern Europe?

Educating them about solving environmental problems	15
Checking nuclear power plants	10
Checking and cleaning up industry	6
Carrying out research	5
Economic assistance	5
Providing Swedish environmental consultants	3
Building sewage plants in Poland and the Baltic states	3
Other	10
Do not know	39

$N=81$

Of greater concern is the lack of information that policymakers have regarding what Sweden's environmental aid to Eastern Europe is used for:

> I am happy that we give environmental aid to Eastern Europe. We have had a long cultural association with many of the nations there.
>
> Q: Do you know what types of projects Sweden funds in the Baltic States and Poland?
>
> I know that they are working on nuclear plant safety, but otherwise I am not sure. [Energy policymaker of a southern Swedish town, October 1993]

Our analysis of the mass media supports this picture of limited information available to the public. The analysis showed that between September 1992 and February 1994 there were only 25 articles discussing the specifics of Sweden's environmental aid to Eastern Europe, and of these articles, 13 discussed the installation of safety devices on nuclear power plants.

To summarize, not surprisingly the respondents in Malmö were more concerned about local environmental problems than about transboundary risk issues. However, they were aware of such transboundary environmental problems as acid rain and radiation, and, more interestingly, industrial waste. The respondents were very altruistic ("we should save the environment") but did not know what in fact the aid was being used for. Like Swedish policymakers, however, the public was well aware that aid to Eastern Europe could serve to decrease risks to themselves. Self-interest appears to be a strong motivating force for environmental aid.

2.7 Conclusions

Environmental aid from Western Europe to the ECE countries for the primary purpose of reducing environmental risks has become an important instrument for transboundary risk management in Europe. This study has examined the effectiveness and equity of Swedish aid targeted at improving the safety of the Ignalina nuclear power plant from the point of view of policymakers and the public in both Sweden and Lithuania.

The findings of our empirical study, which was based on in-depth interviews, a media analysis, and questionnaires to policymakers and the public in Sweden and Lithuania, show a great deal of support for direct and targeted aid to Ignalina from Sweden. However, in many cases this support is qualified. The Swedes, like their Lithuanian counterparts, are mainly concerned about local environmental issues, yet aid to Eastern Europe that also reduces local risks is well accepted. The Swedes were also altruistic: there was as much support on the part of the Swedes for aid that benefits the recipients in Lithuania as for aid that benefits the Swedes. Moreover, it might have been expected that the Swedes would be more concerned about transboundary risks than their Lithuanian counterparts, but this finding was not borne out by the survey results.

In many respects, these results parallel the findings of the survey of the public in Hungary and Slovakia concerning the future of the Gabcikovo hydropower station (see Chapter 6). Many of the survey respondents on both sides of the river appeared to be altruistic. Although both countries viewed themselves as losers vis-à-vis the other country, the general public in both countries overwhelmingly rejected any form of loser compensation. There was a strong willingness on the part of the public on both sides of the river to move ahead with the project in a mutually beneficial way.

In the case of aid to improve the safety of the Ignalina plant, both the Swedes and the Lithuanians are beneficiaries. Yet, the Lithuanian public may resent aid that benefits the donors, especially if they feel that the funds could be used to reduce more serious local risks. Some evidence of this resentment was apparent from the interviews and responses to the questionnaire. Although the Lithuanian policymakers generally viewed Ignalina is a major risk problem and an appropriate recipient of Swedish aid, a comment made by the director of the Ignalina power station is revealing: "As long as the Swedes are concerned [about Ignalina] and pay for their concern, we will be concerned as well." Moreover, the Lithuanian respondents to the questionnaire mentioned pollution to the rivers, air, and sea as serious environmental problems more frequently than they mentioned the Ignalina nuclear power plant.

Finally, Swedish aid to Lithuania appears to be promoting cooperation and mutual respect between authorities in the two countries. On the whole, Lithuanian policymakers were supportive of the prioritization of Swedish aid to the Ignalina plant and of Swedish environmental aid in general. However, they did express concern that they were not always adequately consulted.

Notes

[1] Unless otherwise indicated, throughout this paper the term "East European neighbors" refers to the area encompassing St. Petersburg and its hinterland, the three Baltic states (Estonia, Latvia, and Lithuania), and Poland.

[2] In 1996, for example, Ignalina had five safety incidents that rated a 1 on the International Nuclear Event Scale (INES), and 17 incidents rating a 0; in comparison, Sweden's 12 reactors together had a total of 5 incidents rating a 1 and no zero-rated incidents.

Acknowledgments

We would like to thank the following people, who provided comments on earlier drafts of this paper and contributed with valuable background material: Birgitta Dahl, Gunter Grabia, Laura Kelly, Lars-Gunnar Larsson, Joanne Linnerooth-Bayer, and officials at the Lithuanian Environment and Energy Ministries, the Swedish Nuclear Inspectorate, and the Swedish Board for Radiation Protection. This report was funded by a grant from the Swedish Council for the Planning and Coordination of Research.

References

Crona, E., 1994, af Ugglas besöker Ignalina, *Svenska Dagbladet*, 18 May, p. 13 [in Swedish].

Danish–Swedish Environmental Committee, 1994, *Försurningsproblemene i Sydsverige*, Swedish Ministry of Environment, Stockholm, Sweden [in Swedish].

EBRD (European Bank for Reconstruction and Development), 1994, *Nuclear Safety Account*, EBRD, London, UK.

Holmberg, S., 1988, *Svenska folkets åsikter om kärnkraft och slutförvaring efter Tjernobyl*, National Board for Spent Nuclear Fuel, Stockholm, Sweden [in Swedish].

Karlsson, G., 1993, PCB larm om Ostersjöfisk tonas ner, *Dagens Nyheter*, 16 November, p. A5 [in Swedish].

Lithuanian Energy Institute, 1995, Least-Cost Power Sector Development Programme, Interim Report, Lithuanian Energy Institute, Kaunas, Lithuania.

Löfstedt, R.E., 1993, *Dilemma of Swedish Energy Policy Implications for International Policy Makers*, Avebury Press, Aldershot, UK.

Löfstedt, R.E., 1994, Environmental aid to Eastern Europe: Swedish and Estonian perspectives, *Post Soviet Geography*, 35(10):594–607.

Löfstedt, R.E., 1995, What factors determine Sweden's provision of environmental aid to Eastern Europe, *Global Environmental Change*, 5(1):41–49.

Löfstedt, R.E., 1996a, Fairness across borders: The Barsebäck nuclear power plant, *Risk: Health, Safety and Environment*, 7:135–144.

Löfstedt, R.E., 1996b, Risk communication: The Barsebäck nuclear plant case, *Energy Policy*, 24(8):689–696.

Löfstedt, R.E., 1996c, A review of Sweden's environmental aid to Eastern Europe: Criticisms and possible solutions, in R.E. Löfstedt and G. Sjöstedt, eds, *Environmental Aid Programmes to Eastern Europe*, Avebury, Aldershot, UK.

Löfstedt, R.E., 1997, Sweden: The dilemma of a proposed nuclear phase-out, in U. Collier and R.E. Löfstedt, eds, *Cases in Climate Change Policy: Political Reality in the European Union*, Earthscan, London, UK.

Lundgren, L.J., 1991, *Försurningen på Dagordningen*, Sweden's Environmental Protection Agency and the Swedish Council for the Planning and Coordination of Research, Stockholm, Sweden [in Swedish].

Majone, G., 1985, The international dimension, in H. Otway and M. Peltu, eds, *Regulating Industrial Risks*, Butterworths, London, UK.

Nistad, J.H., 1993, Kärnkraftsäkerhet i Ignalina-ett led i ett regionalt samarbetsprogram, Report for the period 1 July–31 December [in Swedish].

Nistad, J.H., 1994a, Kärnkraftsäkerhet i Ignalina-ett led i ett regionalt samarbetsprogram, Report for the period 1 January–31 March [in Swedish].

Nistad, J.H., 1994b, Kärnkraftsäkerhet i Ignalina-ett led i ett regionalt samarbetsprogram, Report for the period 1 April–30 June [in Swedish].

Nistad, J.H., 1995a, Kärnkraftsäkerhet i Ignalina-ett led i ett regionalt samarbetsprogram, Report for the period 1 January–31 March [in Swedish].

Nistad, J.H., 1995b, Kärnkraftsäkerhet i Ignalina-ett led i ett regionalt samarbetsprogram, Report for the budget year 94/95 [in Swedish].

Paskevicius, V., 1995, Reorganization of the Lithuanian state power system, *Lithuania Energy News*, 1(1):12–14.

Salay, J., 1991, *Osteuropas milj: problem och framtidsutsikter*, Naturia, Stockholm, Sweden [in Swedish].

Selander, J., 1996, Ignalinas VD tillbakavisar svenska nedlaggningskrav, *Svenska Dagbladet*, 21 November, p. B2 [in Swedish].

Selander, J., 1997, Allvarliga brister i kvalitetssakringen, *Svenska Dagbladet*, 13 March, p. B1 [in Swedish].

Sjöberg, L., and Drottz, B.M., 1987, Psychological reactions to cancer risks after the Chernobyl accident, *Medical Oncology and Tumor Pharmacotherapy*, 4:259–271.

Svenningsson, P.J., 1994, *Kärnsäkerhet och strålskyddssamarbete med Osteuropa*, The Secretariat for Analysis of Swedish Development Assistance, Stockholm, Sweden [in Swedish].

Swedish Parliament, 1994, *Regeringens proposition 1993/94. Miljö och Naturresursdepartementet*, Swedish Parliament Publications, Stockholm, Sweden [in Swedish].

Taagepera, R., 1993, *Estonia: Return to Independence*, Westview Press, Boulder, CO, USA.

Westerberg, P., 1993, In Swedish Parliament official documents, *Ostersjöpropositionen 1992/93:99*, Swedish Parliament Publications, Stockholm, Sweden [in Swedish].

Williams, A., 1995, Environmental Economist, ERM London (Coordinator of the Lithuanian National Environmental Strategy Task Force).

Chapter 3

Genetically Modified Crops: What Transboundary Harmonization in Europe?

Les Levidow

3.1 Introduction: Harmonization Problems

Throughout the world there has been an intensifying debate about the risks of biotechnology and of genetically modified organisms (GMOs) designed for agricultural use in particular. Most of the first GMOs to be commercialized were herbicide-tolerant or insect-protected crops; many other GMOs are near or at the commercial stage, including virus-resistant crops, viral insecticides, and nitrogen-fixing microbes. In the public debate over genetically modified (GM) crops, economic and environmental issues have been linked in various ways. In dispute is whether GM crops may mitigate the harmful effects of intensive monoculture – or may inadvertently perpetuate them. (For detailed references, see Levidow and Tait, 1991; Levidow, 1996.)

The agro-food industry emphasizes that GM crops offer various benefits by, for example, enhancing economic competitiveness, increasing food production in pace with population growth, and providing environmentally friendly products. Biotechnology companies have adopted the language of environmental sustainability. According to one company, "Our products create value for our customers by helping them to combine profitability with environmental stewardship. For product impact, this means: more productive agriculture, more soil conservation, less insecticide use, less energy, better habitat protection." For example, "in-built genetic information" helps GM crops to protect themselves against pests and disease, thus reducing agrochemical usage (Magretta, 1997; Monsanto, 1997).

Critics warn that GM crops impose unknown ecological risks, reduce the biodiversity of plant cultivars, direct research and development (R&D) according to commercial criteria, and promote the further industrialization of agriculture. In their view, plant breeders have become subordinate to agrochemical companies, whose products perpetuate technological dependence, for example, through an agrochemical–genetic treadmill. In their view, sustainability must mean reorganizing agricultural systems to prevent the monocultural conditions that attract pests and disease.

Transboundary risks have been a focus of European public debate and legislation on GMOs. In the 1980s environmentalists emphasized the prospect that GMOs could carry risks across national borders through biological migration or commercial trade. A major dilemma was how to reconcile transboundary risks with transboundary commerce. In 1990, a European Council Directive was adopted for regulating the deliberate release of GMOs into the environment, especially for granting Community-wide approval of commercial use. It was designed so that risk-assessment criteria could be harmonized among the member states in order to eliminate trade barriers. Under this regime, each product would obtain approval in all member states – or not at all.

The original goal, however, has remained elusive. Europe-wide regulatory procedures have highlighted diverse national criteria for assessing GM crops. Safety claims have provoked dissent grounded in divergent accounts of both the environmental risks of GMOs and their compatibility with sustainable agriculture – which are difficult to reconcile with transboundary commerce. Europe-wide conflicts have focused on agri-environmental issues concerning farmland. Although risk arguments have cited national environmental characteristics, little more has been said about the biological transboundary scenarios of the 1980s risk debate.[1]

By the late 1990s, widespread public protest had led to European procedures that incorporated more stringent risk-assessment criteria, and to the delay of approval of GM crops. Transboundary issues moved beyond the European context, as regulatory delays in the European Union (EU) aggravated trans-Atlantic trade conflicts. According to the proponents of agricultural biotechnology, Europe was basing its regulation on politics rather than on science.

With respect to a European transboundary risk management regime, this chapter argues the following points:

- An apolitical risk assessment is impossible to achieve, since the relevant science is always framed by environmental values, including some concept of sustainable agriculture.
- Regulatory legitimacy depends on publicly deliberating environmental standards, rather than trying to remove expert judgements from politics.
- A legitimate harmonization depends on accommodating diverse agri-environmental scenarios within technical standards.
- This case exemplifies a more general crisis of the technicist harmonization model that underlies Europe-wide legislation and official expertise.

The technicist harmonization model is elaborated in the next section; the regulatory conflicts over GM crops are analyzed in Sections 3.3 and 3.4.

3.2 Technicist Harmonization Model

Risk debates can be analyzed at three related levels: at the level of factual evidence on the probabilities and consequences; at the level of institutional performance, expertise, and experience; and at the level of worldviews and value systems (Renn and Levine 1991; see also Chapter 9).

At the highest level, where the conflict is defined by different social values, decision making requires a fundamental consensus on the issues that underlie the risk debate. As long as value issues remain unresolved, even the best technical expertise and the most profound competence cannot overcome social, cultural, and political value conflicts. Risk management agencies tend to reframe higher-level conflicts as lower-level ones.

Ultimately, they focus the discussion on technical evidence, for which the regulatory agency claims superior expertise (Renn and Levine, 1991; see also Chapter 9).

At the same time, technical evidence remains inseparable from world-views about nature and society. This feature has been theorized as a "framing" that underlies all risk knowledge. In seeking and organizing more facts about risk, we make sociopolitical choices, for example, about what potential harms to prevent and, therefore, about what opportunities to forgo. According to Jasanoff, "We can hardly order, rearrange, or usefully supplement our knowledge about risk without incorporating these issues into a clear, framing vision of the social and natural order that we wish to live in" (1993: 129).

Indeed, often at issue is the acceptability of technological choices. Protest tends to reframe technical issues as institutional issues about normative frameworks – about "how we should live" (Beck, 1992). Consequently, risk debates involve conflicts of accountability over how the potential harm from commodity production "can be distributed, averted, controlled and legitimated" (Beck, 1996). Such conflicts generate expert disagreements: "Risk society is tendentially a self-critical society ... . Experts are relativised or dethroned by counterexperts" (Beck, 1996).

Moreover, as alternative accounts of environmental problems gain public support, official expertise loses any neutral image. Toward a remedy, transboundary institutional arrangements have been seen as an opportunity or even an imperative for enhancing public involvement (see, e.g., Chapter 9). However, such involvement runs counter to prevalent models for European integration.

Expert-based standards have been central to European integration efforts, especially through the project to overcome internal trade barriers. Originally, the European Community (EC) sought to formalize standards, for example, in the annexes of its Directives, but this approach was abandoned as too cumbersome and contentious. Rather than seek uniform standards, the new approach had a more modest goal: mutual recognition of national standards (Pelkmans, 1987; Majone, 1997: 157). Since the mid-1980s, the EC has sought to reconcile diverse national regulations rather than simply standardize them.

At the same time, EC strategists envisaged that national differences would be overcome or reconciled through Europe-wide expertise. Rather than establish a new bureaucracy, European integration would facilitate new expert networks and develop European forms of knowledge, and thus provide authority for Europe-wide policy (Delors, 1992; Barry, 1993). A decentralized, expert-based harmonization would define the new Europe as well as integrate it.

This project has inadvertently politicized expertise:

> Both supporters and opponents of particular regulatory measures usually cast their arguments in the language of "regulatory science" rather than in the more traditional language of interest or class policies. Paradoxically, the very fact that the scientific basis is often uncertain and contestable tends to increase the role of experts at every stage of the regulatory process. [Majone, 1997:157]

Consequently, EC environmental policy has become politicized in several senses. As the "internal market" imperative led member states to make greater environmental commitments in the 1980s, inadequate compliance led to greater disputes and public protests. Paradoxically, the "implementation deficit" can be regarded as a policy success if measured by greater public expectations of higher environmental quality and constant pressure for improvement (Jordan, 1999: 87).

Why is such politicization a problem? According to Majone (1996), EU regulation faces credibility problems that arise when national governments interfere for party-political reasons or for short-term electoral gain, thus intensifying distrust among governments. As a solution, authority has been delegated beyond direct political influence – to independent agencies, to courts, and/or to professional experts. Consequently, regulatory decisions may suffer from a "democratic deficit," lacking democratic accountability and legitimacy.

Nevertheless, by delegating policy to "independent institutions," Majone argues, the EU "would increase the credibility of domestic policies." It would thereby facilitate "the emergence of those networks of national and European regulators which alone hold the promise of resolving the dilemmas of regulatory federalism" (Majone, 1996: 282). Rather than enhance public participation, the EU can enhance a procedural legitimacy by stating clear reasons for decisions (Majone, 1996: 291–294). Although this strategy was intended for all EU policies, it conflicts with other accounts of environmental policy in particular.

According to Wynne, European integration has been dominated by a technicist harmonization model, which presumes that technical criteria have no socio-cultural content.[2] In this model, "risk" is understood as the probability of measurable harm caused by a specific product interacting with its environment or in its context of use. It is assumed that the context will not be changed adversely by the product itself, for example, by economic pressures toward more "efficient" production (Wynne, 1998).

When faced with local variations, Wynne argues, European policy culture tends "to technicise them, as if they were matters of residual technical imprecision rather than of genuine social and cultural indeterminacy" (Wynne, 1998). Scientific descriptions may vary, but only because of differences in resources or biophysical risks. By allowing only for geographical differences in the "natural" environment, EU standards are presumed to stand above culture. Technical criteria are decontextualized from the institutions that frame the issues and that seek legitimacy for decision making. International disharmonies are portrayed as deviations from an ideal, objective, science-based regulation (Wynne, 1998).

Thus value conflicts are technicized as factual disputes. As a different strategy, diverse national approaches can be regarded as resources for constructing European institutions: "Diversity is the strength of Europe, not its weakness or problem" (Renn, 1995: 154).

All those tensions are illustrated by the case study presented here – the European efforts at transboundary risk management of GMOs, particularly for commercial use of GM crops. In this chapter, the following aspects are analyzed: how the EC adopted new legislation for regulating GMOs; how its implementation led to national disharmonies and eventually to more stringent EU-wide regulation; how labeling has become linked to risk, despite attempts to separate these issues; and how US–Europe trade conflicts relate to European ones. The limits of technicist harmonization and the prospects for superseding that model are analyzed in the concluding section.

3.3   GMO Releases: Regulatory Framework

In the 1980s risk debate, environmentalists sought to stigmatize GMOs as an abnormal danger. They attacked the biotechnology R&D agenda and its molecular-level solutions, which attributed socio-agronomic problems to genetic deficiencies (Gottweis, 1998). Biotechnological developments faced potential obstacles from organized protest and from national divergences in regulatory response. In 1986, new Danish legislation banned GMO releases. Protesters in Germany gained much support for a statutory moratorium there, especially through a Parliamentary Commission of Inquiry.

The European Commission assigned the Environment Directorate-General, DG-XI, the task of preparing a Deliberate Release Directive. DG-XI officials argued that a range of divergent regulatory regimes "was not going to help the harmonious development of biotechnology in Europe and would hamper access, in fact, to the entire Community market of 1992" (CBC, 1990: 18). As the solution, the new Deliberate Release Directive 90/220 formed part of the EC's ambitious legislative program for overcoming internal trade barriers under the Single European Act of 1992 (Hildebrand, 1993: 28–36).

For the commercial stage of GM products, the Directive 90/220 procedure led to further debate over regulatory overlaps or gaps with other legislation, in particular

- the Common Catalogue Directive, including National List registration, relevant to any new plant variety (EEC, 1970); and
- pesticide regulation (EEC, 1991), relevant to any herbicide that has a new use, for example, for spraying on an herbicide-tolerant crop.

Their relevance is explained below.[3] Note that legislation enacted under the European Economic Community (until 1995), is labeled "EEC"; subsequent legislation is labeled "EC."

3.3.1 Deliberate Release Directive 90/220

The Deliberate Release Directive 90/220 governs the approval process for all GMO releases. The Directive was officially justified by citing transboundary risks and ecological uncertainty: "Whereas living organisms ... may reproduce in the environment and cross national frontiers, thereby affecting other Member States; whereas the effects of such releases on the environment may be irreversible ... ." It was also justified by the potential threat of transboundary barriers to trade (EEC, 1990: 15).

As a dual solution, the new legislation was designed to prevent both environmental harm and trade barriers. According to the preamble, Directive 90/220 is based on the principle of "preventive action." It aims to "establish harmonized procedures and criteria" for assessing GMO releases. Completion of the internal market must be based on "a high level of [environmental and health] protection" (EEC, 1990). According to the Environment Directorate-General, DG-XI, Directive 90/220 extended "a preventive approach that the Community is taking on environmental and other issues" (CBC, 1990: 18).

For other regulatory sectors, the term "preventive" generally refers to hazards already documented. In contrast, for Directive 90/220, the term implicitly meant "precautionary." Later, an official document established "the precautionary principle" as EC policy (CEC, 1993: 55), which was then cited to defend the Directive against deregulatory pressures.

The Directive has several precautionary features, which are ultimately linked to transboundary commerce. It provides statutory backing for the "step-by-step" principle, which says that controls may be relaxed "only if evaluation of the earlier steps ... indicates that the next step can be taken" (EEC, 1990: 15; cf. OECD, 1986: 29). For each R&D release, prior consent must be obtained from the designated "Competent Authority" of the country in which the release will take place. The applicant must submit an environmental risk assessment, which places the burden of evidence upon the applicant, rather than upon the regulator.

To place a GMO product on the market, the application must be filed in the member state where marketing is expected to begin. If the member state recommends approval, then it becomes the rapporteur. Its favorable opinion is circulated to all other member states, which may request additional information or raise objections. If necessary, a vote is taken in the regulatory committee established by Article 21 and/or in the Council of Ministers. If the European Commission grants approval, then the rapporteur signs the authorization, which then becomes valid for all member states of the European Community.

After a product has gained market approval, Article 16 allows a member state to provisionally restrict its use if there are "justifiable reasons" to believe that the product poses a risk. After three months, the Commission must decide whether the restrictions are justified. Article 16 was intended to accommodate environmental and geographical differences, which were considered the only legitimate reason for national exceptions to the internal market.

Finally, member states must undertake all appropriate measures "to avoid adverse effects on human health and the environment" from GMO releases, such as by reviewing risk assessments, enforcing any conditions imposed on releases, and considering any new information relevant to the risk assessment. Although "adverse effects" were not defined by law, some risks had been discussed since the mid-1980s. A DG-XI-funded report drew an analogy between GMOs and agricultural products whose usage had caused problems such as reduced biodiversity, pathogen invasions, pest resistance, and herbicide resistance (Mantegazzini, 1986: 76–80). With respect to these wide-ranging problems, the Directive leaves ambiguous the breadth of "adverse effects" that must be prevented. It mentions no assessment of benefits, though benefits have been assessed by some member states.

3.3.2   Common Catalogue Directive

Under the Common Catalogue Directive, National Listing is the ultimate gateway to a market for food crops. Any new variety must undergo National List trials for at least two years in order to satisfy the criteria – DUS (distinct, uniform, stable) and VCU (value for cultivation and use). Before a variety can be marketed, it must obtain registration on the National List in a member state; it then becomes a candidate for the EU Common Catalogue (EEC, 1970).

Although the Common Catalogue Directive has no clear relevance to environmental risks, the National List procedure has come under pressure to fill gaps in the Directive 90/220 procedure. For example, it was used to delay National List trials of an herbicide-tolerant oilseed rape after the product obtained approval under Directive 90/220. The procedure was also used to restrict the commercial use of insecticidal maize products after they obtained approval under Directive 90/220. In light of the concerns about tracing GM food back to its source, the Common Catalogue law eventually was amended to require labeling of all GM seeds (EC, 1998c).

3.3.3   Pesticide Directive

Pesticides are approved for specific uses and so require further approval for any new use. If an herbicide-tolerant crop is marketed on the basis of its herbicide tolerance, for example, then its sale depends upon approval of the relevant herbicide for spraying on that crop. Such decisions have rested with each member state under Directive 91/414 on plant protection products (EEC, 1991).

Directive 91/414 was designed mainly for a Europe-wide case-by-case safety evaluation of active substances, for example, according to toxicological criteria. If and when an active substance is added to Annex I, it gains advantages from a mutual recognition procedure across member states, which then have less discretion in restricting its use. However, the Directive provides no clear means to evaluate the relative safety of alternative herbicides, nor the wider environmental effects of defoliating wildlife habitats with broad-spectrum herbicides, for which herbicide-tolerant crops are designed.

The spread of pesticide resistance has become a general issue. Directive 91/414 mentioned pesticide-resistance management and was later amended to specify the duty of applicants: "Where there is evidence or information to suggest that in commercial use the development of resistance is likely, applicants have to provide a management strategy designed to minimize the likelihood of resistance or cross-resistance" (EEC, 1993: 33). This duty applies only to pesticides listed in Annex I.

In the mid-1990s it seemed that broad-spectrum herbicides not listed in Annex I (such as glufosinate and glyphosate) might soon come into commercial use on herbicide-tolerant crops. If so, resistance genes could become widespread in the environment, without any clear requirement to manage resistance. For GM crops, safety claims argued that the inadvertent spread of glufosinate-tolerance genes and plants would be acceptable on the grounds that such plants could still be controlled by glyphosate, the active substance in Monsanto's Roundup (see Section 3.4.1).[4]

Such claims came under challenge. Some member states emphasized regulatory gaps between GMO legislation and pesticide legislation. As an administrative solution, they sought to evaluate the resistance management and overall environmental implications of broad-spectrum herbicides within Directive 90/220.

3.4   Disputing "Adverse Effects"

In implementing Directive 90/220, member states have had to make a judgement on the acceptability of plausible undesirable effects. Such a judgement has been necessary because the 1990 GMO legislation was enacted prior to any evidence of harm, even prior to any agreement about how to define the "adverse effects" to be prevented. Of course, acceptability judgements arise for any technological system, for example, regarding the carcinogenic effects of hazardous chemicals. For GMOs, however, the normative judgement is firstly qualitative: if an undesirable effect is not officially classified as "adverse" or as "harmful," then by definition there is no "risk," much less any issue about its acceptability.

Health issues have been important for GM crops intended as human food or animal feed. A general concern has been that the inserted gene might produce a novel substance that turns out to be allergenic. When a gene from the Brazil nut was inserted into another crop, researchers found evidence of allergenicity, so product development was discontinued. Debate has continued over what scientific methods would be adequate to detect allergenicity before human consumption of GM foods (e.g., Clydesdale, 1996).

More controversial is the insertion of antibiotic-resistance marker (ARM) genes to help identify GM plant cells in the laboratory. Such genes could inadvertently transfer from an unprocessed food product to gut micro-organisms, thus jeopardizing clinical use of the antibiotic. For ARMs, disagreements over "adverse effects" could be overcome by redesigning the GMO with a different marker gene.

In the case-by-case assessment of GM crops for cultivation, national authorities have disagreed over the acceptability of potential effects. Generally at issue are the sorts of agricultural–environmental effects that were anticipated long beforehand (e.g., Mantegazzini, 1986: 76–80). According to advocates of market approval, such effects should be regarded as agricultural or economic problems, rather than as "adverse effects" under GMO legislation. Such normative judgements have been implicitly accepted by the EU-level Scientific Committee for Plants.

Debate has continued over how to manage plausible undesirable effects at the commercial stage. Issues include how to define the boundary or overlap between GMO legislation and other legislation, how to define "adverse effects" under Directive 90/220, and how to extend precautionary measures through the commercial stage. As public protest intensified against GM crops in 1997–1998, risk arguments and risk research circulated across national boundaries, contributing to oppositional networks (e.g., FoEE, 1996–1998).

In response, some member states changed their original stance favorable to normal commercialization of GM crops. This shift destabilized previous safety decisions and pushed regulatory procedures toward greater precaution (Levidow et al., 1999a). The conflicts are well illustrated by two ongoing controversies concerning the market approval of herbicide-tolerant oilseed rape and insecticidal maize.

3.4.1   Herbicide-tolerant oilseed rape

Oilseed rape has been genetically modified to tolerate glufosinate ammonium, the active substance in Basta, a broad-spectrum herbicide that is considered to be relatively benign. During 1996–1997, the European Commission issued marketing consents for such products under Directive 90/220, yet no such products had been permitted for commercial cultivation by the end of 1999. In this section we examine why this was the case.

UK safety claim

In 1994, Plant Genetic Systems (PGS) sent the UK Competent Authority an application to mass produce glufosinate-tolerant oilseed rape without any safety restrictions. One risk issue was the possibility that the glufosinate-tolerance gene could spread via volunteers or hybridization with related species, thus jeopardizing the efficacy of the corresponding herbicide. According to the company, the likelihood was "extremely low" and the consequences were "negligible." That is, the spread of the herbicide-tolerance gene "may exclude certain uses of such products [glufosinates] for broad weed management," however, given that they "are not used today for the control of volunteer oilseed rape in subsequent cropping, no particular problems are anticipated" (PGS, 1994).

In other words, glufosinate-tolerant weeds could still be controlled by glyphosate sprays. The PGS risk assessment did not claim to resolve the ecological uncertainty about whether gene transfer could create herbicide-tolerant weeds. Rather, by judging such an effect to be acceptable, the risk assessment made its predictability less important.

The UK advisory committee considered all the pathways by which glufosinate-tolerant oilseed rape or its weedy relatives could generate volunteers in subsequent crops. They categorized this scenario as an "agricultural problem," because it could be controlled and/or avoided by the farmer who planted the original GM crop. Echoing the company's claim, the Advisory Committee on Releases to the Environment (ACRE) argued that such an effect would be acceptable: namely, that "sufficient other herbicides or management practices existed for the control of [glufosinate-tolerant] volunteers ... and therefore there would be no harm to man's property arising from this situation" (ACRE, 1995: 7). On that basis, the UK Competent Authority became the EU-level rapporteur, forwarding the application with a favorable opinion to DG-XI.

In response to the UK proposal, several countries criticized the PGS risk assessment – for example, for accepting the potential loss of glufosinate as a weed-control agent and for failing to evaluate the overall implications for herbicide usage. Some countries emphasized their own geographical–environmental characteristics which contributed to the ecological uncertainties. In particular, Denmark cited its own research, which demonstrated a significant capacity of oilseed rape to hybridize with *Brassica campestris*, a widespread weed in Denmark (e.g., Mikkelsen *et al.*, 1996).

In the ensuing debate, the United Kingdom argued that such uncertainties had no relevance to the risk assessment for two reasons: First, the potential loss of glufosinate would not be an "adverse effect" on the environment. Second, "secondary" or "indirect" effects on overall herbicide usage would be due to management practices, not to the crop, so these effects would come instead under pesticide regulation.

The UK arguments were accepted by most member states and by the DG-XI (1995). As some member states argued, however, the EC Pesticide Directive provides no means to evaluate overall effects of herbicide usage; nor does it impose a clear duty to prevent the spread of herbicide resistance. Thus a normative dispute intersected with a boundary dispute over regulatory gaps between two EC Directives. Nevertheless, the PGS application gained a qualified majority vote of member states and was granted commercial approval (EC, 1996; for full references, see Levidow *et al.*, 1996, 1997).

Blockage in France and the United Kingdom

For the same product, PGS sent an application for unrestricted commercial use to the French Competent Authority in 1995. For herbicide-tolerant oilseed rape in general, the French advisory committee perceived "no uncertainties about an identified or potential risk." Rather, it emphasized "unknowns about socio-economic consequences," that is, the prospect of generating herbicide-tolerant weeds (Kahn, 1996). According to its chairman, "The term 'environment' should be understood in a broad sense: herbicide-resistant weeds can be an environmental problem for the relevant agrosystem ... " (A. Kahn, personal communication, 11 April 1996).

Given those concerns, the committee recommended that market approval be granted only on a five-year basis, with mandatory monitoring of commercial usage. Nevertheless the French Competent Authority recommended approval of the PGS seed with no special conditions for commercial use. The European Commission then granted approval for all commercial uses (EC, 1997c).

Meanwhile, conflict arose over putting the PGS oilseed rape into National List trials with other herbicide-tolerant seeds. The French advisory committee asked that each variety be tested separately to prevent any cross-pollination and thus the risk of multiple-herbicide tolerance. In response, the plant variety registration committee argued that the three crops must be tested together in order to focus on the new characteristic inserted. A long impasse followed (Roy and Joly, 2000).

After protest mounted against GM crops in France in 1997, the government reversed its stance and declined to sign the final EU-wide authorization. As a scientific rationale, the government cited the prospect of outcrossing to weedy relatives, as well as new scientific evidence (Chevre *et al.*, 1997). In July 1998, France declared a two-year moratorium on commercial use of any GM crop that could interbreed with weedy relatives, for example, oilseed rape and sugar beet. This decision temporarily resolved the internal conflict over National List trials, while accommodating public protest. The European Commission subsequently demanded that France honor its original commitment and sign the authorization.

As in France, debate intensified over GM crops in the United Kingdom as well. Commercial use of herbicide-tolerant crops in particular was opposed by government-funded conservation agencies as well as by many nongovernmental organizations (NGOs). They warned that broad-spectrum herbicides would damage field-margin habitats essential for wildlife, thus threatening biodiversity, and that inadvertent hybridization could lead to adverse changes in herbicide usage. In response, the agricultural supply industry formulated voluntary guidelines for preventing the inadvertent spread of herbicide-tolerance genes from GM crops (BSPB, 1998).

Amid rising opposition, in 1998 the UK government agreed to assist a "managed development" of herbicide-tolerant crops. Commercial cultivation of such products would begin on a limited scale, accompanied by ecological monitoring. Henceforth the government's advisory committee would consider the possible resultant changes in agronomic practice and the subsequent effects on biodiversity. GMO regulators would seek evidence that the herbicide sprays cause no more harm to wildlife habitats than present practices do. Otherwise, any marketing consent for the crop could be revoked on the basis that such harm would constitute an "adverse effect" under Directive 90/220.

Thus the United Kingdom reversed its earlier stance on the boundary between GMO and pesticide legislation. Moreover, the normative baseline for biodiversity effects became a policy issue. Critics were invited to evaluate the scientific methods and criteria for monitoring potential harm. Thus further precautions were imposed to test plausible effects whose acceptability remained at issue. (For detailed references see Levidow *et al.*, 1999b; Levidow and Carr, 2000c).

3.4.2   Insecticidal maize

Since the 1980s biotechnology companies have been inserting toxin genes from the naturally occurring microbial pesticide *Bacillus thuringiensis* (Bt) into other microbes and into crops. There has been concern that long-term exposure to such insecticidal crops could intensify selection pressure for resistant insects; if so, this effect would shorten the useful lifespan of the product. Insect resistance might also reduce the future utility of naturally occurring microbial Bt, thus exhausting a natural resource as a future option for sustainable agriculture.

The insect-resistance problem first became a practical issue when Ciba-Geigy (later Novartis) requested market approval for a Bt maize product. Its risk assessment suggested that commercial use was needed to help clarify how to slow resistance. As the national rapporteur, France argued that any Bt-resistant insects could still be controlled by other means, such as by reverting to chemical insecticides. Also controversial was the insertion of an ARM gene – in particular, an ampicillin-resistance gene with a microbial promoter – as the gene could be expressed if inadvertently transferred to a gut micro-organism, for example, if the product is used as animal feed.

Despite objections from many member states, the product was approved by the European Commission. According to its decision, insect resistance "cannot be considered an adverse environmental effect, as existing agricultural means of controlling such resistant species of insects will still be available" (EC, 1997a; cf. SCP, 1996). The company sent DG-XI a letter agreeing to monitor commercial use for insect resistance. After much delay due to protest in France, the rapporteur signed the authorization in February 1998.

After the Ciba-Geigy/Novartis maize gained approval, Austria and Luxembourg banned the product under Article 16 of Directive 90/220. Austria presented more evidence for the risks that had been raised by other member states; it also cited a Swiss study indicating risks to lacewing, a beneficial predator of insect pests (Hilbeck *et al.*, 1998). In response, DG-XI drafted a Commission proposal that would require Austria and Luxembourg to lift their bans. This proposal did not gain a qualified majority among member states, so the Commission lacked the political authority to pursue the matter at the European Court of Justice (ECJ).

Moreover, other member states placed restrictions on the Ciba-Geigy/Novartis Bt maize. The Italian government temporarily banned the product until the company presented a plan to delay insect resistance (Terragni and Recchia, 1998). After National List trials were completed in France and Spain, those countries granted the product a time-limited registration but required monitoring for all the risks that had been debated in the Directive 90/220 procedure (France, 1998; Spain, 1998; Todt and Lujan, 2000). The French Environment Ministry established a broadly based *biovigilance* committee to evaluate the monitoring methods (Roy and Joly, 2000).

After the first season's plantings in France and Spain, another obstacle arose. NGOs argued that the original approval was invalid because the French authorities had failed to evaluate risks of the ampicillin-resistance marker gene, though it was later evaluated and declared safe by an EU-level scientific committee (SCAN, 1996; SCF, 1996). In September 1998 the French constitutional court, le Conseil d'État, accepted the NGOs' argument and ruled that the French signature on the EU-wide authorization was invalid. Le Conseil d'État asked the ECJ to clarify a member state's authority to revoke a consent. (Eventually the ECJ ruled that the French signature was valid, though this ruling left open the option for France to cite new evidence as grounds for a ban.)

At the same time, some market-stage precautions were being formalized more precisely. In Monsanto's application for market approval for a Bt maize crop under the Directive 90/220 procedure, it agreed to monitor commercial use for insect resistance. An EU-level committee evaluated and endorsed specific monitoring methods (DG-XI EGBtIRM, 1998). Monsanto later submitted a more specific plan for cultivation methods to minimize selection pressure for resistant insects. The EU's Scientific Committee on Plants regarded the plan as "adequate to delay resistance," while implying that such an effect would anyway be an agricultural problem rather than environmental harm (SCP, 1998a).

Ultimately, the European Commission mentioned the monitoring commitment in the recital of the marketing consent (EC, 1998a). This explicit mention responded to demands from some member states, as well as from Directorates-General VI and XXIV, for Agriculture and Consumer Affairs, respectively. DG-XI regarded the company undertaking as a statutory obligation under Directive 90/220; thus market-stage precautions became semi-mandatory for plausible effects whose acceptability remained at issue.

Non-target harm also remains an issue of predictability and acceptability. After seeing the Swiss study on lacewing, the EU's Scientific Committee on Plants assessed Pioneer's Bt maize; it stated that any harm to non-target arthropod insects would be less than the present harm from chemical insecticides (SCP, 1998b). In other words, the Committee accepted the present harm from chemical-intensive agriculture as the normative baseline for the effects of GM crops – even though not all maize is sprayed with chemical insecticides.

3.4.3 Mediating conflicts

For the contentious cases described above, regulatory boundaries and environmental norms were in dispute. Marketing applications and their regulatory advocates defined "adverse effects" in a relatively narrow way, so that the risk assessment did not have to resolve predictive uncertainties about some plausible undesirable effects. Other regulators defined "adverse effects" more broadly, for example, as a basis to hold products accountable to criteria of sustainable agriculture and/or to ban their commercial use. In the extreme case of Austria, its national policy has promoted organic agriculture, which is widely regarded as being incompatible with GM crops (Torgersen and Seifert, 2000).

Since the mid-1990s "the precautionary principle" has become a consensual rhetoric, though with divergent accounts of the relevant uncertainties. Unsurprisingly, policy actors have interpreted the principle to justify their own stance toward GMOs. Some emphasize the prospect of irreversible ecological changes; others emphasize undesirable effects on (or of) agricultural practices, for which a meaningful test would be difficult before the commercial stage. Using a rhetoric of precaution, various regulators have advocated unconditional approval of GMOs, conditional approval, or even a total ban.

GMO regulation also brings to light national differences in regulatory styles – for example, means of using scientific evidence, constituting expertise, and seeking legitimacy for decisions (Levidow and Carr, 1996, 2000b). To some extent, a broader definition of "adverse effects" correlates with greater public access to value judgements in the risk assessment – as has been the case in Denmark since the 1980s (Toft, 1996) and as has occurred more recently in France and the United Kingdom. However, German precautionary measures have an "elite" style (Dreyer and Gill, 2000; see also Chapter 5).

Given the regulatory conflicts, market-stage precautions have provided a potential compromise (Levidow *et al.*, 1999a). Monitoring and cultivation protocols are becoming mandatory, for example, as companies give written undertakings under Directive 90/220 or as National List registration imposes such requirements. These measures provide a further means of testing potential effects and debating their acceptability.

To clarify the legal basis for market-stage precautions, Directive 90/220 has been redrafted. Under an early redraft, each marketing consent is granted for a time-limited period with a monitoring requirement. The notifier must submit a detailed plan to "identify any relevant direct, indirect, immediate or delayed effects ... ." (CEC, 1998a). The wording was eventually clarified to encompass any effects from "changes in use or management" as compared with a non-GM product (ENDS, 1999). Thus a revised Directive would formalize regulatory changes already under way to require market-stage monitoring of broadly defined "adverse effects."

3.5   GM Food and Labeling

Regulatory conflicts have arisen from public pressures for comprehensive labeling of GM crops and food. NGOs have promoted the consumers' right to make an informed choice about the source of their food. This demand has many aspects – for example, a reaction to the BSE scandal, a general distrust of official safety claims, the traceability of any harm, public accountability, and scrutiny of food according to its production method. As grounds for mandatory labeling, NGOs variously emphasized the new technological process of genetic modification, scientific uncertainty, inherent risks, etc. Some NGOs oppose GM foods by claiming that they are inherently unsafe and that their safety can never be shown by scientific evidence (e.g., Greenpeace, 1997).

The first test case was the Monsanto Roundup Ready soybean, genetically modified to tolerate glyphosate, a broad-spectrum herbicide. Like its non-GM counterpart, the Monsanto soybean would be cultivated in the United States, exported to Europe, and then used in processed foods and animal feed. When Monsanto requested EU approval, labeling demands came from NGOs and some member states. Industry argued that segregation would be unnecessary and expensive, though a fundamental aim was to avoid stigmatizing GM products. The product gained EU market approval with no labeling requirement (EC, 1996).

When the Monsanto soybean reached Europe in unlabeled mixed shipments in late 1996, it met with protest, boycotts, and consumer demands for non-GM alternatives. Under public pressure to label any GM ingredients, some food retailers did so or else found non-GM sources. Some non-GM soya was specially obtained from across national borders; for example, some Danish companies supplied soya to German companies.

When UK retailers requested non-GM soya from their US suppliers, the request was denied on the grounds that it was impractical. Nevertheless, one UK supermarket chain eventually obtained non-GM soya from Brazil and Canada, at no extra cost. Some retailers used these supplies quietly, while others emphasized that their products were "non-GM." Similar issues arose for the Ciba-Geigy/Novartis maize (EC, 1997a), though this has been used less in food products and more as animal feed.

Meanwhile, several marketing applications for GM products were being criticized and delayed on the grounds of inadequate labeling. National regulators disagreed about whether to require more specific labeling than was proposed by the applicant, for example, to require the words "genetically modified" to appear on the packaging. In 1997–1998 the EU imposed general labeling requirements, which have successfully avoided such conflicts among member states.

In particular, Directive 90/220 was amended to require that GM seeds be fully labeled to indicate their source and characteristics; mixed or uncertain sources could be labeled as "may contain GMOs," so that GM seeds need not be segregated (EC, 1997d). In effect, the labeling requirement also applies to GM grain used as animal feed if processing has not eliminated all biologically viable material. The labeling information was intended to facilitate environmental monitoring of GM crops and subsequent labeling through the food chain – that is, traceability.

Regarding GM food, the Novel Food Regulation requires a "GM" label if the food contains biologically viable material, or if scientific techniques can demonstrate that a novel food is "no longer equivalent" to one previously consumed (EC, 1997b).[5] Later legislation clarified such "equivalence": soya or maize must be labeled if any GM DNA or protein is detectable; mixtures or uncertain sources may be labeled as "contains GM" (EC, 1998b). The latter option obviates any need to segregate or test supplies.

Despite the new rules, the food trade has been complicated by continuing public protest and diverse commercial practices. Some European suppliers have applied a "GM" label to soya or maize ingredients obtained from any country where GM crops are cultivated – initially the United States and Canada, and later Argentina as well. Exceptions include highly processed products that contain no DNA or protein, such as oilseed rape and lecithin.

Yet consumer groups have demanded process-based labeling of all GM food, that is, any food containing ingredients derived from GM crops. Such a system would depend on documentation rather than detectability criteria. Some supermarket chains have accommodated these demands, thus going beyond EU legal requirements. In 1999 the Danish food industry agreed to adopt process-based labeling (Toft, 2000). Germany established a similar system for validating claims of "GM-free" food. Consequently, a "GM" label (or its absence) may have different meanings across companies or EU member states.

Another problem is adventitious contamination. Despite efforts to segregate non-GM soya, most soya-based products contain some detectable "GM" contamination and so require a "GM" label under the 1998 EU criteria (EC, 1998b). Thus trade practices have conflicted with the law. Because the same "GM" label – or its absence – could have different meanings across member states, retailers proposed that the law be amended so that a "GM" label would not be required for contamination below a certain threshold, initially set at 1% (EC, 2000). Symbolically, such a threshold indicates the company's intention to segregate supplies; most NGOs demand a level below 1%.

Amid all these maneuvers, the link between risk and labeling has remained contentious. Officially speaking, regulators deny any such link for approved products. In that vein, "GM" rules were separated from risk regulation and put under general labeling law (e.g., EC, 1998b).

Unofficially, however, the rules have been used by those who try to link "GM" with uncertainty or risk. Rather than facilitate the transboundary circulation of GM food, the labeling rules have turned out to deter their sales and to encourage non-GM or "organic" alternatives. By 1999 most food retail chains – and even some food processors – were phasing out GM ingredients from their own-brand products.

3.6   EU–US Trade Conflicts

EU–US trade conflicts over GM products have resulted from trans-Atlantic regulatory differences, which in turn are related to cultural meanings of agriculture. US farms are seen as analogous to factories, sharply demarcated from wilderness and nature conservation areas. Although European agriculture also uses chemical-intensive methods, farmland is widely regarded as an integral part of the environment – as an aesthetic landscape, a wildlife habitat, local heritage, a peasant resource, and a traceable guarantor of food quality.

The EU–US cultural difference has been accentuated by a recent divergence in agricultural policy. The US government has emphasized high-productivity, low-cost production for export. It has pressed other countries to reduce price supports for agriculture and actively promoted biotechnology through measures such as broader patent protection. These US policies came in response to pressure from multinational companies, which have sought to enhance the market for high-productivity agricultural inputs (such as GM seeds), to drive down the price of bulk food commodities, and to obtain multiple sources of inputs for the global food processing industry (McMichael, 1998).

In contrast, EU policy has been moving toward less-intensive, higher-quality production that favors greater caution toward biotechnology (CEC, 1997: 27–29; Haniotis, 1997). This tendency was reinforced by the

1996 crisis over "mad cow disease" and subsequent food scandals. These episodes undermined public confidence in food regulation, while arousing suspicion toward any claims for more efficient food production, especially from biotechnology.

Consequently, the United States has generally subjected GM products to less precautionary criteria than have some European countries, especially their more stringent approaches in the late 1990s. For herbicide-tolerant oilseed rape, the US procedure did not consider the weed-control and wider environmental implications that were controversial in Europe. For the Ciba-Geigy/Novartis Bt maize, the US procedure ignored the ampicillin-resistance risks that attracted European objections. For Bt crops in general, US authorities accepted company evidence as adequately demonstrating that non-target insects would not be harmed; in contrast, European regulators requested more evidence. After US NGOs protested that Bt crops could generate selection pressure for resistant insects, US regulators eventually began to regulate this risk; European regulators discussed how to adapt the US precautions or go beyond them.

Many GM products gained US commercial approval in the mid-1990s and were included in mixed shipments to Europe; thus the entire shipments became suspect. For example, in late 1996 US shipments containing the Ciba-Geigy/Novartis Bt maize were crossing the Atlantic Ocean before the EU had granted market approval. The US Department of Agriculture publicly protested the regulatory delay as a "non-tariff trade barrier"; DG-I Commissioner Leon Brittan warned Europe that the United States would challenge any EU blockage at the World Trade Organization (WTO). Such statements lent credence to NGO claims that GM products were being approved to expedite trade, regardless of any scientific arguments about safety issues.

Although the EU soon approved the Ciba-Geigy/Novartis Bt maize (EC, 1997a), similar conflicts occurred after additional GM maize products entered US cultivation and grain traders declined to segregate them. In 1998 Spain and Portugal, two substantial importers of US maize, temporarily had to find alternative sources until all the US products gained EU approval (EC, 1998a). In mid-1998, after Swiss scientists reported evidence that Bt maize could harm the lacewing, a beneficial insect, the European Commission declined to approve such a product from Pioneer Hi-Bred, as well as several others.

Given that US grain exports have mixed sources, transboundary risk management is dependent upon clarifying product identity – for example, via labeling or testing – even in cases where such measures are not legal requirements *per se*. Whenever an EU–US transboundary issue arises at a national frontier, EU member states are legally required to enforce Directives. In such ways, EU regulatory delays intensify US–EU transboundary conflicts.

Given the various GM maize products in US cultivation in the late 1990s, grain merchants could not legally export mixed shipments of unprocessed grain to Europe. According to some estimates, US farmers lost US$200 million in maize sales to Europe in 1998–1999. US government officials again indicated that they might bring a complaint against the EU to the WTO disputes procedure. If the WTO judges that EU delays lack a scientific rationale, then the United States could impose financial sanctions, for example, retaliatory tariffs of 100% on selected European goods.

Under the General Agreement on Tariffs and Trade (GATT)–WTO agreement, the grounds for an import ban remain open to interpretation. Restrictive trade measures can be justified if they are necessary to protect human, animal, or plant life or health (Article XX, b) or for "the conservation of exhaustible natural resources" (Article XX, g). These measures should not constitute "a means of arbitrary or unjustifiable discrimination among countries where the same conditions apply, or a disguised restriction on international trade" (GATT, 1994: 38).

According to the US account of "sound science," the EU would face a stringent burden of evidence – for example, in demonstrating that the banned product threatens a truly "exhaustible" resource. Along with other proponents of agricultural biotechnology, the US government has advocated "science-based regulation." Its officials have criticized Europe for basing regulation on politics rather than science.

However, such a distinction is misleading. Risk regulation unavoidably makes judgements about what "environment" must be protected, what uncertainties matter for risk assessment, and what research could clarify them. Such judgements are inherently cultural and cannot be reduced to a single objective basis; purely "science-based regulation" can never be achieved. Moreover, given the pressures from industry and NGOs, US approval decisions are no less political than European delays (Levidow, 1999). A similar pattern can be seen in US–EU differences over other agricultural technologies (Vogel, 1997:60–62).

3.7   Conclusion: What European Integration?

In the European transboundary risk management of GM crops, pervasive conflicts reflect contending accounts of sustainable agriculture. When GM crops initially gained commercial approval, regulatory policy was framed by the imperative to enhance European economic competitiveness and agricultural efficiency, while regarding GM crops as beneficial for the environmental sustainability of intensive agriculture. This framework was challenged by NGOs, some regulators, and eventually by mass public protest. In response, more stringent standards have been devised; regulatory delays and extra controls have accommodated diverse environmental norms.

The EC's original 1990 legislation for regulating GMOs was designed to link market integration with environmental protection, especially against transboundary risks. Community-wide product approval would allow national exemptions (if at all) only on grounds of different environmental contexts. This framework rested upon a technicist harmonization model, which eventually developed into a crisis.

When the first GM crops obtained EU-wide commercial approval in the mid-1990s, official risk assessments were framed within an implicit commitment to intensive monoculture. Its inherent hazards were taken for granted as a normative baseline. Some undesirable effects were deemed either acceptable or irrelevant to GMO regulation. Future crop-protection options were regarded as interchangeable and therefore dispensable, regardless of their relative environmental advantages. There was no clear administrative responsibility for evaluating the overall herbicide implications. On this basis, regulatory harmonization technicized different cultural–environmental values across Europe; safety claims conceptually homogenized the European environment.

However, member states disagreed over what was meant by the statutory requirement to prevent "adverse effects" from GMOs. These disagreements focused on undesirable agri-environmental effects of cultivating GM crops within each country. Objectors were accused of raising "agricultural" or "non-risk" issues, as distinct from the "product safety" issues that justified commercial approval.

By 1997–1998 the early objections gained impetus from growing public protest. After activists targeted GM food, industry agreed to more stringent labeling criteria, which in turn deterred a European market for "GM"-labeled food. Protestors also denounced GM crops as contrary to sustainable agriculture, circulated new evidence of risk across Europe, and catalyzed mainstream organizations to adopt similar arguments. GM products have been stigmatized – not simply as contaminated, but also as pollutants themselves (cf. Chapter 5).

In such ways, the protest challenged the EU's regulatory framework and institutional competence. Lacking legitimacy, the EU's risk-management procedure could no longer be implemented as before. It was effectively suspended amid continuing disputes over risks of GM crops, both within and among member states. EU regulatory delays blocked US imports, thus aggravating trans-Atlantic trade conflicts.

Accommodating European public protest, some national governments have incorporated greater precaution into their risk-assessment frameworks, especially in the United Kingdom and France. National regulators broadened the practical definition of the "adverse effects" that must be prevented, increased the burden of evidence of safety regarding such effects, and recruited broader expertise. They devised market-stage precautions to fill regulatory gaps in the EU-level regulation. They invited pressure groups to evaluate the scientific methods and precautionary criteria for environmental testing.

These regulatory changes have been superseding the technicist harmonization model. Regulatory procedures are pressed to reconsider environmental norms, for example, using less intensive farming methods as a baseline of comparison. National precautionary measures have been formalized in the EU-level regulatory procedure for GM crops: by evaluating all "indirect effects" related to agricultural practices, risk-assessment procedures could encompass diverse norms.

What does this case mean for expert authority and the legitimacy of EU decisions? An apolitical risk assessment is impossible to achieve, since the relevant science is always framed by environmental values, including some concept of sustainable agriculture. Regardless of its formal independence, official expertise has had little capacity to legitimize decisions, especially since expert bodies reinforced the normative commitment to intensive agriculture in the mid-1990s.

Opening up such norms, member states eventually devised greater precaution for evaluating GM crops. These measures expressed Europe-wide concerns over sustainable agriculture, rather than self-interested deviations from some neutral expertise. Therefore legitimacy depends upon clearly accommodating public debate over environmental standards, rather than trying to separate expert judgements from politics (cf. Majone, 1996).

In that vein, policy advisors have suggested ways to incorporate public concerns into environmental policy at an early stage. For example, "openness at this framing stage allows people to question assumptions about the character of environmental issues and the scientific understanding upon which analysis is based. Framing of the issues ... needs to be more socially intelligent" (RCEP, 1998). Likewise, US government advisors have proposed deliberative approaches whereby potential antagonists seek to reconcile their divergent framings (Stern and Fineberg, 1996). Technological design choices can be deliberated as social norms (e.g., von Schomberg; see also Chapter 9).

Such a process has been under way for the transboundary risk management of GM crops. Legitimate European integration can be attained only by publicly deliberating technical standards as sociopolitical choices for future agri-environmental systems.

Notes

[1] As a notable exception, such transboundary risks were cited for an early product, an anti-rabies viral vaccine that was sprayed in the countryside in Belgium near France (McNally, 1994, 1996).

[2] In a similar vein, some critics have used the term "technocratic" instead. For example, technocracy is "a wide-ranging administrative system that is legitimated by reference to scientific expertise rather than tradition, law, or the will of the people. To what extent technocratic administration is actually scientific is another matter" (Feenberg, 1999: 4). This chapter uses the term "technicist," more aptly describing an administrative practice that cites technical expertise to justify policy, rather than "technocratic," which could imply that technical experts decide policy.

[3] There were also boundary disputes between Directive 90/220 and the Novel Food Regulation (EC, 1997b), though these have little relevance to the environmental issues analyzed here.

[4] That scenario took a further twist a few years later, when the European Commission proposed delaying any decision to include glyphosate in Annex I of Directive 91/414: " ... after application for the intended uses and in the correct manner, harmful effects on arthropods ... cannot be excluded," for example, several predators of insect pests (CEC, 1998b). If member states agree, then they will less readily accept the loss of glufosinate as a future option for weed control.

[5] This labeling criterion is distinct from "substantial equivalence," which qualifies a novel food for a simplified risk-assessment procedure under the same regulation.

Acknowledgments

This chapter arises from a study, "Safety Regulation of Transgenic Crops: Completing the Internal Market?," funded by the European Commission, DG-XII/E5, contract BIO4-CT97-2215, during 1997–1999. Essential information and analysis was provided by our research partners in 10 EU member states. The essay represents only the views of the author. The full reports are available at http://www-tec.open.ac.uk/cts/bpg.htm.

References

ACRE, 1995, *Advisory Committee on Releases to the Environment: Annual Report No. 2, 1994/95*, Department of the Environment, London, UK.

Barry, A., 1993, The European Community and European government: Harmonization, mobility and space, *Economy and Society*, **22**(3):314–326.

Beck, U., 1992, *Risk Society: Towards a New Modernity*, Sage, London, UK.

Beck, U., 1996, Risk society and the provident state, in S. Lash, B. Szerszynski, and B. Wynne, eds, *Risk, Environment and Modernity*, Sage, London, UK.

BSPB, 1998, Guidelines for Growing Newly Developed Herbicide Tolerant Crops, British Society of Plant Breeders, June, Ely, Cambs, UK.

CBC, 1990, *The Impact of New and Impending Regulations on U.K. Biotechnology*, Cambridge Biomedical Consultants, Cambridge, UK.

CEC, 1993, *Towards Sustainable Development*, 5th Environmental Action Programme; also in *Official Journal of the European Communities*, C 138 (17 May):5–98.

CEC, 1997, *Agenda 2000: For a Stronger and Wider Union*, published as *Bulletin of the European Union*, supplement 5/97, Commission of the European Communities, Brussels, Belgium.

CEC, 1998a, Proposal for a European Parliament and Council Directive amending Directive 90/220/EEC, on the Deliberate Release into the Environment of Genetically Modified Organisms, *Official Journal of the European Communities*, C 139 (4 May):1–23.

CEC, 1998b, *Glyphosate*, Volume 1, Pesticides Safety Directorate/ECCO-Team, Commission of the European Communities, 12.12.98, Brussels, Belgium.

Chevre, A-M., Eber, F., and Renard, M., 1997, Gene flow from transgenic crops, *Nature*, **389**:924.

Clydesdale, F.M., ed., 1996, Allergenicity of foods produced by genetic modification, *Food Science and Nutrition*, **36** (special supplement).

Delors, J., 1992, *Our Europe: The Community and National Development*, Verso, London, UK (translated from 1988 French edition).

DG-XI, 1995, Draft document on the Assessment of the Environmental Impact of Herbicide Use Linked to the Placing on the Market of Genetically Modified Herbicide-Tolerant Plants, Document XI/763/95, Revision 1 (undated).

DG-XI EGBtIRM, 1998, Expert Group on Bt IRM, Working document on Monitoring of ECB Resistance to Transgenic Bt-maize, January, Directorate-General for Environmental Protection, Brussels, Belgium (typescript).

Dreyer, M., and Gill, B., 2000, Germany: Continued elite precaution alongside continued public opposition, *Journal of Risk Research*, **3**(3):219–226.

EC, 1996, Commission Decision 96/281/EC of 3 April 1996 Concerning the Placing on the Market of Genetically Modified Soybeans...., *Official Journal of the European Communities*, L 107 (30 April):10.

EC, 1997a, Commission Decision 97/98/EC of 23 January 1997 Concerning the Placing on the Market of Genetically Modified Maize, *Official Journal of the European Communities*, L 31 (1 February):69–70.

EC, 1997b, Regulation 97/258/EC of 27 January 1997 Concerning Novel Foods and Novel Food Ingredients, *Official Journal of the European Communities*, L 43 (14 February):1–6.

EC, 1997c, Commission Decision Concerning the Placing on the Market of a Genetically Modified Oilseed Rape, in conformity with Council Directive 90/220/EEC, *Official Journal of the European Communities*, L 164 (6 June):38–39.

EC, 1997d, Commission Directive 97/35/EC of 18 June Adapting to Technical Progress for the Second Time Council Directive 90/220/EEC, *Official Journal of the European Communities*, L 169 (27 June):72–73.

EC, 1998a, Commission Decision Concerning the Placing on the Market of a Genetically Modified Maize (Zea mays line 810), pursuant to Council Directive 90/220/EEC, *Official Journal of the European Communities*, L 131 (5 May):32–33. [Monsanto dossier C/F/95/12-02].

EC, 1998b, Council Regulation 1139/98 Concerning the Compulsory Indication on the Labeling of Certain Foodstuffs Produced from Genetically Modified Organisms..., *Official Journal of the European Communities*, L 159 (3 June):4–7 [replaces EC, 1997e].

EC, 1998c, Council Directive 98/95 amending [previous directives] on the Common Catalogue of Varieties of Agricultural Plant Species, *Official Journal of the European Communities*, L 25 (1 February).

EC, 2000, Commission Regulation 49/2000 amending Council Regulation 1139/98..., *Official Journal of the European Communities*, L 6 (11 January):13–14.

EEC, 1970, Directive du Conseil 70/457/CEE concernant le catalogue commun des variétés des espéces de plantes agricoles, J.O. des Communautés européen, L 225 (12 octobre):1–6.

EEC, 1990, Council Directive 90/220/EEC on the Deliberate Release to the Environment of Genetically Modified Organisms, *Official Journal of the European Communities*, L 117 (8 May):15–27.

EEC, 1991, Council Directive 91/414 Concerning the Placing of Plant Protection Products on the Market, *Official Journal of the European Communities*, L 230 (19 August):1–32.

EEC, 1993, Directive 93/71 amending Directive 91/414, *Official Journal of the European Communities*, L 221 (31 August):27–34.

ENDS, 1998, The spiralling agenda of agricultural biotechnology, *ENDS Report*, **283**:18–30.

ENDS, 1999, Overhaul of EC regime for regulating GMOs, *ENDS Report*, **294**:50–52.

Feenberg, A., 1999, *Questioning Technology*, Routledge, London, UK.

FoEE, 1996–1998, various *Mailouts*, Friends of the Earth Europe Biotechnology Programme, Brussels, Belgium.

France, 1998, Arrêté du 5 février portant modification du Catalogue officiel des espèces et variétés de plantes cultivées en France (semences de maïs), *Journal Officiel*, 33:2037, 8 February [registration of two varieties based on Ciba's Bt maize, corresponding to EC, 1997a].

GATT, 1994, *The Results of the Uruguay Round of Multilateral Trade Negotiations: The Legal Texts*, GATT Secretariat, http://www.wto.org/, Geneva, Switzerland.

Gottweis, H., 1998, *Governing Molecules: The Discursive Politics of Genetic Engineering in Europe and in the US*, MIT Press, Cambridge, MA, USA.

Greenpeace, 1997, *From BSE to GMOs: Science, Uncertainty and the Precautionary Principle*, http://www.greenpeace.org.uk.

Haniotis, T., 1997, The Economics of Agricultural Biotechnology: Differences and Similarities in the US and the EU, presentation at Integrated Crop Management Conference, 17–18 November, Ames, Iowa, by the First Secretary (Agriculture), European Commission Delegation to the US.

Hilbeck, A., Baumgartner, M., Padruot, M.F., and Bigler, F., 1998, Effects of transgenic Bt corn-fed prey on mortality and development time of immature *Chrysoperla carnea*, *Environmental Entomology*, **27**(2):480–487.

Hildebrand, P., 1993, The European Community's environmental policy, 1957–1992, in D. Judge, ed., *A Green Dimension for the European Community*, Cass, London, UK. [special issue of *Environmental Politics*, 1(4), 1992].

Jasanoff, S., 1993, Bridging the two cultures of risk analysis, *Risk Analysis*, 13(2):123–129.

Jordan, T., 1999, The implementation of EU environmental policy: A policy problem without a political solution?, *Environment and Planning C*, 17(1):69–90.

Kahn, A., 1996, Evaluation du risque et dissémination volontaire d'organismes génétiquement modifiés: l'expérience francaise, *Natures-Sciences-Sociétés Dialogues*, 96(2):144–145, NSS Association, Paris, France.

Levidow, L., 1996, Simulating Mother Nature, industrializing agriculture, in G. Robertson *et al.* (*BLOCK*), eds, *FutureNatural: Nature, Science, Culture*, Routledge, London, UK.

Levidow, L., 1999, Regulating Bt maize in the USA and Europe: A scientific-cultural comparison, *Environment*, 41(10):10–22.

Levidow, L., and Carr, S., eds, 1996, Biotechnology Risk Regulation in Europe, special issue of *Science & Public Policy*, 23(3):133ff.

Levidow, L., and Carr, S., 2000a, UK: Precautionary commercialization of GM crops?, *Journal of Risk Research*, 3(3):261–270.

Levidow, L., and Carr, S., eds, 2000b, Precautionary regulation: GM crops in the EU, special issue of *Journal of Risk Research*, 3(3):187–285.

Levidow, L., and Tait, J., 1991, The greening of biotechnology: GMOs as environment-friendly products, *Science and Public Policy*, 18(5):271–80; reprinted in V. Shiva and I. Moser, eds, 1995, *Biopolitics: A Feminist and Ecological Reader on Biotechnology*, Zed, London, UK.

Levidow, L., Carr, S., von Schomberg, R., and Wield, D., 1996, Regulating agricultural biotechnology in Europe: Harmonization difficulties, opportunities, dilemmas, *Science & Public Policy*, 23(3):135–157.

Levidow, L., Carr, S., von Schomberg, R., and Wield, D., 1997, European biotechnology regulation: Framing the risk assessment of a herbicide-tolerant crop, *Science, Technology and Human Values*, 22(4):472–505.

Levidow, L., Carr, S., and Wield, D., 1999a, Market-stage precautions: Managing regulatory disharmonies for transgenic crops in Europe, *AgBiotechNet*, 1:1–8, http://www.agbiotechnet.com/reviews/April99/Html/Levidow.htm.

Levidow, L., Carr, S., and Wield, D., 1999b, Regulating biotechnological risk, straining Britain's consultative style, *Journal of Risk Research*, 2(4):307–324.

Magretta, J., 1997, Growth through global sustainability: An interview with Monsanto's CEO, Robert Shapiro, *Harvard Business Review*, Jan–Feb:79–88.

Majone, G., 1996, *Regulating Europe*, Routledge, London, UK.

Majone, G., 1997, From the positive to the regulatory state: Causes and consequences of changes in the mode of governance, *Journal of Public Policy*, 17:139–167.

Mantegazzini, M.C., 1986, *The Environmental Risks from Biotechnology*, Pinter, London, UK.

McMichael, P., 1998, Global food politics, *Monthly Review*, 50(3):97–111.

McNally, R., 1994, Genetic madness: The European rabies eradication programme, *The Ecologist*, 24(6):207–212.

McNally, R., 1996, Political problems: Genetically engineered solutions: The socio-technical translation of fox rabies, in Ad van Dommelen (ed.), *Coping with Deliberate Release: The Limits of Risk Assessment*, International Centre for Human and Public Affairs, Hengelo, Netherlands.

Monsanto, 1997, *Report on Sustainable Development*, Monsanto Company, St. Louis, MO, USA.

Mikkelsen, T.R., *et al.*, 1996, The risk of crop transgene spread, *Nature*, 380:31.

OECD (Organisation for Economic Co-operation and Development), 1986, *Recombinant DNA Safety Considerations*, OECD, Paris, France.

Pelkmans, J., 1987, The new approach to technical harmonization and standardization, *Journal of Common Market Studies*, 25(3):249–69.

PGS, 1994, A New Hybridization System in Oilseed Rape (*B. napus*): Application for Consent to Market Genetically Modified Organisms, ref. no. C/U.K./94/M1/1, unpublished document, submitted to by Plant Genetic Systems to DoE, February.

RCEP, 1998, *21st Report: Setting Environmental Standards*, Cm 4053, Her Majesty's Stationery Office, London, UK.

Renn, O., 1995, Style of using scientific expertise: A comparative analysis, *Science & Public Policy*, 22(3):147–156.

Renn, O., and Levine, D., 1991, Credibility and trust in risk communication, in R. Kasperson and P.J. Stallen, eds, *Communicating Risk to the Public*, Kluwer Academic Publishers, Dordrecht, Netherlands.

Roy, A., and Joly, P-B., 2000, France: Broadening precautionary expertise?, *Journal of Risk Research*, 3(3):247–254.

SCAN, 1996, Report of the Scientific Committee on Animal Nutrition on the safety for animals of certain genetically modified maize lines notified by Ciba-Geigy, DGVI, 13 December.

SCF, 1996, Scientific Committee on Food, Opinion on the potential for adverse health effects from the consumption of genetically modified maize, DGIII, 13 December.

SCP, 1996, Opinion of the Scientific Committee on Pesticides on the genetically modified maize lines notified by Ciba-Geigy, DGVI, 13 December.

SCP, 1998a, Opinion of the Scientific Committee on Plants regarding Monsanto's MON10 Bt maize (C/F/95/12-02), 10 February. Full texts available at http://europa.eu.int/en/comm/dg24.

SCP, 1998b, Opinion of the Scientific Committee on Plants regarding Pioneer's MON9 Bt, glyphosate-tolerant maize, 19 May.

Spain, 1998, Ministerio de Agricultura, Orden de 23 de marzo por la que se dispone la inscripción de variedades de maz en el Registro de Variedades Comerciales, 26 marzo, *Boletin Oficial del Estado*, **73**:10193–95, 10289–90 [registration of two varieties based on Ciba's Bt maize, corresponding to EC, 1997a].

Stern, P.C., and Fineberg, V., 1996, *Understanding Risk: Informing Decisions in a Democratic Society*, National Research Council, Committee on Risk Characterization, National Academy Press, Washington, DC, USA.

Terragni, F., and Recchia, E., 1998, Italy: Precaution for environmental diversity?, Report on Italy, Safety Regulation of Transgenic Crops: Completing the Internal Market?, coordinated by the Open University, Milton Keynes, UK.

Todt, O., and Lujan, J., 2000, Spain: Commercialization drives public debate and precaution, *Journal of Risk Research*, **3**(3):237–245.

Toft, J., 1996, Denmark: Seeking a broad-based consensus on gene technology, *Science & Public Policy*, **23**(3):171–174.

Toft, J., 2000, Denmark – Potential polarization or consensus?, *Journal of Risk Research*, **3**(3):227–235.

Torgersen, H., and Seifert, F., 2000, Austria: Precautionary blockage of agricultural biotechnology, *Journal of Risk Research*, **3**(3):209–217.

Vogel, D., 1997, *Barriers or Benefits? Regulation in Transatlantic Trade*, Brookings Institution, Washington, DC, USA.

von Schomberg, R., ed., 1998, *Democratizing Technology: Theory and Practice of a Deliberative Technology Policy*, International Centre for Human and Public Affairs, Hengelo, Netherlands.

Wynne, B., 1998, Does Europe Have to be Reductionist?, paper delivered at the SPSG/ESRC Conference, March.

Chapter 4

Transboundary Air Pollution: Lessons for Useful Analysis

Anthony Patt

4.1　Introduction

European countries have repeatedly succeeded at agreeing to reduce transboundary air pollution of various forms.[1]　In the Second Sulphur Protocol to the Convention on Long-Range Transboundary Air Pollution (LRTAP), which addresses sulfur emissions causing acid rain (UN/ECE, 1994), the negotiators arrived at an innovative solution.　Non-uniform emission cuts would achieve progress toward the science-based "critical loads" – a level of sulfur deposition that essentially results in no observable environmental impact – at the least possible cost across the continent. Not only did many countries pledge to reduce their emissions substantially more than their neighbors – Germany, for example, promised to reduce emissions by 87%, while Greece promised only 4% reductions – without compensation for asymmetric burdens, but they have largely followed through with implementing their promises.

　　A defining feature of the European acid rain case, and the 1994 Sulphur Protocol in particular, is the reliance on formal analysis and integrated assessment modeling. In this chapter, different analytical methods that contributed to the policy success story are compared. What types of information were useful to negotiators in providing the groundwork for consensus? What types of information were less useful, and why? In this international context, where the negotiations were more complex and the issues broader than in many local contexts, negotiators succeeded when they narrowed the problem frame significantly. Achieving consensus may also have been related to the narrow focus of negotiators on "bright lines," or apparently natural targets for pollution control, rather than on more ambiguous targets that required consensus on human values. A comparison of the transnational negotiation process with the process of reducing the same pollutants at the local level indicates that bright lines, informed by natural science rather than economic balancing, were far more influential in the transboundary context, whereas balancing approaches were more attractive at the local level.

This chapter first describes the problem of acid rain as it has evolved from a local issue to a transboundary one and briefly summarizes the institutional frameworks for international regulation. In the next section, the types of analysis that have informed international solutions to acid rain in Europe are examined. Next, the same set of pollutants in a more local context, the Black Triangle region of Central Europe, are discussed and the use of analysis in the two contexts is compared. Lessons to policymakers engaged in planning and designing assessments for future transboundary issues are offered in the concluding section.

4.2   Acid Rain: From Local Effects to Transboundary Regulation

Acid rain – more accurately known as *acidifying deposition* – is the most notorious impact of a class of air pollutants that affect local and distant places. Two by-products of industrial activity, sulfur dioxide (SO_2) and nitrogen oxides (NO_x), can remain airborne for several days, and they react chemically in the atmosphere to produce acid rain. With sunlight providing the reactive energy, NO_x combines with volatile organic compounds (VOCs) to form ground-level ozone (O_3). Through biological processes, ammonia (NH_3), a by-product of agricultural activities, converts into compounds that contribute to both acidification and eutrophication. Other compounds, such as methane (CH_4) and carbon monoxide (CO), are also part of the web.

At high enough concentrations, each of these compounds can adversely affect health, damage building materials, and impair visibility. Concentrations are naturally higher in the immediate vicinity of the sources, even where steps are taken to minimize local effects, such as building taller smokestacks. In Central Europe, SO_2 has a mean residence time in the atmosphere of one day; if it reacts to form sulfate particles it has a residence time of two to three days (Hordijk *et al.*, 1990). In this time frame of one to three days, sulfur can easily travel 1,000 kilometers (km) in high-speed upper-atmosphere winds. But the one-day mean residence time is an average, and a significant portion of the SO_2 travels only a short distance before precipitating out of the atmosphere. For this reason, people first recognized these pollutants as local phenomena. As Farrell and Keating (1998) discuss, problems such as ground-level ozone and particulate smog first became important in the mid-1800s, a result of intense coal burning in urban and industrialized areas. The naked eye and the open nose could detect the pollution, with dense clouds hanging over cities, odors in the air, and occasional extreme events in local pollution causing identifiable fatalities. With a gradual shift in Western Europe from coal to oil and natural gas as the primary fuel for residential heating, transportation, and electricity generation, the problem of urban air pollution had become less obvious by the late 1960s.

In 1968, the Scandinavian scientist Svante Odén published the first article attributing Swedish acidification to pollution from the United Kingdom and Central Europe (Odén, 1968). Although at first his reports went largely unnoticed and his funding was cut (Hordijk *et al.*, 1990), within a few years both the scientific and policy-making communities, not to mention the general public, began to take notice. VanDeveer (1998:10) argues that Odén's language and images "captured public and scientific interest and imagination in parts of Western Europe," helping to put the acid rain issue on the environmental agenda. Odén's message represented an important change in how people thought about pollution. As Alcamo *et al.* state:

> Consider how we cling to the notion that the countryside is a place of fresh air and a healthy natural environment. The city, with its smokestacks, vehicles, contaminated water, is the place of pollution. Yet the reality is that we are in a new era of pollution problems – the old era was one of localized pollution near cities, and of individual problems such as polluted rivers or contaminated urban air. In the new era, pollution covers vast regions far from pollutant

sources, and affects simultaneously water, air, and soil. Rather than an image of polluted cities surrounded by fresh-air countryside, a more realistic picture is that of a vast polluted air basin over all Europe. [Alcamo *et al.*, 1990:21]

The old problems associated with air pollution were most obvious in urban areas, and governments treated them locally. The new kind of pollution, however, crossed political boundaries and required international cooperation. The idea that pollution was more than a local problem reached prominence during the 1972 United Nations Conference on the Human Environment (UNCHE) in Stockholm. It was at the Stockholm conference that UNCHE Principle 21 emerged, which has shaped the issue of transboundary pollution ever since:

> States have, in accordance with the Charter of the United Nations and the principles of international law, the sovereign right to exploit their own resources pursuant to their own environmental policies, and the responsibility to ensure that activities within their jurisdiction or control do not cause damage to the environment of other states or of areas beyond the limits of their national jurisdiction. [UN, 1973]

In response to evidence that transboundary pollution caused long-range effects, the Organisation for Economic Co-operation and Development (OECD) launched a program to monitor long-range pollution. By the mid-1970s the OECD study had concluded that long-range transport of sulfur did occur, with countries such as Norway, Sweden, and Austria receiving more than half their sulfur deposition from abroad (OECD, 1977). Responding to this situation was more problematic, however, for both scientific and political reasons. Nobody could identify what policy responses would be sufficient to curb acid rain, and so an extensive research program would be necessary to lay the groundwork for regulation. Politically, the OECD did not include the prime pollution-generating countries of Eastern Europe, whose emissions demonstrably traveled west. The OECD, therefore, was not the proper institution to handle the business of regulation. Furthermore, countries such as the United Kingdom and West Germany, also major pollution exporters, did not agree with the OECD findings and would not agree to limits prior to the completion of more research.

In 1978 and 1979, representatives agreed on the LRTAP Convention, which was distinct from the OECD. The United Nations Economic Commission for Europe (UN/ECE), based in Geneva, provided logistic support. As an incentive for countries such as West Germany and the United Kingdom to join LRTAP, the initial calls for emission reductions were limited and vague. Instead of regulating emissions from the start, LRTAP would serve as a forum for research and further negotiation. The network of monitoring stations originally associated with the OECD took the name of the Co-operative Programme for Monitoring and Evaluation of the Long-Range Transmission of Air Pollutants in Europe (EMEP), received funding from the United Nations Environment Programme (UNEP) and the World Meteorological Organization (WMO), and associated itself with LRTAP. Delegates began the process of negotiating the first LRTAP protocols, the specific obligations to reduce emissions.

This process began in 1982 when Norway, Sweden, and Finland proposed a uniform 30% cut in sulfur emissions. They gradually convinced other countries to agree to this measure through a process Levy (1993) has called "tote-board diplomacy," applying slow but steady diplomatic pressure on countries to join their "30% club." At a 1985 meeting in Helsinki, 21 LRTAP nations signed the First Sulphur Protocol, agreeing to reduce emissions or transboundary fluxes by at least 30%. Other protocols, at first based on uniform obligations, soon followed. At a 1988 meeting in Sofia, Bulgaria, the ministers agreed to freeze NO_x emissions from both industrial and mobile sources at 1987 levels and to implement certain best available technology (BAT) standards. In 1991, nations signed a protocol to reduce VOCs by 30%. In 1994 they finalized the Second Sulphur Protocol, which required nonuniform levels of emission reductions designed to achieve the greatest benefit at the lowest cost. In 1998, LRTAP negotiators signed a protocol for persistent organic pollutants (POPs) and heavy metals.

Until recently, the European Union (EU) and its legislative arm the European Commission (EC) left the acid rain issue to LRTAP. One exception has been the Large Combustion Plant Directive, based largely on German legislation that requires BAT to be installed in new electricity generating facilities. In 1997, however, DG-XI and the Council released a new strategy to combat acidification (Council of the European Union, 1997). This strategy, which should form the basis for future Directives, adopts an effects-oriented cost-minimizing approach and specifically recognizes a multiple-pollutants approach to assessment and regulation. Work on directives consistent with the strategy is proceeding in parallel with current LRTAP negotiations toward a multiple-pollutants protocol, and both efforts are relying on the same set of scientific analysis and assessment.

4.3   Long-Range Acidification: Critical Loads, Cost Optimization, and Economic Analysis

The scientific research in the early 1980s specifically addressed the validity of such across-the-board reductions in sulfur emissions. The four questions for research were "(1) Did sulfur dioxide travel long distances? (2) Did airborne deposition of sulfur dioxide harm rivers and lakes? (3) Did airborne sulfur dioxide harm forests and crops? (4) Would proposed domestic abatement measures bring comparable improvements in foreign environmental effects?" (Levy, 1993:80). The early research provided affirmative answers to these questions, though not without some political struggle. For example, the United Kingdom had been accused of being "the dirty man of Europe," after it failed to join the 30% club and as representatives from the British Central Electricity Generating Board (CEGB) continued to question the effects that British emissions were having on Scandinavian lakes. It took a combined research effort started in 1984, the Anglo-Scandinavian Surface Waters Acidification Program, to finally resolve the issue. Involving 300 scientists from 30 institutions in 3 countries (Norway, Sweden, and Britain), the report finally concluded that transboundary pollution did occur and could be reduced (Mason, 1992).

There were holes in the simplicity of this approach large enough to block passage of tighter emission limits. The primary reason that the United Kingdom gave for not signing the First Sulphur Protocol was its lack of scientific credibility. Surely, their representatives said, LRTAP could come up with a regulation that did not rely on an arbitrary reduction (30%) from an arbitrary base year (1980) (Boehmer-Christiansen and Skea, 1991). To some extent the first NO_x Protocol avoided this problem by giving countries flexibility in choosing the base year and in adopting an emission freeze rather than a 30% cut. Analysis of acid rain that took into account the asymmetric positions of nations with respect to sources and receptors of compounds such as SO_2, the vulnerability of their soils to acidifying compounds, and the ability to reduce emissions at modest economic costs became important during negotiations for the Second Sulphur

Protocol. If nations such as the United Kingdom were going to agree to further costly emission reductions, they needed to know that such reductions would be worthwhile and necessary. A brief review of the analysis on which LRTAP relied is useful here; for a more in-depth description of the use of different analytical frameworks, see Patt (1999).

4.3.1   Critical loads

In the early 1970s, scientists reported that many systems do not show sensitivity to low levels of pollutants (Wiklander, 1978). Time-sensitive thresholds occur because natural systems are able to chemically neutralize accumulating acidifying deposition at a certain rate. Depending on local geology, different soils can withstand different amounts of acidifying deposition before showing effects. A "critical load" is an amount of pollution that a given place can absorb before showing adverse effects, roughly equivalent to its buffering capacity (Nilsson and Grennfelt, 1988). By ensuring that depositions remain below critical loads, policymakers could in principle prevent damage and solve the problem of acid rain. Again, Scandinavian scientists led the way, discussing the concept of critical loads in the early 1980s. By 1988, LRTAP had adopted critical loads as a framework for future analysis and the achievement of critical loads as the overriding goal of regulation. By 1994, LRTAP nations had agreed to the Second Sulphur Protocol with its ambitious nonuniform commitments.

How did the achievement of critical loads become the target for European acid rain policy when other targets, such as health benefits or economic balancing, were vying for attention? Levy (1993:102) suggests that critical loads "focus negotiators" on scientific issues: "While no one is so naive as to think politics will disappear, there is the hope that the process will be more productive because critical loads will reduce much of the arbitrariness and uncertainty." Critical loads would prove to be a useful concept for generating consensus around discriminatory emission reduction targets. Critical loads gained acceptance for different reasons in different countries (Patt, 1999). Scandinavian policymakers embraced the concept of critical loads because it provided a clear rationale for the strongest possible emission reductions elsewhere in Europe. Early research had indicated that Scandinavian lakes could receive about 3 kilograms of sulfur depositions per hectare per year before showing signs of acidification. This amounted to an 80% reduction from the deposition levels then taking place. In the wake of this finding, Swedish scientists began a strong campaign advocating the critical loads concept, justifying it on its politically neutrality (Eliassen, 1998). In 1986, the Nordic Council of Ministers (NCM) accepted critical loads as a guiding principle for acidification policy and presented the concept to LRTAP.

A second group of countries, including the United Kingdom and Germany, agreed to the critical loads concept because it appeared to be a way of avoiding action, at least temporarily. British industry, for example, foresaw a lengthy process of scientific research as a prerequisite to negotiating a policy based on critical loads (Ågren, 1998b). They may also have believed (wrongly) that achieving critical loads would not require extensive British emission cuts and thus would be less costly than another uniform reduction similar to the First Sulphur Protocol (Hordijk, 1998; Kakebeeke, 1998). The Germans had a history of promoting technological standards, as opposed to performance standards, and of exporting the technology to meet those standards. Convinced that critical loads would be more difficult to implement and enforce than a simple technology standard, they supported critical loads as an alternative to another flat and arbitrary emission cut (Ågren, 1998a). Nonetheless, they were committed to strong international regulation of acid rain (Boehmer-Christiansen and Skea, 1991). By supporting critical loads in the short run, the Germans may have believed that technology standards would emerge as the eventual regulatory instrument.

The Soviet Union supported critical loads primarily for ideological reasons. They accepted any regulatory approach based on natural science and were highly suspicious of approaches that involved economic balancing (Hordijk, 1998). They may also have believed, like the British, that critical loads would require few obligations on their part, since the prevailing westerly winds meant that only a small fraction of their emissions traveled to Scandinavia (Kakebeeke 1998; Hordijk 1998). The Soviets' participation in LRTAP was crucial, so their support for critical loads influenced others.

4.3.2   Cost optimization

Scientists succeeded in identifying critical loads targets for negotiators to agree to. The research, as it unfolded across Europe, took many years, but it also indicated that substantial emission cuts were necessary. A major appeal of the critical loads approach was that it was nonarbitrary, and LRTAP negotiators quickly focused on another nonarbitrary means of achieving critical loads: cost optimization. This required integrating information not only on effects and transport, but also on the costs of emission reductions in countries across Europe, through cost-effectiveness analysis (CEA).

The most important analytical tool for negotiating the Second Sulphur Protocol was the Regional Acidification INformation System (RAINS), an interactive and highly accessible computer model developed at the International Institute for Applied Systems Analysis (IIASA) outside Vienna. Midway through their work, the RAINS team came to the following conclusions, which became the basis for LRTAP negotiations:

1.   Doing what is planned is not enough.
2.   However, the planned reductions are better than nothing.
3.   Doing our best would be worthwhile.
4.   But the best will be expensive
5.   Cooperation saves effort and money.
6.   If you're not sure about points (1) to (5), use the RAINS model yourself (Alcamo *et al.*, 1990:11).

Over time, LRTAP took on an organizational structure to accommodate and promote CEA and the use of integrated assessment models, such as RAINS. As *Figure 4.1* shows, the main work of LRTAP occurred in separate working groups (WGs), which served as loci for separate task forces (TFs) and international cooperative programs (ICPs). Individual countries assumed leadership roles for each task force, often reflecting that country's primary area of concern or technical expertise. The Effects WG had TFs looking at each of the downwind ecological impacts of acid rain, the more prominent and official ones being ICPs. The Strategies WG housed the TF on Integrated Assessment Modelling (TFIAM) and, later, the TF on Economic Aspects of Abatement Strategies (TFEAAS). Overall, LRTAP's structure reflected its mission to handle the transboundary problem of acid rain, as opposed to the more local and regional health problems associated with high concentrations of pollution or ground-level ozone. In the work toward the Second Sulphur Protocol, the Strategies WG became the most politically important, and it relied extensively on the TFIAM, which in turn was in constant communication with the modelers at IIASA and elsewhere. Detailed analysis to support a nonarbitrary solution to the critical loads problem became a central feature of LRTAP. While the TFIAM used results from two other integrated assessment models, the Abatement

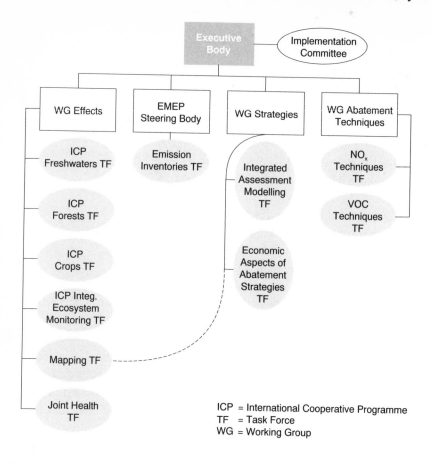

Figure 4.1. LRTAP organizational structure (Wüster, 1998).

Strategies Assessment Model (Apsimon *et al.*, 1994) and the Coordinated Abatement Strategy Model (SEI, 1991), it was the RAINS model that became the primary analytical tool. How did the RAINS model become the most important, and how did it come to center on the CEA cost-minimization objective?

IIASA initiated the RAINS project in 1983, prior to the popularization and adoption of critical loads targets, as a model that combined available information on energy emissions, transport, and deposition (Alcamo *et al.*, 1984). The following year, Leen Hordijk, an econometrician from the Netherlands, took over leadership of the project, and expanded the RAINS model to include effects on soils, lakes, groundwater, and trees,

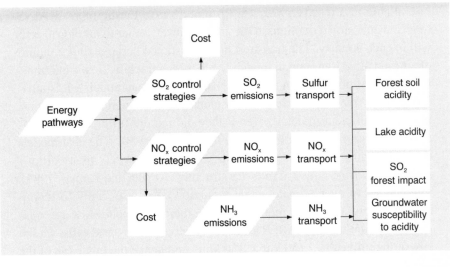

Figure 4.2. Schematic of the RAINS model (after Alcamo *et al.*, 1990).

as well as economic analysis. Hordijk recognized early on that for the RAINS model to produce useful results at a rapid pace, it would have to rely on imperfect data and simplify the physical and economic systems it studied. These simplifications would leave room for skeptics to challenge RAINS' reliability, and Hordijk took preemptive moves to boost the model's credibility.

Figure 4.2 shows the general structure of the RAINS model. Moving left to right, RAINS could perform scenario analysis by predicting the impacts of different energy pathways, control strategies, and emission levels (the slanted boxes). Moving right to left, the model could perform cost optimization, starting with acceptable levels for the right-hand boxes and translating these into the least-cost scenarios for the slanted ones. In either case, however, the RAINS' predictions were only as reliable as its input data and its assumed relationships between boxes, and these were far from perfect. For instance, RAINS incorporated national emissions data gathered by EMEP, which in turn originated from both countries' self-reporting and EMEP monitoring (Batterman *et al.*, 1986). One problem with this was that the Soviet Union refused to provide EMEP with detailed point source information for coal use and sulfur, fearing that doing so would reveal the location and size of its defense-related steel industry (Hordijk, 1998). In general, 20–50% of sulfur emissions data were unavailable in any given year (di Primio, 1998). Furthermore, RAINS modeled emission reductions at the national level, rather than for grid cells within each country. The transport model assumed homogenous columns of air (so-called Lagrangian models), rather than tracking flows and transformations of pollutants in three dimensions (Eulerian models). It is interesting that American modelers and scientists considered the Lagrangian models insufficient in detail, even if they did require far greater amounts of data and knowledge (Eliassen, 1998; Wüster, 1998). The cost models used nationally supplied data – again less than completely trustworthy – and assumed time-constant industry structure (Amann and Kornai, 1987). This tended to overestimate actual reduction costs, especially for countries that were able to be more flexible in their approaches toward emission control (Wüster, 1998). RAINS analyzed effects by grid cells, yet the size of the grid cells – 150 km × 150 km – and hence the precision of the results was far less exact than with other models, such as those developed by and for the United Kingdom (Hordijk, 1998). Finally, RAINS made no attempt to quantify its uncertainty levels, such as by providing confidence bounds on its estimates (Hordijk, 1998).

Therefore, it was no surprise that people criticized the RAINS model for being too simplistic (Eliassen, 1998; Hordijk, 1998), and Hordijk anticipated this. He invited both scientists and policymakers to a series of review meetings where the RAINS team addressed the criticisms (Hordijk, 1998). He successfully argued that the simplifying assumptions were necessary to achieve useful results at a pace fast enough to keep up with LRTAP's demands. These results, while somewhat inaccurate, were still satisfactory and were not biased toward any particular country or region (Eliassen, 1998). The RAINS model emerged as the dominant integrated assessment model (IAM) because of the speed at which it was developed (possible with its simplifying assumptions), because it came from an international research institute (and thus could be viewed as politically neutral), because of its scientific credibility (addressed specifically by Hordijk), and because members of its modeling team frequently left IIASA to work with LRTAP directly (such as Hordijk, who went from IIASA to head the TFIAM). Other models existed, but they proved less influential than RAINS.

While the popular conception of RAINS was that it suggested optimal ways to reach pollution targets, in truth it also influenced the choice of those targets in the first place. The RAINS modelers conducted early scenario analyses and demonstrated that achieving critical loads would be virtually impossible. Working with the TFIAM, they changed the goal for sulfur regulation from critical loads to a messier concept known as *5% critical loads*. A RAINS grid cell achieves 5% critical loads when 95% of the grid cell, based on the distribution of soil types within the cell, can withstand more deposition than the cell on average is receiving. When the RAINS modelers again showed that even with the maximum feasible reductions (MFRs), 5% critical loads were not within reach, the task force adopted a new target concept known as *gap closure*. A policy would achieve 50% gap closure, for example, if under the policy those cells exceeding 5% critical loads (as of 1990) made it half-way toward the 5% critical loads target. As negotiations toward the Second Sulphur Protocol progressed, the TFIAM, with the help of the RAINS team, examined the implications of a wide variety of gap closure targets. Eventually, the Strategies WG used the RAINS-derived cost-effective scenario for 60% gap closure as a starting point for negotiating the 1994 Second Sulphur Protocol. The RAINS model showed that by using nonuniform emission cuts – different countries reducing emissions by different amounts – Europe as a whole could achieve 60% gap closure much less expensively than would be possible with uniform cuts. *Table 4.1* shows the substantial differences among countries under the Second Sulphur Protocol. As Patt (1999) states, the "combination of the critical loads concept and the RAINS model allowed negotiators to justify non-uniform sulfur emissions cuts as being politically neutral, scientifically sound, and a smart alternative to arbitrary fixed-percentage reductions."

4.3.3 Economic analysis

LRTAP's regulation of transboundary acid rain, relying as extensively as it did on formal analysis, illustrates the limitations of a third basis for analysis: economic cost-benefit analysis (CBA). The limitations were both methodological (the difficulty categorizing and measuring the economic costs of acid rain) as well as political (the difficulty presenting economic data as being impartial in the same way as the critical loads and other natural science data). The LRTAP experience highlights how difficult the task of using economic analysis can be in the transboundary case, even when negotiators are open to creative solutions.

Table 4.1. Second Sulphur Protocol requirements for 2010.

Country	Emissions, kilo-tons SO_2 /year	Percentage reduction from 1980 levels
Austria	78	80
Belarus	370	50
Belgium	215	74
Bulgaria	1,127	45
Czech Republic	632	72
Denmark	90	80
Finland	116	80
France	737	78
Germany	990	87
Greece	570	4
Hungary	653	60
Ireland	155	30
Italy	1,042	73
Luxembourg	10	58
Netherlands	106	77
Norway	34	76
Poland	1,397	66
Portugal	294	3
Russian Federation	4,297	40
Slovakia	240	72
Slovenia	71	70
Spain	2,143	35
Sweden	100	80
Switzerland	60	52
Ukraine	1,696	56
United Kingdom	980	80

Source: UN/ECE, 1994.

Unlike CEA to meet critical loads targets, the full use of economic analysis measures both the costs of acid rain, in terms of the ecological and other damage it causes, and the costs of reducing emissions, in terms of decreased industrial activity. By convention, economists express the costs of acid as the benefits of acid rain reduction. Economists then convert these benefits into the quantitative metric of money, based on an understanding of people's preferences and hence the prices they would be willing to pay for environmental improvement. The optimal target lies at the point of reduction where the marginal cost and benefit curves intersect.

Table 4.2. Increasing marginal costs of SO_2 abatement.

Annual abatement cost, 10 bln DM	Emission reductions from 1980 levels, %	European area exceeding 5% critical loads, 10 mln km²	Annual cost per additional hectare protected, DM
0	27	1.343	0
10	52	0.427	152
20	60	0.162	468
30	68	0.120	3,676
40	77	0.114	25,000

Source: Apsimon *et al.*, 1997.

As *Table 4.2* shows, in the absence of any explicit policy to control SO_2, emissions would fall 27% by 2010 as a result of endogenous technological change and the shift toward low-sulfur fuels. As the total amount of money spent to reduce emissions increases, the amount of additional land protected falls, even when that money is spent in a cost-effective manner. The right-hand column of *Table 4.2* shows that the marginal cost of protecting land rises substantially as the total amount of emission reduction increases. Likewise, according to economists, making sure that the last few hectares achieve critical loads is likely worth no more than, and maybe less than, making sure that a much larger area of less vulnerable land achieves critical loads. Thus, the marginal benefits of reducing emissions are constant, or perhaps even falling. At some point short of 100% gap closure, the marginal cost of emission reduction is likely to surpass the marginal benefit, and it makes sense to set regulation no higher than this point. As economists note, the Second Sulphur Protocol's target of 60% gap closure may well approximate this point (Apsimon *et al.*, 1997). CBA, however, holds the promise of reducing the error even further and providing a justification for regulating to a particular level that is based not on expert judgment but on popular values.

While the strategy for conducting accurate and credible CBA is simple, the logistics are difficult (Pearce and Nash, 1981; Tietenberg, 1988; Hanley and Spash, 1993). Economists must predict the costs of reducing emissions to different levels, much as the RAINS modelers did. But they must also predict the economic benefits of these emission reductions. This involves not only understanding the physical and biological effects of reducing emissions – such as critical load attainment – but also the relative value to people of those changes. For non-market goods – from ecosystem health to visibility to human health – the practical ability of economists to assign monetary values is limited. The transboundary and transcultural character of acid rain exacerbates this difficulty. Norwegians may care greatly about the health of lake trout, whereas Italians may value it significantly less. Obviously, there is a strategic advantage for the Norwegians to say publicly that they value lake trout highly, since doing so will lead to a result that reduces pollution in Norway largely at the expense of others. Therefore, for strategic reasons, national spokespersons may not reveal their true values or preferences. In addition, the result of different preferences across national frontiers is that a trout in Norway is worth substantially more than a trout in Italy. To correct for this, economists can express their results with a wide range of uncertainty, such that a trout is valued at somewhere in between the Norwegian and Italian expressed values. Either way, the credibility of economic assessments as a tool for negotiation shrinks in comparison with alternatives such as critical loads.

Early in the LRTAP regime, many people wanted to see CBA guide the negotiation of protocols (UN/ECE, 1982). For example, one committee within LRTAP (since disbanded), the Group of Experts on Cost-Benefit Analysis, emphasized "the importance of informing policy-makers of the increasing availability of operational methods for estimating environmental benefits in monetary terms and recommended that countries make increased use of these methods in their policy-making" (UN/ECE, 1985). An OECD (1981) report examined costs and benefits of reducing SO_2 to 1974 levels by 1985. The cost would be US$2.7 billion in annual investment. They estimated the benefits with respect to agriculture, lake fishing, and building materials at US$1.2 billion per year. They calculated human health benefits as falling somewhere in the range of US$600 million to US$14.4 billion. With a range of benefits so large, the report was not useful for LRTAP negotiators (Ågren, 1998b), and they chose to pursue the simpler, and speedier, course of uniform emission reductions (Kakebeeke, 1998). Further efforts in the 1980s to conduct CBA met with similar problems. One report to the UN/ECE examined how CBA could benefit international decision making, but it fell short of actually assigning costs or benefits (UN/ECE, 1981). Another set of reports focused on the methodological difficulties of obtaining credible benefits estimates, even as they attempted to value clean air in Germany (Schultz, 1985; UN/ECE, 1985). A third report measured economic benefits by assuming that *national responses* to acid rain revealed that country's preferences, and thus the costs associated with these responses set a minimum value for economic benefits (Klaassen and Jansen, 1989). This report does not appear to have proved influential. A fourth report, from Canada, attempted to measure benefits but failed to credibly quantify its results (UN/ECE, 1990). Slowly, even the Group of Experts on Cost-Benefit Analysis began turning their attention to CEA, in response to calls in this direction from the LRTAP Executive Body (UN/ECE 1983, 1988) and in keeping with the critical loads work then under way. The end of the line for CBA, at least temporarily, came in the early 1990s (Førsund, 1998). The Norwegian LRTAP delegation organized a conference to review whether CBA could be useful for acid rain analysis. At the 1991 conference in Oslo, the Soviet delegation objected strongly to the use of CBA, based on ideological principles opposing market-oriented solutions. As Soviet participation was crucial, that was enough to signal the end of CBA (Amann, 1998).

Economic analysis has seen a revival in recent years, in conjunction with efforts to arrive at a multi-pollutants LRTAP protocol and EC Directive. The LRTAP Executive Body stated a desire to "raise the profile" of CBA, particularly the measurement of economic benefits of regulation (UN/ECE, 1995). The Group of Experts on Cost-Benefit Analysis, now in its third incarnation as the Task Force on Economic Aspects of Abatement Strategies, has renewed its work measuring the benefits of regulation and attempting to advise policy (UN/ECE 1992, 1993; Pearce 1998). The hope for economic analysis is that it can point out which impacts – including ecosystem loss, visibility degradation, building material damage, human morbidity and mortality, and reduced agricultural yields – are most significant. This, in turn, would suggest the appropriate relative levels of regulation for the different pollutants (Apsimon and Warren, 1997). It is significant that health effects of regulation dominate the benefits side of the cost–benefit equation; they surpass ecosystem and other benefits by a factor of 1,000 (UN/ECE, 1998). Warmer countries, such as Italy, Spain, and France, where ground-level ozone can be a problem, benefit the most from further emission cuts. Even with this analysis, the main impetus for regulation continues to come from the Scandinavian countries, rather than the Mediterranean ones (Ågren, 1998b). Assessments such as those by Holland and Krewitt (1996) and Apsimon *et al.* (1997) may prove useful, although those involved believe it unlikely that regulatory policy will shift from critical loads in the near future (Apsimon, 1998). Countries still perceive the problem as one of acidification, rather than other effects such as health. Critical loads analysis continues to be an integral part of LRTAP and EC negotiations (Amann *et al.*, 1997). However, a crisis may be looming, since people apparently value their own health more than they do the health of lakes and streams. To the extent that we do make comparisons between different types of impacts, as practitioners of CBA have done, we see that major problems with air pollution remain where the people are – in the cities, near the sources of emissions.

4.4 Local Acidification: The Black Triangle

The so-called Black Triangle, where the Czech Republic, Poland, and Germany meet, highlights the conflicting perceptions between air pollution as a long-range transboundary issue versus a local and regional issue. Home to 32 million people over an area of 186,000 km^2, the industrial output of the region is one of high material flows: mining, steel, chemical manufacturing, and petroleum refining. The results of these activities are striking. During the 1980s, Poland, East Germany, and Czechoslovakia had the highest use of coal per capita in Europe and accounted for almost 40% of the SO_2 emissions outside the Soviet Union. Together with Hungary and Bulgaria, they also had the highest SO_2 emissions per capita (Grübler and Nakićenović, 1992). Poland's per capita SO_2 emissions were 10 times higher than those of most Western countries (Löfsted, 1998). While parts of Europe far downwind feel the effects of the Black Triangle's emissions, it is the region itself that suffers most, having the highest airborne concentrations of SO_2, and the greatest rate of SO_2 deposition, in Europe (Touvinen *et al.*, 1994). As Anderberg (1996) states, "reductions outside of the region have only a marginal effect, while emission reductions here are of great importance for the deposition in many other regions."

The Black Triangle is a legacy of East European central planning, isolated from international competition and lacking the technological advances that brought sulfur emissions in Western Europe down during the 1980s. Compared with that of Western Europe, the economy of the Black Triangle was energy intensive, relying primarily on local resources such as high-sulfur coal burned in outdated plants where efficiency was poor. In Poland, for example, coal accounted for 77% of primary energy consumption and 97% of electricity generation in 1992 (International Energy Agency, 1994). With the collapse and restructuring of heavy industry in the region has come a concomitant fall in emissions. Still, the problem of local air pollution is far from over. In the Katowice area of Poland, air concentrations were four times the safe levels for SO_2, five times those for cadmium, and eight times those for lead (Nowinska, 1996).

4.4.1 International coordination

Continuing to resolve the problem of air pollution and its effects in the Black Triangle necessitates the coordination of national and international efforts. The countries in transition simply cannot invest to the extent that OECD countries can; in 1993 Poland invested US$22 per capita for environmental protection, compared with US$268 per capita in Germany. A range of international programs help Poland and the Czech Republic, accounting for 25% of environmental investment in Poland but much less – no more than 5% – in the Czech Republic (Novy, 1996). For example, with Poland's Ecofund program, creditor countries convert a portion of Poland's national debt into investment to tackle four environmental problems: greenhouse gas emissions, transboundary air pollution, Baltic Sea pollution, and loss of biodiversity. European multi- or bilateral environmental aid programs – such as the EU's PHARE program, World Bank contributions, and the European Bank for Reconstruction and Development – typically prioritize transboundary air and water pollution while rarely funding projects aimed at local air pollution or water problems (World Bank, 1993; Novy, 1996). There may be indirect benefits for local problems, arising from the transfers of technology and expertise to monitor pollution emissions and effects; but the message is clear that international institutions care primarily about transboundary pollution.

Finally, the Black Triangle countries belong to the various international regimes that regulate transboundary and global environmental problems, such as LRTAP. One important new initiative in this area is the biannual "Environment for Europe" conference, out of which comes the Environmental Action Programme for Central and Eastern Europe (EAP). The EAP prioritizes environmental issues and, unlike LRTAP, has a history of ranking problems in terms of their human health impacts. The EAP stresses the importance of eliminating high local concentrations of SO_2 and heavy metal emissions, as well as minimizing the localized and regional effects of combinations of pollutants, such as the NO_x and VOCs that combine to produce ozone.

4.4.2 Public opinion in the Black Triangle: Health and fairness

The EAP is not alone in stressing the importance of human health as a necessary consideration of environmental improvement. In contrast with the LRTAP regime and its strongest members –West European countries such as Norway, the Netherlands, and Germany – policymakers in areas with high local concentrations of air pollution stress the importance of human health and the issue of fairness toward local residents in setting environmental policy. There are good reasons for this. In Poland, for example, infant mortality is the third highest in Europe, and deaths caused by infection are the second highest, with heavy metal pollution, poor air quality, and other effects of coal burning being largely to blame (Osuch-Jasczewska and Baczynska-Szymocha, 1992). East European policymakers express concern about the international aid they receive, in that it prioritizes transboundary issues over local health issues.

A study by Löfsted (1998) highlights these issues. Löfsted interviewed ranking Polish policymakers, as well as more than 100 citizens in Katowice, a Polish city in the Black Triangle. He tested three hypotheses: (1) that policymakers are concerned about both local and transboundary effects of air pollution, but that they are becoming less concerned about the transboundary risks over time; (2) that Polish citizens are aware of the transboundary pollution caused by Polish power plants; and (3) that both policymakers and citizens feel that more attention ought to be paid to local health risks, as opposed to transboundary pollution. His findings confirmed these hypotheses. Polish "policymakers are well aware of the effects of Poland's pollution problems on nations beyond its borders, but feel that local environmental problems should receive first priority" (Löfsted, 1998:336). He found that citizens, too, "were more concerned about local rather than transboundary environmental problems" (Löfsted, 1998:336).

Löfsted finds two features of decision making that contrast with West European processes. First, Polish policymakers expressed enthusiasm about a risk-based approach toward ranking environmental problems, introduced to them by the United States Environmental Protection Agency. As one official at the Ministry of the Environment told Löfsted, "[w]e have to take into consideration the concerns of local people and policy makers when we set up environmental funding strategies. They are the ones who suffer the most. People must always be prioritized over Swedish forests"

(Löfsted, 1998:335). This risk-based approach, then, is one that prioritizes human health and, like CBA, compares the relative benefits of treating different environmental problems. Second, Polish citizens showed willingness to compare the costs of controlling pollution with the benefits of reducing it. Citizens saw the coal-fired plants as being of immense value for providing power and heat, and did not want to close them down to improve the environment. Indeed, the Polish citizens demonstrated the status quo bias so often found in decision making that considers disparate costs and benefits (Samuelson and Zeckhauser, 1988; Patt and Zeckhauser, forthcoming). People wanted to keep existing coal-fired plants in operation, but did not want the government or industry to construct new ones (Löfsted, 1998).

4.5 Discussion: Transboundary and Local Criteria for Action

4.5.1 Transboundary acid rain: Bright lines and few trade-offs

Transboundary acid rain has distant and ill-defined effects resulting from well-dispersed pollution. As Alcamo *et al.* (1990) suggest, to understand the acid rain problem we must challenge our notion of pollution being concentrated and noxious. It took scientists decades to realize that transboundary acid rain existed at all, and longer still to understand the causal pathways for its effect and the potential for stopping it. The effects are not necessarily salient for most people. Thus, to a citizen or even a policymaker in the United Kingdom, it was not obvious that British coal plant emissions were killing Scandinavian fish, much less combining with other pollutants to cause harmful regional effects. We should expect, in this situation, the pull of the status quo bias to be especially strong – why make a change when nothing is obviously wrong? But a series of decisions – LRTAP protocols – has been made. What went right?

Europeans started at a simple level with the uniform emission cuts inherent in the First Sulphur Protocol and the freeze of the NO_x Protocol. Once there was consensus that countries ought to do something – anything – the agreement easiest to achieve was one involving uniform commitments. The fact that most countries would reach the target on their own helped matters: agreeing to do nothing, and do it uniformly, was an attractive target. But matters became more difficult with calls for further cuts in emissions, as the Scandinavians started pressing for in the early 1990s. The effects were still not salient, but the reductions that would be needed were potentially costly; moreover, with greater knowledge about transboundary emission flows, countries were now situated asymmetrically.

The Scandinavians supported critical loads for strategic reasons: they imported a large fraction of their pollution and had the most sensitive soils. What does not fit the strategic model is why other countries in Europe agreed to use critical loads. The only way that countries such as the United Kingdom, which exported a large fraction of pollution and would likely be called upon to reduce emissions significantly, might agree to further cuts would be to achieve an attractive target for Europe as a whole. The goal of "no observable impact" became that line. The concept of 5% critical loads was not well understood (Hordijk, 1998) and not significantly different from the true critical loads attainment target. Furthermore, European policymakers saw gap closure as an intermediate target on the way toward critical loads attainment. The attractiveness of ridding the continent of all acid rain effects – implicating fairness as a fundamental value as well – made up for the lack of salience of long-range pollution in the lives of ordinary Europeans.

The standard economic model of decision making assumes that in the face of scarcity, people make trade-offs to satisfy their competing desires. Recent work in behavioral economics and decision theory has shown that this is approximately correct, but that people also make decisions according to well-established "heuristics and biases," and tend to favor particular types of outcomes that the economic model does not explain well (Kahneman and Tversky, 1974; Tversky and Kahneman, 1979; Thaler, 1991). When risks and uncertainties are not well understood, when either the costs or benefits of a decision are not salient, and when feedback is slow or nonexistent, people are more likely to favor particular outcomes, even at the expense of internal consistency in their decisions (Zeckhauser, 1986). With European transboundary pollution, negotiators faced this type of situation. We can view the concept of critical loads as a "bright line" around which people could achieve consensus, one that did not require them to agree on the more difficult issues related to different value systems.

Bright lines give the appearance of saliency to an outcome and make attractive, if not optimal, targets for human behavior. For example, DeGeorge *et al.* (1999) find that corporate managers of publicly traded companies manipulate reported earnings at the expense of long-term profitability. They try to meet specific targets such as positive net profits, the prior year's earnings, or earnings levels predicted by stock market analysts. Camerer *et al.* (1997) examined the behavior of New York City taxi drivers. They found that the drivers work many hours on slow days, but stop work early on busy days. Of course the drivers could earn more money working fewer total hours by working the same number of hours each day, and could do better still by working long hours on busy days and quitting early on less profitable days. But the taxi drivers appeared to want to satisfy a bright line – earning a particular sum of money each day – even at the expense of a higher average wage. Thus people choose natural bright line targets for their decision making to simplify the problems they must face. These targets are salient indicators of success – such as positive profits or achieving an income quota – but they often do not represent the full complexity of the problem.

Economists would say that the best decision is one that respects peoples' values and their trade-offs between competing objectives. But the methodology that respects popular values, cost-benefit analysis, was relatively unattractive as a decision-making methodology in European acid rain negotiations. There are several reasons. First, the process of economic valuation explicitly introduces popular preferences into politics, and these preferences are likely to vary considerably across national borders. In contrast, targets based on critical loads imply a judgment that ecosystem preservation is worthwhile, but beyond that do not depend on people's relative preferences. Second, economic analysis has methodological difficulties in terms of fixing reliable and credible price tags on the benefits of emission reductions. Economists must often express these valuations with wide margins of uncertainty, and this makes them less useful to policymakers who need a single number to guide their decisions. Cost-effective critical loads attainment suffered similar difficulties, but because policymakers viewed the underlying process as less political and value laden, they were willing to accept a great deal of uncertainty and model simplification in order to move ahead quickly with the negotiation process. Third, economic analysis deliberately avoids bright lines. Optimal solutions occur when marginal cost is equal to marginal benefit, which is rarely an intuitive target for most people. Economic analysis explicitly recognizes that some pollution is optimal, and this is an unattractive concept for many people. In contrast, the concept of critical loads offers the attractive and natural target of a complete solution to the acid rain problem, although in the process of doing so it narrows the problem definition significantly.

4.5.2   Local air pollution: Willingness to make trade-offs

Whereas in the transboundary context it was necessary to simplify the problem to one of long-range acidification and the solution to one of critical loads attainment, in the Black Triangle there has been a relative willingness to consider the problem in ways that take into account popular preferences among competing social objectives. The issue of local pollution is less abstract than its long-range cousin: emissions from the nearby power plant are causing pollution right where we would expect. People do not need to sort through the more complicated causal pathways inherent in long-range ecosystem degradation, and the political channels for action are more direct and do not require international cooperation.

In the Black Triangle, people focused less on the absolute target that critical loads analysis represents and were more willing to consider trade-offs between different risks in accordance with popular values. Health benefits, what people seem to care about most, defined the relative merits of competing proposals. Even though critical loads attainment might be possible, it has not captured people's attention as a bright line for decision making. Instead, people are eager to use risk-ranking methods to achieve a balanced policy that achieves more uniform marginal benefits across a range of health problems. Furthermore, ordinary citizens are willing to compare the costs and benefits of different levels of pollution control; while they would like to be rid of all pollution, they do not want this at the expense of losing their industrial base or electric power.

4.6   Conclusion: Useful Analysis for Transboundary Problems

Policymakers have demonstrated that they are not willing to base emission reduction targets on economic CBA. In the course of LRTAP negotiations, efforts to value the different benefits of pollution control in order to make trade-offs and to fine-tune the reduction targets to an optimal level did not prove useful. Policymakers did not want to base their policies on the diverse set of values and preferences found in the transboundary context for decision making, and they narrowed the problem definition to include only acidification effects. Critical loads and cost-effective solutions provided an attractive set of targets around which policymakers could reach consensus. Negotiating policies to achieve these targets required large amounts of scientific data and integrated assessment modeling, but the most useful research, such as the RAINS model, avoided consideration of public values and preferences.

Health issues seem to be extremely important to policymakers in the Black Triangle, where the same set of pollutants generate far more significant and visible local effects. In contrast, in Western Europe the impact of air pollution on human health is less clear, and while recent analyses have shown that reducing emissions will benefit health greatly, this is less obvious a conclusion than in the Black Triangle. The difference in the Black Triangle, however, is that the public and policymakers have embraced the ranking of relative risks and the making of trade-offs.

Policymakers should think carefully about how they use the time and funds available for environmental research and assessment. In transboundary cases, it has proved expedient to center assessment on bright lines within narrow problem frames, such as critical loads. Solutions that appear to be based on natural science may be no more free of politics and competing values than those grounded in economics, but they have allowed the leaders of countries that sacrificed more in Europe – such as the United Kingdom or Germany in LRTAP's Second Sulphur Protocol – to justify their actions to their citizens. Attaining critical loads was an extremely attractive target; the experts could confidently look forward to eliminating all effects of air pollution on European ecosystems. In contrast, CBA may be more useful in cases where policymakers and the public will accept trade-offs and more ambiguous targets. These situations are likely to involve local pollution, where costs and benefits of regulation are both salient, and where a more homogenous citizenry can more easily agree on value-laden trade-offs between competing objectives.

Note

[1] Wettestad (1997) provides a useful synopsis of the large literature examining European transboundary air pollution.

References

Ågren, C., 1998a, E-mail to the author, Swedish NGO Secretariat on Acid Rain.

Ågren, C., 1998b, Telephone interview with the author, Swedish NGO Secretariat on Acid Rain.

Alcamo, J., Kauppi, P., Bosch, M.B., Runca, E., 1984, Acid Rain in Europe: A Framework to Assist Decision Making, WP-84-032, International Institute for Applied Systems Analysis, Laxenburg, Austria.

Alcamo, J., Shaw, R., and Hordijk, L., eds, 1990, *The RAINS Model of Acidification: Science and Strategies in Europe*, Kluwer Academic Publishers, Dordrecht, Netherlands.

Amann, M., 1998, Interview with the author, International Institute for Applied Systems Analysis, Laxenburg, Austria.

Amann, M., and Kornai, G., 1987, Cost Functions for Controlling SO_2 Emissions in Europe, WP-87-065, International Institute for Applied Systems Analysis, Laxenburg, Austria.

Amann, M., Bertok, I., *et al.*, 1997, Third Interim Report: Cost-effective Control of Acidification and Ground Level Ozone, International Institute for Applied Systems Analysis, Laxenburg, Austria.

Anderberg, S., 1996, The Economic and Environmental Development in the Black Triangle Region: An All-European Problem, Unpublished manuscript presented at the conference Transboundary Risk Management in Europe: Theory and Reality, 6–8 October, Warsaw, Poland.

Apsimon, H., 1998, E-mail to the author, Centre for Environmental Technology, Imperial College, London, UK.

Apsimon, H. and Warren, R., 1997, Abatement Strategies to Reduce Particulate Concentrations across Europe, Imperial College, London, UK.

Apsimon, H., Warren, R., and Wilson, J., 1994, The abatement strategies assessment model-ASAM: Applications to reductions of sulphur dioxide emissions across Europe, *Atmospheric Environment*, **28**(4):649–663.

Apsimon, H., Pearce, D., and Özdemiroglu, E., eds, 1997, *Acid Rain in Europe: Counting the Cost*, Earthscan, London, UK.

Batterman, J., Amann, M., Hettelling, J.-P., Hordijk, L., Kornai, G., 1986, Optimal SO_2 Abatement Policies in Europe: Some Examples, WP-86-042, International Institute for Applied Systems Analysis, Laxenburg, Austria.

Boehmer-Christiansen, S., and Skea, J., 1991, *Acid Politics: Environmental and Energy Policies in Britain and Germany*, Belhaven Press, London, UK.

Camerer, C., Babcock, L., Loewenstein, G., and Thaler, R., 1997, Labor supply of New York City cabdrivers: One day at a time, *The Quarterly Journal of Economics*, **112**:407–442.

Council of the European Union, 1997, Council Conclusions on a Community Strategy to Combat Acidification, The Council of the European Union, Brussels, Belgium.

DeGeorge, F., Patel, J., and Zeckhauser, R., 1999, Earnings management to exceed thresholds, *Journal of Business*, 72(1):1–33.

di Primio, J., 1998, Data quality and compliance control in the European air pollution regime, in D. Victor, K. Raustiala, and E. Skolnikoff, eds, *The Implementation and Effectiveness of International Environmental Commitments: Theory and Practice*, MIT Press, Cambridge, MA, USA.

Eliassen, A., 1998, Interview with the author, Norwegian Meteorological Institute, Oslo, Norway.

Farrell, A., and Keating, T., 1998, Multi-jurisdictional Air Pollution Assessment: A Comparison of the Eastern United States and Western Europe, Harvard University BCSIA ENRP Discussion Paper E-98-12, Cambridge, MA, USA.

Førsund, F., 1998, E-mail to the author, Department of Economics, University of Oslo, Norway.

Grennfelt, P., Hov, O., and Derwent, D., 1994, Second generation abatement strategies for NO_x, NH_3, SO_2 and VOCs, *Ambio*, 23(7):425–433.

Grübler, A., and Nakićenović, N., 1992, *The Economic Map of Europe*, International Institute for Applied Systems Analysis, Laxenburg, Austria.

Hanley, N., and Spash, C., 1993, *Cost-Benefit Analysis and the Environment*, Edward Elgar Publishing Limited, Aldershot, UK.

Holland, M., and Krewitt, W., 1996, Benefits of an Acidification Strategy for the European Union, Draft 3, European Commission Directorate-General XII, Brussels, Belgium.

Hordijk, L., 1998, Interview with the author, Wageningen Institute for Environment and Climate Research, Wageningen Agricultural University, Netherlands; former Head of IIASA's Transboundary Air Pollution Project; former chair of the LRTAP Task Force on Integrated Assessment Modeling.

Hordijk, L., Shaw, R., and Alcamo, J., 1990, Background to acidification in Europe, in J. Alcamo, R. Shaw, and L. Hordijk, eds, *The RAINS Model of Acidification: Science and Strategies in Europe*, Kluwer Academic Publishers, Dordrecht, Netherlands.

International Energy Agency, 1994, Electricity in European economies in transition, Organisation for Economic Co-operation and Development, Paris, France.

Kahneman, D., and Tversky, A., 1974, Judgment under uncertainty: Heuristics and biases, *Science*, 185:1124–1131.

Kakebeeke, W., 1998, Interview with the author, Ministry of Housing, Spatial Planning and Environment, The Hague, Netherlands.

Klaassen, G., and Jansen, H.M.A., 1989, Economic Principles for Allocating the Costs of Reducing Sulphur Emissions in Europe, United Nations Economic Committee for Europe Executive Body for the Convention on Long-Range Transboundary Air Pollution, Group of Economic Experts on Air Pollution, Geneva, Switzerland.

Levy, M., 1993, European acid rain: The power of tote-board diplomacy, in P. Haas, R. Keohane, and M. Levy, eds, *Institutions for the Earth Sources of Effective International Environmental Protection*, MIT Press, Cambridge, MA, USA.

Löfstedt, R., 1998, Transboundary environmental problems: The case of the burning of coal in Poland for heating and electricity purposes, *Global Environmental Change*, **8**(4):329–340.

Mason, B., 1992, *Acid Rain: Its Causes and Effects on Inland Waters*, Clarendon Press, Oxford, UK.

Nilsson, J., and Grennfelt, P., 1988, Critical Loads for Sulphur and Nitrogen, Nordic Council of Ministers, Copenhagen, Denmark.

Novy, M., 1996a, International Actions to Combat Pollution in the Black Triangle and Katowice Regions, WP-95-155, International Institute for Applied Systems Analysis, Laxenburg, Austria.

Nowinska, Z., 1996, Soil Contamination in the Katowice District and its Implications to the Human Exposure and the Economy, Institute of Ecology of Industrial Areas, Katowice, Poland.

Odén, S., 1968, The Acidification of Air and Precipitation and its Consequences in the Natural Environment, Swedish National Science Research Council, Stockholm, Sweden.

OECD, 1977, The OECD Programme on Long-Range Transport of Air Pollutants, Organisation for Economic Co-operation and Development, Paris, France.

OECD, 1981, The Costs and Benefits of Sulphur Dioxide Control: A Methodological Study, Organisation for Economic Co-operation and Development, Paris, France.

Osuch-Jasczewska, R., and Baczynska-Szymocha, H., 1992, Health status of children and young people, *Aura*, **11**:31–32.

Patt, A., 1999, Separating analysis from politics: Acid rain in Europe, *Policy Studies Review*, **16**(3/4):104–137.

Patt, A. and Zeckhauser, R. (forthcoming), Behavioral perceptions and policies toward the environment, in R. Gowda and J. Fox, eds, *Judgments, Decisions, and Public Policy*, Cambridge University Press, Cambridge, UK.

Pearce, D., 1998, Letter to the author, Chair, LRTAP Task Force on Economic Aspects of Abatement Strategies, University College, London, UK.

Pearce, D., and Nash, C., 1981, *The Social Appraisal of Projects: A Text in Cost-Benefit Analysis*, Macmillan Education Ltd., Basingstoke, UK.

Samuelson, W., and Zeckhauser, R., 1988, Status quo bias in decision making, *Journal of Risk and Uncertainty*, 1:7–59.

Schulz, W., 1985, Bessere Luft, was ist sie uns wert? Eine gesellschaftliche Bedarfsanalyse auf der Basis individueller Zahlungsbereitschaften, Umweltbundesamt, Berlin, Germany [in German].

SEI, 1991, An outline of the Stockholm Environmental Institute's Coordinated Abatement Strategy Model, CASM, Stockholm Environmental Institute at York, Heslington, York, UK.

Thaler, R., 1991, *Quasi-rational Economics*, Russell Sage Foundation, New York, NY, USA.

Tietenberg, T., 1988, *Environmental and Natural Resource Economics*, second edition, Scott Foresman & Co., Glenview, IL, USA.

Touvinen, J-P, Barrett, K., Styve, H., 1994, Transboundary Acidifying Pollution in Europe: Calculated Fields and Budgets 1985–93. EMEP/MSC-W Report 1/94, The Norwegian Meteorological Institute, Blindern, Norway.

Tversky, A., and Kahneman, D., 1979, Prospect theory: An analysis of decision under risk, *Econometrica*, 47:263–291.

UN, 1973, Report to the UN Conference on the Human Environment, Stockholm, Sweden, 5–16 June 1972, United Nations, New York, NY, USA.

UN/ECE, 1981, Methodological Approach to the Economic Assessment of Environmental Damages, Senior advisors to United Nations Economic Commission for Europe governments on environmental problems, Geneva, Switzerland.

UN/ECE, 1982, Cost-benefit Analysis of Alternative Programmes for Sulphur Emissions Control in the ECE Region: Methodological Approach and Data Requirements, Interim Executive Body for the Convention on the Long-Range Transport of Air Pollution, Geneva, Switzerland.

UN/ECE, 1983, Meeting on Cost-Benefit Analysis of Sulphur Emission Control, United Nations Economic Committee for Europe Executive Body for the Convention on Long-Range Transboundary Air Pollution, Geneva, Switzerland.

UN/ECE, 1985, Report of the Second Session, United Nations Economic Committee for Europe Executive Body for the Convention on Long-Range Transboundary Air Pollution, Group of Experts on Cost and Benefit Analysis, Geneva, Switzerland.

UN/ECE, 1988, Cost-impact and Economic Impact Analyses of Different SO_x and NO_x Abatement Strategies, United Nations Economic Committee for Europe Executive Body for the Convention on Long-Range Transboundary Air Pollution, Group of Economic Experts on Air Pollution, Geneva, Switzerland.

UN/ECE, 1990, Economic Benefits of a Cleaner Environment. Geneva, United Nations Economic Committee for Europe Executive Body for the Convention on Long-Range Transboundary Air Pollution, Group of Economic Experts on Air Pollution, Geneva, Switzerland.

UN/ECE, 1992, Economic Aspects of Abatement Strategies, United Nations Economic Committee for Europe Executive Body for the Convention on Long-Range Transboundary Air Pollution, Working Group on Strategies, Geneva, Switzerland.

UN/ECE, 1993, Economic Aspects of Abatement Strategies, United Nations Economic Committee for Europe Executive Body for the Convention on Long-Range Transboundary Air Pollution, Working Group on Strategies, Geneva, Switzerland.

UN/ECE, 1994, Protocol to the 1979 Convention on Long-Range Transboundary Air Pollution on Future Reductions of Sulphur Emissions, United Nations Economic Committee for Europe Executive Body for the Convention on Long-Range Transboundary Air Pollution, Geneva, Switzerland.

UN/ECE, 1995, Economic Evaluation of Benefits of Abating Nitrogen Oxides and Related Substances, United Nations Economic Committee for Europe Executive Body for the Convention on Long-Range Transboundary Air Pollution, Working Group on Strategies, Geneva, Switzerland.

UN/ECE, 1998, Economic Assessment of Benefits, United Nations Economic Committee for Europe Executive Body for the Convention on Long-Range Transboundary Air Pollution, Working Group on Strategies, Geneva, Switzerland.

VanDeveer, S., 1998, European Politics with a Scientific Face: Transition Countries, International Environmental Assessment, and Long-Range Transboundary Air Pollution, Harvard University BCSIA ENRP Discussion Paper E-98-09, Cambridge, MA, USA.

Wettestad, J., 1997, Acid lessons? LRTAP implementation and effectiveness, *Global Environmental Change*, **7**(3):235–249.

Wiklander, L., 1978, The sensitivity of soils to acid precipitation, in T.C. Hutchinson and M. Havas, eds, *Effects of Acid Precipitation on Terrestrial Ecosystems*, Plenum Press, New York, NY, USA.

World Bank, 1993, Environmental Action Programme for Central and Eastern Europe, The World Bank, Washington, DC, USA.

Wüster, H., 1998, Interview with the author, Secretary for Working Group on Strategies, LRTAP Secretariat, UN-ECE, Geneva, Switzerland.

Zeckhauser, R., 1986, Comments: Behavioral versus rational economics: What you see is what you conquer, *Journal of Business*, **59**(4):S435–S449.

Chapter 5

Cultures of Uncertainty – Transboundary Risks and BSE in Europe

Brian Wynne and Kerstin Dressel

5.1 Introduction

Contrary to a common stereotype of "modemity" and its negative impacts, transboundary risks are not a new phenomenon. Since ancient times, trade and travel have entailed international circulation of infectious diseases and environmentally damaging plant and animal species. However, the development of (admittedly fragile) notions of global identity associated with economic global interdependence and environmental globalization of "common risks," such as global climate change, has in some respects increased the stakes involved, as the negotiation and dispute of responsibility for generating such risks and controlling them properly becomes intertwined with more complex and ambitious political–economic units, such as the Organisation for Economic Co-operation and Development

(OECD), the European Union (EU), and bodies with growing transnational legal powers like the World Trade Organization (WTO). The possible evolution of new collective identities superseding or complementing the nation-state – at both the supra- and subnational levels – has increasingly been influenced by the shape of such risk dispositions. The EU has been a prominent testing ground for such processes, as an explicit but contested ambition of political as well as economic unity has colored its evolution through the negotiation of new issues such as transboundary risks.

Risk is about these political and cultural identity processes as well as about physical harm, as the normal culturally sustained contours of trust and responsibility in existing institutions are exposed and challenged by – and reflected in the construction of – new kinds of risk issues. One such issue was that of bovine spongiform encephalopathy (BSE), a previously unknown cattle disease that emerged in the United Kingdom in the mid-1980s. Normally such new connections between human practices, natural agents, and physical processes are first encountered in arenas where their implications and reverberations can be limited, and institutions are allowed time to adapt to and shape the new realities with minimal disruption to existing commitments and identities. In the BSE case, however, the United Kingdom's reactions, which in the prevailing political culture were assumed to be adequate to contain the problem, proved to be utterly inadequate despite considerable assistance from the European Commission (EC). The ramifications generated a profound international crisis of political trust and mutual loyalty among EU member states that went far beyond the immediate issue of public safety which became its focus.

The crisis over BSE, or "mad cow disease," erupted for the EU in April 1996, when exports of British beef were banned worldwide. This occurred days after the UK government had undergone a dramatic about-face and, on 20 March – after years of repeated denials of any risk to humans from the recognized transmissible spongiform encephalopathy in British cattle – acknowledged that cases of a new variant (nv) of the human encephalopathy, Creutzfeld-Jakob disease (nvCJD), might be caused by exposure to BSE. The resulting EU imposition of a worldwide ban on its products plunged the British beef industry into potential disaster and provoked an already rampant anti-EU faction of a struggling Tory government into unprecedented hysteria against alleged foreign, particularly German, irrationality and anti-British conspiracy.

In fact, the EU only followed the UK government's position; and indeed the EC had for some years been adopting a largely pro-UK stance in the face of earlier BSE-inspired bans on British beef imports by the United States, Australia, Russia, Canada, and other EU partners such as German state governments. However, as the extent and audacity of previous UK denial and the unnecessary risk this had imposed on customers became apparent, and as the correspondence between the UK stance on precaution and uncertainty in this case and its unpopular stance on other EU environmental issues became clear, political mistrust of and derision for the UK's official stance on BSE combined with resentment at its self-righteous anti-EU political stance. Thus the EC's initially mollifying and deferential orientation toward the United Kingdom was engulfed by escalating official confrontation and open hostility, with the Union's regular business and its larger unification agenda being jeopardized across the board by threat and counter-threat. The intensity of these reactions was undoubtedly amplified by structural features of the issue: the risk was materially embodied in a physically mobile and commercially exchanged consumer product that was a central part of the population's diet and was consumed more or less daily, whose origins were essentially difficult to demarcate, and which was easily exchanged for alternatives by uncertain consumers, with huge effects on the producing industry. Although it was largely confined to the British cattle herd and arose solely from UK causes, the BSE issue presented the EU with a risk problem for which it had little precedent or experience.

Not only British beef, but all European beef was tainted with the stigma of risk, so that fluid, complex coincidences and conflicts of interest and identity emerged across national boundaries. Continental European farmers were desperate to dissociate themselves and their beef from their UK counterparts. Yet European consumers showed little propensity to distinguish national sources of beef, so that sales of all beef were badly hit throughout Europe, reflecting a suspicion that reliable labeling and attribution of origins in such an industry were not a realistic basis for reassurance. The responses to the crisis also showed uncertainties and conflicts between member states, the EU, and even regional units of government (e.g., German *Länder*) over sovereignty and "legal competence" to exercise policy control over different aspects of the issue. Complicating matters more in this transboundary risk management arena were the evident, though implicit, differences across national boundaries between cultural approaches to scientific knowledge and its limits in public policy.

As we attempt to show in this paper, with respect to risk issues the experience of the BSE problem demonstrates the significance of a lack of close and precise cultural unity within the EU regarding issues such as the nature of valid public knowledge; the relationship between knowledge, uncertainty, and responsibility; and the role, possibilities, and purpose of science as a public policy resource. These institutional and cultural differences left a crucial lacuna where there should have been substantial underpinning to common institutional commitments to ways of handling the different elements and manifestations of the crisis. This is not to imply that unification at this cultural level in Europe is therefore desirable or realistic, nor that it would have superseded conflicting economic or political interests where these arose. It is widely acknowledged by academics and policy actors that in the BSE case different kinds of knowledge and uncertainty make political decision making extraordinarily difficult. However, we wish to elaborate this framework to argue that different underlying cultural presuppositions are in play that are unrecognized by their (at this level) innocent proponents, but that fundamentally affect what counts as knowledge or what justifies commitments in each national system, and that confuse the interactions which occur at a more superficially rational level between these cultural idioms.

The most prominent difficulty crippling the BSE case – namely, handling the trade-offs of public health risk against economic interest in the face of highly uncertain knowledge of effects and processes, and the uncontrollable public reactions to any risk, however remote – overlies more subtle cultural dislocations over knowledge and its social roles and limits. These cultural dimensions implicitly also deal with questions of distribution of responsibility between science, industry, and different elements of the public sphere, and with needed negotiation of the proper license to be given to instrumentalism as the guiding normative force of public knowledge and policy. This highlights national policy cultural differences over how to recognize and implement new ways of dealing with ignorance and non-knowledge in actual policy. We therefore deal with this theoretical issue and describe its empirical manifestations. In this respect, the issues raised by the BSE crisis are shared to varying degrees by a range of other international risk problems, where the identity, authority, and scope of national, international, and local institutions are in flux and effectively under negotiation through the historical process of such issues. They therefore pose challenging questions about the relationships between transboundary risks, uncertain scientific knowledge, institutional structures, and political commitment and responsibility in late modern societies.

5.2 The Emergence of BSE in the United Kingdom

BSE was first detected in 1985 in Britain and described as a new cattle disease in 1987. It became a notifiable disease in 1988 in Britain and in 1990 in the EU. The first article suggesting the possibility of transmission of the cattle disease by dietary means to humans was published in 1988 in the *British Medical Journal* (Holt and Phillips, 1988). This article became a key reference for critical voices inside Britain wishing to emphasize the risk from consumption of infected beef products. At the same time the official UK line was very reassuring: British beef is safe to eat. But nobody knew for sure. Official UK expert inquiries gave expressions of confidence whose subtle qualifications could be ignored by high-profile media and ministerial references to them as scientifically demonstrating zero-risk. Officials attempted to obliterate any sense of risk with statements such as that of a government veterinary scientist asserting that transmission to humans was as "unlikely as being struck by lightning" (Bradley, 1988, cited by Holt, 1998). Yet such statements were repeated in the face of mounting evidence of the unanticipated mobility of the still-unknown infective agent across more and more species boundaries, of its apparent resilience in ambient environmental media, of its possible transmission from mother to calf, and of a growing number of observed cases of a new variety of human CJD which (unlike the known version) seemed to match the form of brain pathology that BSE showed in cattle.

The whole BSE issue, festering and occasionally bubbling up from beneath this intensifying official UK effort to contain and deny it, erupted uncontrollably in March 1996, when the secretary of health, Stephen Dorrell, and the agriculture minister, Douglas Hogg, took the unusual step of making a joint statement that "there remains no scientific proof that BSE can be transmitted to man by beef, but ... the most likely explanation at present is that these cases [of nvCJD] are linked to exposure to BSE before the introduction of the specified bovine offal ban in 1989" (Dorrell, 1996).

Britain has had about 176,000 confirmed BSE cases and over 70 diagnosed victims of nvCJD as of summer 2000. The other European countries have had several hundred BSE cases with numbers currently rising in Portugal and France, which imported infected cattle-feed from the United Kingdom, and, with the possible exception of France, no cases of nvCJD. The public perception of risk aroused by BSE seems to be very different in various countries. For example, one year after the March 1996 announcement, British consumer confidence as measured by beef consumption had improved from 40% down on pre-announcement figures to 16% down (MLC, 1997:6). By contrast, in Germany, where there have been six cases of BSE, the national beef market has suffered a reduction of about 30% since 1990 (Deutsche Landwirtschafts-Gesellschaft-Wintertagung, January 1998).

5.3   Risk and Borderline Knowledge

As economic interrelations become globalized, the density and extent of transboundary risk problems are likely only to grow, requiring a corresponding increase of transboundary concertation. One approach is to do as the WTO and EU have typically done, which is to legally require nation-states to respect politically loaded commitments to risk assessments originating elsewhere. If scientific risk knowledge were truly value free and objective, the political loading would not exist and the universal sovereignty of risk assessments in this way might be unexceptionable. But the risk assessments may well be premised upon or framed by value commitments and social assumptions that are locally inspired, not universally valid or accepted. In this case, the science acts as a covert vehicle for imposing contentious political commitments upon a wider international arena and avoiding democratic debate and accountability. Thus scientific knowledge and its tacit social underpinnings, especially the meanings attributed to uncertainty in different parts of an increasingly transboundary network of exchange and interdependency, come to be focal issues for analysis.

To this end, in this paper we focus on the relations between what is unknown, perhaps what we can never know, and how knowledge (and uncertainty) is represented and recognized or ignored in different national risk policy cultures. To describe our "not-knowing," we use the term *borderline knowledge* (Dressel, 1997a). With this term we refer not only to the general differentiation between nations and cultures, but also to that between categories and dimensions. For example, there might be a borderline (in a "real" and in a figurative sense) in what is accepted as knowledge that is recognized by one party as a cognitive, cultural, or interests boundary, but that might be perceived only as "knowledge" by another party. Exclusions and boundaries may occur not only by deliberate commitment, but as a knock-on effect of material cultural and subcultural differences.

The idea of borderline knowledge reflects our attempted modification of Beck's fruitful "non-knowledge" concept (see Beck, 1996) to make it less cognitivist and more culturally attuned. Beck differentiates between five dimensions of non-knowledge:

- Selective perception and mediation of knowledge
- Uncertainties of knowledge
- Possibilities of mistakes and errors
- Inability to know
- Unwillingness to know

With this conceptualization of non-knowledge – which he argues acts as an agent for nature by reflecting unanticipated consequences of commitment (e.g., to a new technology) back onto political institutions – Beck extends the discussion of the status of knowledge in late modern societies. He goes beyond the classical ideas of simple modernity (and indeed of Giddens' notion of reflexive modernity), which focus exclusively on positive knowledge. Although our empirical application of Beck's "non-knowledge" idea to the British BSE case led to some conceptual critique and important modifications, we have suggested elsewhere (see Dressel, 1997b) that Beck's concept has proved fruitful. On the other hand, the emphasis on cognitive dimensions in Beck's formulation of non-knowledge has limitations in understanding policy on risk management in national and international contexts. To take one example, is the "unwillingness to know" dimension treated as a universal one in Beck's approach, and what is its relationship with his separate category of "inability to know"? Social and cultural contingencies may well result in different framings of what is recognized and counts as a risk, as well as what is recognizable as knowledge and ignorance. Similar considerations might apply to the other categories of non-knowledge that Beck posits.

Beck's five dimensions of "non-knowledge" fail to make the fundamental (if empirically entangled) distinction between (i) explicit knowledge as a discursive (instrumental) tool and expressible object of deliberative reflection by social actors (where lack of knowledge is also endemic), and (ii) embodied knowledge, which is part of taken-for-granted practices – which is usually part of a whole social process, but which is not, and is not capable of being, reflected upon or explicitly addressed by its actor-subjects. The latter refers to material culture as routinized, habituated forms of practice, relationships, and cognitions that are bound up with an actor's self-identity. Its boundaries with the first type of knowledge, which encapsulates the conventional notion of knowledge as object, are intrinsically ambiguous and contingent, as social action pushes such boundaries at different times and places in one direction or the other.

In attempting to grasp the concept of "non-knowledge" or ignorance, we have identified a third form of "knowledge," what we have called (iii) "virtual knowledge." Like embodied knowledge, this is also bound up in social and technical practices. It is the knowledge or belief *implied to exist* by dint of the practical commitments and behaviors of a given social group. Thus, for example, if cattle-feed manufacturers add animal remains to feed, they *imply* a positive belief either that no infection of the animal feed will result, or that if it did, it could go no further (e.g., not to live animals or their human consumers). It is in this domain of not only unstated but unconscious "virtual knowledge" or "virtual propositional claim" that many of the confusions and problems over scientific knowledge and decision making occur. This is because the range of such *virtual knowledge* always stretches well beyond what we can know or test (it is potentially infinite in open systems, whereas knowledge is always finite) and – crucially for the self-conscious and too-often self-congratulatory explicit scientific treatment of uncertainty – beyond what can be known as uncertainty. Not only does "virtual knowledge" equate to non-knowledge in an intellectual sense, it also creates the material and social space for nasty surprises and unanticipated damage effects. Moreover, it creates profound confusion after the fact about who was responsible for such (as it turned out, rash) commitments, because the boundaries of ignorance and uncertainty were confused before the nasty surprise occurred. It is in this ambiguous space, however, that we would like to posit cultural differences deriving from recognized differences between the Anglo-Saxon and the continental cultural traditions, these differences having important practical policy consequences relating to "precaution."

All these distinctions can be accommodated in, but do not clearly correspond to, the five dimensions of non-knowledge identified by Beck. Beck's theoretical framing focuses on the cognitive dimension. It misses the *cultural* dimension of unreflected and unconsciously learned social and technical practices, cultural routines and habits, and moral identities (see also Wynne, 1994). Instead, it appears that non-knowledge is solely the flip side of knowledge, where more knowledge implies less non-knowledge and vice versa. Indeed, at least four of Beck's five categories appear to assume deliberate selection, filtering, and other means of actively, calculatingly creating conditions of non-knowledge, while we wish also to add the important extra, cross-cutting dimension of knowledge as culture. In our cultural conceptualization of (non-)knowledge as borderline knowledge, ignorance is an embodied element of knowledge. Ignorance is seen as a particular form of signification or meaning that creates the complementary lack of meaning, which as it were occupies the same space but, for reasons of cultural incompatibility, is usually not recognizable and open to the knowledge subject, but is taken for granted. Once knowledge is seen as inalienably bound up in practical culture – in the way that Kuhn described scientific disciplinary cultures and post-Kuhnian science studies have elaborated – non-knowledge has to be seen as a human predicament that is universal in principle but always culturally and practically (though unknowably) defined. In other words, the very process of establishing the conditions of knowledge is also a process of creating a particular human identity, moral engagement, and culture, and this is an unavoidably selective and limiting cognitive process (thus simultaneously creating ignorance), just as it is this same condition which creates that knowledge's coherence and (qualified) usefulness.

If we are to understand the relationship between knowledge, risk perception, uncertainty, and policy decisions in international contexts, it is essential that we analyze the "... social mechanisms of closure around particular logical constructions [which] have to occur in order to complete the otherwise incomplete logical construction of local knowledge-forms" (Wynne, 1992:123). The cultural process is where the intrinsic commitments required to give any knowledge coherence and structure occur, and where, at the very same time, ignorance, exclusion of knowledge, and a "lack of meaning" are created.

To summarize, knowledge and ignorance are always shaped by national and/or cultural contexts. What counts as knowledge in a specific

context is subject to a cultural intrinsic labeling praxis, which, furthermore, is dependent on power relations. By directing attention to this cultural dimension of (non-)knowledge production, we are not dismissing
the cognitive, deliberative, or "interests" dimension. Rather, we are emphasizing an important but often overlooked dimension and arguing for
a more complex relationship between the cognitive and the cultural. In
distinguishing this culturally grounded "non-knowledge" concept, we use
the term "borderline knowledge."

5.4   The Institutional Handling of BSE in the United Kingdom

The first cases of cattle with conspicuously uncoordinated behavior, uncontrollable staggering, and falling were noticed in 1985 by a veterinary
practitioner in southwest Britain.[1] The symptoms, the incubation period,
and the cause of this eventually fatal disease were not known. Even at the
writing of this chapter, the disease agent – thought to be a deformed brain-
protein, or prion – remains an unknown quantity. After more cases arose,
the government's Central Veterinary Laboratory (CVL) was called in. The
CVL confirmed the diagnosis of a hitherto unrecognized cattle disease of
the family of encephalopathies. The British *Veterinary Record* from 31
October 1987 published an article by Wells *et al.* from CVL, in which
they described this disorder and coined the term "bovine spongiform encephalopathy" (Wells *et al.*, 1987). By the end of 1987, 420 cases of BSE
had been confirmed around the country, though it was still not a notifiable
disease and all cattle products (beef, milk, meat, bone meal, etc.), even
from infected herds, entered the human food and animal feed chains as
usual.

In 1988 the British Ministry of Agriculture, Fisheries and Food
(MAFF) set up an ad hoc scientific advisory committee chaired by an
eminent academic biologist, Professor Sir Richard Southwood, to investigate BSE. The "Southwood Committee" comprised four distinguished
scientists, none of them expert in the relevant field. Following the first
meeting of the Southwood Committee in June 1988, several recommendations for urgent actions were given confidentially to MAFF but were
not published until February 1989. These were to destroy the carcasses of
infected animals, with compensation; to impose a ruminant feed ban (feed
containing animal remains); and to establish a standing expert committee

for evaluation of and advising on research. The UK government introduced the feed ban in July 1988 (although it was valid for ruminants, it was
still allowed to be fed to other animals); the compulsory "slaughter-with-
compensation policy" came into effect in August 1988; and the standing Consultative Committee on Research (the Tyrrell Committee) was established in February 1989. Moreover, as a precautionary measure, the
milk of suspected animals was destroyed after December 1988 (Southwood's Report of the Working Party on Bovine Spongiform Encephalopathy, 1989). The Southwood Committee was especially concerned about
the potential risks for infants from infant food containing processed meat.
However, their recommendation to prohibit specific bovine residues in infant food was implemented only one year later by the UK government
(European Parliament, 1997:11).

The general conclusions of the Southwood Committee were as follows: "From present evidence, it is likely that cattle will prove to be a
'dead-end host' for the disease agent and most unlikely that BSE will
have any implications for human health. Nevertheless, if our assessments
of these likelihoods are incorrect, the implications would be extremely serious" (Report of the Working Party on Bovine Spongiform Encephalopathy, 1989:21). With respect to the possible spread of the disease, including
to other countries, the Report stated, "Assuming there is no vertical or hor-
izontal transmission, the strict adherence to the regulations preventing the
incorporation of infective material in calf and cattle feed should . . . lead to
a fall in the number of new cases and on present evidence . . . the disease
is likely to be extinct in Great Britain."

As it turned out, the dominant "dead-end host" assumption was a crucial unfulfilled condition of the reliability of the qualified reassurances
from these scientists. In the hands of other experts it became a far less
conditional statement, and its transmission and repetition across the differentiated networks of multiple scientific and professional communities
gradually allowed its conditional origin to become invisible. In June 1989,
MAFF announced the intention to remove specified bovine offals (SBO)
from cattle over 6 months old from the human food chain. In November
1989, the British government implemented the SBO ban: 16 months after
the protection of cattle and other ruminants they started protecting people
in the United Kingdom and elsewhere.

In the face of more than 7,000 confirmed cases of BSE in the United
Kingdom in 1989, and almost no scientific knowledge about the nature of

the disease, the transmission or reproduction of the pathogen, or methods of treatment or live diagnosis, several countries responded by banning British cattle and beef. The United States was the first to ban British beef imports in 1989, followed by Canada, Australia, New Zealand, and Russia in 1990. Similarly, the EU (initiated by Germany) restricted exports of British cattle, SBOs, and cattle organs under the age of six months to European member states. Nevertheless, or perhaps because of these bans and the threat they posed to the British beef industry, British politicians and civil servants continued to reassure the public in Britain and elsewhere that there was no risk at all from the consumption of British beef products and that the bans lacked any rational basis. For example, David MacLean, then the British food minister, stated that "the cow disease does not pose a health risk to humans. We are not in the business of subjecting our people to unsafe food" (*New York Times*, 24 January 1990). Similarly, Keith Meldrum, former government chief veterinary officer, said in his statement to the Standing Veterinary Committee of the EU in September 1990, "But we say that there is no risk, or indeed any proof of such a risk" (European Parliament, 1997:10).

Whatever reassurance such statements had succeeded in creating, ripples of uncertainty began again in February 1990 when MAFF released a press notice stating that under experimental conditions BSE was transmitted to other cattle and to mice (European Parliament, 1997:91). The assumption of the infected cow as a "dead-end host" (i.e., that the infective agent was confined to the single animal and destroyed or completely immobilized when the animal was slaughtered) started to erode, although this opinion continued to be officially expressed for years afterward, for example, in the SEAC Report of 1995 (Spongiform Encephalopathy Advisory Committee, as the Tyrrell Committee was later called). John Gummer, then agriculture minister, tried to reassure the public by feeding British beef to his four-year-old daughter Cordelia in front of TV cameras. But it was not only representatives from the realm of agriculture who reacted. Kenneth Clarke, then health minister, dismissed the new scare and the further evidence of species boundary crossing that inspired it with the statement, "We are completely confident there is nothing wrong with beef, despite this crazy public scare."

The year 1990 could also be called the "year of the dissenters" in the British BSE case. With more than 1,000 BSE cases being officially notified per month, and the lowest beef consumption rate in Britain since

1962, dissenters from the official reassuring line received much more public attention than ever before. They asked for precautionary measures while the government, MAFF, and scientific advisory bodies were convinced that there was, at worst, only a very remote "theoretical" risk to humans from this novel cattle disease. The critics experienced varying degrees of neglect, marginalization, intimidation, and thwarting of their research and careers (for more details, see Dressel, 1997c).

The period between 1991 and 1995 saw a gradually escalating background of concern and reaction over BSE. Several significant news "events" occurred as the numbers of infected cattle rose relentlessly despite the official assumption that this increase would stop after the 1989 ruminant feed ban. Recorded cases eventually peaked in 1993, with 1,000 confirmed cases per *week*. Seventy-five percent of all recorded BSE cases occurred between 1990 and 1994 (European Parliament, 1997:5). Background concern about the falsehood of the key "dead-end host" belief erupted from time to time, fed by news that BSE had jumped the species barrier, naturally or experimentally, to marmoset monkeys, a cheetah, a puma, pigs, antelopes, deer, cats, and mice. The main buttress for officials and scientists who continued to believe that, this unexpected mobility notwithstanding, BSE posed no risk to humans was the experience of widespread scrapie, a BSE equivalent, in British sheep flocks over more than two centuries with no epidemic of human spongiform encephalopathy despite unrestricted consumption of at-risk sheep tissues and organs. Even if the infective agent did – against official scientific assertions – cross the human species barrier, so this analogy was taken to indicate, it was not necessarily infective to humans. Whatever official reasons were given for denying a risk to humans from BSE, this informal reasoning has been given time and again as the main logic of the UK official faith that there was no risk. A national stir was caused in 1993 when it became public that two dairy farmers, both with BSE cases in their herds, died of CJD (it was only in autumn 1997 that these were confirmed as cases of classical CJD and not the new variant CJD associated with BSE).

The public's demand for more open information about the risks to humans – for example, the amount of infected meat already consumed – was ignored in favor of increasingly questionable yet increasingly strident reassurances by governmental bodies. Many local education authorities exercised their own precautionary views by banning beef from school meals, to the dismay of the UK farming lobby and the government. In the face of mounting public concern and gathering rejection of government assurances, large advertising and promotional campaigns were started, for example, by the British Meat and Livestock Commission (MLC), aiming to restore consumer confidence in British beef (1.9 million BSE Questions & Answers leaflets, 10,000 posters, and 10,000 Safeguarding our Beef leaflets were distributed; MLC, 1996). These did not claim directly that British beef was safe to eat, nor that there was no risk of human transmission, but maintained simply that British beef is best. However, in another context, the MLC organized meetings for the British meat industry and retailers and members of the government's independent Spongiform Encephalopathy Advisory Committee to keep "the industry up to date on the science and facts, [and to] provid[e] reassurance for them to pass on to their customers" (MLC, 1996:5). By 1994, at least 30 countries had banned imports of British cattle and, after a statement by the German health minister, Horst Seehofer, expressing his concern regarding BSE's impact on public health, meat consumption dropped by 30% in Germany (*Veterinary Record*, 21 May 1994:535).

The first two new variant (nv) CJD victims appeared in 1995. CJD is typically a disease of old people. Worldwide, only four cases of CJD in young people had ever been described. The United Kingdom had two atypical teenage victims of CJD in one month, and the number increased dramatically until March 1996, by which time 10 similar cases were identified in the United Kingdom (with some others still uncertain). Rob Will and others from the CJD Surveillance Unit submitted an article to the *Lancet* stating, "These cases appear to represent a new variant of CJD, which may be unique to the United Kingdom. This raises the possibility that they are causally linked to BSE. Although this may be the most plausible explanation for this cluster of cases, a link with BSE cannot be confirmed on the basis of this evidence alone" (Will *et al.*, 1996: 921). The same line was taken in the government announcement of 20 March 1996 that although there was no scientific proof, the most likely explanation for these unusual cases was BSE. However, the crucial part of this fundamental change of position on the human risks was that it could be claimed that these risks were under control and bounded, as the supposed sole risk factor, contaminated feed, had supposedly been eradicated five years earlier with the ban of SBO, and this ban was believed to have been effectively implemented.

This point was lost in the general melee of concern, where the effectiveness of such attempted reassurances depended on a vanished public belief in government assertions about feed controls being fully implemented, about the impermeability of the cattle–human species barrier, and about the general inability of the BSE agent to infect humans. Thus this announcement precipitated the biggest blow to consumer confidence, to beef farmers, and the beef industry. The rest of 1996 was dominated by frantic activity and deep political and economic ramifications for other issues altogether, inside and outside the United Kingdom.

5.5   EU Responses and Reverberations

Only days after the UK's announcement of 20 March, the EU banned all movement of live cattle and bovine products (including embryos and semen) of British origin – not only inside the Community but also on the world market. The EU ban provoked a fury of anti-EU sentiment in the United Kingdom, with the virulently anti-Europe right wing of the Conservative Party exploiting this foreign scapegoat – Bonn or Brussels – to split the government benches in Parliament and forcing ministers to adopt an aggressively disruptive stance within all EU processes. The backlash from Europe was fierce and firm, to the apparent shock of UK ministers, who by mid-summer 1996 were looking for ways to effect a face-saving retreat from this extreme and politically all-embracing symbolic posturing.

On BSE itself, however, the UK government continued to pursue its scientifically self-righteous stance of martyr to European irrationality with respect to the proper disciplines of science-based policy. It turned on the EC for implementing the April ban, describing it as scientifically unjustified because, as far as it was concerned, British beef was now safe since controls on contaminated feed and removal of offals from the human food chain had been implemented years earlier. However, this "scientifically based" UK claim rested on several ambitious assumptions, for example, assumptions about the source of the infective agent in contaminated feed, the incubation period, the confinement of the agent to the tissues singled out for removal from human food, the dead-end host status of infected cattle, the supposed fulfillment in practice of formally specified regulations about notifying infected cattle, complete slaughter-house removal of specified tissues and organs, and rendering and feed industry practices.

Unlike UK practice, which was to slaughter only animals identified as being infected by BSE, continental European practice was to slaughter all of any herd where even a single case of BSE was found. Critical UK scientists such as Richard Lacey argued that the more precautionary continental practice should be required in the United Kingdom, too, even if it meant slaughtering 6 million cattle, thus stoking the conflict between UK and continental European approaches. The question of how much of the British herd to cull, and the related question of what to believe about the transmission of the BSE agent, soon became the main point of negotiation and disagreement between the United Kingdom and the EU. UK culling policy for potentially infected animals was intensified in April 1996 in a belated bid to stop the EU export ban. However, it proved unpersuasive to most other EU agriculture ministers, beset as they now were by desperate domestic farmers and consumers demanding far more militant anti-British-beef action.

British policy lost further credibility in the EU when it emerged that the otherwise respected British penchant for taking practical realities seriously beneath the glow of formal rules and symbolic statements of policy had broken down in the BSE case. Through the negotiations of what was a realistic culling target for the British herd, it was revealed that the much-trumpeted earlier UK legislation concerning BSE controls in slaughter-houses and feed manufacture – the key reassurance that the risk was past and absolutely bounded – was still not being properly enforced by governmental institutions. For example, until August 1996 no legal penalties existed to back up the ruminant feed ban of 1988 (European Parliament, 1997:8). Instead, renderers and the meat and agriculture industries were relied upon to fully implement what were extensive and arduous regulations, with little effective inspection or enforcement. Moreover, the United Kingdom not only continued but doubled exports of presumably infected meat and bone meal to EU countries in 1989 – after introducing its own feed ban in 1988 (European Parliament, 1997:8). It is also known that an inspection mission of the EU carried out in July 1996 "revealed the non-existence of the checks on shipments of beef products to the Member states" by the United Kingdom (European Parliament, 1997:14).

The Florence Summit of the European Heads of Government in June 1996 was supposed to be taken up by the new EU treaty being negotiated after Maastricht. Instead the BSE crisis took over, with the United Kingdom threatening to disrupt not only the Summit but routine EU business across all areas of policy unless the beef ban was lifted. A document of over 100 pages was submitted from MAFF detailing all UK measures to control the risks and spread of BSE, as an argument that everything necessary was already being done. However, instead of convincing EU partners to relax restrictions, this offensive only exacerbated their anger at the UK's stance. Isolated, the UK government was forced to accept a further increase of the "selective cull programme" (now almost 150,000 head of cattle). However, it was not until December 1996 that the British Parliament approved this culling program and started to implement it. Prime Minister John Major's hope, mentioned at the Florence summit, of a lifting or easing of the EU global embargo was further damaged by new scientific evidence from MAFF in July 1996 that maternal transmission between cow and calf, hitherto denied, had been found in 10% of cases from a long-term cohort study. As if to try to mitigate this blow, a study by Oxford scientists was released with calculations claiming that BSE would die out naturally soon after the turn of the century, and that the more intensive culling demanded by the EU would make little difference to this projected rate of decline ("Oxford Study," Anderson *et al.*, 1996).

With these important fluctuating new scientific findings and arguments being introduced before the implications of previous findings had been clarified and digested, the higher rate of culling reluctantly agreed to by the United Kingdom after the Florence Summit in the hopes of lifting the ban was effectively suspended. In any case, the culling was in trouble because finances and the disposal of huge numbers of carcasses had become major practical obstacles. In October 1996, Collinge *et al.* found evidence that the pathogen of nvCJD is more similar to BSE than to any other form of CJD (Collinge *et al.*, 1996:685–690). However, only publication of the research results one year later reinforced the conclusion that the agent that causes nvCJD is indeed identical with BSE: "in effect, [n]vCJD is human BSE" (Almond and Pattison, 1997:437). There is still an enormous lack of knowledge about what this means for human risks: "At present we cannot calculate the average incubation time of BSE in humans; nor is it possible to estimate the amount of infectivity ... required to infect a human. ... Finally, these latest results also do not tell us anything more about the route by which the victims of [n]vCJD were infected" (Almond and Pattison, 1997:438). But whereas these and related scientific uncertainties and areas of ignorance were effectively interpreted in the UK policy culture as good reasons to discount real risks, elsewhere – for example in Germany – they were seen as good reasons to take precautions, since large-scale infection and damage could not be ruled out.

Such basic differences in policy response to knowledge limitations in the face of health risk and threat to commercial commitments were rooted in broader and deeper cultural differences. It is reasonable to suggest that the manifestation of these deeper, unarticulated differences created larger shock waves and intersected with a substantial number of cross-cutting issues precisely because they contradicted the implicit expectation, under conditions of modernity, of the dissolution of traditional differences of this kind and confounded the surrounding expectation and partial experience of greater interdependence, collective concertation, and unity of Europe. These under-recognized cultural differences, including differently institutionalized concepts of science and rational policy, simply had more to disrupt than they might have in earlier, less unified times.

Faced with the concerted EU rebuttal of what they had presented as a rational, scientifically based policy that (despite the now-acknowledged nvCJD risk) British cattle, beef, and beef products like gelatin no longer posed a risk to European or other consumers, the reflex reaction of UK policy experts was to lampoon the EU as unscientific, irrational, and anti-British, even though up to March 1996 the EU had been defending the United Kingdom's actions as responsible and sound against the concerns of individual member states. The United Kingdom's ire soon settled more intensely on Germany, which had the most militant consumers and where state governments had already taken their own initiatives against British beef. "Germans ban UK beef" was headlined across national daily newspapers in Britain, and counter-allegations of unreported BSE cases in the German cattle herd were made in the UK press to argue for bans on EU beef in the United Kingdom. The UK's dismissal of the EU and especially Germany as unscientific and prone to public hysteria only amplified transboundary political mistrust and misunderstanding, and thus undermined any basis for transboundary coherence in handling the problem.

The deeper underpinnings of the construction of logical reasoning are well indicated in a late turn of UK policy. The fact that Britain had in the past exported (legally and illegally) enormous amounts of BSE-infected meat and bone meal as well as live infected cattle to other EU member states combined with the fact that Britain has undoubtedly the most extensive and (formally) rigorous legislation concerning BSE, including the removal of possible infectious material, led the new UK government to the following conclusions in late 1997:

- Though "mad cow disease" is perceived almost exclusively as a British problem, there must be more cases of BSE elsewhere because of the previous extensive export of British meat, bonemeal, and cattle. Either these cases are not recognized as such, or they are simply hidden by other countries.
- Taking into account these facts, along with the less stringent removal of high-risk material in most other member states, beef products of these countries are likely to be more infectious than British beef products.
- Therefore, the UK government will require the same regulations elsewhere in the Community as are in place in Britain, otherwise the United Kingdom will unilaterally ban EU beef imports to prevent the spread of BSE to humans in Britain.

In other words, the United Kingdom, itself banned from exporting beef products for many years because of the risk of nvCJD from British beef, started banning beef imports from abroad for the very same reasons those countries had banned British beef!

In January 1998 the European Commission agreed to a partial easing of the British beef ban. This conditional exemption applied to herds that could be documented as free from BSE. The UK government had tried to avoid the costs and practical difficulties of such a scheme, proposing instead that all British cattle under two years old must be BSE free, since they had been born well after the 1991 feed ban, and so should be freed without the passport requirement. But at least two crucial conditions were implied by this assertion: first, that the incubation period was known to be less than two years, and, second, that no vertical cow–calf transmission, nor indeed any other environmental transmission between generations, takes place. These assumptions were not shared by most EU partners, and the second had even been contradicted by UK government research. Unlike their UK counterparts, those EU partners recognized the seriousness of the uncertainties and potential error costs involved. This decision had to be approved by a two-thirds majority at the EU's Standing Veterinary Committee, if passed, it would be the first step toward easing the worldwide export ban (MAFF News Release, 14 January 1998).

5.6   Institutional Problems within the EU

So far we have focused on the issues as they unfolded between the United
Kingdom and the EU, especially with respect to Germany, and how scientific risk knowledge became bound up with larger transboundary political
and cultural processes. However, there were also some interesting issues
within the EU – a supposedly transboundary policy entity. These problems relate not just to the potential confusion caused by an extra "layer"
of government with attendant uncertainties about distributions of responsibility, but also to the inevitable reduction of public transparency, especially when most actors engaged in attempts to scapegoat others and avoid
responsibility themselves.

It was quite evident that several EU institutions also downplayed the
danger of BSE transmission to humans. In July 1996, The European Parliament, as constitutional public watchdog of the Commission, set up an
ad hoc inquiry to "investigate alleged contraventions or maladministration
in the implementation of Community law in relation to BSE" (European
Parliament, 1997:4). The report of the inquiry made a devastating appraisal of the handling of the BSE crisis by both the UK government and
the European Commission. It concluded that incompetence and coordinated conspiracy, including hiding of facts, led to the mismanagement of
the risks from BSE. For example, compartmentalization between several
Commission Directorates was a major obstacle to coping coherently with
the BSE issue. The BSE affair was handled by several different Directorates, each with its own priorities and relationships with national and
sectoral interests, including the Directorates for Agriculture, Industry, Environment, Research and Science, Consumer Protection, and Health and
Safety. Moreover, various institutions were entrusted with management of
the situation: the EU Council and the Directorates of the Commission, the
Scientific Veterinary Committee, and the Standing Veterinary Committee,
not to mention the member state governments. The complex intersections
of national perspectives, sectoral interests (including expert disciplinary
cultures), and the different EU bodies' perspectives and interests undoubtedly made the effective management of the issue more difficult – although
this complexity and its damaging effects on transparency and accountability are typical of all such EU issues.

A particular institutional handicap was the "consensus principle" inside the Scientific Veterinary Committee. Opinions of the Committee are
adopted by consensus, thus excluding dissenting views. In the best case,

divergent opinions are attached as notes to the minutes of the meeting, if they are mentioned at all. The European Parliament Report gives a fascinating example of how this expert consensus is effected, and how minority opinions were suppressed in the BSE saga. The assumption by EU officials that formal EU law was sovereign over scientific truth and debate is illustrated in the treatment of the dissenting view of Arpad Somogyi, a professor from Germany, expressed in a meeting of the Scientific Veterinary Committee in November 1994 and annexed to the minutes of the meeting. This recording of his dissent over a safety question led to the following letter from Guy Legras, director-general of DG VI (Agriculture), to the German minister of health:

> ... I was surprised, therefore, to be informed that some German had continued to put forward the view that meat from British cattle born before 1/1/91 in herds which had a case of BSE should not be put into the human food chain. This view was expressed to an international meeting ... . I find it quite unacceptable that officials of a national government should seek to undermine Community law in this way, particularly on such a sensitive subject. ... I would ask, therefore, to ensure that this debate is not continued, particularly in an international forum ... ". [EP Report, Part A-Annexes, 1997:111]

Overall, the EC and the Council of Ministers followed the UK government position that unless there was positive scientific evidence that BSE causes nvCJD in humans, the existing measures had to be adequate. Even more than in national government processes, within the Commission it was feasible – and indeed a part of routine Commission culture – that such a stance could be so unaccountable to wider scientific critique, even though its establishment for so long (until March 1996) can be seen as an adventitious capture of a key advisory mechanism by the particular UK policy commitments embedded within this "scientific" stance.

5.7 EU Institutional Culture and BSE

It is tempting to follow convention and interpret all the commitments and manipulations of the EU BSE saga as resulting from the exercise of deliberate interests and intentions, some of which, of course, went astray, but which were nevertheless strategically and consciously chosen. Without denying the importance of such interests, and supporting the normative stance that this kind of explanation corresponds with the need to attribute responsibility for consequences where appropriate, we argue nevertheless that such interests emerge out of a particular cultural background and become institutionalized into routinized patterns of "taken for granted" thought and behavior that are no longer deliberated and chosen with those putative interests in mind. We have already described many cases of what can be treated as deliberate actions or inactions reflecting particular unacknowledged interests. Below we describe some additional cases and then discuss – empirically and analytically – the complex interplay of interests and cultural factors in this transboundary risk arena.

The lack of institutional coordination within the EU only enabled what could be described as "deliberate" action inside EU institutions and allowed the UK government to hamper any coordinated and effective protective action. For example, although diverse national delegations – in particular the German and French delegations – expressed their concern with respect to BSE and directly requested action, the EU Agriculture Council did not deal with BSE at all between June 1990 and July 1994. The European Parliament Report marked this situation as "an indictment of its inability or, at least, of its lack of determination to manage this issue" (European Parliament, 1997:20f.). This is particularly astonishing because BSE was at its height during this period, and the parties demanding collective EU action included the most powerful EU nation-states. Indeed, it is a measure of the significance of the EU as a transboundary political entity that powerful nation-states like France and Germany felt the need to try to obtain a formal EU mandate for blocking UK exports rather than create national legal bans (they could have made a case for unilateral national action based upon claims of threat to public health), as this would have contravened key legal pillars of the EU internal market and provoked retaliatory action which would have threatened the very basis of the EU.

The European Commission was indeed a major downplayer of the BSE risk. The European Parliament's inquiry committee accused the EC of giving priority to defending the single EU market in beef and beef products, and of being so obsessed with protecting this central European institution that "it has tried to follow a policy of downplaying the problem" (European Parliament, 1997:23). For example, in April 1994 the EC stated unequivocally that "the measures already in place fully protect animal and public health" (see *Veterinary Record*, 30 April:458). The EU Consumer Protection Service had already warned the Commission of the possible risk to humans from BSE and asked for action long before March 1996, but nothing happened. In 1996 it also became public that in 1990 a civil servant of the Commission's Directorate-General for Agriculture (DG–VI) gave an explicit order to the Standing Veterinary Committee to conceal any risk concerning BSE and to give "disinformation to the press" (*Süddeutsche Zeitung*, 9 July 1996).

The strong dominance of British scientists on the Scientific Veterinary Committee, and its BSE subgroup, seems to have made it difficult for the Commission to take clear measures against the prevailing UK denial of risk. From 1989 to March 1996 the Scientific Veterinary Committee maintained the consistent position that the risk of humans developing a human form of BSE did not exist or, if it existed at all, was remote and theoretical (European Parliament, 1997:32). This well-known UK government position was formulated by, among others, Ray Bradley, chairman of the Scientific Veterinary Committee, Subgroup BSE, and until 1991 head of UK's governmental Central Veterinary Laboratory (see above) and after that a UK government consultant.

After the European Parliament Report, BSE food safety had to be separated from the Agriculture Directorate and transferred to a strengthened Consumer Affairs Directorate (DG–XXIV). Even the Scientific and the Veterinary Committees will have to report to the new Food Safety Directorate (*The Economist*, 22 February 1997).

5.8 Interests and Culture

Although the transboundary dimensions of BSE as a risk issue are far larger than we are able to fully describe here, we have examined this case of a transboundary risk with the selective aim of examining the relationship between conventional interests-based forms of explanation of such issues and more cultural factors. The aim of this is not to propose cultural factors as complete alternatives to interests, but to deepen our understanding of how non-knowledge, in Beck's sense, arises and is played out as a crucial but hitherto under-recognized condition of the general predicament of risks and their policy handling. Thus we focus on the social, institutional, and cultural contexts in which the BSE issue was played out, and we look for factors that produced and shaped it as a transboundary risk crisis in the EU and beyond.

Here we use the term culture in a modest way to mean beliefs and forms of knowledge and epistemic commitments (about the proper purposes of knowledge, which shape the criteria for determining validity) that have become unself-conscious, routinized, habitual, taken-for-granted forms of practice, including technical and cognitive practices. They are no longer subject to deliberate conscious choice and decision, and they have become the fabric of moral identification for their subject agents. Thus, as Kuhn described it for scientific disciplinary subcultures, those cognitive, technical, and practical commitments become the normative framework of reflection on and interpretation of experience and new observation, not the object of such critical deliberation. This is why we believe it is crucial to go beyond both interests-based historical explanations and cognitivist forms of explanation that are consistent with the idea of deliberate knowledge choices. In focusing on unstated cultural dimensions, our analytical aim is thus to generate more collective self-awareness of taken-for-granted commitments which are exercised in and reproduce particular forms of society as if they were natural when they are actually human normative commitments.

Of course, many developments in the BSE history can only be described as deliberate action based on interests – whether explicit or in some way hidden and needing to be analytically imputed to their agents. The foregoing account gives evidence relevant to this interpretation. But our main focus is on less obvious, more subtle and routinized practices, assumptions, and commitments embedded as constitutive in institutions and local cultures, whose international and domestic reverberations made BSE the "biggest crisis British policy has suffered since the Suez crisis" (Erik Millstone, personal communication, 9 February 1998). It was also one of the most serious issues ever to confront the EU: "Since the beginning of the European Community, no debate has affected the daily life of individuals as much as this one. We must not underestimate the damage that the BSE crisis is causing among the general public, in particular the questioning of the food chain; and the eventual number of deaths remains an unknown quantity" (European Parliament, 1997:22). We conclude by discussing how borderline knowledge (as a culturally defined condition), political decision making, and transboundary risks are intertwined in the BSE case.

We identify two main cultural dimensions in the BSE affair. One has to do with the ways in which beliefs, claims, and commitments that one can plausibly suppose to be shaped by specific interests, whether explicit or imputed, and for which there is evidence, however fragile, for deliberation and rationalization, can be seen to depend for their existence upon particular prior cultural contexts, that is, a set of taken-for-granted habitual practices, identities, relationships, assumptions, and beliefs. The second has to do with the different ways that intrinsic culturally defined limitations of knowledge are recognized and how this affects divergent policy commitment over uncertainty and precaution between Anglo-Saxon and continental European policy cultures.

5.8.1 Interests and culture

We wish to emphasize that specific interests, imputed or more directly identifiable, are only conceivable and feasibly exercised in a background of corresponding taken-for-granted cultural commitments. Thus not all interests and deliberations are thinkable in all cultural settings, though we would want to leave the notion of "correspondence" flexible here. Thus it is only such a cultural context that makes the more interests-based claims and choices conceivable and potentially effective.

For example, we would argue that the identifiable – and costly – intimacy over BSE between UK government concerns, policies, and claims, and those of the British beef industry can be seen as a classic case of private interests tacitly at work inside government, illegitimately to the detriment of public protection. We would not want to contradict this analytical assertion, but to elaborate it. This close industry–government relationship has been a distinct feature of UK policy since the 19th century. It is constituted not just of a succession of ad hoc examples, but also of a host of rationalizing beliefs, assumptions about trust and behavior, normative expectations of industrial actors, and projected implicit models of others such as the public at large. These facets are woven into a historically evolved formal texture of consistent legislation and formal regulations (for example, the traditional UK policy style of imprecise technical criteria), all part of a wider cultural pattern. This is "cultural" in our terms in that many of its most important features are not chosen but are taken for granted and part of a certain identity on the part of UK policy and industrial actors (as when they, with self-satisfaction, contrast their UK identity in this respect with their continental and US counterparts). Thus the close industry–government mutuality of interests that was evident in the UK's BSE risk management was politically feasible, or rather assumed to be feasible, just because it was cultural – it was performed without much, if any, reflection as being the "natural" way of conducting affairs. Indeed, it was just this unreflected-upon and unchosen cultural form, and its manifestation in extreme forms of denial, complacency, conviction, and manipulation, that so deeply alienated domestic and international political subjects alike. It may not have been so extreme and unsubtle had it been more calculated and deliberate – that is, less culturally shaped.

To give another example of this interests–culture relationship, it was only the preexistence of a deeply rooted culture in the United Kingdom of deference and institutional charisma (presumed public authority and respect) that allowed MAFF to imagine it could conceivably get away with the extreme hegemonic control that it exercised over information, research, and interpretation of the unfolding BSE experiences. (As of July 1988, all infected cattle material is the legal property of MAFF; they have legal control and ownership over all BSE material. If researchers want to work with infectious material, they need the permission of the ministry to work on this issue and the ministry must agree to provide infectious material.) Deliberate misinformation was premised on an arrogant and reductionistic preexisting institutional culture which assumed officialdom to be more legitimate and more competent to judge than any other agent and, what is more, that one such particular agent was more competent to cultivate public truth on a matter of such complexity and uncertainty than a pluralistic melting pot of open and equally legitimate and contending ideas. These commitments, the springboard for more specific interests, are of a more cultural kind. This is not to argue deterministically that a given cultural setting of this kind mechanically determines the supremacy of particular corresponding deliberate interests, but that it does (however imprecisely) set a selective field for the emergence and predominance of a bounded range of such interests.

It is also true that the relationship between imputed interests and culturally embedded commitments is mutual and unstable, in that cognitive assumptions and epistemic principles, perhaps at one time chosen and deliberated with given interests in mind, may gradually become assimilated as part of routine practice in a given area, perhaps also defining the identity of that area. They come to be part of what constitutes that culture and the identity of its subjects. Thus one could say that the possibility that putting sheep and cattle remains in British animal feed might cause unknown and unknowable effects for cattle and for those who ultimately consumed their meat was thought about at the time it was introduced – albeit too briefly as it turned out – but went underground as an issue. (Thus, for example, the UK Soil Association criticized the practice at the time, but as it did not have specific damage pathways to point to, its criticism did not raise public awareness and gain wider attention.) Thus the notion that this "feed-cannibalism" was safe for herbivorous cattle and their human consumers became an implied or virtual belief, tacitly enculturated into the particular routine, taken-for-granted material culture of British feed, farming, meat, and meat-products industries.

A further cultural feature of UK science and policy that intersected with more interests-based commitments was the way in which MAFF was able not only to restrict access to supposedly open, universalistic scientific information and even basic research material, but also to restrict the channels of official advisory expertise to very narrow cadres of recognized authority, severely reducing the richness of confusion of wider scientific debates, deliberations, and uncertainties. Again, one can plausibly account for this suffocatingly reductionist conferral of legitimacy to only a selected part of the full intellectual spectrum as a deliberate interests-driven commitment by MAFF officials and ministers, those interests not being hard to identify. But it was a set of commitments, claims, and initiatives that was only conceivable to its authors from within a culture where this general pattern of behavior was already assumed to be legitimate, proper, and even efficient.

The reason it became important to emphasize and clarify these more cultural dimensions is partly because the salient issue transcended the boundaries of such cultural idioms. If the issue had remained only a UK matter, there would have been no contradiction between this particular cultural style and its constitutive assumptions and human commitment, and another set of clashing commitments. However, there did arise just such a clash, as traditional UK approaches were forced to interact with, and confront, continental European ones. Our argument is that this was a "blind" clash, leading to confusion, transboundary bad faith, and more general mistrust precisely because those cultural features were cultural; that is, because they were not reflected upon and deliberated, but were implicit, unself-consciously held, and embedded in commitments that were animated by human moral cultural identifications.

5.8.2   Uncertainty and ignorance as cultural conditions

The BBC2 TV program "Mad Cows and Englishmen," originally broadcast 23 February 1998, recorded some key evidence of differences between Anglo and German cultural framing of the public policy basis for
decision in the face of "actionable uncertainty." By actionable uncertainty,
we mean a sufficient degree of recognized uncertainty about a null hypothesis of cause and effect (such as "BSE in British cattle cannot cause
human risk") that leads responsible policymakers to act to prevent further
risk (e.g., to ban cattle and beef movement or sale). This can of course be
expressed the other way round: What counts in each culture as *evidence*
justifying commitment?

Interviews with the German government's chief veterinary officer and
with his UK counterpart and other UK officials underlined a sharp and
systematic contrast between the empiricist form of UK definitions of uncertainty and the more abstract German understanding of "actionable" uncertainty. This seems to correspond with the stronger instrumental culture
of prediction and control in the UK policy-science system. The interviews
repeatedly exposed the taken-for-granted UK policy view of effective scientific certainty about the lack of species transferability of the BSE agent,
and hence the lack of risk to humans, whereas the German counterparts
saw that the abstract possibility of such species crossing represented a serious, that is, "policy-actionable," scientific uncertainty. The UK policy-
scientists frequently talked of the "lack of evidence" for this possibility,
hence the "unscientific" nature of the German position. However, embedded within this UK perspective was a very empiricist definition of what
constituted actionable uncertainty – there had to be positive empirical evidence for it, as opposed to theoretically derived possibility or even indirect
evidence like species transfer in other species (e.g., the cat case in 1990).

This form of cultural construction of recognized uncertainty, we argue,
is connected with the particular hold in the UK science-policy culture of
the defining principles of instrumental prediction and control, and of empiricism as a defining UK intellectual tradition, one fully documented in
the history of science and in contrast with its German counterpart of ide-
alism. The German acceptance that the abstract possibility of the existing
knowledge – or, more accurately, the assumptions embodied in existing
practices – being wrong equals actionable uncertainty corresponds with
the acceptance that existing knowledge does not offer a complete system
of prediction and control of nature, and may embody contingency, which

would imply acknowledgement of limitations of such control and prediction. This German cultural embodiment of indeterminacy in policy rationality may in turn reflect the wider intellectual traditions of continental philosophy, in which human and natural sciences are seen as fundamentally united, unlike in Anglo traditions. In the latter, there is a strong confidence in the control of reality with existing scientific knowledge, and this seems to be reflected in the confidence with which UK policy advisers belittle the uncertainties of their own knowledge. It may also be a factor contributing to the unquestioning confidence of UK policy advisers that when formal rules assuming controlled practices in slaughter houses, etc., were elaborated, these formal definitions were empirical reality, in contrast to German perceptions, which did not reify formal knowledge to anywhere near the same extent.

Differences in cultures of risk definition and management of this kind are increasingly important in international trade and policy, not only because risk networks extend internationally, as in beef trade, but also because the assumptions are that political systems extend their practical norms consistently across international arenas like the EU. Yet we are only beginning to get into focus some of the more subtle but profound cultural differences, even in apparently universal rational discourses of science, which fracture these empires of economic interdependency. The expectation that growth of global systems of exchange, including their concomitant exchanges of risks of all kinds, could exist without need and pressure for cultural convergence toward homogenization was a naive delusion whose impossibility and unacceptability are now manifesting in the kinds of international confusion exemplified in the BSE case. Transboundary risks are not only material and intellectual management challenges, but are quintessentially about fundamental human identities.

5.9 Conclusions

We do not wish to imply that a culturalist theoretical perspective offers a complete alternative to a more cognitivist, deliberative, or interests-based approach to understanding the dynamics of the transboundary risk processes described in this paper. In many respects such an approach, if exclusivist in this way, would be an alibi for any such deliberating subject to claim exemption from responsibility for actions and commitments. We want to supplement the analytical discourse which takes it, or at least implies by default, that all human commitment, interaction, and disposition of power and resources is made up of interests, deliberations, and choices or decisions. Interests are also often implicit and have to be inferred like cultural factors.

We have chosen to stress culture because so many important features of such risk issues, especially the predicament of non-knowledge and how it is handled, have developed by unreflexive elaboration of existing familiar routines and culturally comforting behaviors, beliefs, and assumptions. These risk definition and management networks stretch across dangerously unrecognized dislocations in taken-for-granted human commitments and cultural patterns of a most routine and mundane sort. The consequences of this lack of reflexive awareness of the dislocated and obscured human underpinnings of parochial but pretentious cultures of rationality are potentially devastating in their wider effects on crucial human conditions of trust, mutual respect and recognition, cohesiveness, and loyalty – the essentials of any international institutional viability.

The interwovenness of interests and culture frequently can be seen in the empirical accounts of this case study. For example, the typical UK response to the EU ban – that it was "a German plot" or evidence of German hysteria in the face of risk – can be interpreted as expressing a hidden interest to defend the economic and political interests of maintaining a thriving British beef industry. There is ample circumstantial support for such a view, but these putative "interests" as deliberated positions and as forces deliberately if tacitly deployed in constructing intellectual rationalizations merge with recognizable, already established (of course, unevenly so) xeno-skeptic or -phobic UK cultural dispositions, especially anti-German ones. Indeed, this kind of argument has been exercised by UK policy and scientific actors as a recognized keystone of a distinctly British policy culture in many areas of international environmental regulation where the United Kingdom has been accused of being too cavalier or complacent about risks and uncertainties. These are part of a certain nationalistic UK cultural tradition and identity, with unreflected, non-deliberated moral and intellectual force. The very repetition of this discourse as legitimated and authoritative within such policy networks encourages its assimilation as a taken-for-granted, routinized constitutive element of the identity of such actors and their policy style.

Other examples drawn from official forms of argument exemplify the same ambiguous intertwining of commitments that can be interpreted as deliberated and chosen, and those that are more to be seen as prevailing taken-for-granted, habituated expressions and reproductions of practical lifeworlds. The assertion that crucial official regulations – for example, about slaughterhouse isolation of specified offals – were reliably and comprehensively implemented is one such taken-for-granted assumption. This could easily be seen as a deliberate and knowing misrepresentation, especially given the evidence of shelving or suppression of critical reports on this issue; but it can also be seen as a consistent part of a larger syndrome of advisory academic scientists' naivete about questions of real-world practicalities when assessing risks (e.g., Wynne, 1989). This pervasive tendency can plausibly be explained as a function of the artificial, controlled, and ideal-world conditions under which scientific observation and theoretical analysis or debate typically must be conducted. As such, it is a habituated cognitive stylistic commitment, a part of scientific culture. We do not claim that all of the dramatic mistakes and events of the BSE issue can be explained as cultural in this sense, but we do claim that they cannot be adequately explained without invoking such factors beyond and interwoven with more deliberated, instrumental commitments.

Perhaps the most fundamental dislocation of transboundary framings of the issues in the BSE case – and one most directly relevant to the theoretical issues of reflexivity and non-knowledge – concerns cultural differences over how uncertainty or ignorance underlying positive scientific knowledge is conceived and treated in practice. Here we identify an important difference between the UK approach and the typical continental European one, as manifested especially in the predominant German stance.

In the typical UK approach to uncertain scientific knowledge of risks and consequences, the risk mechanism or damage pathway has to be specified and accepted as realistic even if the estimated probabilities of harm may be very low. Uncertainty has to be focused on something concretely identified, and indeed has to be quantifiable if at all feasible; ignorance in the sense of unknowns is disqualified from this framework, since by definition we cannot describe what we do not know. However, this UK approach – which automatically excludes abstract uncertainties or knowledge limitations from policy or advisory responsibility – is not universal. It appears not to be characteristic of German and other continental

European ways of defining precautionary environmental risk policies, where precautionary intervention to regulate some activities is taken in the absence of demonstration of concrete possible damage pathways but where there exists an abstract "theoretical" risk. It was precisely this term that UK officials and advisers used to dismiss the need for more serious action to protect beef consumers.

In other words, the UK policy culture reflected a pragmatic, empiricist, and instrumental style of thought and practice that is part of a much deeper set of intellectual traditions in science and in cultural traditions more broadly. Empiricism eschews the abstract and theoretical, authenticating concrete demonstration instead. The pragmatism and instrumentalism of UK intellectual traditions also correspond to the radical divorce of the natural sciences from the human disciplines – the humanities being where indeterminacy and contingency can be recognized, but the sciences, including increasingly the social sciences, being framed epistemically in instrumental, behaviorist, and deterministic form.

Continental European traditions have always integrated the natural and human disciplines more strongly, and the sciences have been markedly and systematically less empiricist and more abstract and idealist. This epistemic commitment in academic and intellectual circles has colored normative commitments in political culture more broadly, giving authority and recognition to corresponding forms of knowledge in policy and public debate. Along with the greater recognition of human indeterminacy from the more integrated relationship between natural and human knowledge, this more abstract epistemic culture has meant a greater capacity in the political culture at large in continental European systems to recognize the intrinsic limitations of knowledge, hence ignorance, even if this cannot be specified.

The EU has rightly been regarded as the most well-developed transboundary political unit for developing and implementing policies across a whole range of social, environmental, economic, technical, political, and even cultural arenas. Yet even in such a relatively cohesive, historically close, and articulated entity, there are many extensive dimensions of basic ways to see itself and constituent-part mutual understandings that are deeply under-recognized. Moreover, the demanding conditions of integrity, legitimacy, and viability of rational risk management systems are also woefully poorly understood. The rampant drive for economic nirvana through global free trade followed by the realization of attendant risks and the establishment of universal regulatory regimes to control those risks, despite its culture-neutral pretensions, is itself an unstated cultural project of gargantuan hubris, and of consequential proliferating risks which will never be attributed to their proper responsible agents.

Notes

[1] Although some propose that MAFF (Ministry of Agriculture, Fisheries and Food) already knew about BSE (Stephen Dealler, interview by author, 26 June 1997; Helen Grant, interview by author, 9 June 1997; Richard Lacey, interview by author, 23 June 1997; see also BBC2 program *Mad Cows and Englishmen*, originally broadcast 15 February 1998).

References

Almond, J., and Pattison, J., 1997, Human BSE, *Nature*, **389**(2):437–438.

Anderson, R.M., Donnelly, C.A., Ferguson, N.M., Woolhouse, M.E.J., Watt, C.J., Mawhinney, S., Dunstan, S.P., Southwood, T.R.E., Wilesmith, J.W., Ryan, J.M.B., Hoinville, L.J., Hillerton, J.E., Austin, A.R., and Well, G.A.H., 1996, Transmission dynamics and epidemiology of BSE in British cattle, *Nature*, **382**:779–788.

Beck, U., 1996, Wissen oder Nicht-Wissen? Zwei Perspektiven reflexiver Modernisierung, in U. Beck, A. Giddens, and S. Lash, eds, *Reflexive Modernisierung: Eine Kontroverse*, Suhrkamp, Frankfurt/M., Germany.

Collinge, J., Sidle, K.C.L., Meads, J., Ironside, J., and Hill, A.F., 1996, Molecular analysis of prion strain variation and the aetiology of 'new variant' CJD, *Nature*, **383**:685–690.

Consultative Committee on Research into Spongiform Encephalopathies, Ministry of Agriculture, Fisheries and Food, Department of Health, 1989, *Tyrrell Report*, Interim Report, June 1989, London, UK.

Dealler, S., 1996, *Lethal Legacy: BSE – The Search for the Truth*, Bloomsbury, London, UK.

Dorrell, S., 1996, Statement by the Secretary of State for Health on BSE/CJD, House of Commons, 20.3.1996, London, UK.

Dressel, K., 1997a, Borderline Knowledge – Ideas for a New Concept in Dealing with Non-Knowledge, unpublished draft, Munich, Germany.

Dressel, K., 1997b, Facing non-knowledge: The BSE case in Britain, *Proceedings of Uncertainty, Knowledge and Skill Conference*, Limburg University, 6–8 November, Limburg, Belgium.

Dressel, K., 1997c, Facing Non-Knowledge – Why Talking of Risk Could be Full of Hazards, The BSE-Case in Britain, paper given at the Media, Risk and the Environment Conference, 3–4 July, Cardiff, UK.

European Parliament, 1997, Report on alleged contraventions or maladministration in the implementation of Community law in relation to BSE, without prejudice to the jurisdiction of the Community and national courts, Part A, Luxembourg.

Holt, T.A., 1988, Statement for the BSE Committee of Inquiry, Statement 20, 23.2.1998, London, UK, http//www.bse.org.uk.

Holt, T.A., and Phillips, J., 1988, Bovine Spongiform Encephalopathy, *British Medical Journal*, **296**:1581–1582.

Hughes, S., 1998, Protecting health: Can the UK do better?, in S.C. Ratzan, *The Mad Cow Crisis: Health and the Public Good*, UCL Press, London, UK.

MLC (Meat and Livestock Commission), 1996, *Annual Report & Accounts 1996*, Milton Keynes, UK.

MLC (Meat and Livestock Commission), 1997, *Annual Report & Accounts 1997*, Milton Keynes, UK.

Southwood, R., Department of Health, Ministry of Agriculture, Fisheries and Food, 1989, Report of the Working Party on Bovine Spongiform Encephalopathy, London, UK.

Wells, G.A.H., Scott, A.C., Johnson, C.T., Gunning, R.F., Hancock, R.D., Jeffrey, M., Dawson, M., and Bradley, R., 1987, A novel progressive spongiform encephalopathy in cattle, *Veterinary Record*, 31 October:419–420.

Will, R.G., Ironside, J.W., Zeidler, M., Cousens, S.N., Estibeiro, K., Alperovitch, A., Poser, S., Pocchiari, M., Hofman, A., and Smith, P.G., 1996, A new variant of Creutzfeld-Jakob Disease in the UK, *Lancet*, **347**:921–925.

Wynne, B., 1989, Frameworks of rationality in risk management: Towards the testing of naive sociology, in J. Brown, ed., *Environmental Threats: Social Sciences Approaches to Public Risk Perceptions*, Pinter, London, UK.

Wynne, B., 1992, Uncertainty and environmental learning: Reconceiving science and policy in the preventive paradigm, *Global Environmental Change*, June:111–127.

Wynne, B., 1994, Scientific knowledge and the global environment, in M. Redclift and T. Benton, eds, *Social Theory and the Global Environment*, Routledge, London, UK.

Chapter 6

A Transborder
Environmental Controversy
on the Danube:
The Gabcikovo–Nagymaros
Dam System

Anna Vari and Joanne Linnerooth-Bayer

6.1 Introduction

The Gabcikovo–Nagymaros Project on the Danube River has given rise to
one of the most controversial transborder risk disputes in Europe. In 1977,
a treaty between Czechoslovakia and Hungary was signed to build two hydroelectric dams: the Gabcikovo dam in Slovakia and the Nagymaros dam
on the Danube Bend near Budapest. Particularly on the Hungarian side,
where the project was linked to the unpopular socialist rule, there were
strong protests on the part of scientists, environmental groups, and the
public. It was feared that the dams would damage the valuable ecosystem
of the region, threaten the underground water reserves on which more than

a million Hungarians depend, and jeopardize the rights of the Hungarian minority living in Slovakia. Fifteen years after signing the treaty, Hungary unilaterally withdrew.

On the Slovak side, where the project was linked more closely to aspirations for independence and national pride, it was viewed as supplying needed energy, improving navigation and flood control, and replacing coal-burning and nuclear power stations. After Hungarian withdrawal from the treaty, the Slovaks continued with a revised version of the project, diverting the river to a power station at Gabcikovo. In 1994, the two countries filed a lawsuit with the International Court of Justice. The Court recently declared both the renunciation of the 1977 treaty and the diversion of the river illegal and instructed the two countries to negotiate an agreement on an environmentally sound technical solution and financial compensation.

Viewing this controversy as Hungarian political dissent versus Slovak nationalism is an oversimplification. There are conflicting views and expert evidence about the benefits and risks of the project on both sides of the river, as well as conflicting claims of responsibility, liability, and property rights. Moreover, the over 20-year conflict has coincided with massive political upheavals in the Danube region – the disintegration of the Soviet Union, the reunification of Germany, the separation of Slovakia from the Czech Republic, and the devastating war in the former Yugoslavia (Linnerooth-Bayer, 1990, 1993; Linnerooth-Bayer and Murcott, 1996). The conflict has mirrored some of the most emotional issues of these decades: environmental degradation, sustainable economic development, minority rights, and the inviolability of international borders.

This chapter describes the history of the Gabcikovo–Nagymaros conflict, the views and arguments of the stakeholders on both sides of the border, the uses made of scientific expertise, and the attempt to involve the public. The dispute spans the transition from communist to democratic regimes and illustrates the difficulties of redefining the roles of government authority and expertise during the institutional flux. The Gabcikovo–Nagymaros dam issue served to shape the institutional transition, but did so differently in the two countries. As shown in Chapter 5 with respect to the bovine spongiform encephalopathy (BSE) issue, the difficulties in negotiating an agreement overlie more subtle cultural dislocations over knowledge and its social roles and limits.

We argue that in Hungary and later in Slovakia, these cultural dislocations constrained the problem and state negotiations to a single construction of the issue that conflicted with the construction of the problem on the other side of the river. In Slovakia, this dam project was viewed as modern, technologically advanced, and symbolic of a growth-oriented economy, whereas in Hungary, the risks and benefits of the project were viewed from a post-modern, environmentally oriented perspective (Nagy, 1992:56). We suggest that this gridlock might have been circumvented by involving the culturally diverse groups of non-state actors. Participants in these loosely coupled networks can be very innovative in many small ways without having to face the challenge of accepting or rejecting one narrowly defined negotiating position.

This case illustrates the potential value of a deliberative process that takes account of the ideas and opinions of the public. While the views of the general public in Hungary and Slovakia did not influence the policy negotiations in this case, it is clear from the survey reported in this chapter that these views would have been valuable input to the otherwise stalemated negotiations. In many ways, the Gabcikovo controversy parallels that of the debate on Swedish aid to the Ignalina nuclear power plant. In both cases, the public appears to accept a "victim pays" approach to resolving issues in a mutually beneficial manner.

6.2 The History of the Gabcikovo–Nagymaros Project

6.2.1 The conception of the project (1950–1977)

Planning for a joint Hungarian–Czechoslovakian hydroelectric power project on the Danube River began in the early 1950s, but it was not until 1977 that the two countries signed a treaty for the construction of the Gabcikovo–Nagymaros barrage system,[1] which was to consist of three dams and two hydroelectric power plants (see *Figure 6.1*). The Danube would be dammed at Dunakiliti in Hungary to flood an area of 60 square kilometers (km^2). From there, the water would be routed downstream from the dam to a 720 megawatt (MW) hydroelectric plant at Gabcikovo. From the Gabcikovo plant, the watercourse was to be routed back in an 8 kilometer (km) canal on Slovak territory to join its old Danube bed. International water traffic would be diverted to the canal, and the 31-km-long

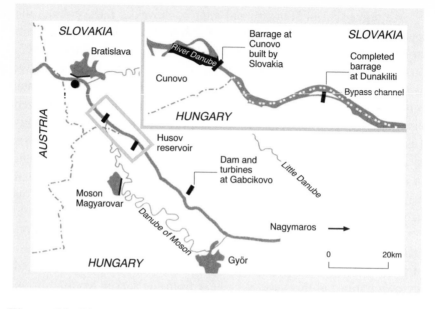

Figure 6.1. The Gabcikovo–Nagymaros dam project.

section of the old Danube riverbed would have only 2.5% of its original average flow (Galambos, 1992). About 100 km downstream from the
mouth of the canal, a second and considerably smaller hydroelectric plant
was planned at Nagymaros in Hungary. The water of the river would be
retained in the reservoir at Dunakiliti and released twice a day. A main
purpose of the Nagymaros dam was to compensate for the large changes
in the water level caused by this "flushing" (Galambos, 1992:74).

    The political and economic circumstances of the 1970s were espe-
cially conducive to the decisions of both governments to enter into a contract for the construction of this dam system. In the communist era, large
projects were a symbol of economic progress, and environmental considerations were not on the social or political agenda. The rationale for the
project was primarily economic. The dam system would improve navigation on the Danube and to the North Sea via the planned Danube–
Maine–Rhine canal, an argument that was also of interest to the Soviet
Union. Flood danger was a particularly persuasive argument that was
put to good use by the water management authorities of both countries.
Only later did the argument for electricity production dominate the political discourse. According to the Czechoslovakian–Hungarian bilateral

agreement, the two countries were to share the construction work and costs equally, as well as the expected 3,775 million kilowatt-hours (kWh) per year of electricity produced (Galambos, 1992:74).

The water authorities in both countries played a significant role in the inception of the project. In Hungary, the National Water Management Office and its background institutions had a staff of over 70,000 people at that time (Fleischer, 1993). The organizational momentum for the dam projects was powerful, yet not open to public scrutiny. As Fleischer observes, the Gabcikovo–Nagymaros project was "a sort of side show for most of the period: its preparation was reported not through open planning, but rather by professional representation at international talks on the matter, and through hints hidden in international specialists declarations" (Fleischer, 1993:431). The political decision to accept the dam plan was made with little opposition. It was, in the words of Fleischer,

> no coincidence that this occurred precisely in a period when a centrally directed force to restore order was gathering strength in opposition to the limited economic reforms which had been unfolded since 1968; when sociologists who had begun to connect social problems with the peculiarities of the political regime were forced to emigrate; and when the (one-) party ideology declared that the economists were wrong and that the impact of the oil price explosion could not affect the socialist countries. [Fleischer, 1993:432]

Later, the Gabcikovo–Nagymaros project in Hungary would come to symbolize the circumstances under which it was conceived.

6.2.2 Hungarian protest and suspension of the works at Nagymaros (1978–1989)

Shortly after the bilateral treaty was signed and construction had begun in Czechoslovakia, public and professional debates over the project started. In 1981, an article harshly criticizing the project was published by a Hungarian biologist, Janos Vargha, who later became a leading figure of the environmental movement (Vargha, 1981). During a temporary suspension of the project, the Hungarian Academy of Sciences prepared a review that favored postponing or canceling the project; however, the study was not published since the Hungarian Parliament had made an undisclosed decision in favor of its completion (Fleischer, 1993:431).

This period of suspension marks the beginning of political protest in Hungary, which eventually would contribute to the fall of the communist system. Environmentalists in Hungary and Austria, and later in Czechoslovakia, actively criticized the project, expressing their concerns about its long-term environmental consequences. Specifically, the environmentalists claimed that operation of the power stations would result in the contamination of subsurface water reserves in the area (the largest underground freshwater reserve in Europe), impede the use of bank-filtered water (the main source of drinking water in the region), change the quality and level of groundwater and surface waters, and lead to serious damage to agriculture, forestry, fishing, and flora and fauna. The project would threaten the sustainable economy in the affected regions (Galambos, 1992).

In Hungary, public debates were held in university clubs and professional associations, and the first grass-roots environmental group in Hungary, later to become the unofficial Danube Circle, was established. The movement collected more than 10,000 signatures in support of a petition addressed to the Parliament and government demanding a halt to the construction. In response, the political leadership toughened its position and prohibited public discussion of and publications against the project. This ban did not, however, dissuade the Danube Circle from publishing a bulletin of information, and in 1985, the Danube Circle received the Right Livelihood Award, or the so-called Alternative Nobel Prize (Galambos, 1993).

In the meantime, Hungarian authorities turned to Austria for help in financing the Nagymaros dam project, bringing a third country into this transboundary conflict. Protesting against Austrian financing of the project, a "Danube Walk" was organized by the Danube Circle and the Austrian Greens. The violent disruption of this protest by the Hungarian police was internationally condemned. Although it was not obvious at that time, the police action was a last display of strength by the Hungarian authorities (Fleischer, 1993:435). Despite the protest, an agreement was reached in which Austrian banks would supply loans for the construction of the project in return for 70% of all building contracts (Galambos, 1993:181). Hungary would repay the loans by delivering electric energy to Austria (Fisher, 1993). In August 1988, the Austrian companies began construction at Nagymaros.

Public attention still centered on Hungary and focused on the planned Nagymaros dam. In September 1988, the World Wildlife Fund and the Danube Circle organized a two-day international conference on the environmental impacts of the project. Despite international concern and the first mass demonstration against the project, the Hungarian Parliament voted to continue the project. In the words of Fleischer, this vote along party lines "openly, spectacularly and completely discredited the government" (Fleischer, 1993:436).

As the Hungarian debate heated up, simultaneous demonstrations against the project took place in 27 capitals around the world. The momentum of this grass-roots movement triggered a political struggle within the leadership of the Socialist party, and Miklos Nemeth, a prominent reformist, became Hungary's prime minister. In the spring of 1989, the Hungarian government unilaterally announced that it would suspend construction work at Nagymaros to conduct further studies and to explore project alternatives.[2] A government study with international experts concluded that a complete cancellation of the project was more favorable in the long run since the potential costs and risks of the project outweighed the projected benefits (Hardi *et al.*, 1989). Supported by this study, Nemeth announced a prolonged suspension of construction at Nagymaros and at the Dunakiliti dam and offered alternatives to the project. These were rejected by Czechoslovakia in a diplomatic note (Galambos, 1993:184).

6.2.3 Hungary's abrogation of the 1977 treaty and Slovak resolve to continue (1989–1992)

The collapse of the Soviet Union in 1989 fundamentally changed the relations between Hungary and Czechoslovakia. The environmental groups in Czechoslovakia were granted freedom of speech, and a Slovak group launched the first major protest rally against the Gabcikovo project in which more than 60,000 people took part, forming a chain along the Danube between Hainburg in Austria and Komarom in Hungary. Spurred by this momentum, Austrian, Czechoslovakian, and Hungarian environmentalists adopted the Danube Charter calling for the establishment of a trilateral nature reserve to protect the Danube landscape. They also demanded a halt to construction at Gabcikovo.

The new political leadership in Czechoslovakia was more receptive to ecological concerns than the previous leadership, but remained intent on completing construction at Gabcikovo because of the huge sums of money already invested and because construction work was allegedly 90% complete. Commenting on this "sunk costs" argument, Nagy writes that the government "used the genuinely myopic argument that the project must be completed because it is already begun. Politicians in Prague have repeatedly admitted that in the light of present knowledge the investment would not be started now, but since it is close to completion, it should be operated" (Nagy, 1992).

After the first free elections in 1990, the new Hungarian leadership took concrete steps to withdraw from the project by making a quick and costly deal with Austria under which it would pay the Austrian firms US$240 million as compensation for expenses and lost profit (Galambos, 1993:188). A different route was taken, however, by the first freely elected Czech government. After an expert assessment, the responsible ministry recommended so-called Variant C, or the completion of the Gabcikovo hydroelectric station with a smaller reservoir at Kortvelyes. The influential Environmental Committee of the Slovak Parliament also accepted Variant C as a temporary, provisional solution, provided that ecological and other conditions were met. The Hungarian government rejected this provisional solution.[3]

The focal point of environmental protest moved steadily to Slovakia, especially to Csallokoz, the region potentially most affected by the Gabcikovo dam. In February 1991, the mayors of 82 towns in this area addressed a petition to the governments in Prague and Bratislava and to President Havel requesting the project's termination. This seemingly pro-Hungarian stance is complicated by the fact that the villagers in this area are largely of Hungarian descent, adding a complicating transboundary dimension to the conflict (Williams, 1994).[4]

In May 1992, the Hungarian government unilaterally declared a termination of the 1977 treaty.[5] Czechoslovakia, on the other hand, confirmed its intention to complete the Gabcikovo plant. In the case that the two sides were unable to agree, Czechoslovakia's stated intention was to implement the project in a go-it-alone effort – Variant C – diverting the Danube onto Slovak territory. The Slovak government's determination to proceed with the implementation of Variant C, in spite of technical and financial difficulties, was greatly underestimated by the Hungarians, many of whom viewed the proposal as a bluff. The implementation prospects were improved, however, after an offer from a private Austrian financier to raise half the necessary capital for completing the Gabcikovo project. With this offer, Austria was again involved in the transborder conflict.

In Slovakia, the nationalist and separatist Democratic Movement for Slovakia formed a government headed by Vladimir Meciar. By early November 1992, the diversion of the Danube was declared completed by the Czech and Slovak authorities. Hungary's foreign minister declared that the river's diversion and the completion of the related structures violated Hungary's sovereignty and territorial integrity, breaching international law (Williams, 1994:17). Slovakia referred to the work completed so far as temporary and reversible (Williams, 1994:17).

In May 1994, the two governments filed a lawsuit with the International Court of Justice in The Hague. The two critical questions were whether the 1977 treaty would continue in force and whether Slovakia could unilaterally pursue the provisional solution in light of the Hungarian renunciation of the 1977 treaty. The Vienna Convention on the Law of Treaties provides several grounds for the abrogation of a treaty.[6] Williams argues that the customary international law doctrine of "a fundamental change of circumstance" might have been the most effective justification for Hungarian withdrawal from the treaty, since a number of changed circumstances affected the viability of the project, including improved energy conservation technologies, the shift away from heavy industry, the shift of East European trade away from the former Soviet Union toward Western Europe, and the dissolution of the Warsaw Pact affecting military benefits of the project (Williams, 1994).

6.2.4 Mitigating the damage (1992–1997)

Both countries recognized that it would be many years before they could expect a decision from the Court and, in the meantime, the countries would have to cooperate in dealing with the environmental consequences of the operation of the Gabcikovo hydropower station. The most pressing concern to the Hungarians was the dramatic decrease in the amount of water discharged into the old riverbed, which decreased groundwater levels and threatened drinking water supplies. If the branches of the Danube were to dry up, the 320 km^2 nature reserve at Szigetkoz would be devastated. Throughout the history of the project, environmentalists were concerned mainly about the long-term consequences of the project, particularly the risks to natural ecosystems, whereas local residents were more concerned about short-term economic impacts to agriculture, forestry, hunting, fishing, and tourism.

Although technically it was not possible to restore 95% of the water, as was being demanded by the Hungarians, many felt that only an amount approaching this could prevent irreversible environmental damage (TED, 1995:7). In 1995, Slovakia agreed to charge 400 cubic meters of water per second (m^3/sec) to the original Danube bed (compared with an average flow of 2,000 m^3/sec before the diversion) and 40 m^3/sec to the Mosoni-Danube (TED, 1995:7). In turn, the Hungarians agreed to build a submerged weir aimed at temporary mitigation of the negative impacts of the diversion of the Danube. With these measures in place, many claim that the project has actually improved the environment of the region (Pearce, 1994). Particularly on the Slovak side, the wetland area around the canal has more water than previously, and the ecosystem appears to be improving. Recharging the wetland and creating the reservoir at Cunovo has also replenished underground water reserves. Still, the issue of environmental damage has not been resolved, since the Hungarians claim that the negative effects will become apparent in 3 to 15 years. They claim that the water level is too high close to the project and too low farther downstream, which over time will have detrimental effects on the vegetation. The Hungarians also fear that the dirty water standing in the reservoir will eventually infiltrate into the underground reservoir (Pearce, 1994).

6.2.5   The decision of the International Court of Justice (1997)

On 25 September 1997, the International Court of Justice announced its decision regarding the case of the Gabcikovo–Nagymaros Hydroelectric Dam System. The Court found both Hungary's withdrawal from the 1997 treaty and Slovakia's implementation of Variant C by diverting the Danube to be illegal. The Court did not accept the Hungarian argument that the resulting ecological situation made it necessary to stop construction work in 1989. Nor did the Court appreciate Hungarian concerns regarding potential damage to the drinking water reserves and other ecological values. On the other hand, the Court decided that the diversion of the Danube violates international law.

The Court suggested that the two countries again initiate negotiations, the basis of which should be the original treaty. However, the Court did not prescribe any specific technical solution. Neither the construction of the Nagymaros dam nor the demolition of the Gabcikovo power plant is mentioned in the verdict. The two parties were instructed to give high priority to environmental issues and to the provision of sufficient water for the old riverbed. The verdict also recognized that both parties have incurred major financial losses, and therefore the two countries should not seek compensation from each other. Finally, the Court declared that if the two countries were unable to negotiate an agreement within six months of the Court's ruling, either of them could reapply to the Court, which would then make decisions regarding the specific issues.

The Court's decision was accepted differently in the two countries. In Hungary, many were disappointed that the Court did not recognize the ecological issues. In Slovakia, the decision was interpreted as a major "victory of law and justice." Initially, arguments supporting the completion of the project became stronger in both countries, but recently Hungarian opposition has again surfaced. The government elected into office in 1998 has rejected any sharing of the electricity generated at Gabcikovo and continues to demand that at least 50% of the water be restored to the original river bed. Since there is a strong desire on the part of both countries to join the European Union, many are frustrated by this seemingly endless controversy.

6.3 The Nature of the Transboundary Conflict

In many ways, the Gabcikovo conflict is typical of environmental risk controversies. In its more than 20-year history, the debate, which has been characterized by multiple stakeholders with conflicting interests and values, has become increasingly polarized between the proponents and opponents. Independent expertise was brought in late in the controversy and interpreted differently by the conflicting parties depending on their values and interests. On only a few occasions did expertise play a significant role in influencing important decisions. The political discourse, therefore, adds to the accumulating evidence that the "facts" of the case are intrinsically intertwined with values, which according to cultural theorists are related to "worldviews." The technologically optimistic, growth-oriented worldview and discourse of the Slovak authorities irreconcilably clashed with the post-modern, ecological sustainability worldview and discourse of the Hungarian authorities.

The increasingly divergent paradigms or "hegemonic discourses" on the part of the authorities in the two, and later three, countries fueled the transborder conflict. What is particularly intriguing in this case is the radically changing official discourse in Hungary as opposed to the constancy of the discourse in the Czechoslovakia and later Slovakia. The intractability of two or more official discourses or stances is one eventuality that distinguishes transboundary from national risk management. In contrast to national conflicts, at a transboundary level diverging official, political discourses can emerge with no effective institutional structures for their resolution. In Chapter 5, Brian Wynne and Kerstin Dressel illustrate the different discourses and administrative cultures existing in Germany and the United Kingdom, which contributed to inhibiting a coordinated risk management strategy for BSE in the European Union.

In the Gabcikovo case, the changing official discourses are perhaps best illustrated by the respective roles of the powerful water authorities. As Hungary became committed to the abandonment of the project, the official arguments of the water authorities became increasingly critical. Gyorgy Tatar, Hungary's chief commissioner for dams, has argued strongly against the project and warned of the long-term environmental risks (Pearce, 1994:30). The Slovak authorities have continued to stress the current successes of the project and to express a great deal of technological optimism. In the words of Miroslav Liska, a senior engineer on the Slovak project, "We have always said that if there were ecological problems with the Gabcikovo scheme, we would find engineering solutions to them, and we have been proved right. You can call this a fix-it philosophy. Environmentalists oppose it. But it is not irresponsible. We know problems can be solved" (quoted in Pearce, 1994:30).

Hungary incurred enormous economic losses in order not to have the dams. The main official justification was to avert the risk of catastrophic environmental consequences. It is a mistake, however, to view the Hungarian government's stance and discourse as solely environmentally motivated. Indeed, the positions of all the political parties have steadily de-emphasized environmental considerations in view of declining public support for the environment and increased concern over the economy. In addition, the strength of the newly formed industrial lobbies has resulted in government support of a number of environmentally questionable projects, for example, extending the operation of brown coal and lignite power stations and building new highways. But as Fleischer states, the Gabcikovo–Nagymaros project remains the exception simply because its symbolic political content is such that any party reversing the earlier decision risks losing its credibility (Fleischer, 1993:438).

Thus, it is important to understand the strong opposition to the project in Hungary as being rooted in and motivated by both environmental concerns and political aspirations – and a changing hegemonic world-view. The attention and mass support this issue received from the public throughout the 1980s went hand-in-hand with the declining legitimacy of socialist rule. Indeed, the Danube movement was viewed as a thin disguise for support for the revolutionary forces that would eventually contribute to the radical changes in the political system. In 1989, the year the communist system fell, Vargha had this to say about the project: "For us, the energy and water lobbies represent the Stalinist structure. Water projects here are paramilitary, centralized, undemocratic and monolithic" (quoted in Pearce, 1994:28). Not surprisingly, after the free elections of 1990, when political opposition became legal and economic recession pushed environmental issues into the background, public interest in the Gabcikovo–Nagymaros issue decreased significantly. Today, environmental groups no longer enjoy the popular support they did in the 1980s (Tamas, 1995:51).

In sharp contrast to Hungary, and in spite of some internal opposition to the dams, the official Czechoslovakian and later Slovak discourse remained constant. The project would reduce dependence on polluting coal-burning power plants and unsafe nuclear power plants in favor of a clean source of energy to modernize their industrial economy. When nationalist movements became stronger in Slovakia, the Gabcikovo plant was celebrated as a major achievement of Slovak technology and a symbol of Slovak development and independence. Not surprisingly, the Green Party and others opposing the dam have frequently been labeled as traitors of Slovak interests (Galambos, 1993:206). As was observed by Nagy (1992), the long-standing controversy reflects two distinctly different worldviews. In Slovakia, the hegemonic dialogue has been one of technological optimism and technological fixes to ecological problems, whereas in Hungary the dominant discourse has been post-modern and environmentally oriented.

6.4   Cultural Plurality and Transboundary Risk Management

These two worldviews dominated the official discourse and locked the two countries into their intractable, polarized positions. Through much of the negotiating history, Hungary has insisted on total abandonment of the project while (Czecho-) Slovakia has insisted on the fulfillment of the 1977 treaty. The negotiations between the two governments can thus be characterized as being predominantly position based as opposed to interest based (Moore and Delli Priscoli, 1989). Interest-based bargaining involves parties in a collaborative effort to find solutions that meet mutual needs and satisfy mutual interests. Rather than uncompromisingly maintaining polar positions, the national representatives might instead have searched for creative alternatives to meet their energy, environmental, social, and political needs. That is, both sides might have benefited from an agreement that promoted collaboration rather than conflict.

In many respects, the failed negotiations resulted from the immaturity of the democratic systems of both countries. Indeed, in Hungary the parliamentary decision to cancel the 1977 agreement was internally criticized as too severely limiting the negotiating position of the government. There were some attempts at amending the decision, but the political significance of the Danube project made it impossible for Parliament to retract from its position of canceling the agreement (Fleischer, 1993:439). Likewise, the uncompromising resolve of the Slovaks to continue with the provisional solution only added fuel to the controversy and blocked any attempts at a joint resolution.

It can be argued that the locked-in positions and interest-based bargaining were inevitable given the exclusion of nonofficial parties from the process. The negotiating agendas were constrained to reflecting the official rhetoric and construction of the problem by the political powers. Yet, from the beginning, the environmental risks of the project have been constructed differently by officials, environmentalists, and the public on both sides, and the views are far from homogeneous within borders.

With diverse constructions of the issue within the policy, expert, environmentalist, and local communities, it is not clear where the interests of the two feuding countries lie. This partly explains why the realist model of transboundary decision making has failed to resolve the conflict. According to the realist model, individual nation-states determine their policy agendas and negotiating positions according to their self-interest, and the respective governments come together to generate transboundary agreements based on a consensus or compromise of interests. While this model adequately describes the process leading to many international conventions, according to Rayner (1993) it can easily lead to polarization and a failed consensus. For example, the realist model was unsuccessful in securing an international protocol banning chlorofluorocarbons in aerosols to accompany the 1985 Vienna Convention for the Protection of the Ozone Layer (Rayner, 1993:22).

An alternative model of international decision making is the regime or polycentric decision model, which is already operating for many international environmental issues. In this model, there is no one national decision maker constrained to one construction of the national interest. Rather, there are many groups or stakeholders in each country, and they form coalitions with culturally compatible actors in the other countries. According to Rayner (1993), this model allows international constituencies to reach consensus on various aspects of complex problems without committing nation-states to inflexible positions. Participants in these loosely coupled networks can be very innovative in many small ways without facing the challenge of accepting or rejecting a single big treaty.

These networks, especially between environmental groups on both sides of the river as well as between national experts, also existed in the negotiating history of the Gabcikovo–Nagymaros controversy, but they were not integrated into the negotiating process, which remained faithful to the realist model. Without allowing for the innovations that these networks might have brought to the process, the nation-state actors became polarized in their positions. Indeed, in what follows we show that the non-state actors, and particularly the local population on both sides of the river, were innovative in assessing options to resolve the conflict and far more willing to accept mutually beneficial compromises than their political counterparts.

6.5 Resolution of the Conflict: The Role of the Public

Involving the affected public in disputes about large-scale investments is a common practice in Western industrialized countries (Renn *et al.*, 1995), but it can prove problematic at a transboundary level (see Chapter 9). In

Hungary and Slovakia, there has been little effort to inform the affected public about the decisions made with regard to the Gabcikovo dam issue, much less to involve the public in the policy process. An exception was a project undertaken in 1994 by Reflex Environmental Association, a large grass-roots organization (Reflex, 1995) that launched a public communication program involving the Hungarian and Slovak residents of the Szigetkoz and Csallokoz regions.[7] This project was undertaken after completion of the Gabcikovo station but before mitigation measures were put into place to restore some water to the dried-out riverbed. The project was aimed at eliciting public input to guide a comprehensive impact assessment study in the region and formulating recommendations for reducing the negative consequences of the operation of the Gabcikovo power plant.

The first phase of the project included separate meetings for the general public, local government officials, and representatives of local and regional research institutions, environmental organizations, and other specialists of environment and nature protection. Hungarian and US experts facilitated the meetings. The purpose of the public meetings was to elicit opinions with regard to the experienced and anticipated impacts of the Gabcikovo plant; to the possibilities of prevention, mitigation, and compensation of damages; and to an acceptable decision process for elucidating short- and long-term interventions. At this time in Hungary's political history, a broader intention of the public meetings was to promote the democratization process.

Public meetings were held in five villages of the Szigetkoz region. The most serious concerns about the repercussions of the Gabcikovo plant mentioned at the meetings included damage to agriculture (e.g., drying out of wells), fish stocks, forests, buildings, and recreation and tourism (e.g., making swimming impossible). There was also concern about the social consequences, including the loss of local self-esteem, loss of future prospects, out migration, and anger and bitterness. The participants at the public meetings also expressed concern about the lack of public information and the failure to take account of local experience and knowledge in central government decisions associated with the Szigetkoz region. There was a general feeling that key decisions were made "above the heads of the local population," without considering their knowledge and interests. Participants also expressed distrust of the scientific experts and policymakers, doubting their competence and fairness. Some felt that the mitigation efforts undertaken by the government were insufficient, and others complained about the lack of promised compensation and support. Finally, many of the participants thought that the Hungarian–Slovak hostilities had been unnecessarily incited to serve political purposes. The locals were generally more interested in collaboration than conflict, and they thought that only an agreement with the Slovaks could ensure any improvement in environmental conditions.

Two meetings were also organized for local government officials, the first for the mayors of the villages of Szigetkoz and the second for both Hungarian and Slovak mayors. The mayors urged bilateral negotiations with the Slovaks in order to achieve an appropriate amount of water – at least 50% of the original amount – in the Danube. Some supported the construction of submerged weirs and the partial or complete filling of the Dunakiliti reservoir; some even supported the completion of the Nagymaros dam. Participants found that the negative environmental consequences of the Gabcikovo plant were very similar on both sides of the border, while the positive impacts (e.g., new jobs, development of infrastructure and tourism) were experienced mainly on the Slovak side. It was suggested that Szigetkoz and Csallokoz be treated as a "border-free" ecological region where prevention and mitigation activities are co-ordinated.

Three meetings were organized for the representatives of academic institutions, environmental organizations, and other local experts involved in studying the impacts of the diversion of the Danube in the Szigetkoz region. In contrast to the public meetings, the expert meetings were characterized by conflict and tension among the participants. Most experts had already committed themselves to one or the other side of the controversy. In spite of existing conflicts, participating experts stressed the need for continued dialogue. Many also spoke of the need to agree on goals and priorities rather than on concrete actions.

Experts were invited to review and revise a study prepared by the Institute for Scientific Research on Water Management (VITUKI, 1994) on variants of temporary water supplement. Participants of this meeting agreed that the study did not meet basic professional standards, since it used a multiple-attribute analysis without assigning weights to the various attributes. However, the group was not willing to review the study because there was a general perception that the decision on building a submerged weir and putting the Dunakiliti locks in operation had already been made by the government and that the study as well as the debate in the Parliament served only for window dressing. Indeed, the recommendations of VITUKI were accepted shortly after the expert meeting, and it was this study that was used to justify the January 1995 bilateral agreement on mitigation.

The local public realized that a decision had been made "above their heads" again. Therefore, most of the local experts decided to withdraw from the public participation program. Reflex Environmental Association recognized that conducting environmental impact assessment studies without involving the local experts would be in conflict with the objectives of the public participation program, therefore they decided to terminate the program in 1995 (Reflex, 1996).

The meetings showed that the population on both sides of the river viewed the controversy as political rather than technical in nature. They noted that there still was no comprehensive impact assessment and that the scientists disagreed on the long-term consequences of the project. Opinions expressed at the meetings indicated that cooperation between the Hungarians and the Slovaks would be more feasible at the local level than at the national level. Unfortunately, decisions on the project remained highly centralized on both sides of the Danube, and this led to the termination of local initiatives.

6.6   Public Views on the Conflict: The Results of a Questionnaire

The opinions expressed by the public participation initiative raise the question of whether the local citizens on each side of the river could contribute to a negotiated settlement to the conflict. As this chapter has shown, the governmental negotiations were gridlocked insofar as both sides refused to compromise their respective positions. Moreover, the positions of both countries were, as the local population recognized, tied to political aspirations and agendas. Predictably, these agendas influenced the expertise commissioned and the results of this expertise.

With little guidance from the International Court of Justice, the resolution of the conflict at this time will require difficult decisions over a range of alternatives – from accepting the status quo to abandoning the entire project to completing the project in its entirety, with the possibility of compensation to one or both of the countries. The desirability of these alternatives will greatly depend on the assessments of the environmental consequences. Thus, trust in the experts with different affiliations will be central to a negotiated settlement.

In a 1995 survey of the population in the affected regions of both Slovakia and Hungary, the views of the citizens on the fairness of selected alternatives and the objectivity and motivations of the experts were solicited (Tamas, 1995). One thousand people in each country were given a written questionnaire with the questions presented and discussed below. Both the Hungarian and Slovak samples were divided into four groups of approximately equal size according to their distance from Gabcikovo (The closest group of communities is located in the immediate vicinity of Gabcikovo; the farthest communities are at a distance of about 50 km.)

In the first question, the respondents were asked to assess the following six alternatives to resolving the conflict:

- Slovakia continues to operate the power plant according to the status quo.
- Slovakia continues to operate the power plant and compensates Hungary for any environmental and economic costs incurred.
- Slovakia abandons the Gabcikovo plant and restores all the water to the Danube.
- Slovakia abandons the Gabcikovo plant and receives compensation from Hungary for its losses.
- Slovakia operates the power plant at a reduced rate.
- Both countries complete the entire Gabcikovo–Nagymaros project as originally planned.

These particular alternatives were selected because they reflect those that have been raised in the political discourse.

The respondents were asked to evaluate the fairness of each of these alternatives on a scale of 1 to 5 points. In *Table 6.1*, the averaged response of the most- and least-affected Hungarian and Slovak groups, and the average of both samples, are reported.

In light of the respective governmental positions, the results of this question are both revealing and surprising. *On average, both the Slovaks and the Hungarians viewed the continued operation of the Gabcikovo power plant, but at a reduced rate, to be the best alternative to the conflict.* This alternative would restore some increased amount of water to the old river bed, but would not disrupt the Slovak operations. Interestingly, this

Table 6.1. Public views on the fairness of various outcomes of the conflict.

Outcome	Hungarians			Slovaks		
	Most affected	Least affected	Aver-age	Most affected	Least affected	Aver-age
Slovakia operates power plant	1.93	1.61	1.80	2.70	4.30	3.17
Slovakia operates power plant and compensates Hungary	2.86	2.66	2.77	3.15	2.45	2.91
Slovakia abandons power plant and river is restored	2.39	1.95	2.24	1.57	1.18	1.64
Slovakia abandons power plant and receives compensation from Hungary	1.65	1.54	1.60	1.94	1.65	1.84
Slovakia operates power plant at reduced rate	4.28	4.39	4.40	4.36	4.19	4.21
Both countries complete entire GNBS project	3.53	4.30	3.73	3.46	4.12	3.51

Ratings based on a scale of 1 (low) to 5 (high).

alternative was ranked high by those most and least affected on both sides of the river.

The only rival faction promoting a more radical approach to the conflict was the least-affected Slovaks. They gave a relatively high ranking to the status quo with Slovakia continuing to operate the power plant, as well as to the completion of the entire project. *None of the groups on either side of the conflict viewed compensation in any form as a (relatively) attractive proposition.*

In a second question, the respondents were asked to give their views on the motivations of the environmentalists. This question was of interest because of the ambiguous role the environmental concerns have played with the government and the public throughout the conflict. Although environmental concerns have continually justified the Hungarian government's stance, in the early years the public's hidden agenda was political dissent from the communist system. The local population also appears fickle in its support of the environmentalists, with early allegiance and then rejection when the environmentalists did not support remediation measures to restore water to the Danube. An important issue is the extent to which the public trusts the motivations of the environmentalists.

Table 6.2 shows the responses of the public to the various motivations of the Hungarian and Slovak environmentalists. *The results show that*

Table 6.2. Public views on the motives of the environmentalists.

| | Agree (%) | |
Objectives	Hungarians	Slovaks
Protecting nature	77.9	82.2
Serving political parties	23.2	28.2
Protecting future generations	72.5	79.2
Pursuing their own interests	21.6	25.8
Protecting people living near the Danube	65.1	67.5
Pursuing foreign interests	12.6	21.1

*a large majority of the Hungarians and Slovaks viewed the motivation
of the environmentalists to be that of protecting nature, protecting future
generations, and (to a somewhat lesser extent) protecting the people living
near the Danube.* Interestingly, the results of the Hungarian and Slovak
samples did not differ significantly, with the exception that more Slovaks
viewed an important environmentalist motivation to be that of pursuing
foreign interests. This is not surprising since throughout the conflict the
Hungarian environmentalists dominated the protests and were supported
by the World Wildlife Fund and many other international environmental
groups.

In the third question, the respondents were asked to give their views
on the objectivity of selected expert groups from their Academy of Sciences, government, universities, environmental groups, and water management authorities. They were also asked to evaluate expertise from the
other country, from Western countries, and from the International Court
of Justice.

Table 6.3 shows that the majority of Hungarians and Slovaks evaluated their Academy of Sciences, water management authorities, and environmentalists as sources of objective expertise. The majority of citizens
of both countries, however, had little faith in the objectivity of the government experts, and in Hungary there was little support of the university
experts. Perhaps most surprising were the stark differences in the views of
the objectivity of experts in the other country on the part of the Hungarian
and Slovak samples. *While only about 10% of the Hungarians viewed the
Slovak experts as objective, around 68% of the Slovaks viewed the Hungarian experts as objective.* This does not appear to be a generally greater
respect for expertise of all kinds on the part of Slovaks since, on average, they viewed their own Academy of Sciences as being less objective

Table 6.3. Public views on the objectivity of experts.

Expert affiliation	Agree that experts are objective (%)	
	Hungarians	Slovaks
Academy of Sciences	82.7	71.5
Government	24.9	30.4
Universities	40.5	69.0
Environmental movements	70.9	76.9
Water management	80.9	75.3
Other country	9.9	68.4
Western countries	47.1	73.5
International Court of Justice	47.2	69.3

than did the Hungarians. The environmentalists thus appear to enjoy more credibility with both publics than the experts of their government, and many Slovaks appear to have greater trust in the Hungarian experts than in their own. This finding may indicate a great deal of sympathy for the Hungarian position on the part of the Slovaks.

6.7   Conclusions

The Gabcikovo–Nagymaros dam project has developed into one of Europe's longest and most complex transborder environmental conflicts. In many ways, the three-decade-long conflict reflects the turbulent and uncertain political environment of the Danube region. The project was conceived in an era of socialist optimism about large-scale industrial and energy projects with little awareness of the environmental costs. Public opposition, which led to the cancellation of the project on the Hungarian side, was motivated as much by political dissent from the communist system as by concerns about the environment. The emerging democracies in Slovakia and Hungary were too immature to maintain flexible and adaptive negotiating positions. This inflexibility, coupled with the lack of involvement of the various actors, led to the entrenchment of both sides in single and conflicting constructions of the problem solution and thus its resolution.

Even recognizing the historical circumstances, however, one is struck by a number of disturbing aspects of the progression and current status of this project, namely,

- Hungary and Slovakia may both be losers. Hungary bears environmental costs from the reduction of water in the Danube, must finance costly mitigation efforts, and receives no compensating benefits from the project. While expert opinion is mixed, Slovakia's electricity benefits may come at a higher environmental and social price than would have been the case with alternative schemes.
- The new governments have also lost badly needed credibility and public trust. Local residents in both countries feel that their concerns have not been adequately addressed. Nor were nongovernmental organizations (NGOs) involved in the process in a constructive way. The public survey showed a willingness on the part of citizens on both sides of the river to reach a constructive compromise on the conflict, which demonstrates that the political apparatus is out of touch with citizen concerns.
- International institutions have proved inadequate to deal with this issue in a timely and effective manner. The decision by the International Court of Justice took several years, which only served to prolong the conflict. Moreover, the decision of the Court has not resolved the conflict, but has incited old debates.

Although the verdict on the environmental damage from the project is still out, the project failed from the standpoint of ensuring an equitable distribution of the costs and benefits, involving the public, and creating trust in the newly formed democratic governments. Several features of this failure have been particularly noteworthy, namely, the role of scientific experts, international negotiations, third-party involvement in resolving the conflict, and the role of informal networks in the negotiating process.

Because of the highly politicized nature of the debate, the involvement of scientific experts proved rather ineffective for reducing the disagreements between the countries. This is not unique to transboundary conflicts; it is widely documented that experts often justify and solidify party positions rather than build consensus based on scientific "facts." Indeed the generation of facts or knowledge often only intensifies the disagreement among experts and ultimately the conflict (Levidow, 1994). In this case, completely different uses were made of expertise by the authorities on either side of the river with remarkably contrasting constructions of the environmental risks. Yet, looking closer, one finds that many of the actors and groups in the process shared the same problem definition and concerns with their counterparts on the other side of the border. The lack of consensus between technical experts throughout the process strengthens the view that scientific uncertainty can and is used as a symbolic element of strategic argument (Campbell, 1985).

The international negotiations lacked a creative focus on jointly solving the energy needs of the respective regions and countries with minimum environmental damage and social disruption. Instead of taking an interest-based approach, the negotiating parties retreated into counter positions, and the conflict degenerated into a zero-sum proposition. Moreover, few channels were open to more informal, and often creative, communication and input from Hungarian, Slovak, and Austrian NGOs (e.g., local communities, civil organizations, environmental groups, private firms). Although, as we have shown, the non-state actors and particularly the local population on both sides of the river were innovative in assessing options to resolve the conflict, the 20-year negotiation proceeded with little public input. The national decision makers became increasingly constrained to a single construction of the problem that conflicted with the construction of the problem on the other side of the river. In Slovakia, this construction was modern, technologically optimistic, and growth oriented, whereas in Hungary, the risks and benefits of the project were consistently constructed with a post-modern, environmentally oriented worldview (Nagy, 1992:56). A more participative, networked approach to the negotiations could have involved the many groups or stakeholders in each country and taken advantage of their coalitions with culturally compatible actors in the other countries. This might have allowed the national policymakers to reach consensus on various aspects of complex problems without committing nation-states to inflexible positions. Participants in these loosely coupled networks can be very innovative in many small ways without facing the challenge of accepting or rejecting one narrowly defined solution.

Throughout the 20-year conflict, there has been little effort made to inform or involve the affected communities and environmental groups in the decision process. The efforts by Reflex Environmental Association to conduct a dialogue with the local public appeared encouraging at the start, but later failed because the governments of both countries continued to disregard the importance of public information and involvement. The survey of public opinion demonstrated the public's willingness to consider the situation of the other side and to work out a mutually beneficial package for resolving the conflict.

The entrenchment of both countries in their positions, a "sunk costs" mentality, the lack of adequate institutions for dealing with the conflicting interests, and the barriers for NGOs and the public to influence the process eventually led to a lawsuit. However, the decision of the International Court of Justice has not resolved the conflict. It has instructed Hungary and Slovakia to negotiate an agreement under difficult circumstances. Regardless of the eventual outcome, a timely and constructive dialogue with and the involvement of the affected and interested parties may have resulted in greater benefits in terms of the credibility of both governments, their long-term political future, and the provision of energy from an environmentally and socially acceptable source.

Notes

[1] Treaty between the Hungarian People's Republic and the Czechoslovak Socialist Republic Concerning the Construction and Operation of the Gabcikovo-Nagymaros System of Locks, 16 September 1977, 1109 U.N.T.S. 236.

[2] Application of the Republic of Hungary v. The Czech and Slovak Federal Republic on the Diversion of the Danube River, at 3, ICJ (22 October 1992).

[3] Protocol of the negotiations between the governmental representatives of the Hungarian Republic and the Czech and Slovak Federal Republic on issues related to the Gabcikovo-Nagymaros Barrage System on 6 September 1990 in Bratislava and on 17–18 October 1990 in Budapest.

[4] Application of Hungary, *op cit.*, note 2, p. 5.

[5] Application of Hungary, *op cit.*, note 2, p. 5.

[6] Vienna Convention on the Law of Treaties, opened for signature 23 May 1969, 1155 U.N.T.S. 331 (entered into force 27 January 1980).

[7] Sponsors of the project included the Regional Environmental Center for Central and Eastern Europe, the Charles Stewart Mott Foundation, the German Marshall Fund, and the Environmental Partnership for Central and Eastern Europe.

References

Campbell, B.L., 1985, Uncertainty as a symbolic action in disputes among experts, *Social Studies of Science*, **15**:429–453.

Fisher, S., 1993, The Gabcikovo-Nagymaros Dam controversy continues, *International Relations*, **2**:7–12.

Fleischer, T., 1993, Jaws on the Danube: Water management, regime change and the movement against the Middle Danube Hydroelectric Dam, *International Journal of Urban and Regional Research*, **17**:429–443.

Galambos, J., 1992, Political aspects of an environmental conflict: The case of the Gabcikovo-Nagymaros Dam System, in J. Kaekoenen, ed., *Perspectives on Environmental Conflict and International Relations*, Pinter, London, UK.

Galambos, J., 1993, An international environmental conflict on the Danube: The Gabcikovo-Nagymaros dams, in A. Vari and P. Tamas, eds, *Environment and Democratic Transition: Policy and Politics in Central and Eastern Europe*, Kluwer Academic Publishers, Dordrecht, Netherlands.

Hardi, P., 1989, The Hardi Report: Summary for the Council of Ministers of an experts review concerning the ecological, environmental, technical, economic, international and legal issues of the Bos-Nagymaros Barrage System, Budapest, Hungary.

Levidow, L., 1994, Biotechnology Risk Controversy: Depoliticizing Uncertainty, Paper presented at the Conference of the European Association for the Study of Science & Technology, Budapest, Hungary, August.

Linnerooth-Bayer, J., 1990, The Danube River Basin: Negotiating settlements to transboundary environmental issues, *Natural Resources Journal*, **30**: 629–660.

Linnerooth-Bayer, J., 1993, Current Danube River events and issues, *Transboundary Resources Report*, **7**:7, International Transboundary Resources Center, Albuquerque, NM, USA.

Linnerooth-Bayer, J., and Murcott, S., 1996, The Danube River Basin: International co-operation for sustainable development, *Natural Resources Journal*, **36**:631–657.

Moore, Ch., and Delli Priscoli, J., 1989, Alternative Dispute Resolution (ADR) Procedures, Handbook, US Army Corps of Engineers, Washington, DC, USA.

Nagy, B., 1992, The Danube dispute: Conflicting paradigms, *The New Hungarian Quarterly*, Winter:56–65.

Pearce, F., 1994, Dam truths on the Danube, *New Scientist*, September:27–31.

Rayner, S., 1993, Governance and the Global Commons, Discussion Paper 8, The Centre for the Study of Global Governance, London School of Economics, London, UK.

Reflex Environmental Association, 1995, The Szigetkoz Public Communication Project, Progress Report, February.

Reflex Environmental Association, 1996, Conflict Prevention, Conflict Research, Conflict Management, Gyor, Hungary.

Renn, O., Webler, T., and Wiedemann, P., eds, 1995, *Fairness and Competence in Citizen Participation: Evaluating Models for Environmental Discourse*, Kluwer Academic Publishers, Dordrecht, Netherlands.

Tamas, P., 1995, Transborder Environmental Conflict at the Danube Barrage System, Report to the European Union, Hungarian Academy of Sciences, Institute for Social Conflict Research, Budapest, Hungary, p. 51.

TED (Trade and Environment Data Base), 1995, Case Studies: Hungary Dam (case number 34, Hungarian Dam Controversy), http://gurukul. ucc.american.edu/ted/Hungary.htm, p. 7.

Vargha, J., 1981, Egyre távolabb a jotol (Departing from the Good), *Valosag*, 11/1981.

VITUKI (Institute for Scientific Research on Water Management), 1994, *Analysis of Various Methods to Resolve Water Supplement on the Szigetkoz*, VITUKI, Budapest, Hungary.

Williams, P.R., 1994, International environmental dispute resolution: The dispute between Slovakia and Hungary concerning construction of the Gabcikovo and Nagymaros Dams, *Columbia Journal of Environmental Law*, **19**:1–59.

Chapter 7

Transboundary Risk Management in the South: A Nepalese Perspective on Himalayan Water Projects

Michael Thompson and Dipak Gyawali

Transboundary risks, like all risks, are socially constructed, which means that the orthodox management approach, based on the clear separation of facts and values, cannot be followed. What the transboundary risks really are, and what people variously perceive them to be, can never be fully and unambiguously distinguished, and this means that we need an approach that treats them for what they are: an entanglement of facts and values. In this chapter we try to develop this approach (drawing on cultural theory) by focusing on the dynamics of trust and mistrust that are generated by the interactions between the physical flows and the human inhabitants of the southern slopes of the Himalaya. We begin by discussing the interplay of water and social life and then focus on two specific sets of risks within that interplay: high dams and unwelcome silt.

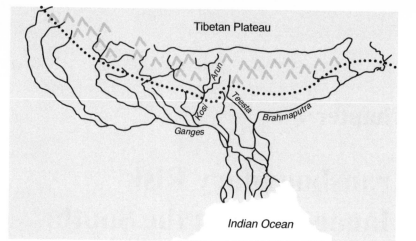

Figure 7.1. The physical flows. The dotted line shows where rivers debouch onto the plain. Southern (i.e., non-Himalayan) tributaries omitted.

7.1 The Physical Flows

Water and suspended solid material flow down the southern slopes of the Himalaya, across the plains, through the delta, and into the Indian Ocean. The water itself actually originates in the Indian Ocean, falling as monsoonal snow and rain on the mountains and plains. It therefore goes round and round: as a solid or liquid on the downward part of its cycle and as vapor on the upward part. The suspended material, however, makes a one-way journey,[1] much of it being deposited along the way and some of it not coming to a final rest until it is thousands of kilometers out into the Bay of Bengal (*Figure 7.1*).

Though they may look like little squiggles on the map, these rivers are enormous, cutting their way down from the crest of the Himalayan Range (at 8,000 meters) to the Gangetic Plain (at a few tens of meters above sea level) in just 100 or so kilometers. As a silt transport system the rivers are without equal.[2] Indeed, the plain and the delta are their creations: the alluvium they have deposited is 5,000 meters (m) deep, and their suspended silt forms a plume that reaches as far as Sri Lanka – 3,000 kilometers (km) across the Indian Ocean. And on this plain and delta there live around half a billion people, which, of course, brings us to the political boundaries.

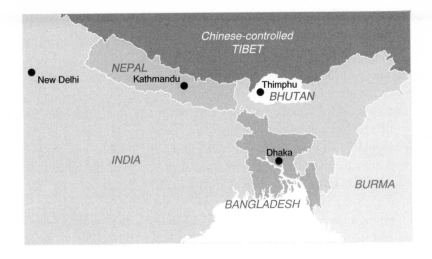

Figure 7.2. The political boundaries.

7.2   The Political Boundaries

The first point that must be made about the national boundaries of the region is that they are far from fixed. The second is that, except for those at the eastern extreme (between Burma and India, and between Burma and Bangladesh), they do not follow the watershed. So the boundaries keep on moving and, wherever they move to, the physical flows career across them (*Figure 7.2*). These two characteristics are not unique to the Himalaya–Ganga system. We find them around the Baltic and along the Danube, and the student of transboundary risk management would be well advised to regard these characteristics as the norm and to treat those instances where one, the other, or both are absent as fleeting and unstable exceptions.

The following points will serve to give some feel for the fluidity of the boundaries depicted in *Figure 7.2*:

- Fifty years ago India, Pakistan, and Bangladesh were a single unit: the "jewel in the crown" of the British Empire.
- Less than 40 years ago Tibet was an independent nation (*de facto*, certainly, and, many would argue, *de jure* also).
- Less than 30 years ago there was a small Himalayan nation – Sikkim – which is now a part of India, and there was a part-nation – East Pakistan – that is now Bangladesh.

- Over the past 50 years there have been wars between India and Pakistan, between India and China, and between East Pakistan and West Pakistan.
- There are long-running separatist struggles along the entire length of the Himalaya – from Kashmir in the west to Nagaland in the east.
- Expansionist claims and fears are rife. China claims large parts of territory that India sees as hers, there are fears of a "Greater Nepal,"[3] there are ethnic expulsions in Bhutan, and there are fences against illegal immigration in the area of the narrow neck of Indian territory that separates Bangladesh and Nepal.

Turning now to the relationship between these fluid political boundaries and the physical flows, we should note that not one of these great rivers lies wholly within the undisputed territory of just one nation. Most are shared between India and Bangladesh, and some (the Arun, for instance) are also shared by Nepal and Chinese-controlled Tibet. Each country, wary of the floods, droughts, and aggraded riverbeds that may be unleashed upon it, and aware of the asymmetry of the risks that are inherent in these flows, refers to its upstream neighbor as "the upper riparian." In the case of the Arun – perhaps the most awesomely powerful of all these rivers – Bangladesh has an upper riparian (India), India has an upper riparian (Nepal), and Nepal has an upper riparian (Chinese-controlled Tibet).

From this brief sketch, we can see that the region is not without its transboundary problems. Moreover, complicating matters still further, the physical flows do not stay in the same place:

- The Ganges and the Brahmaputra, though they share the same delta, used to make their separate ways to the sea. But in 1830 the Brahmaputra, in a dramatic earthquake-inspired leap of more than 100 km, captured the Ganges, with the result that their waters now mingle for the final 200 km of their journey.
- Three great rivers – the Sun Kosi, the Arun, and the Tamur Kosi – merge just before they debouch onto the plain. Their combined waters – the Sapta Kosi (sometimes just called the Kosi) – create an enormous alluvial fan, part of which is in Nepal, part in India. The Kosi creates this fan by continually diverting itself with the barriers of silt that it deposits as its rate of flow decreases. Over the

past 250 years it has shifted itself more than 100 km westward. If it met the Teesta and the Brahmaputra in the past, it now meets the Ganges (Chapman and Thompson, 1995; Bandyopadhyay and Gyawali, 1996; Hofer and Messerli, 1997).

Currently, the Kosi is confined to the western edge of its "inland delta" by being "jacketed" by 125-km-long embankments on either side. This jacket has now been in place for 40 years, and the result is that the *bed* of the river, at certain stretches within these embankments, is about two to four meters above the surrounding countryside. Whether the Kosi will continue on its journey, or begin to sweep back eastward is anyone's guess, but one thing is certain: it will not stay where it is! And when it decides to move, it will take villages and cities with it (Mishra, 1997).

- The Ganges and its tributaries, when not "jacketed" by man-made embankments, meander from bank to bank, with their main stems capturing one or the other of their braided channels. Huge silt islands (called *chars* or *diyaras*), which are extremely fertile, are created or destroyed every year in a dynamic cycle that those who inhabit this region see as echoing the cycle of life and death (Barua, 1997).

Humans intervene at every point within this dynamic physical system – building barrages here, removing forest there, putting water in at one place, taking it out at another, on and on – which means that, whenever anything changes, it is possible to blame somebody for it. Very often, in the absence of any clear, objective understanding of the vast and complex processes at work (and quite often in its presence) people choose the answer they would like: "The upper riparian did it!" So the blame for the devastating floods of 1988 in Bangladesh was put squarely on the poverty-ridden subsistence farmers in the hills of Nepal. It was their felling of the forests for fuelwood and to provide more terraced fields to support their ever-expanding population that, by destabilizing the fragile mountain slopes, had caused the disastrous floods. That the Ganges' and Brahmaputra's flood peaks, which normally come a month apart, coincided that year was conveniently ignored. So, too, was the fact that this simultaneous cresting coincided with a high tide in the Bay of Bengal. So, too, was the fact that this vast surge of water was further amplified by the drainage constrictions in the floodplain that have been created in recent years by road construction (Hofer, 1997).

7.3 Transboundary Risks and Sustainable Development

The first obstacle to development – sustainable or unsustainable – is the appalling history of mistrust in what is euphemistically known as "the cooperative development of Himalayan water resources."[4]

- Much of the public discourse in Nepal between December 1991 and September 1996 – a discourse that tied up the Parliament, the Supreme Court, and three successive governments – was dominated by what was perceived to be a "bum deal" with India over the waters of the Mahakali, the river that forms Nepal's western border with India (Gyawali and Schwank, 1994). This mistrust had its roots in another perceived "bum deal," the Sarada Treaty with British India (the river's name changes with the bank you are standing on) which dates back to 1910–1920.
- The Mahakali is only one of the many rivers that originate in the Nepal Himalaya and flow into the Ganges in India. The other major river systems of Nepal include the Kosi and the Gandak, both of which were the subject of deals in the 1950s that are similarly perceived by many Nepalis as being heavily weighted in India's favor.
- The Farakka Barrage, built by India just upstream of where the Ganges enters Bangladesh, is routinely blamed for just about every misfortune that befalls Bangladesh. That the relevant Indian hydrological data enjoy the same security classification as data from its nuclear weapons program does little to improve Bangladesh's relations with its upper riparian.
- In 1987, following that year's serious floods in Bangladesh, Britain's minister for overseas aid, Chris Patten, announced a special grant for afforestation in Nepal, thereby adding his country's weight to the increasingly suspect theory that the upper upper riparian's hill farmers were to blame.[5]

However, regardless of their mistrust for one another, Bangladesh, its upper riparian (India), and its upper upper riparian (Nepal) are all in much the same predicament when it comes to the development problems they will face in the next few decades.

7.3.1 Getting to the demographic transition

Demographers can tell us with considerable confidence that, barring the onslaught of some 21st century equivalent of the Black Death,[6] the rural population of the middle Ganges plain will double – from 385 million to around 685 million – between now and the year 2031, and that the urban population will increase fivefold – from 50 million to around 250 million (Chapman and Thompson, 1995). This burgeoning urban population will need *all* the surface water, and the chances are it will get it! There is no instance anywhere in the world (except, some argue, in California) where rural water interests have prevailed over urban interests. So where will the growing rural population get its water – water that it needs, among other things, to keep the urban population fed? The answer is *groundwater*. Much of the water that is deposited on the Himalaya and on the plains finds its way to the ocean *beneath* the surface, and there is enough groundwater (provided it is carefully managed) to meet the rural population's needs. But the groundwater is "down there," and it requires energy to get it to the surface. Where will that come from?

Human and animal power have been used for this task for centuries; more recently, they have been joined by pumps (powered by diesel oil or by electricity generated from fossil fuels or from nuclear power). All of these modern technologies have serious sustainability problems. Solar power, and perhaps hot fusion (or, more plausibly, natural gas, either discovered locally or piped in from the Caspian region),[7] may eventually bail everyone out, but the only renewable resource that currently can be harnessed is the surface water itself as it thunders down from the Himalaya. This hydropower potential is truly immense, comparing favorably with oil-rich places like Saudi Arabia and the North Slope of Alaska, but there are problems (technical and political, and the two are inextricably intertwined) in realizing that potential.

7.3.2 Institutional plurality and the building of trust

Since the hydropower potential is mostly in the mountainous countries – Nepal and Bhutan – while the growing population, industry, and agriculture that need the energy are in the low-lying countries – India and

Bangladesh – the rapid development of these stupendous water resources will require a high level of international trust and cooperation. But, just because all this trust and cooperation is absolutely vital, does not mean that it will be forthcoming. Indeed, negotiations between these sovereign nations have been so unproductive that some wags have suggested that much money could have been saved at these meetings if each of them had sent, not a delegation, but a fax stating, "We reiterate our previous position"!

This stagnant and trust-sapping discourse has now been significantly transformed. Since the advent of democracy in Nepal in 1990, other voices have been able to make themselves heard and power no longer runs in the old-style channels. Here we will mention just two instances of this major shift in the distribution and flow of power.

The first is the dramatic expansion in the number and variety of stakeholders in the debate. Now, in addition to the familiar state actors, there are entrepreneurial academics (from both sides of the border); nongovernmental organizations, or NGOs (both local and international); and environmentalists (homegrown and exotic).[8] Cacophony, of course, is not always constructive, but in this case it has been. What hitherto had been accepted as self-evident has now been questioned by actors with perspectives and refractive indices that are very different from those that gave rise to the traditional pattern of thinking. Nation-state actors who had labored long and hard under assumptions about future demand for water and energy, and who had agreed on projects that ostensibly met those demands, now face awkward (that is, assumption-challenging) questions that, for all the discomfort they may cause, open up all sorts of hitherto unconsidered options and close off many of those options that previously had gone through (or been stalemated) "on the nod."

The most celebrated among these is the Arun-3 project, a run-of-river hydroplant in the upper reaches of the Arun River within Nepal. A coalition of activist groups (the Alliance for Energy, Nepal, for instance, and the International Rivers Network based in California, as well as Germany's Urgewald and the UK's Intermediate Technology Development Group) was able to mount a successful campaign against the World Bank and the Nepal government, who together were pushing this project. The essence of the argument put forward by these non-state actors was that the proposed Arun-3, at almost US$1.1 billion (almost twice the annual revenue of the government), was too risky for the country, which would be better served by a series of smaller alternatives that were technically more sound, economically less risky, and development-wise more conducive to the building of national capacity (Gyawali, 1997; Pandey, 1995). A related argument (advanced by other NGOs) was that a pristine Arun valley, with a host of great Himalayan peaks around its head (Makalu, for instance, and Baruntse) and a catchment stuffed with a fair proportion of the world's biodiversity (pheasants, for example, and musk deer and many of the plants that have made the English garden what it is) would be worth a great deal more to Nepal than one with an Arun-3 and the access road needed for its construction.

In August 1995, after two years of struggle, the new president of the World Bank, James Wolfensohn, pulled out of the project, confessing that it was too great a risk for Nepal to bear – a decision that, by some accounts (e.g., Vidal, 1995), was joyously received in towns and villages across the length and breadth of Nepal. As a result of this "killing" of Arun-3, a set of six smaller projects is now under way in Nepal. These six projects will produce a third more power than Arun-3 in less than half the time for almost half the cost and across six different districts of Nepal.[9] (The government of Nepal, however, vows to revive Arun-3, for reasons of prestige, and the Ministry of Water Resources has recently called for proposals from foreign investors.)

The second major shift in the distribution and flow of power centers on the decision by Nepal's coalition government and the government of India to push ahead with the ratification of the Mahakali Treaty. The Mahakali River (as we have already mentioned) forms Nepal's western border with India, except for a 4,000-acre stretch of the Nepali bank which in 1920 was traded to British India for a similar area of forestland elsewhere. On this swapped piece of bank the British built the Sarada irrigation project, which diverts about 93% of the river's flow to the Indian state of Uttar Pradesh, leaving some 7% to Nepal.

In 1984, India began construction of the 120 megawatt (MW) Tanakpur power plant; by 1988, it was complete, with the exception of two details that still needed to be addressed. The first was the diversion, inherent in the Indian power plant's design, of the remaining 7% of the river's flow into the Sarada irrigation channel. This, of course, would deny Nepal the modest share it had been allocated under the 1920 treaty – water that Nepal had used to supply its Mahakali irrigation project. After much haggling, India agreed to modify the design so that the water flowed back into the river. The second detail was that, for the power plant to be completed, Nepal would have to allow India to use a 577 m strip of its territory for the construction of what was known as the weir's "left afflux bund." Without that, it would be impossible to channel the river toward the sluice gates.

The devil, as they say, is in the detail: in this case, the two details. Because India had maintained all along that this was an Indian project and no concern of Nepal, these details, each of which made clear that it was *not* just an Indian project, rankled many Nepalis. Indeed, these two details dominated the Nepal government's agenda, and the front pages of Kathmandu's exuberant free press, for months.

Eventually, in December 1991, in a desperate effort to resolve the crisis, the Nepali Congress government (the first government elected after the restoration of democracy in 1990) reached what it called an "understanding" with India. This understanding (which was, of course, a treaty) allowed India to construct the left afflux bund in exchange for 150 cusecs of water and 10 million units of electricity from the power plant. The understanding was promptly challenged in court as a breach of Article 126 of Nepal's constitution, which requires such treaties to be ratified by a two-thirds majority in Parliament. The court upheld the challenge.

What we see in these continuing efforts to conclude a Mahakali Treaty is the democratization of decision making in an area – the cooperative development of Himalayan water resources – where, until 1990, decision making had taken place on an "uncontested terrain." Almost a century's worth of Nepali disgruntlement, which previously could not obtain a hearing, is now able to express itself. The result, you could say, reveals the true scale of the political risks (and, in many instances, the physical risks as well) that are involved in these large-scale transboundary agreements.

When the Nepal Congress government, fatally weakened by its efforts to push through its "understanding," finally fell in 1994, it was replaced by a minority communist government. This new government came up with a "package deal" in which Nepal, in return for various additional benefits (70 million units of electricity and some more water) would give India permission to build, farther upstream on the Mahakali, the 6,480 MW Pancheswar multipurpose project, complete with its 315 m high dam. The speed with which this new deal (which links the already troublesome Tanakpur project with the vast new Pancheswar project) has been proposed, and the method by which its ratification process was carried out, has split all the main Nepali parties into opposing political camps. Public opinion in Nepal is likewise split into those who think this "package deal" is an even worse deal than those that have preceded it and those who think it will make Nepal "if not an Asian tiger, then at least an Asian leopard."[10] Not surprisingly, this communist government has now fallen.

There is, however, a silver lining to this crisis-ridden cloud, which is that the now-pluralized discourse has exposed risks that previously were hidden. And, in the very process of exposing those risks, it has revealed new opportunities and new options. Stagnation has been replaced with a hyperactive free-for-all that Nepalis call "democracy on fast-forward."

7.3.3 The silver lining

In the case of Arun-3, the risk was to the financial stability of Nepal (and, ultimately, to its sovereignty). In the Mahakali case, the risk was to the viability of democracy in Nepal. The silver lining in the Arun-3 case is that Nepal can do much better with its set of six smaller projects (including a joint private investment by an American IPP – independent power producer – and a Nepali five-star hotel; see Shakya, 1998). Moreover, it is now going to be much more difficult for single-mission outfits to push through their single-minded solutions. On the other hand, as the blitzkrieg ratification of the Mahakali Treaty shows, these old ways of thinking and acting are not going to disappear overnight. If building a 201 MW project (Arun-3) at US$1.1 billion was too risky for Nepal, what hope is there that it will be able to bear the risk of a project 30 times bigger (Pancheswar) in a fifty–fifty cost-sharing partnership with India? Nor has Nepal ever had to face so massive an involuntary resettlement of its citizens. How will that be managed equitably, especially now that all those displaced by development have the vote? And how will Nepal deal with a monopsony market – India – if it does not wish to give away its sites at the cost price? These and many other questions are bound to be asked in the days ahead by the same vociferous actors who put a stop to Arun-3.

But, it will be objected, if the dams are all cancelled, what hope is there for the sustainable development of the region? This is where the technical arguments (and their entwinement with the political arguments) come in. Many of the non-state actors argue that the required generating capacity can be achieved more quickly, more safely, and at a lower cost by the incremental growth of smaller-scale (often village-level) hydro-projects, more than 400 of which are already up and running (Pandey,

1994). On top of that, this technological solution, unlike the proposed mega-projects, involves no transboundary risks: technical, financial, or related to sovereignty. A solution, roughly along these lines, has now replaced Arun-3, and the promised result is more, cheaper, and better-distributed power available sooner than was promised by Arun-3.

One of the most striking features of the whole water-harnessing debate – and it is a feature that holds for transboundary risks generally – is that preferences for the various technical options are not evenly distributed among the various participants. National ministries, the World Bank, the European Union, and giant corporations find their way unerringly to the large-scale, capital-intensive solutions; NGOs, environmental activists, and grassroots campaigners zoom in on the small-scale and labor-intensive solutions. Less obvious, and somewhere in between these extremes, there are all sorts of innovative and genuinely competitive businesses (often Nepali businesses) eager to try their hands at cheap-and-cheerful solutions: cheap enough to attract the punters, cheerful enough to show a profit. Until the debate is pluralized, these small- and appropriate-scale solutions simply are not considered, and the technology of water harnessing marches off down the sort of inflexible path that helped bring the Soviet Union to its knees.

So the very act of pluralizing the debate, thanks to the markedly different technological commitments that each kind of actor brings to it, shifts the whole process of technological decision making away from inflexible paths and toward flexible ones. And, within that debate, transboundary risks provide us with a means of assessing the various technological solutions that are all the time being urged by some actors and resisted by others. It is not a straightforward assessment, however, because the various actors have different perceptions of the risks (and benefits) that are involved. Indeed, in emphasizing some risks (and benefits) and in minimizing others, each actor manages to define the problem in such a way that it nicely matches the solution that actor is eager to provide. So the assessment process is essentially argumentative. Though it often reduces the uncertainties, revealing some perceived risks to be "beyond the pale," it never decides, once and for all, who is right. In other words, it is a way of handling, and making the most of, *irreducible ignorance*.

These three argumentative positions, a little more formalized, constitute the three "active biases" – *hierarchy* (pro-large-scale), *egalitarianism* (pro-small-scale), and *individualism* (pro-appropriate-scale) – within the typology of ways of organizing and their supporting ways of constructing reality that is proposed by cultural theory (Thompson *et al.*, 1990; Schwarz and Thompson, 1990; Rayner and Malone, 1998). Exclude any one (worse still, any two) of these biases, cultural theory predicts, and you will lock yourself into technological inflexibility and lay yourself open to all sorts of unwelcome surprises. That, essentially, is the conceptual framework around which this chapter is built.

7.4 High Dams

Most of the high dams currently being proposed in Nepal are at the points where the Himalayan rivers debouch onto the plain (Dixit, 1995). Consequently, they are just a few miles from the Indian border, and if any one of them were to burst the loss of life (mainly Indian life) would be cataclysmic. They are also just upstream of some of the most sacred sites of the Hindu world – Hardwar, for instance, in the Uttar Pradesh hills and Barahakshetra in eastern Nepal – which means that those Hindus who were not themselves drowned would still experience a profound loss.

These proposed dams all lie in one of the most seismically active tracts in the world, many of them in the "seismic gap" – the area between Dehra Dun and Kathmandu – where an earthquake of major proportions is currently predicted (Bilham, 1994). Such an earthquake (8+ on the Richter scale), seismologists have recently discovered, can have a ground acceleration of more than 1g. This means that if the ground is moving downward, anything lying loose on its surface – a boulder, for instance, or a high dam and the massive volume of water behind it – will be left up in the air. The catastrophic failure of such a dam, with 20 km^3 of impounded water, just a few miles upstream of one of the most densely populated plains in the world, would hardly be a firm step in the direction of sustainability!

But there is an even worse scenario: deliberate rupture. While there is only one dam in the world (just inside North Korea) that was actually built as a weapon, any dams that are built for other purposes can easily be converted into weapons. In 1993, Serbian militia forces detonated explosions in the inspection galleries of a dam, with the aim of killing some 22,000 Croatians in the villages downstream. Their efforts, mercifully, were thwarted by the actions of one man (a Captain Gray of the British Army, who surreptitiously lowered the level of the water, thereby averting the expected failure). Engineers are now discussing the need to build

dams without inspection galleries, thereby lessening the risks from deliberate ill will but increasing the likelihood that accidental weakening will
go undetected (Mihill, 1995).

Thus we are not being overly fanciful if we imagine the rise of some
Himalayan Hitler, who, in pursuit of his dream of a Greater Nepal, is
prepared to detonate, simultaneously, 20 high dams, each full to the brim.
Hiroshima and Nagasaki would be insignificant sideshows compared with
this (and, once the waters had subsided and the corpses had rotted away,
there would be a good deal more *lebensraum* than was available in the
Sudetenland).[11]

Thinking the unthinkable in this way has its uses. At the very least, it
suggests that if there is a technological alternative that would allow us to
avoid these "ill-will risks" (and that is what the hitherto excluded voices –
the egalitarian and the individualist – each in its own way, are arguing),
then we should not let it go unconsidered. So cultural theory is pointing
out that although transboundary risk management involves a lot of science
and a great deal of economic calculation, it is essentially a matter of institutional design: arranging things so that all the voices are heard and their
interaction is constructive. In other words, there is a very direct link between technology and democracy: inflexible technologies are inherently
undemocratic; flexible ones are inherently democratic. To investigate this
link a little further, we now turn to the second of our sets of transboundary
risks: unwelcome silt.

7.5   Unwelcome Silt

"Losing Ground" – the title of a book by Eric Eckholm (1976) – nicely
captures the way in which the whole environment-and-development problem has been framed. A mushrooming population in the mountains of
Nepal has no option but to remove the trees and terrace ever steeper hill-
sides to create enough agricultural land to feed itself. But, in doing so,
these subsistence farmers increase the amount of land slippage and erosion, which leads to even more silt in the mountain torrents and even
worse flooding when that silt reaches the plains of India and the delta
in Bangladesh.

This argument, rather more formally stated, is the theory of Himalayan
environmental degradation, a theory so compelling and so intuitively

appealing that it has defined the problem ever since the first major international conference on the environment (in Stockholm in 1972). It has also defined the solution – resettlement and reforestation in Nepal – and has justified an asymmetrical disbursement of aid, with the small root of the vast problem (Nepal) receiving the lion's share for this particular activity. On top of that, in distinguishing between those nations that are "risk receivers" and those that are "risk givers," it has justified finger pointing and saber rattling in a region that has enough troubles already.

Now, 20 years after it was enunciated, this theory is in tatters. Not one of the vicious circles it comprises stands up to examination (Thompson *et al.*, 1986; Ives and Messerli, 1989). Two decades of aid projects (and millions and millions of dollars) have been directed at what is, and all along was, demonstrably not the problem. This is, perhaps, the classic example of bad science for public policy: the ascendancy of a theory that was unquestioned because it was so self-evidently true to a bunch of environmentally concerned scientists and to a community of development aid professionals. Each deluded the other, and together they managed to exclude all those perspectives that could have shown them the error of their ways.

It is the forces of nature, operating over millions of years, not the recent activities of an expanding human population in the hills of Nepal, that are putting the silt into the rivers. Such contribution as may be provided by the hill farmers is insignificant when viewed against the relentless payload of this vast natural conveyor belt (and recent research shows that these human actors are probably doing more to retard this flow of silt than to accelerate it). Nor, of course, is the silt always unwelcome: if there had not been any silt there would not be any Bangladesh! Whether or not you want silt depends, as Dixit (1997) has shown, on who you are. It depends on *where* you are too, of course, but even those who are in the same place can have very different perceptions of the physical flow to which they are all subject. Dixit, a hydrologist, has used cultural theory to tease out the different ways those in the plains perceive and evaluate the 95 million m^3 of suspended sediment (103 million m^3 if bedload is included) that is brought down from the hills each year by the Kosi.

The first three sets of perceptions correspond to cultural theory's "active biases": those associated with the hierarchical, the individualist, and the egalitarian solidarities, respectively. The fourth corresponds to one of the two "passive biases": that associated with the *fatalistic* solidarity.

1. *The Department of Irrigation.* "Silt is a danger to be controlled."
    This hierarchical outfit is charged by the Indian government with a
    single mission: to build embankments, irrigation canals, dams, and
    related hydraulic structures. In the early 1950s, it clearly saw that
    the solution to the Kosi's silt problem lay in "jacketing" the river
    with long embankments on each side, with a barrage on the Nepal
    border as the main hydraulic controlling structure. Irrigation was
    later added on to make the project more attractive for funding, and
    the entire undertaking was seen as a temporary solution, a way of
    controlling the problem until the massive Kosi high dam was built,
    farther upstream, to provide the permanent solution. This expen-
    sive dam, in one of the poorest and most seismically active parts of
    the world (southern Nepal – northern Bihar), is nowhere in sight,
    but the implementation of the temporary solution has locked the De-
    partment of Irrigation into this permanent solution. Only if the Kosi
    high dam is built will the risks that are every year being piled up by
    the temporary structure be removed. There is no alternative!

    The jacketing of the river has caused it to deposit its massive sed-
    iment load between the two embankments, instead of across the
    much wider floodplain (it has also, of course, put a temporary stop
    to the river's self-diverting processes, which propel it westward, and
    eventually back eastward, across its massive alluvial fan). The river
    is now "perched" high above this floodplain, chronically attacking
    both embankments and diverting a significant proportion of its silt
    into the irrigation channels beyond those embankments. Because the
    Department of Irrigation is in the business of controlling, the biggest
    risk, so far as it is concerned, is a loss of control. It therefore looks to
    the esoteric knowledge and skills of its certified experts. In the view
    of these experts, the best control structure, and therefore the best so-
    lution – a solution to which everyone should consent and adhere –
    is the massive Kosi dam in the lower hills (which would function as
    a silt trap) and government-sponsored afforestation measures in the
    middle hills (which would stop the population in the hills of Nepal
    from cutting down the trees). This solution is triply attractive be-
    cause, as well as removing the risks that are continuously building
    up, it provides huge amounts of electricity and a great volume of
    regulated water (which can then be used for irrigation and possibly
    to promote navigation as well).

2. *The Zamindars* (large landowners). "Silt is opportunity." Long-practiced in the individualistic art of keeping himself free from any form of *raj* – British or Indian Congress – the Zamindar looks on the bright side of life. If silt *is* a problem then it can probably be by-passed by using tubewells: he has the capital, understands the technology, and has the personal network needed to gain permission for their installation. Such technological innovations may even obviate the need for the Kosi high dam (and all the hierarchical controls that would come with it). And, if the dam does not come about, he will continue to make money by obtaining petty contracts for the removal of silt from the irrigation channels (and, perhaps, not-so-petty contracts for digging out the perched bed of the river itself). On the other hand, if the dam does come, there will be plenty of other contracts.

3. *The Ganga Mukti Andolan* (the Ganges Liberation Campaign). "Silt is a diversion from other evils in our midst." This activist campaign aims to capture the moral high ground and, like the canary that falls off its perch when the methane level in the coal mine rises above a certain level, raises the alarm about impending dangers. Growing straight out of the tradition that goes back to Gandhi himself, in his early struggles in the Champaran district of northern Bihar, these egalitarian activists (and the many other local groups like them) argue that the poor do not benefit from either of these solutions: the hierarchical (controlling silt) or the individualistic (taking advantage of silt, one way or another). The silt is natural and would kill the Kosi high dam in a very short time. And the danger that this dam would pose to the downstream areas if it were to fail renders it wholly unjustifiable. Neither solution addresses the real problem, which is seismicity, not silt, together with the inequitable social relations that are sustained by the structural corruption in the canal works.

4. *The Ryots* (the sharecroppers on the Zamindars' lands, landless laborers, or victims of debt bondage). "Silt is one among a host of woes about which we can do nothing in this life." At the bottom of the discourse heap, and seldom heard, are those who find themselves marginalized by the organizational efforts of those who *are* able to make themselves heard – the hierarchists, the individualists, and the egalitarians. The *ryots*, busy coping with their everyday problems of

survival, elect not to devote any of their efforts to changing things that they are powerless to change. Silt is only one of the many adverse, day-to-day conditions to which they are subject, and it is coped with as and when it comes: in the extreme, by migration or death.

Choose just one of these definitions of problem and solution and you inevitably discard all the wisdom and experience that is contained within the other three. You also pile up for yourself all sorts of difficulties in implementation and governability, since those who do not share the chosen definition of the problem are unlikely to consent to its solution. Hubris – the denial of the uncertainty that is so clearly revealed by this fourfold plurality – then results in all sorts of surprises that could have been avoided had this single solution not been imposed. The alternative, of course, is not to choose just one solution, thereby recognizing the true scale of the uncertainty and instituting the *argumentative style* of decision making – the style that, we have been arguing, is evident in the contested terrain on which the debate over "developments" such as Arun-3 is now being conducted. A single solution, we concede, is neat and noiseless, but, as our final example shows,[12] it comes at far too high a price.

Kulekhani – the largest existing reservoir in Nepal – is a 60 MW hydroelectric project with a 114 m high dam with a gross reservoir volume of 85 million m^3 and a dead storage volume of 12 million m^3. It was completed in 1981 at a cost of US$120 million. This was not a homegrown venture; it was an international affair, in which the hierarchists – national aid donors and HMG (His Majesty's Government, as the then undemocratic regime in Nepal was called) – had managed to exclude the individualists and the egalitarians from the decision-making process, thereby ensuring a terrain that was both quiet and uncontested. In July 1993, a massive cloudburst deposited 540 millimeters of rain on the Kulekhani catchment in a period of just 15 hours (about an inch and a half of rain an hour). There was massive landsliding and considerable loss of life, but the dam itself held. Its contents, however, were much altered.

This one, 15-hour event (and such cloudbursts, though mercifully localized, are not uncommon) filled up the dead storage with 5 million m^3 of sediment. This was on top of a pre-cloudburst sedimentation rate that was 10 times greater than the design estimate. The result is that the projected life of the reservoir has now shrunk from the design estimate of

100 years to 15 years. Efforts funded by Japanese loans are currently under way to redesign a sloping intake above the dead water level and undertake watershed protection measures (the original project was Japanese designed and led). This will reduce the effective reservoir volume but allow it to function for a few more years, at about 30% of the cost of the original project! As an example of technological inflexibility, the Kulekhani project is probably unrivaled anywhere in the world (though high-rise system-built housing in Britain might have the edge on it [see Collingridge, 1992]), and the question it raises is, How much more of this sort of development aid can a poor country like Nepal afford to receive?

7.6 Conclusion

Transboundary risks emerge in different parts of the world and have all sorts of characteristics that are particular to those various localities. Nonetheless, they do exhibit some universal features. Therefore, lessons learned in one place often transfer to another. Ill will is one example. That a mafia boss in Lithuania, whose son had been imprisoned, credibly threatened to blow up the Ignalina nuclear power station alerts us to the possibility that dams, in Croatia or Nepal or wherever, that were built with the best of intentions may be turned into weapons of mass destruction.

But transboundary risks are not something we can simply draw a line around and then manage. It is never simply a question of tightening existing procedures and devising clever new ones for monitoring compliance or punishing infringement. Such measures are inevitably snarled up in competing technological preferences, in contending and contradictory systems of knowledge, in rival institutional commitments, and in varying perceptions of the risks involved and thus of the responses required. In other words, we are dealing with entanglements, and the challenge is to find ways of treating them as entanglements. Plurality, contradiction, argumentation, contention, and agreements that look like clumsy compromises, we suggest, are clear indicators that you are treating these entanglements for what they are. Conversely, if you find yourself with just a single definition of the problem, watch out!

The most important practical implications of cultural theory, of course, have to do with how to actually institute the argumentative style. In this paper we have been able to do little more than "unpack" some of the transboundary risks in the Himalayan region and show how they are entangled (often in a trust-sapping and democracy-destroying way) with the institutional arrangements, both homegrown and international, that aspire to manage them. Plurality – the non-exclusion of any of the "voices" – is clearly the first essential, but we have barely broached the question of how this plurality can emerge and be constructively harnessed to reduce technological inflexibility and enhance security at every level (from family hearth to nation-state to international regime). This question, however, is discussed (in general terms) in Ney and Thompson (1999) and (in relation to water in the Himalayan region) in Gyawali (1998).

Notes

[1] Though, in the very long run, even this can go round and round, as the Earth's tectonic plates perform their awesome dances. Indeed, it is the eruption from volcanoes of carboniferous rocks laid down on seabeds many millions of years ago that completes the long-term carbon cycle, as it is called.

[2] For an ambitious framing, in terms of what they call *Himalaya–Ganga*, of the environment-and-development challenge, see Gyawali and Dixit (1994). We use *Ganga* in the South Asian sense as encompassing all the waters that flow from the Himalaya. This, of course, includes the river that those who are not South Asian call the Ganges (an anglicized corruption, it is believed, of the honorific *Ganga-ji*). To distinguish between the whole and the part, we use *Ganges* when speaking of this particular river. For a more complete account of all these physical processes, see Chapter 1 of Chapman and Thompson (1995).

[3] See, for instance, the March/April 1993 issue of *Himal* devoted to this topic, as well as correspondence in the subsequent issue of that journal.

[4] Taken from the title of an international conference held in Kathmandu in February 1993; selected papers were published in a special issue of *Water Nepal*, 4(1), September 1994.

[5] As we explain later in this paper, the orthodox view, since at least the early 1970s, was that the cause was man-made and lay in the hills. This was seriously questioned in 1985 (Thompson and Warburton, 1985) and very quickly shown to be without foundation. There was no evidence that human activity in the mountains was worsening the flooding in the plains and delta, and considerable evidence that it was not. This bold assertion may appear to be contradicted by Blaikie (1985), but see Blaikie (1988).

[6] Acquired immunodeficiency syndrome (AIDS), in the developing countries (which cannot afford the treatments available in developed countries) may be precisely this.

[7] Natural gas, of course, is not carbon free, but it is by far the least offensive of all the hydrocarbon fuels.

[8] This is the so-called Patna Initiative, after the venue of its first meeting (Behera *et al.*, 1997). A key event within that process was the 1993 Kathmandu meeting on "The Co-operative Development of Himalayan Water Resources." Many of the contributions to this meeting are assembled in a special issue of *Water Nepal* (1994).

[9] The 201 megawatt (MW) Arun-3 had a 10-year construction schedule (requiring a 120 km road in the High Himalaya) and would have cost US$1.083 billion. The set of smaller alternatives currently under way totals 280 MW at a cost of between US$588 and US$718 million. The alternatives are Kali Gandaki – 144 MW estimated at US$425 million but with tenders coming in at US$350 million; Khimti – 60 MW at US$126 million; Bhote Kosi – 36 MW at US$102 million (estimate at which contract with the private party was made, subsequently subcontracted to a Chinese group for US$49 million); Chilime – 20 MW at US$27 million; Modi – 14 MW at US$26 million; and Puwa – 6.2 MW at US$12 million.

[10] Those opposing the treaty are an unlikely set of bedfellows from the extreme left to the extreme right (who are united on a "nationalist" platform) as well as members of Parliament from the main political parties in favor of the treaty (who defied the party whip with the argument that "the nation is higher than the party"). The statement about Nepal being an Asian leopard is part of the hype put forward by the ruling coalition and by those among the communists supporting this treaty; this particular expression is one of the favorites of Pashupati Rana, the water resources minister.

We can take the opportunity, here, to briefly explain what has happened since then. The communist government fell and was replaced by a center-right coalition, which fell because of internal dissension and was replaced by a left-right coalition of communists and royalists, which subsequently fell because of floor-crossing. Nepal then hosted a center-right coalition, which also fell because its main coalition partner, the centrist Nepali Congress, decided it wanted the premiership. Then came a center-left Congress-communist government, which shuffled between a center-left (nationalist or close-to-royalist) coalition and a center-left (less-than-royalist, and – if one believed its detractors – pro-Indian hence anti-national) one, which was finally forced to go to the polls and end the political circus. The general elections of 1999 brought the centrist Nepali Congress to power with a parliamentary majority, but bickering within the fractious party has forced change of premiership, resulting in a polarization between two camps with every indication of a split in the offing. In early January 1998, the Nepal Communist Party United Marxist Leninists held their five-year congress, in which the issue of the Mahakali Treaty split the party right down the middle and fueled the legitimacy of the Maoist movement. ("See how the bourgeois Parliament sells the interests of the country!")

[11] We no longer have to imagine this Himalayan Hitler. Since we first wrote this paper (1996) he has appeared: 68-year-old Gajendra Narayan Singh is chief of the extreme pro-Indian Nepal Sadvawana Party, which has three seats in the Nepali Parliament and has been a partner in all three coalition governments in Nepal since 1995. In the debate on the Mahakali Treaty, he and his party have always spoken for an immediate ratification. In an interview given to the left-leaning weekly *Jana Ashtha* ("People's Faith") on 4 September 1996, this is what he had to say about how he sees a monopsonistic India agreeing to buying power from Nepal:

> *Jana Ashtha*: You say this [project treaty] is direly needed for India too. What is the benefit for India in this?
>
> Minister: Flood will be controlled in Uttar Pradesh and Bihar of India. They will get irrigation. Such regulation will stop [flood] havoc in India. Since [we are landlocked] other countries cannot come here, so our electricity has to be bought by India, we will also benefit tremendously.
>
> *Jana Ashtha*: Is there a guarantee of that in this Treaty?
>
> Minister: If they go against international norms [by not buying our electricity] we can destroy the dam. If we release all the waters, it will drown India. They will be affected by it. So they will buy our electricity and make arrangements for irrigation. A treaty is by definition a guarantee – they will not have the courage to go against it.

[12] Described in detail in Gyawali and Dixit (1998).

References

Bandyopadhyay, J., and Gyawali, D., 1996, Himalayan water resources: Ecological and political aspects of management, *Mountain Research and Development*, **14**(1):1–24.

Barua, D., 1997, The characteristics and mobility of some major rivers in Bangladesh, *Water Nepal*, **5**(1):109–127.

Behera, N.C., Evans, P.M., and Rizvi, G., 1997, *Beyond Boundaries: A Report on the State of Nonofficial Dialogues on Peace, Security and Co-operation in*

South Asia, University of Toronto–York University Joint Center for Asian and Pacific Studies, Toronto, Canada.

Bilham, R., 1994, The next great earthquake, *Himal*, **7**(3) (May/June):26–30.

Blaikie, P.M., 1985, *The Political Economy of Soil Erosion in Developing Countries*, Longman, London, UK.

Blaikie, P.M., 1988, Environmental crises in developing countries, in P.M. Blaikie and T. Unwin, eds, *Environmental Crises in Developing Countries*, Institute of British Geographers, Developing Areas Research Group Monograph No. 5, pp. 1–6, London, UK.

Chapman, G.P., and Thompson, M., 1995, *Water and the Quest for Sustainable Development in the Ganges Valley*, Mansell, London, UK.

Collingridge, D., 1992, *The Management of Scale: Big Organisations, Big Decisions, Big Mistakes*, Routledge, London, UK.

Dixit, A., 1995, Mapping Nepal's water resource, *Himal*, **8**(4):23 (July/August).

Dixit, A., 1997, Indo-Nepal water resources development: Cursing the past or moving forward, in J.K. Ray, ed., *Indo-Nepal Co-operation Broadening Measures*, Department of History, University of Calcutta, Monograph 13, K.P. Bagchi and Company, Calcutta, India.

Eckholm, E., 1976, *Losing Ground*, Worldwatch Institute, W.W. Norton, New York, NY, USA.

Gyawali, D., 1997, Foreign aid and the erosion of local institutions: An autopsy of Arun-3 from inception to abortion, in C. Thomas and P. Wilkin, eds, *Globalization and the South* (International Political Economy Series), Macmillan, London, UK, and St Martin's, New York, NY, USA.

Gyawali, D., 1998, Patna, Delhi and environmental activism: Institutional forces beyond water conflict in Bihar, *Water Nepal*, **6**(1):67–115.

Gyawali, D., and Dixit, A., 1994, The Himalaya-Ganga: contending with interlinkages in a complex system, *Water Nepal*, **4**(1):1–6.

Gyawali, D., and Dixit, A., 1998, Natural Disaster and Social Resilience: The 1993 Cloudburst over Central Nepal and Community Response to Vulnerability, *Water Nepal*, **6**(2).

Gyawali, D., and Schwank, O., 1994, Interstate sharing of water rights: An Alps-Himalaya comparison, *Water Nepal*, **4**(1):228–236.

Hofer, T., 1997, Meghalaya, not Himalaya, *Himal South Asia*, **10**(5) (Sept/Oct):52–56.

Hofer, T., and Messerli, B., 1997, Floods in Bangladesh: Process understanding and development strategies, Synthesis Paper prepared for the Swiss Agency for Development and Co-operation, Institute of Geography, University of Berne, Switzerland.

Ives, J.D., and Messerli, B., 1989, *The Himalayan Dilemma: Reconciling Development and Conservation*, Routledge, London, UK.

Mihill, C., 1995, British major saved 20,000 in Croatia, *The Guardian*, 16 September.

Mishra, D.K., 1997, The Bihar flood story, *Economic and Political Weekly* (Bombay), **32**(35):2206–2217 (30 August).

Ney, S., and Thompson, M., 1999, Consulting the frogs: The normative implications of cultural theory, in M. Thompson, G. Grendstad, and P. Selle, eds, *Cultural Theory as Political Science*, Routledge, London, UK.

Pandey, B., 1994, Small rather than big: The case for decentralised power development in Nepal, *Water Nepal*, **4**(1):181–190.

Pandey, B., 1995, Because it is there: Foreign money, foreign advice and Arun-3, *Himal*, **8**(4)(July/August).

Rayner, S., and Malone, E.L., eds, 1998, *Human Choice And Climate Change: An International Assessment*, Vols. I–IV, Battelle Press, Columbus, OH, USA.

Schwarz, M., and Thompson, M., 1990, *Divided We Stand: Redefining Politics, Technology and Social Choice*, Harvester-Wheatsheaf, London, UK, and University of Pennsylvania Press, Philadelphia, PA, USA.

Shakya, S., 1998, Power development vision for the twenty-first century, *The Kathmandu Post*, 10 February.

Thompson, M., Ellis, R., and Wildavsky, A., 1990, *Cultural Theory*, Westview, Boulder, CO, USA.

Thompson, M., and Warburton, M., 1985, Uncertainty on a Himalayan Scale, *Mountain Research and Development*, **5**(2):115–135.

Thompson, M., Warburton, M., and Hatley, T., 1986, *Uncertainty on a Himalayan Scale*, Ethnographica, London, UK.

Vidal, J., 1995, Nepalese hail move to scrap huge dam, *The Guardian*, 5 August, p. 12.

Chapter 8

Border Crossings

Jeanne X. Kasperson and Roger E. Kasperson

In a world careening toward a single global economy and a relentlessly interactive world communication system and popular monoculture, it is apparent that, ever increasingly, the sources of health and environmental risks that confront individual nation-states and other political units lie beyond their political boundaries. Technological change – such as the creation of genetically modified organisms (GMOs) and innovations in cybernetic systems – proceeds with widening scales of impact and repercussions beyond national borders, and the effects are becoming ubiquitous worldwide (French, 2000). As symbolized by the political turmoil at the World Trade Organization (WTO) meetings in Seattle in the United States in 1999, international trade, finance, and resource regimes are assuming greater importance in the allocation of global risk. International risk management accords, such as the Kyoto Protocol to the United Nations Framework Convention on Climate Change and the harmonization of regulation in the European Community, portend significant international intrusion into the structure of national industrial systems and policy. Meanwhile, political change reveals divergent trends, as greater integration pertains in some arenas (e.g., the European Community), while greater political fragmentation prevails in many others (e.g., the new states of central Asia), amid a concurrent weakening of national state structure and a strengthening of nongovernmental civil society.

Despite these trends, risk scholars have accorded transboundary risks only limited attention. A host of questions surrounds the incidence, impacts, equity problems, societal responses, and management interventions for the control of transboundary risk. This chapter focuses on the complex dynamics of how the direct biophysical and economic risks associated with transboundary activities interact with social, psychological, and political processes to send signals about these border crossings and how they should be managed. We also explore how social institutions and management authorities process or might process these signals. Following an analytic framework developed in 1988 by Clark University researchers and Paul Slovic and his colleagues at Decision Research (Kasperson *et al.*, 1988; Kasperson, 1992), we envision this inquiry as an analysis of the "social amplification and attenuation" of transboundary risks. We then draw upon this analysis to address the implications of the risk dynamics involved for the communication and management strategies.

As to whether transboundary risks pose distinctive challenges, events over the past two decades have provided dramatic testimony to their far-reaching potential effects and associated management conundrums. The Bhopal accident was not only an Indian tragedy but a wrenching trauma for the global chemical industry as well (Bowonder *et al.*, 1985). In the United States, the Emergency Planning and Community Right-to-Know Act of 1986, passed as Title III of the Superfund Act (SARA), and the extraordinary post-Bhopal efforts of the US Chemical Manufacturers Association were direct results of the accident and its aftermath. Such risk-monitoring and risk-communication requirements were already formally in place in Europe, but the horror of Bhopal kept the implementation of the Seveso Directive high on the policy agenda. Moreover, the subsequent accidents at Sandoz and Chernobyl dispelled any perception that Bhopal could not have happened in Europe. The Chernobyl accident, for its part, removed an innocence concerning the possible reverberations and scale of a nuclear plant accident, and perhaps for technological accidents more generally. The transnational character of the Chernobyl fallout, and in particular the international incidence of hot spots, surprised all of Europe, bared in sharp relief the inadequacy of protective strategies, and may also have stamped indelible imprints upon public attitudes, in Europe and elsewhere, concerning nuclear power technology (Hohenemser and Renn,

1988; Renn, 1988). International efforts to clean up the Baltic have high-lighted the difficulties in implementing international regulatory regimes in countries with disparate economic priorities and capabilities even when broad consensus exists at the policy level (SEI, 1996; Greene, 1998), a situation that undoubtedly presages experience at the close of the 20th century with the faltering of the Kyoto Protocol and not-so-concerted in-ternational efforts to avert global climate change. The controversy during the 1990s with bovine spongiform encephalopathy (BSE), so-called mad cow disease (see Chapter 5), has demonstrated that the social amplification of risk surrounding the handling of the risks involved in an exported food commodity (British beef) can result in dramatic transboundary responses that threaten not only a pillar of a national economy but also stigmatize a national industry and erode social trust in experts and national regula-tory authorities (Powell *et al.*, 1997; ESRC, 1999; Granot, 1999). Finally, the ongoing debate over GMOs, and especially the differences between European and North American views of the risk involved, signals how differences in national risk assessment and regulatory practices can inter-act with broader cultural values and historical political tensions to place transboundary risks at the center stage of debate and conflict.

Here, using the social amplification of risk as a framework of analy-sis and drawing upon empirical evidence from recent examples of trans-boundary risk conflicts, we explore the nature of these growing chal-lenges. We argue that, as with other risk experience, this is not a single problem or challenge but that transboundary risks come in different com-plexes and forms. Distinguishing among them can provide greater clarity about the social amplification-of-risk processes that result and the fea-sibility and likely effectiveness of strategies of managerial intervention, including risk communication, public participation, and precautionary ap-proaches.

8.1 What Is Different about Transboundary Risks?

At first glance, transboundary risks are not much different from other risks. The dangers of industrial accidents, the movement of a radioac-tive plume, or the damage to health associated with ecological exposure to acid deposition do not change because differing political jurisdictions are present. Similarly, the unintended effects of the release of GMOs upon non-target species or upon agricultural systems will cross political jurisdictions. Threats to humans and their environments, in short, neither observe sovereignty nor respect political authority. In this respect, they evince some attributes of common-property resources (Cutter, 1993:67–68). In *World Risk Society*, Beck (1999) goes so far as to claim that "misery can be marginalized, but that is no longer true in the age of nuclear, chemical and genetic technology" (p. 61) and refers to the "border-transcending magnetism" (p. 143) of the risks of these technologies.

But on closer inspection, this simple view of risk dissipates. In fact, even for the direct potential impacts on health and ecosystems, location often matters greatly. Hazardous facilities may be intentionally located at the edges of political jurisdictions, either to export the risk to others (the classic example of this being the downstream contamination of rivers by upstream users), to capitalize on more permissive safety standards in an adjoining political system, or to exploit margins and peripheral regions because they are viewed as expendable and of little importance to political elites and central authorities. The US–Mexico borderland accommodates a remarkable constellation of hazardous *maquiladoras*, drawn to the Mexican side of the border by laxer safety standards and cheaper labor (Sanchez, 1990), whereas the depletion of the Aral Sea for irrigation to benefit the Soviet state through much of the past century represents a clear case of intentional exploitation of a peripheral region (Glazovsky, 1995). Our recent study of long-term environmental change in nine threatened regions around the world found that peripheral location and marginality near borders, whether geographical or sociopolitical, were major contributors to environmental degradation and to tardy and ineffective mitigative responses from central authorities and elites (Kasperson *et al.*, 1995, 1999).

Indeed, the nature of transboundary risks is such that the spatial separation between the area generating the risk and the areas exposed to potentially harmful consequences may exacerbate potential vulnerabilities, thereby increasing risk. As Beck observes, "Beyond the walls of indifference, danger runs wild" (Beck, 1992:46). If those at risk reside in one nation-state and are unaware, or less aware than their neighbors, of the threats posed by hazardous facilities or human activities in another nation-state, they may be ill-prepared for an accident. Emergency communication and response systems may run up against language and cultural barriers, and border-management systems may also be lacking or under-developed. All these deficiencies certainly complicated the Chernobyl accident. To the extent that knowledge of the risk is lacking, communications are vulnerable to boundary obstacles, and unless precautions have been taken for emergency preparedness, an accident or release is likely to produce greater adverse consequences than would otherwise be the case. Put another way, since risk is a joint product of perturbations and events, on the one hand, and the vulnerability of those at risk, on the other, transboundary situations may easily enlarge and exacerbate existing health and environmental risks.

Among the most telling attributes of transboundary risks is their great potential for the social amplification or attenuation of risk. If the source country of the risk and the recipient country have overlays of past conflicts, cultural differences, or ongoing tensions, even minor potential "exports" of risk may generate widespread media coverage, societal attention, public concern, and protests. Ordinary citizens, in short, may have extraordinary risk aversion to even the most minor risks emanating from another party whom they regard as hostile, uncaring, or just plain untrustworthy. Distrust centered on what is perceived to be a lack of competence by those managing the risk or a lack of concern for the health and safety of those across the border will surely heighten the volatility of risk questions and debate. The merest hint that the risk producers are cornering the benefits while transferring the risks to neighbors who receive no benefits is likely to rekindle old tensions and perhaps even generate new demands for compensation, greater risk control, or both. All the above are dramatically at work in public concerns over the "Frankenfoods" and "terminator technology" involved in the export of genetically modified (GM) foods by US corporations to European consumers.

Meanwhile, risk attenuation may also be at work. Where significant benefits accrue to the risk-source region while the risk consequences fall on extraregional peoples or places, managers of the exported risk may be less driven to expend scarce resources for risk control and minimization. Transboundary risks may even become bargaining chips in political negotiations surrounding broader and more complex arrays of interests, and in national differences in the framing of risk problems, assessment procedures, and alternative constructs of precaution. The public may also be less concerned if it knows that the consequences of an uncertain accident are likely to fall elsewhere. Thus, it is quite possible, perhaps even likely, that the processes of risk amplification and attenuation will be simultaneously at work with transboundary risks, with different intensities or effects apparent at different scales and layering of simultaneous amplification and attenuation, so that misperceptions, miscommunication, distrust, and conflict arise more readily and prove to be quite resistant to resolution or accommodation.

8.2 Classifying Transboundary Risks

What defining qualities of transboundary risks shape societal perceptions and responses? How can we usefully sort the apples and oranges in the "basket" of transboundary risks?

Historically, the Organisation for Economic Co-operation and Development (OECD, 1972) has distinguished two principal classes of international pollution:

- *Upstream–downstream pollution*: Upstream (or upwind) countries benefit from the natural export downstream (or downwind) of polluted water (or air), and downstream (or downwind) countries suffer from receiving it. Winners and losers are determined by fortune of location in relation to natural environmental flows and pathways. Upstream donors have little incentive (other than political good will) to control their pollution. Downstream recipients have no control over the pollution they receive, and they generally have a weak political bargaining position and must rely on good will, international pressure, or some trade-off bargaining with the polluter country.
- *Reciprocal pollution*: The costs and benefits of polluting processes are scattered throughout a number of countries, including the source country or countries. This most commonly occurs where the countries involved have unrestricted access to common resources such as air or oceans (which may be shared in practice, although in principle they are continuous, homogeneous, and indivisible). This is the most common form of international pollution, but effective solutions are generally elusive because unresolved conflicts and disagreements over the distribution of social and economic costs and benefits commonly persist.

Of course, a much broader array of transboundary risk situations abides beyond this simple dichotomy and its characteristic focus on one specific type of risk (pollution).

A closer look suggests that a robust classification needs to address a host of special considerations, including equity and fairness, differences in environmental standards, problematic institutional issues, and an apparent potential for the social amplification (or attenuation) of risk. The editors of this volume emphasize in particular whether the risk that crosses the border is a legitimate visitor or an unwelcome trespasser, and whether the very crossing implies the explicit consent of the country that experiences adverse risk consequences. Other distinctions – including the types of re-lease of pollutants, potential major accidents, and differing environmental effects and transport media – merit consideration as well. It has been sug-gested, for example, that a taxonomy of transboundary risks might treat types of risks, transport media, country characteristics, and national versus common-property resources (Linnerooth-Bayer, 1996:170).

Previous social studies of risk (e.g., Kasperson and Stallen, 1991; Rolén, 1996; Stern and Fineberg, 1996) have clearly affirmed the impor-tance of social and political context in risk assessment. Indeed, any mean-ingful discussion of analyzing and managing transboundary risk must be-gin with the explicit recognition that this is neither a single problem nor a single-context type of situation. Recognizing that all sorts of transbound-ary risks abound, we focus in this chapter primarily on those risks that cross national political boundaries. In keeping with the tenor of the vol-ume as a whole, then, we regard transboundary risks as risks that arise when human activities in one or more nation-states threaten current or future environmental quality, human health, or well-being in at least one other nation-state.

We next recognize four different transboundary risk situations, in which the differences entail important aspects of social context (*Fig-ure 8.1*). *Type 1, border-impact risks* involve activities, industrial plants, or developments in a border region that affect populations or ecosystems in the border region on both sides of the boundary. Although such risks, whether from accidents or routine releases, threaten inhabitants or ecol-ogy in this region, they usually do not involve long-distance transport or displacement of the risk. This type of transboundary risk typically is binational, although it may involve more than two countries if multiple boundaries happen to coalesce, as in the Upper Silesia–northern Bohemia

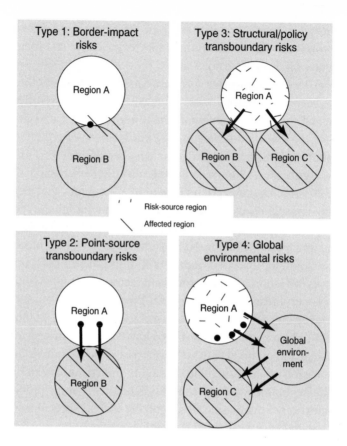

Figure 8.1. A fourfold classification of transboundary risks.

or the Aral Sea regions. Upstream–downstream problems or developments along a shared natural resource are not uncommon (Park, 1991). The development of the Gabcikovo–Nagymaros hydroelectric power stations on the border between Slovakia and Hungary illustrates this type of transboundary risk well, and the nature of the dispute between the two countries suggests the array of issues and dynamics of conflict that this type of transboundary risk often generates (Fitzmaurice, 1996; see also Chapter 6).

Type 2, point-source transboundary risks involve one or several clear point sources of potential pollution or accident that threaten an adjoining country or region (or several countries or regions). The concentration of the risk source at one or several clearly identifiable locations, whether situated close to the border or away from it, provides a sense of problem or focus for perception of risk. The Chernobyl accident, or course, was the archetype of such a risk situation, but Lithuania's Ignalina nuclear power plant and its threat to other Baltic states (see Chapter 2) and the Barsebäck nuclear plant in southern Sweden, once operating a scant 20 kilometers (km) from Copenhagen, exemplify this type of transboundary risk (Löfstedt 1996a, 1996b). Indeed, the Swedish government's 1997 decision to close the Barsebäck plant was motivated in no small part by the continuing public concerns in Denmark over the potential effects of a nuclear accident.

Type 3, structural/policy transboundary risks differ from the foregoing categories in that they involve less identifiable and more subtle and diffuse effects associated with state policy, transportation or energy systems, or the structure of the economy. Such risks typically cross boundaries uninvited, but they can enjoy varying degrees of hospitality, complicity, and consent from the affected countries. Here the stakes, and the risks, are much more dramatic, but access to the risk issues is often more indirect and opaque. Elsewhere, we have described these risks as one type of "hidden hazards" (Kasperson and Kasperson, 1991). The US decision to promote an automobile-based transportation system has had enormous implications for air pollution and acid precipitation in the United States and Canada. The coal-burning industrial structure in England has had extensive environmental effects in the form of widespread acid precipitation in northern Europe. The decision by France to become the nuclear state *par excellence* has imposed transborder risks on the rest of Europe. The forthcoming decisions by China as to the burning of its high-sulfur coal (and under what technological conditions) will have far-reaching implications throughout Asia and, of course, for the global environment itself. And the BSE controversy illustrates how risk management of potentially contaminated beef in the source country (the United Kingdom) and the transfer of risk through long-standing export patterns to European (and other) countries unleashed a worldwide ban and devastation of the British beef industry and subsequent controversy over the lifting of the ban and the assessment of continuing risk (ESRC, 1999; Granot 1999). Here the conflict drew from a history of previous and ongoing tensions between the United Kingdom and the continent.

Although ubiquitous and almost routine, risks in this class share formidable hurdles for risk communication and management. Issues concerning the mix of energy systems, the structure of the economy, and the public policies surrounding industrial ecology, consumption, and environmental protection are traditionally the prerogative of nation-states. Equally, the risks are typically pervasive but opaque – truly hidden hazards. How to communicate and manage such risks involves a quantum level of difficulty that exceeds the ambition of national risk programs and usually entails international negotiation and the construction of international risk regimes.

Type 4, global environmental risks present a still higher bar for risk assessment and management. What distinguishes this class of risks is that human activities in any given region or country, or set of regions and countries, affect many or all other countries or regions, often remote from the source country, through alterations of the global "systemic" environment (Turner *et al.*, 1990). Nearly always, multiple and diffuse sources combine to alter aspects of the global environment through complex pathways of biophysical change in which the exact nature of interactions and causes is highly uncertain. Similarly, although potential effects may be sometimes dramatic and possible to pinpoint by particular geographic distributions (e.g., effects of sea-level rise on the Maldive Islands or Bangladesh), more typically (as in climate change) the potential impacts are murky, the spatial resolution of precise effects poor, and winners and losers difficult to discern. In short, this category of transboundary risk, which rudely intrudes upon national risk agendas, embraces many of those issues most difficult to accommodate.

Increasingly, international regimes and institutions are occupying a central place in producing, structuring, and regulating this class of risks. The European Community, through its harmonization of economic, trade, and environmental policies, is assuming wide authority as a risk allocator and manager. The WTO's efforts to reduce trade barriers are not only opening new markets worldwide but are also generating concerns in many countries over potentially far-reaching impacts on the industrial and agricultural structures, food supply, and patterns of consumption, as well as the environment, many of which may not be to the advantage of the less developed countries. The implementation mechanisms of the Kyoto Protocol – especially the Clean Development Fund, emissions trading, and joint implementation – carry wide potential for international control over national developmental pathways, prompting some developing countries and nongovernmental organizations (NGOs) to charge "environmental colonialism" (Agarwal and Narain, 1999). These increasingly important shapers of worldwide risk patterns are difficult to classify on the involuntary/voluntary transboundary risk continuum. In the political turmoil that beset the 1999 WTO meetings, a primary locus of public controversy was the degree of coercion that some see the organization exercising over smaller states, as well as its alleged exclusion of non-state parties from processes that are rapidly becoming more open arenas for multiple interests and advocates beyond the traditional economic representatives from nation-states.

8.3   The Social Amplification of Risk

The concept of risk amplification and attenuation proceeds from the thesis that risk events, defined very broadly, interact with psychological, social, institutional, and cultural processes in ways that can either heighten or dampen perceptions of risk and shape the risk behavior of institutions, groups, and individual people (*Figure 8.2*). Behavioral responses, in turn, generate secondary and tertiary social or economic consequences, which extend far beyond direct harm to human health or the environment to include significant indirect impacts such as liability, insurance costs, loss of confidence in institutions, stigmatization, or alienation from community affairs (Kasperson *et al.*, 1988; Kasperson, 1992).

Such secondary effects can (in the case of risk amplification) trigger demands for additional institutional responses and protective actions, or, conversely (in the case of risk attenuation), place impediments in the path of needed protective actions. In this usage, "amplification" is a generic term referring to both intensifying and attenuating signals about risk. Thus, alleged "overreactions" of people and organizations receive the same attention as alleged "downplaying."

Risk, in this view, is in part biophysical threats of harm to people and in part a product of social experience and the social processing of risk signals. Hence, all hazardous events are "real": they involve not only transformations of the physical environment or human health as a result of continuous or sudden (accidental) releases of energy, matter, or information, or reports on such transformations, but also perturbations in social and value structures. These events remain limited in the social context unless they are observed by human beings and communicated to others

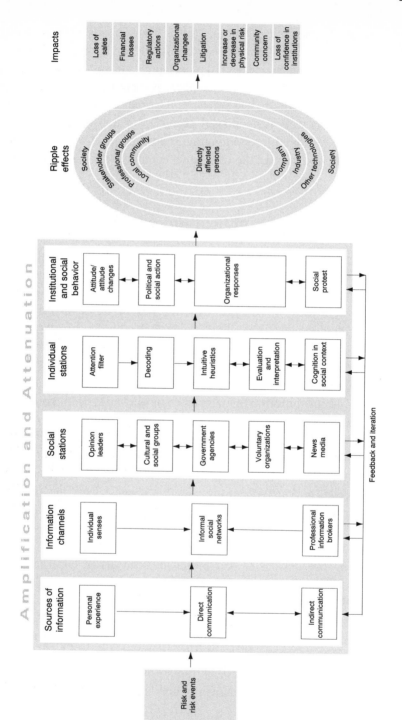

Figure 8.2. The social amplification and attenuation of risk: A conceptual framework.

(Luhmann, 1986:63). The consequences of this communication, the subsequent reframing of risk signals at other social stations, and subsequent social interactions may lead to other physical and socioeconomic transformations, such as changes in technologies, changes in methods of land cultivation, changes in the composition of water, soil, and air, or effects on institutions. The experience of risk is, therefore, both a matter of physical harm and the result of culture and social processes by which individuals or groups acquire or create interpretations of risks. These interpretations provide rules of how to select, order, and explain signals that emanate from the risk experience. Additionally, each cultural or social group selects certain risks and adds them to its strand of worry beads to rub and burnish even as it shuts out other risks as not meriting immediate concern.

The amplification process can take many different paths. It may start with either a physical event (such as an accident), claims by environmental groups, or a report on an environmental or technological risk. Some organizations and individuals also, of course, actively monitor the experiential world, searching for risk events related to their agenda of concerns. In both cases, individuals or groups select specific characteristics of these events or aspects of the associated depictions and interpret them according to their perceptions and mental schemes. They also communicate these interpretations to other individuals and groups and receive interpretations in return. Social groups and individuals process the information, locate it on their agenda of concerns, and may engage in risk-related behavior. Some may change their previously held beliefs or gain additional knowledge and insights and be motivated to take action. Others may use the opportunity to compose new interpretations that they send to the original sources or other interested parties. Still others may find the new information as confirming long-held views of the world and its order.

The individuals, groups, or institutions who collect information about risks communicate with others and through behavioral responses act, in our terminology, as *amplification stations*. It is obvious that social groups or institutions can amplify or attenuate signals only by working in social aggregates and participating in social processes, but individuals in groups and institutions act or react not merely in their roles as private persons but also according to the role specification associated with their positions. Amplification may therefore differ among individuals in their roles as private citizens and in their roles as employees or members of social groups and organizations.

Social institutions and organizations also occupy a primary role in society's handling of risk, whether internal or transboundary in nature, for it is in these contexts that many risks are conceptualized, identified, measured, and managed (Short, 1992:4). In postindustrial democracies, large organizations – multinational corporations, business associations, and government agencies – largely set the contexts and terms of society's debate about risks. These organizations vary greatly in their goals for and commitments to risk management. Freudenburg (1992:13–14) has called attention to breakdowns in internal organizational communications as a contributor to the bureaucratic attenuation of risk, as occurred in the minimization and suppression of a potential risk alert during the early signals from BSE cases. Other studies (e.g., Kasperson and Kasperson, 1993) reveal that large corporations develop very different kinds of organizational cultures that shape their ability to identify and assess the risks of their products and determine if and how these risks will be communicated to other social institutions and the public.

Risk issues are also an important element on the agendas of NGOs concerned with environmental and health issues. The nature of these groups is important in the framings and social constructions of the risk problem and the types of rationality brought to interpretation and to preferred management strategies. To the extent that risk becomes a central issue in a political campaign or a source of contention among social groups, it will be brought to greater public attention and often imbued with value-based interpretations. Polarization of views and escalation of rhetoric by partisans typically occur, and new recruits are drawn into the conflict. These social alignments about risk disputes often outlive a single case and become anchors for subsequent risk episodes, setting the stage for new risk controversies.

Role-related considerations and membership in social groups shape the selections of information that individuals regard as significant. People frequently ignore or attenuate interpretations or signals that are inconsistent with their beliefs or that contradict their values. If the opposite is true, they may well magnify, or amplify, the interpretations, signals, or both. The process of receiving and processing risk-related information by individuals is well researched in the risk-perception literature (Slovic, 1987; Freudenburg, 1988). But this is not sufficient: individuals also act as members of cultural groups and larger social units that codetermine the dynamics and social processing of risk. In this framework, we term these larger social units *social stations of amplification*. Individuals in their roles as members or employees of formal organizations, social groups, or other institutions not only follow their personal values and interpretative patterns, they also perceive risk information and construct the risk "problem" according to cultural biases and the rules of their organization or group (Johnson and Covello, 1987).

Both the information flow depicting the risk or risk event and the associated behavioral responses by individuals and other social stations of amplification generate secondary effects that extend beyond the people directly affected by the original hazard event or report. Secondary impacts include such effects as enduring public perceptions and attitudes, impacts on the local or regional economy, political and social pressure, social disorder, changes in risk monitoring and regulation, increased liability and insurance costs, and repercussions on other technologies. Secondary impacts are, in turn, perceived by social groups and individuals so that additional stages of amplification may occur to produce higher-order impacts. The impacts thereby may spread, or "ripple," to other parties, distant locations, or future generations. Each order of impact will not only disseminate social and political impacts but may also trigger (in risk amplification) or hinder (in risk attenuation) positive changes for risk reduction. The concept of social amplification of risk is hence dynamic, taking into account the continuing learning and social interactions resulting from social experience with risk.

The analogy of dropping a stone into a pond (see *Figure 8.2*) illustrates the spread of these higher-order impacts associated with the social amplification of risk. The ripples spread outward, first encompassing the directly affected victims or the first group to be notified, then touching the next higher institutional level (a company or agency), and, in more extreme cases, reaching other parts of the industry or other social arenas with similar problems. This rippling of impacts is an important element of risk amplification since it suggests that the processes can extend (in risk amplification) or constrict (in risk attenuation) the temporal and geographical scale of impacts.

8.4 Inequity and Distrust: Contributors to the Social Amplification of Transboundary Risks

Since the distinctiveness of transboundary risks, we have argued, arises in part from their unusual potential for social amplification and attenuation, some exploration is needed of the social properties that affect how social institutions and cultural groups process such risks. Two major factors that appear to have particular capability for contributing to social amplification and attenuation are the risk inequities that are involved in the "export" of risk and the distrust that may underlie or accompany risk incidence across boundaries. We begin with some conceptual discussion of the issues that each poses.

8.4.1 Inequity

Challenging complexities and ambiguities surround inequity problems embedded in transboundary risk conflicts. The causes of environmental degradation lie rooted in a variety of basic driving forces, such as agriculture, industrial ecology, population growth, and urbanization. The transforming economies of eastern and central Europe add additional complex problems of social and economic justice. Beneficiaries and motivations are often difficult to discern, and interactions with the physical environment may be poorly understood and highly uncertain. Those likely to be most affected across political boundaries or in other states are often only dimly perceived, and little may be known of their values, capabilities, or living circumstances. Past international conflicts may add an overlay of sociopolitical isolation and tensions.

Then, too, there are the complexities and ambiguities attached to the notion of equity itself (Kasperson, 1983). Equity means different things to different people. Although it is often conceived as the "fairness" of a particular arrangement, the standards and underlying principles of fairness vary. Some see it as a concordance between benefits and burdens; others, as an allocation of burdens to those best able to absorb or deal with them. Some view equity as primarily concerned with the substantive outcomes of an activity or project; others as concerned with the procedures used to make the allocations. What is clear is that equity involves both matters of fact and matters of value, and it is an artifact of culture. And if equity is to be confronted explicitly in fashioning international initiatives for the management of transboundary risk, it will need to capture the diversity of values underlying different perceptions of responsibilities and goals. Whether or not a single principle or set of principles can win endorsement across political boundaries remains in question, and debates about inequity hold great potential for entering into and significantly contributing to the social amplification of risk in transboundary risk debates. In Chapter 5, Wynne and Dressel argue that even though the precautionary principle enjoys wide acceptance in Britain and on the continent, the BSE controversy spawned a myriad of framings of this principle and its application. Similarly, it also highlighted major differences in approaching uncertainty, especially between Britain and Germany.

Transboundary risk controversies may well pose several different types of equity problems, so some conceptual clarification and background are germane. To begin, equity may be defined as the fairness of both the process by which a particular decision or policy is enacted and the associated outcomes. This suggests that any full analysis of equity needs to consider both distributional and procedural equity.

The primary equity issue in transboundary risk situations is likely to be the spatial (i.e., geographical) pattern of benefits and eventual harms associated with a particular set of activities. Thus economic activities can, in principle, be compared as to their spatial pattern of harmful and beneficial impacts among states or other jurisdictions. In simple cases, these empirical patterns serve as a basis for making inferences about the obligations and responsibilities (if any) that beneficiaries have for those harmed and the adequacy of legal structures and institutional mechanisms for meeting these responsibilities. In the siting of a hazardous-waste facility, for example, it is increasingly common to enlist a variety of means to compensate local host communities for bearing estimated risk impacts.

But assessing the geographical distribution of potential transboundary impacts will often be sufficiently complex and uncertain to challenge even carefully developed empirical studies. Estimating such inequities will involve, for example, defining the proportion of lake acidification in Sweden resulting from coal burning in Poland, placing a value on the resulting ecological damage, estimating the probability that an accident at the Ignalina nuclear plant will cause radiological damage in Sweden, defining the distribution of future beneficial and adverse economic impacts that will result from the Gabcikovo–Nagymaros project, or judging the damage attributable to unintended changes in species composition associated with the use of genetically modified organisms in agriculture. In a study of the distributional equity outcomes associated with the West Valley nuclear waste reprocessing plant in the United States, Kates and Braine (1983) found themselves able to provide only a qualitative set of judgments about the magnitude of effects on local, state, and national political jurisdictions. There are very few examples of careful empirical assessments of distributional outcomes associated with the kinds of transboundary risks that are the subject of this volume. Mounting such assessments across political boundaries may prove intractable, as differences in concerns over the risks, variations in assessment methodologies, and conflicting approaches to estimating uncertainty exist will greatly complicate this task and the likely acceptance of findings.

Scoping out the equity assessment is also problematic and likely to spark debates, even about what issues and what history are relevant for equity discussions. Equity, it can be argued, cannot be assessed solely within a particular regime or policy arena. It is inappropriate to divorce coal burning from other types of environmental change and past inequities involved in the previous transboundary interactions of peoples, nations, and economics. Indeed, it will not be surprising if the type of transboundary equity problem that generates greatest concern is the one that has received the least attention, what we refer to as *cumulative geographical inequity*. New inequities that correlate with other past inequities suffered by disadvantaged societies, societies in transition, or marginal groups are particularly pernicious, because their effects are likely to be synergistic and not simply additive. Previous inequities are also almost certain to have increased the vulnerability of some groups to new projects. Thus it should not be surprising when countries of Central and Eastern Europe and those in the Third World object vehemently to admonitions from the Nordic countries, Western Europe, or the United States to reduce future fossil-fuel emissions in order to preserve or improve the well-being of the rest of Europe or the globe as a whole. Cumulative geographical inequities, in short, may well be expected to form the core of many debates over transboundary risks and enter into the suitability or preferability of particular policy options. Moreover, those inequities may be highly relevant to strategies for managerial intervention – particularly, determining who should pay for reducing transboundary risks and where control should be vested in the regulatory regime.

The *procedural equity* of the processes by which transboundary environmental problems have arisen and by which they may be resolved differs from distributional equity issues. Here the concern is with the adequacy and appropriateness of the decision processes and political regimes that have created the risks. People living today, it can be argued, were not part of the considerations involved in decision making or the self-interest that externalized damage and burdens on other places, groups, and generations. Established international institutional mechanisms for addressing such procedural inequities are unavailable, undeveloped, or highly contentious. So achieving procedural equity will be one of the most complex problems surrounding the management of transboundary risks.

8.4.2 Distrust

Addressing transboundary risks that are feared, that overlay previous histories of conflicts and other inequalities, and that contain complex equity considerations calls for high levels of social trust across transboundary participants so that management interventions can go forward. *Social trust*, in our usage, refers to the expectation that other persons, institutions, or states in a social relationship can be relied upon to act in ways that are competent, predictable, and caring (Kasperson *et al.*, 1992). *Social distrust*, equally, is the expectation that other persons, institutions, or states in a social relationship are likely to act in ways that are incompetent, unpredictable, uncaring, and thus probably inimical.

Four key dimensions of social trust, in our view, enter into range and depth of trust-related behavior, and all are highly relevant to the social-amplification processes surrounding transboundary risk situations. Each dimension can play an important role in the development and maintenance of social trust; none is sufficient in itself, however, to ensure the existence of such trust. These four dimensions are as follows:

- *Commitment.* To trust implies a certain degree of vulnerability of one individual or group to another, to an institution, or to another social and political system. Thus, trust relies on perceptions of an uncompromised commitment to a mission or goal (such as protection of the public health) and fulfillment of fiduciary obligations. Perceptions of commitment rest on perceptions of objectivity and fairness in decision processes and on the provision of accurate information.

- *Competence.* Trust is gained only when an institution or another government in a social relationship is judged to be reasonably competent in its actions over time. Although expectations may not be violated if these institutions or governments are occasionally wrong, consistent failures and discoveries of unexpected incompetence and inadequacies can lead to a loss of trust. With regard to the cases treated in this volume, risk managers and institutions responsible for transboundary risks must show that they are technically competent in their mandated area of responsibility.
- *Caring.* Perceptions that an institution or government will act in a way that shows concern for and beneficence toward trusting individuals are critical. Perceptions of a caring attitude are an especially important ingredient where individuals must depend upon authorities in other societies who control the generation of risk. Obviously such perceptions are difficult to achieve even within a nation-state; trust in those who have no formal accountability to individuals cannot be expected to come easily.
- *Predictability.* Trust rests on the fulfillment of expectations and faith. Consistent violations of expectations nearly always result in distrust.

Public perceptions, specific situational contexts, and general societal factors all play important roles in the development of social trust. Thus, the nature of an individual's past interaction with organizations, with social institutions as a whole, and with other societies involved in the transboundary risk will be major influences on the existence of social trust. The degree of trust or distrust that prevails, in turn, will play a major role in the dynamics of social amplification and attenuation of the transboundary risk issues.

8.5   Social Amplification of Transboundary Risks: Cases in Point

The transboundary risk cases treated in this volume provide evidence concerning the social amplification and attenuation processes described above, and we turn to them for preliminary exploration of what can be learned from an initial set of cases.

In Chapter 2, Löfstedt and Jankauskas ask, Why are the Swedes and the other European nations so concerned about Ignalina? Indeed, the question is quite relevant, for despite this Lithuanian nuclear power plant's having design similarities to the Chernobyl plant, the Swedish Nuclear Inspectorate had, by 1995, already allocated 90 million Swedish krona (SEK) to upgrading safety at Ignalina, which funded improvements in fire protection, early-warning radiation systems, monitoring of metal strength, enhancement of operating procedures and maintenance, and establishment of a Lithuanian nuclear inspectorate modeled on the Swedish system. And another SEK 70 million had been allocated for the 1995–1996 budget year. Meanwhile, the plant itself sits a full 700 km from the Swedish coast, which, the Chernobyl accident notwithstanding, affords a substantial cushion of distance from accident risks.

The high level of public concern is, apparently, an artifact of the social amplification of the risk. It is quite evident that even in advance of a serious (or perhaps even minor) accident that would drive levels of public concern and reaction even higher, significant risk amplification has already occurred. The authors report, for example, substantial public worry in Malmö, Sweden, over environmental problems – especially acid rain and industrial wastes – originating in Eastern Europe. One in five respondents in an open-ended solicitation of problems cited "unsafe nuclear power plants." Concerns were even higher about coal burning and acid rain, and fully 92% of the respondents supported Sweden's giving environmental aid to Eastern Europe, with a primary motivation being to protect the Swedish environment from damage.

These concerns among the public appear to outstrip apprehensions among Swedish policymakers, but significant worry exists there as well, particularly among those at the national level. As one environmental spokesperson put it, "... we are heavily affected by transboundary environmental problems. I am especially worried about unsafe nuclear power stations and acid rain. Look what happened with Chernobyl." The social dynamics that have created the high levels of concern among the public and policymakers alike cannot be judged from the data presented, particularly in the absence of any extensive recent media coverage (although Chapter 2 does refer to continuous media reports in the early 1990s about the safety problems of Ignalina). And, of course, virtually all Swedes know for a fact that Swedish lakes have registered dramatic adverse effects as a result of coal burning in Poland. The linkage of the Ignalina plant to the disastrous impacts of Chernobyl, threats of terrorism at the plant, and the pollution of the Baltic more generally all may play a role. Elements of social distrust are also undoubtedly present, as Swedish officials and the public have reservations concerning the competence of Lithuanian managers to operate the Ignalina plant safely. But exactly how media coverage, distrust, concern over nuclear plant risks, and the memorability of the Chernobyl accident interact to shape Swedish perceptions of the transboundary risk posed by the Ignalina plant remains opaque at present.

In contrast to the Swedish response, elements of *both* social amplification and attenuation of risk are apparent in Lithuania. The Lithuanian media have, particularly since Lithuanian independence, given extensive attention to the problems of the Ignalina plant and the risks that it poses. All respondents in the survey of public perceptions in Kaunas had heard of the Ignalina plant, and imagery centered on the problems and perceived lack of safety of the plant. The reality of a Russian-built plant in Lithuania clearly enhanced the negative imagery. Distrust of the responsible authorities was also quite apparent: 63 of 100 respondents in Kaunas reported a lack of trust, although different dimensions or bases for the distrust appeared to be present. Moreover, since Kaunas respondents were concerned about environmental problems generally, it may well be that both the Ignalina plant problems and coal burning are linked to this more generalized concern.

Despite these elements of social amplification in the media, negative imagery, and the distrust of the responsible authorities, attenuation of the risk has also apparently occurred. In an open-ended question of concerns about environmental problems, nuclear power scored well down the list. Generally, Kaunas respondents were more concerned about local problems than transboundary risks, a pattern also apparent among the Lithuanian policymakers interviewed. Most Kaunas respondents opposed closing the Ignalina plant, with many citing the need for electricity as a primary reason. And since the Russians were blamed for imposing the plant on Lithuanians to begin with, many saw the Lithuanians as hapless victims (of Russian transboundary incursions) rather than villains responsible for exporting risk to Sweden.

The Gabcikovo–Nagymaros hydroelectric power plant controversy (see Chapter 6) illustrates several other features of the social amplification of transboundary risks. Environmental activism played a critical role in this controversy, with 60,000 people participating in a 1990 protest rally, and with environmentalists from Austria, Czechoslovakia, and Hungary coalescing into a coordinated political force. Meanwhile, the controversy itself was part of a larger political evolution in Hungary, since it offered a primary means of expressing opposition to the government. Indeed, the amplification potential of the Gabcikovo–Nagymaros conflict waxed and waned in relation to broader political changes in Hungary (Fitzmaurice, 1996). It is clear that social amplification of risk can be heavily influenced by the extent of its incorporation into broader social and political movements.

And by ideology as well. In Chapter 6, Vari and Linnerooth-Bayer show that the public debate over the risks of the dam project became linked to two ideological paradigms. In Hungary, the dam system became so much a symbol of the old regime that opposition became entwined with broader political reform. In Slovakia, in contrast, the project became a symbol of national pride and economic progress. The paradigm divergence provided a political overlay contributing to greater polarization in perception and social valuation of the risk, whereas the lack of international institutions made the emerging conflicts difficult to overcome or resolve.

Transboundary air pollution, an archetypal Type 3 case in our classification, displays a number of distinctive assessment and management challenges associated with its patterns of social amplification, as suggested by Patt (see Chapter 4). Given the importance that notions of equity and fairness take on in a situation with a high national stake in the economic activities generating the pollutants and the far-reaching nature of the effects, as with acid deposition, it is not surprising to witness significant influences on the types of assessments undertaken and the underlying rationale for taking management actions. In the case of acid rain in Europe, the source and type of assessments became very important. The Regional Acidification INformation and Simulation (RAINS) model was adopted as the basis of assessment in no small part because it emerged from an international research institute, IIASA (the International Institute for Applied Systems Analysis), and so could be viewed as more politically neutral than a model generated within one of the contending nations. Similarly, given the diversity of value perspectives pervading the transboundary context of acid rain, a management approach that had the appearance of being based in natural sciences, rather than being a choice among contending values or conceptions of equity, easily won favor. This approach allowed contending countries to justify adoption of the critical-loads targets on quite different bases and rationales – as Patt puts it, a "bright line" on which consensus could be won – including substantial impact reduction (science) sought in Scandinavia, the appearance of avoiding action in the United Kingdom and Germany, and ideological reasons in the Soviet Union. In short, the complexity and intensification of this type of transboundary situation may well shape the types of assessment and management approaches likely to be successful.

The 1986 Chernobyl accident, in our classification a dramatic example of Type 2 transboundary risks, showed significant amplification and attenuation of the risk occurring simultaneously among different elements of the public and different groups within particular nations. Differing patterns of social trust and credibility undoubtedly abetted the marble-cake mix of amplification and attenuation. According to one study (Peters *et al.*, 1987), 60% of all Germans surveyed viewed the federal government and other official institutions as having been totally or partially trustworthy. Public opinion polls in France and Italy revealed that 70% or more of the public distrusted and lacked confidence in official government information sources. In Sweden and the Netherlands, in contrast, trust levels appear to have been higher than in many other parts of the European Community. As Otway *et al.* (1987) point out, the competing and often conflicting information provided by adversarial interest groups and stakeholders compounded the distrust problem and contributed to public misperceptions and confusion. Exploiting Chernobyl either to protect or attack national nuclear energy programs produced a great range of conflicting information and interpretations of the accident and fallout threats (Hohenemser and Renn, 1988). In the welter of discordant communication, unreliable sources often commanded as much or more credibility as reliable sources. During the unfolding of the post-accident responses, industry quickly lost much of its credibility, and governmental sources were not far behind.

The accident suggests that conflicting stances by officials in different nations or political jurisdictions in providing risk information, explaining the risk, and recommending protective actions in transboundary risk settings can easily spawn public misperception, confusion, and distrust. Yet consistency in management responses to risk across national political boundaries will be difficult, perhaps impossible, to achieve. It is also clear that *anticipatory* or pre-emergency communication and education are essential to securing a basic level of preparedness among the potentially affected public. Models for such preparedness programs, including needed communication systems, have been well developed for major industrial accidents, including nuclear mishaps (Sorensen and Mileti, 1995). Although it is a generic risk-communication issue, the need to put transboundary risk and protective measures into context was driven home in the aftermath of the Chernobyl fallout. Quantitative information on risk is unlikely to have the desired effects absent the means to help the public understand the data and to connect the data to protective actions. Finally, it is apparent that in many transboundary settings the public will distrust official information sources across boundaries regardless of how well they do their job. Creative measures to maintain or increase trust and confidence before and during an emergency may need to be a part of transboundary risk-communication programs.

The more recent experiences with the so-called mad cow disease scare in the United Kingdom and the ongoing controversy over GM foods are highly suggestive of both the growing importance of transboundary risks and how volatile they may be (Tait, 1999). The BSE case provides additional confirmation of how transboundary risk setting can complicate risk management and drive social amplification of the risk as a result of differences in risk-assessment practices. In Chapter 5, Wynne and Dressel show, for example, that the United Kingdom's approach to uncertainty demands the specification of the risk mechanism or damage pathway and concrete identification of uncertainties, whereas practices on the continent, and especially in Germany, accord more credence to abstract "theoretical" risks. Furthermore, continental traditions have involved substantial integration of the social and the natural sciences, whereas assessment practices in the United Kingdom have been strongly rooted in the physical sciences and empirical analyses. This setting facilitated the rapid resort to characterizations in the United Kingdom of European risk managers, and especially those in Germany, as "unscientific" and prone to "overreaction" and "hysteria." In turn, continental perceptions emphasized the lack of precautionary procedures in the United Kingdom, given a food-supply risk fraught with poor knowledge and high uncertainty.

Whereas the BSE case entails considerable "risk amplification mirroring," as noted above, it also suggests the propensity of conflict over transboundary risks to escalate latent patterns of historical tensions and distrust into overt conflict. In doing so, it points to the high potential of transboundary risks to drive stigmatization processes. So while British consumers' trust in their own officials' management of BSE risks underwent a dramatic decline between 1991 and 1995, the 1996 European Union (EU) ban on the movement of all live cattle of British origin unleashed nationalistic loyalty and a fury of anti-EU sentiment in the United Kingdom and, subsequently, a powerful backlash from European countries (see Chapter 5). The furor of media coverage and loss of credibility of British risk managers drove further escalation of risk concerns and caused extensive damage to the "identity" of British beef, whereas the rising political mistrust and misunderstanding undermined whatever basis might have existed for creating common approaches to risk management.

Some of these same connections between transboundary risks and social amplification processes are apparent in the controversy over the export of GM foods from the United States to Europe. Specifically, transboundary effects are apparent in the risk assessment process, patterns of distrust, and stigmatization of GM foods. As Levidow notes in Chapter 3, European regulatory approaches perforce have had to proceed in the face of divergent accounts of the risk and differing notions of sustainable agriculture (Persley and Siedow, 1999). Debates have involved varying assessments of the scope of "indirect adverse effects" of GM crops, with Denmark, France, and the United Kingdom all moving toward greater use of value judgments (see Chapter 3). Even here, however, individual nations have interpreted the precautionary principle in different ways to justify their own policy stances on the use of GMOs or living modified organisms (LMOs). And surely the fact that the United States, and a US corporation (Monsanto), has been in the lead in the use of GM foods builds upon historical antipathy to the "invasion" of US fast foods and popular culture on the European continent. But it is also the case that these intercontinental conflicts become more intractable as a result of the difference in US regulatory approaches to GM foods and agricultural strategy, in which the United States emphasizes earlier approval and a less precautionary strategy than that prevailing in Europe. Then, too, the transboundary setting facilitates the entrance of a diversity of highly contentious value positions (Stirling and Mayer [1999] found, for example, no fewer than 117 criteria emerging in judgements about GM crops and other alternatives). Meanwhile, by the 1980s a maturing European political movement had already succeeded in stigmatizing GM foods, so that current labeling strategies represent not only a means for making risk more voluntary but a powerful means for extending the visibility of the stigma (i.e., the marking).

From the exploration of empirical evidence concerned with the social amplification and attenuation of transboundary risks, we identify several propositions that merit testing in further research:

- Compared with other risk problems, transboundary risks have distinctive properties likely to intensify the social amplification and attenuation of risk, enlarging the gaps between expert assessment and public perceptions and making them more volatile and difficult to manage.
- Because transboundary risks occur across national risk management programs with varying approaches to and practices of assessment, values will pervade assessment procedures and interact with other dimensions of political conflict.
- A "mirror" structure in social processing of risk is likely to be a common pattern in such situations, with social attenuation in the risk-source region and social amplification in the risk-consequence region.
- This "mirror" structure will frequently be accompanied, and further complicated, by a scale-related "layering" of intensity of effects, with attenuation most pronounced at the local scale and amplification most pronounced at the national scale.
- Equity problems and social distrust will play a more powerful role in the social amplification of transboundary risks than they do with most other types of risk problems, and risk amplification may reveal an intensification of asymmetrical influence of trust-building and trust-destroying events.
- Contextual effects, particularly those involving previous political animosities and ongoing sociopolitical movements, will more extensively shape the social dynamics of risk amplification and attenuation than with other types of risk.

In the next section, we consider the implications of the attributes of transboundary risk for risk communication and management.

8.6 Managing and Communicating Transboundary Risks

Since, as we note above, communicating to the public *within* a country or *across* borders about the same transboundary risk raises a number of different problems, it is appropriate to distinguish among these problems. We enlist our fourfold categorization of transboundary risks to examine communication and management challenges, as summarized in *Table 8.1*.

8.6.1 Border-impact risks

Although border-impact risks take many forms, they typically have their greatest impacts in the border regions. They also commonly occur in frontier areas on the periphery of states or political jurisdictions, areas often viewed as marginal or expendable by the state or political elites at the center. Disputes over natural resources present at the boundary are common, as the many international conflicts over upstream–downstream uses of rivers, diversion of waters, rights to fishing grounds located just outside territorial limits, or border locations for hazardous industries suggest. Borders will continue to be targets for the siting of hazardous industrial facilities, because of either their peripheral situation or their status as the meeting ground that divides differing legal or economic systems (and, thus, many involve differing regulatory structures or contrasting labor costs). Disputes over border developments have a strong potential for amplification of risks through connections to national political movements and agendas, as occurred at the Gabcikovo–Nagymaros hydroelectric power plant project on the Hungary–Slovakia border (see Chapter 6). Linkages with national politics may provide an overlay to escalating polarization in risk perception and social response to the risk, thereby adding to the obstacles to arriving at binational or multinational agreement over the project.

Concerning risk communication about this category of risks, certain problems (e.g., language barriers, cultural differences, institutional fragmentation) common to many transboundary risks are likely to be present. Institutional structures, regulations, and standards will often vary on opposite sides of a border. The strategy, level, and content of communication will often need to diverge. Political groups within each country may exploit boundary risk issues for national agenda setting.

Much will depend upon the nature of relations between the two adjoining states and the nature of relations among groups or interests within

Table 8.1. Communicating risks across borders: A profile of differentiated challenges.

Type of transboundary risk	Nature of hazard	Affected public	Key communication issues
Border-impact risks	Hazards usually localized in border regions; conflicts over resource use, allocation, or depletion; impacts often near-term in nature	Concentrated among border peoples, with more diffuse impacts at regional or national levels; potential perception of threats to national security	Hostile relations between boundary states may impede communication; past history important; interests of ethnic subgroups may be present
Point-source transboundary risks	Clearly identifiable risk source(s); distance decay of effects may occur; accidents and toxic releases dominant problem	Layered impacts, some in proximate location, others in more distant locations across borders; benefits dissociated from risk, raising equity problems	Identifiable and visible risk sources; emergency preparedness and warning systems important; trust issues often involved; risks may be strongly socially amplified
Structural/policy transboundary risks	Diffuse and opaque risk sources; long delay in emergence of hazards and lag times in effects common; diffuse management responsibility	Highly distributed within risk-source state and affected transborder areas; future generations may be major risk bearers	Few rights for redress currently exist; difficult to link risks with economic structure or public policy; linkages to future impacts often opaque
Global environmental risks	Highly variable though potentially catastrophic; long time lines; widely distributed risk sources; large uncertainties; effects on global commons	Often remote in space and time; winners and losers often opaque; conflicting values and priorities surround risks and benefits; risks overlay other socioeconomic problems; vulnerable groups	Few established transborder communication links; hazards accumulate slowly; episodic extreme events; equity and distrust problems exacerbate effects

the boundary area itself. The risk debate may easily mirror or take on ingredients of these ongoing relations, especially if long-standing tensions and conflicts are in play. Issues of distrust or inequity in such situations may generate intense amplification. On the other hand, if binational relations have long been amicable, as is true of the Great Lakes management regime in North America (Beierle and Konisky, 1999), then an innovative participatory approach to transboundary risk regime building may become possible.

8.6.2   Point-source transboundary risks

The Chernobyl experience typifies, if in extreme form, this class of transboundary risk. A few dominant sources of risk, readily identifiable, define the risk situation. From a management perspective, efforts can focus on ameliorating the risk. It may even be comparatively easy to identify winners and losers. From a communications perspective, consultations and negotiations with the peoples at risk from the concentrated risk source are advisable.

As with all transboundary risks, significant impediments may be present. Difficulties in communicating across jurisdictions will still prevail. Lack of trust in the safety management at the facility may intensify public concerns over hazards and generate significant social amplification of the risks. Past tensions or hostilities may erode even well-intentioned communication efforts by the risk-source country. Nonetheless, of the four types of transboundary risks we have identified, this is likely the easiest to manage, although risk-communication discussions in the aftermath of Chernobyl suggest this is not always the case.

8.6.3   Structural/policy transboundary risks

Arguably, this may be the most difficult and formidable arena for transboundary risk management and communication. First, the sources and causes of the hazards are typically multiple, diffuse, indirect, and opaque. The structure of an economy focused on heavy manufacturing, using high inputs of energy and exercising few environmental controls, as occurred with Soviet policy in Russia and Eastern Europe, has pervasive and long-term effects. Agricultural systems supported by high chemical inputs may have to endure long-term environmental effects, and, probably, reduced crop yields as well. The extensive import by China of highly inefficient and polluting automobiles from Singapore and elsewhere has environmental ramifications in Korea, Japan, and globally. National population policies, despite their evident roles as "drivers" of environmental change, remain the prerogative of individual nation-states. GM foods regulated and exported through existing international agreements represent a new transboundary risk issue of high volatility and one almost certain to remain contentious far into the future.

Such transboundary matters did not preoccupy international risk-management regimes during the second half of the 20th century. Indeed, the Science Advisory Board of the US Environmental Protection Agency (USEPA, 1987) concluded that further progress on environmental protection in the United States depended on a shift of focus from "end-of-pipe" cleanup to intervention in the structure of the economy and basic social and economic policy. But these issues will be very much on national and international environmental agendas in the 21st century. Since national economic policies and structures have been extensively protected by national sovereignty, they have thus far largely escaped extranational intervention. But as the environmental interdependence of nations becomes progressively more visible, questions of national security, as has already happened, will be progressively linked with environmental cooperation. This will inevitably cause states to confront both basic policies and structures of economy and trade policies, and the growth of nongovernmental actors and global civil society may well challenge existing national and international regimes and institutions in these risk arenas. These transboundary risks, in short, may have a "forcing" potential for institutional change.

Meanwhile, transboundary risk issues remain formidable in their own right. Linking environmental and human health effects with different mixes of energy systems, transportation choices, social-welfare arrangements, aging populations, or urbanization policies entails a level of assessment beyond the capability of most current approaches to risk analysis. Imagine communicating about risk "residuals" that involve such a complex array of economic, social, and health effects. Putting risk "in context," in the current fashion, will be an interesting challenge to the assessors. Communicating the assessment results and linking them to policy choice and to diverse and far-flung publics will likely confound the most optimistic of risk communicators. Yet, arguably, this may be the most important of the transboundary risk problems.

8.6.4   Global environmental risks

The distinctive property of these risks, which share much in common with the previous class of transboundary risks, is that they produce their effects through alteration of the global risk system as a whole. For the purpose of this analysis, we treat what elsewhere we term "cumulative global environmental risks" (Turner *et al.*, 1990) as falling within our Type 3 risks discussed above.

Again, the major risk sources are associated with basic population and economic structures and policies. But the environmental effects are registered through alterations of basic biogeochemical flows, particularly when human alterations produce larger fluctuations than those attributable to natural variability. The obstacles confronting risk communication are imposing: the risk sources are widely distributed and historically cumulative, the links between human activities and changes in climate, atmosphere, oceans, and biosphere generally are opaque and poorly understood, large uncertainties complexify the pattern of effects, the links between risk sources and affected peoples are often remote in space and time, and management options lie embedded in larger problems of growing global inequalities and conflicting views of responsibility and values. The ramifications, or "signals," of emerging risks are often episodic, shrouded by expert debate and disagreement, and prone to unwelcome future surprises.

Communicating about such risks is already under way in various countries. Interestingly, a highly interactive global mass media and Internet system may work to overcome the plethora of hurdles that might impede recognition by the world's people of their common stake in addressing these issues. As a Gallup Poll of members of the public in 24 countries unexpectedly demonstrated, concern about environmental degradation throughout the world is much more pronounced than might have been expected (Dunlap *et al.*, 1993). And there are indications that threats to the planetary environment as a whole may constitute a special category of concerns to members of the public throughout the world. Perhaps, as our study of nine environmentally threatened regions throughout the world abundantly suggests (Kasperson *et al.*, 1995), the particular problem of communicating such risks lies less with evoking public concern than with mobilizing and articulating such concern through national political systems focused on differing economic and political goals and possessing very different political cultures.

So managing transboundary risks clearly entails different complexes of problems. Although significant progress in national programs and international legal regimes is evident in particular regions and risk domains, current efforts are but the early stage in what is a rapidly growing collection of international regimes (Victor *et al.*, 1998). As with many other international environmental risk problems, the *rate* of the mounting challenge will continue to pose daunting challenges to these emerging international responses. At the same time, it is apparent that an international imperative to communicate at least certain types of risks across national borders is routinely interwoven into the international fabric of risk responsibilities. At the end of January 2000, delegates from 135 countries produced a new biosafety protocol to regulate the transboundary movement of GMOs, now LMOs (Blassing, 2000). The Cartagena Protocol on Biosafety (IER, 2000; also http://www.biodiv.org/biosafe/protocol) speaks to a global awareness and willingness to share the risks (and benefits) of an eminently transboundary risk. The document may well validate a claim that "a plural world citizenship is soaring with the wind of global capitalism at its back" (Beck, 1999:17). To be sure, "informed consent" and democratic principles figure prominently. The tremendous growth in NGOs worldwide and communications technology, especially the Internet, is providing infrastructure to this changing ethic. Yet the rapid growth in transboundary risks is clearly substantially outpacing managerial responses and policy innovations.

References

Agarwal, A., and Narain, S., 1999, Kyoto Protocol in an unequal world: The imperative of equity in climate negotiations, in K. Hultcrantz, ed., *Towards Equity and Sustainability in the Kyoto Protocol*, Stockholm Environment Institute, Stockholm, Sweden.

Beck, U., 1992, *Toward a New Modernity*, Sage Publications, London, UK.

Beck, U., 1999, *World Risk Society*, Polity, London, UK.

Beierle, T.C., and Konisky, D.M., 1999, Public Participation in Environmental Planning in the Great Lakes Region, Discussion Paper 99–50, September, Resources for the Future, Washington, DC, USA.

Blassing, R., 2000, Countries agree on Biosafety Protocol regulating transboundary movements of GMOs, *International Environment Reporter*, **23**(3):71–72.

Bowonder, B., Kasperson, J.X., and Kasperson, R.E., 1985, Avoiding future Bhopals, *Environment*, **27**(7):6–13, 31–37.

Cutter, S.L., 1993, *Living with Risk: The Geography of Technological Hazards*, Edward Arnold, London, UK.

Dunlap, R.E., Gallup, G.H., Jr., and Gallup, A.M., 1993, *Health of the Planet: Results of a 1992 National Opinion Survey of Citizens in 24 Nations*, George H. Gallup International Institute, Princeton, NJ, USA.

ESRC (Economic and Social Research Council) Global Environmental Change Research Programme, 1999, *The Politics of GM Food: Risk, Science and Public Trust*, Special Briefing No. 5, University of Sussex, Falmer, Brighton, UK.

Fitzmaurice, J., 1996, *Damming the Danube: Gabcikovo and Post-Communist Politics in Europe*, Westview Press, Boulder, CO, USA.

French, H.F., 2000, *Vanishing Borders: Protecting the Plant in an Age of Globalization*, Earthscan, London, UK.

Freudenburg, W.R., 1988, Perceived risk, real risk: Social science and the art of probabilistic risk assessment, *Science*, **242**:44–49.

Freudenburg, W.R., 1992, Nothing recedes like success? Risk analysis and the organizational amplification of risk, *Risk: Issues in Health and Safety*, **3**(3):1–35.

Glazovsky, N., 1995, The Aral Sea, in J.X. Kasperson, R.E. Kasperson, and B.L. Turner, II, eds, *Regions at Risk: Comparisons of Threatened Environments*, United Nations University Press, Tokyo, Japan.

Granot, H., 1999, Facing catastrophe: Mad cows and emergency policy-making, *International Journal of Mass Emergencies and Disasters*, **17**(2):161–184.

Greene, O., 1998, Implementation review and the Baltic Sea regime, in D. Victor, K. Raustiala, and E.B. Skolnikoff, eds, *The Implementation and Effectiveness of International Environmental Commitments: Theory and Practice*, MIT Press, Cambridge, MA, USA.

Hohenemser, C., and Renn, O., 1988, Chernobyl's other legacy: Shifting public perceptions of nuclear risk, *Environment*, **30**:4–11, 40–45.

IER (International Environment Reporter), 2000, Text: Final draft of Biosafety Protocol approved at Montreal meeting on Biological Diversity Convention, January 29, *IER*, **23**(3):125–134.

Johnson, B.B., and Covello, V.T., eds, 1987, *The Social and Cultural Construction of Risk*, Reidel, Dordrecht, Netherlands.

Kasperson, J.X., and Kasperson, R.E., 1993, Corporate culture and technology transfer, in H. S. Brown, P. Derr, O. Renn, and A. White, *Corporate Environmentalism in a Global Economy*, Quorum Books, Westport, CT, USA.

Kasperson, J.X., Kasperson, R.E., and Turner, B.L., II, eds, 1995, *Regions at Risk: Comparisons of Threatened Environments*, United Nations University Press, Tokyo, Japan.

Kasperson, R.E., ed., 1983, *Equity Issues in Radioactive Waste Management*, Oelgeschlager, Gunn, and Hain, Cambridge, MA, USA.

Kasperson, R.E., 1992, The social amplification of risk: Progress in developing an integrative framework of risk, in S. Krimsky and D. Golding, eds, *Social Theories of Risk*, Praeger, Westport, CT, USA.

Kasperson, R.E., and Kasperson, J.X., 1991, Hidden hazards, in D.C. Mayo and R. Hollander, eds, *Acceptable Evidence: Science and Values in Hazard Management*, Oxford University Press, Oxford, UK.

Kasperson, R.E., and Stallen, P.-J., eds, 1991, *Communicating Risks to the Public: International Perspectives*, Kluwer, Dordrecht, Netherlands.

Kasperson, R.E, Renn, O., Slovic, P., Brown, H., Emel, J., Goble, R., Kasperson, J.X., and Ratick, S., 1988, The social amplification of risk: A conceptual framework, *Risk Analysis*, **8**(2):177–187.

Kasperson, R.E., Dominic G., and Tuler, S., 1992, Social distrust as a factor in siting hazardous facilities and communicating risks, *Journal of Social Issues*, **48**(4):161–187.

Kasperson, R.E., Kasperson, J.X., and Turner, B.L., II, 1999, Risk and criticality: Trajectories of regional environmental degradation, *Ambio*, **28**(6):562–568.

Kates, R.W., and Braine, B., 1983, Locus, equity, and the West Valley nuclear wastes, in R.E. Kasperson, ed., *Equity Issues in Radioactive Waste Management*, Oelgeschlager, Gunn, and Hain, Cambridge, MA, USA.

Linnerooth-Bayer, J., 1996, Fairness in dealing with transboundary risks, in R. E. Löfstedt and G. Sjöstedt, eds, *Environmental Aid Programmes to Eastern Europe*, Avebury Studies in Green Research, Ashgate, Aldershot, UK.

Löfstedt, R., 1996a, Fairness across borders: The Barsebäck nuclear power plant, *Risk: Health, Safety & Environment*, 7(2):134–144.

Löfstedt, R., 1996b, Risk communication: The Barsebäck nuclear plant case, *Energy Policy*, **24**(8):684–686.

Luhmann, N., 1986, *Ökologische Kommunikation*, Westdeutscher Verlag, Opladen, Germany.

OECD (Organisation for Economic Co-operation and Development), 1972, *Problems of Trans-Frontier Pollution: An OECD Record of a Seminar on the Economic and Legal Aspects of Trans-Frontier Pollution*, OECD, Paris, France.

Otway, H., Hasstrup, P., and Cannell, W., 1987, *An Analysis of the Print Media in Europe Following the Chernobyl Accident*, Joint Research Centre of the Commission of the European Community, Ispra, Italy.

Park, C., 1991, Trans-frontier air pollution: Some geographical issues, *Geography*, **76**(335-1):21–35.

Persley, G.J., and Siedow, J.N., 1999, *Applications of Biotechnology to Crops: Benefits and Risks*, Issue Paper no. 12 (December), Council for Agricultural Science and Technology, Ames, IA, USA.

Peters, H.P., Albrecht, G., and Hennen, L., 1987, *Reactions of the German Population to the Chernobyl Accident: Results of a Survey*, Jül-Spez-400/Translation (May), The Nuclear Research Centre Jülich, Jülich, Germany.

Powell, D., and Leiss, W., with Whitfield, A., 1997, Mad cows or crazy communication?, in *Mad Cows and Mother's Milk: The Perils of Poor Risk Communication*, McGill-Queen's University Press, Montreal, Quebec, Canada.

Renn, O., 1988, Public responses to Chernobyl: Lessons for risk management and communication, in *Uranium and Nuclear Energy: 1987*, The Uranium Institute, London, UK.

Rolén, M., 1996, *Culture, Perceptions, and Environmental Problems: Interscientific Communication on Environmental Issues*, Swedish Council for Planning and Coordination of Research, Stockholm, Sweden.

Sanchez, R.A., 1990, Health and environmental risks of the maquiladora in Mexicali, *Natural Resources Journal*, **30**(1):163–186.

Short, J.F., 1992, Defining, explaining, and managing risks, in J.F. Short and L. Clarke, eds, *Organizations, Uncertainties, and Risk*, Westview Press, Boulder, CO, USA.

Slovic, P., 1987, Perceptions of risk, *Science*, **236**:280–285.

Sorensen, J.H., and Mileti, D.S., 1995, Pre-emergency information programs for accidents at nuclear power plants, in D. Golding, J.X. Kasperson, and R.E. Kasperson, eds, *Preparing for Nuclear Power Plant Accidents*, Westview Press, Boulder, CO, USA.

Stern, P.C., and Fineberg, H.V., eds, 1996, *Understanding Risk: Informing Decisions in a Democratic Society*, National Academy Press, Washington, DC, USA.

Stirling, A., and Mayer, S., 1999, *Rethinking Risk: A Pilot Multi-Criteria Mapping of a Genetically Modified Crop in Agricultural Systems in the UK*, SPRU, University of Sussex, Falmer, Brighton, UK.

SEI (Stockholm Environment Institute), 1996, *Baltic 21: Creating an Agenda 21 for the Baltic Sea Region, Main Report*, SEI, Stockholm, Sweden.

Tait, J., 1999, *More Faust than Frankenstein: The European Debate About Risk Regulation for Genetically Modified Crops*, SUPRA Paper no. 6, August, Scottish Universities Policy Research and Advice Network (SUPRA), University of Edinburgh, Edinburgh, Scotland.

Turner II, B. L., Kasperson, R.E., Meyer, W.B., Dow, K., Golding, D., Kasperson, J.X., Mitchell, R.C., and Ratick, S.J., 1990, Two types of global environmental change: Definitional and spatial issues in their human dimensions, *Global Environmental Change*, **1**(1):14–22.

US National Research Council, 1989, *Improving Risk Communication*, National Academy Press, Washington, DC, USA.

USEPA (United States Environmental Protection Agency), 1987, *Unfinished Business: A Comparative Assessment of Environmental Problems*, USEPA, Washington, DC, USA.

Victor, D.G., Raustiala, K., and Skolnikoff, E.B., eds, 1998, *The Implementation and Effectiveness of International Environmental Commitments: Theory and Practice*, MIT Press, Cambridge, MA, USA.

Chapter 9

Public Participation across Borders

Ortwin Renn and Andreas Klinke

9.1 Introduction

Transboundary risks have gained significant public attention over the past decade, particularly since the Chernobyl accident and the resulting spread of nuclear fallout throughout Europe. In addition, the recent debate about global climatic changes and the ongoing debate about acid rain have contributed to a worldwide awareness about cross-national risks. The issue of transboundary risk touches upon the main concepts of fairness and equity (Renn *et al.*, 1996). The risks originate in one country, the effects materialize in another country. There are controversies about the health impacts, long-term consequences, institutional trust, cultural values, and economic disadvantages associated with transboundary risks. However, the main focus of the debate is on institutional mechanisms that guarantee international cooperation and trust (Slovic *et al.*, 1993). Hence the perceptions of risk and fairness are the driving agents of the debate.

Honest and effective risk communication is an important prerequisite for promoting the necessary institutional means for international cooperation and trust building. Informing the public in all affected countries may help to clarify the issues involved, but it cannot resolve international conflicts about risks, particularly if benefits and risks are distributed unequally among the affected populations. Furthermore, cultural differences, differences in legal and political traditions, and divergent value commitments and interests of the general public tend to lead to intense conflicts between national governments and between the affected populations on both sides of the national boundaries. Resolving these conflicts necessitates a process in which stakeholders and affected citizens are given the opportunity to take part in the decision. Cooperation of citizens beyond national boundaries is a rarely disputed goal among risk managers (Fiorino, 1990; Renn et al., 1993). There is, however, a controversy about the desirable structure and appropriate process of participation. Furthermore, the role of the public and its mandate in decision-making processes are highly debated (Dienel, 1978; Barber, 1983; Pollak, 1985; Lynn, 1986; Kasperson, 1986; Chen and Mathes, 1989; Fiorino, 1989; Renn et al., 1991). In addition, the legal and political regulations with respect to transboundary risks leave little space for extended cross-national participation projects. Are there any means available to address these transboundary risks in a democratic fashion? Is it possible to involve citizens in a decision-making process that spans national boundaries?

The fact that public participation has become a relevant subject in the international political discourse illustrates one of the main items at the Fourth Ministerial Conference about the Environment for Europe, held in Aarhus, Denmark, in June 1998.[1] About 54 environment ministers were involved in an extensive debate about a Convention on Access to Information, Public Participation in Decision-Making and Access to Justice in Environmental Matters. Such a convention should include rights of citizens and nongovernmental organizations (NGOs) with respect to access to information on the environment, participation through hearings in environmental decisions, and access to justice. As a result, many citizens of countries in both the East and West, as well as NGOs, would be enabled to affect the environmental decision-making processes.

In this chapter, we focus on the structural conditions and requirements for organizing public participation processes. First we analyze the structure and functions of risk debates and explore styles of argumentation characterizing three different levels of such debates. Second, we propose a model for public involvement that we believe is appropriate for cross-national risk management. Third, we discuss the possibilities for implementing such a model given the legal and political constraints of international regimes. Before reaching our final conclusions, we briefly summarize the results of two case studies: one that can be interpreted as a success story and the other an example of a failure to find a satisfactory solution to transboundary risk problems. The long-term cooperation between the United States and Canada concerning freshwater resources illustrates what conditions need to be met to initiate successful participation across borders. In contrast, the case of the Mochovce nuclear power plant near the Austrian–Slovak border demonstrates the difficulties and obstacles that impede the establishment of public participation across borders.

9.2   The Three Levels of Risk Debate

Before looking at the requirements for useful international risk debate, it is important to focus on the substance of risk debates in general. Although topics vary from risk source to risk source, most risk debates reflect three major issues (Funtowicz and Ravetz, 1985; Rayner and Cantor, 1987):

- Factual evidence and probabilities
- Institutional performance, expertise, and experience
- Conflicts about worldviews and value systems

Figure 9.1 is a graphical representation of this model using a modified version of the original categories (taken from Renn and Levine, 1991). The first level of risk debate involves factual arguments about risk probabilities and the extent of potential damage. If the problem is a lack of technical knowledge on the part of the public, procedures should focus on informing the public about the consensual expert opinions. In this case, participation is equivalent to successful risk communication. While scientists and risk managers are most comfortable with this type of debate, it is rare in real-life conflicts.

The second, more intense level of debate concerns institutional competence to deal with the risks. At this level the focus of the debate is on the distribution of risks and benefits, and the compatibility of the proposed solution with current economic and social conditions. This type of debate does not rely on technical expertise, although reducing scientific uncertainty may be helpful. The emphasis on personal and institutional judgments and experience requires more than risk communication; it needs

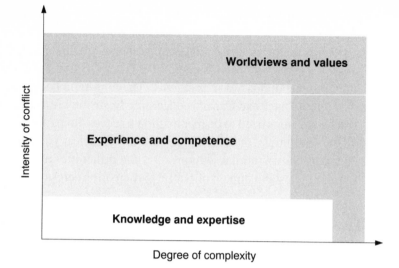

Figure 9.1. The three levels of concern in risk debates.

input from stakeholder groups and affected populations. Approval in this situation is gained by showing that the risk management institution has been competent, effective, and open to public demands.

At the third level the conflict is defined by different social values and cultural lifestyles and their impact on risk management. In this case, neither technical expertise nor institutional competence and openness are adequate conditions for public involvement. Decision making here requires a fundamental consensus on the issues that underlie the risk debate. The nature of the discussion and conflict resolution methods should vary depending on the level at which the risk debate takes place. As long as value issues remain unresolved, even the best technical expertise and the most profound competence cannot overcome social, cultural, and political value conflicts. There is, however, a strong tendency for risk management agencies to reframe higher-level conflicts as lower-level ones: third-level conflicts are presented as first- or second-level conflicts, and second-level conflicts are presented as first-level ones. This is an attempt to focus the discussion on technical evidence, in which the agency is fluent (Dietz *et al.*, 1989). Citizens who participate in the discourse are thus forced to use first-level (factual) arguments to rationalize their value concerns. Unfortunately, this is often misunderstood by risk managers as "irrationality"

Table 9.1. Rules of a rational discourse.

Rule setting	Reaching consensus on the procedure the participants want to employ to derive the final decision or compromise, such as majority vote or involvement of a mediator (Majone, 1979)
Evidence	Basing factual claims on the "state of the art" of scientific knowledge and other forms of legitimate knowledge; in the case of scientific dissent, all relevant camps should be represented (Rushefsky, 1984)
Argumentation	Interpreting factual evidence in accordance with the laws of formal logic and argumentative reasoning (Habermas, 1971)
Disclosure of values	Disclosing the values and preferences of each party, thus avoiding hidden agendas and strategic game playing (Renn, 1986)
Fair bargaining	Attempting to find a fair solution whenever conflicting values or preferences occur, including compensation or other forms of benefit sharing (Bacow and Wheeler, 1984)

on the part of the public. Frustrated, the public retreats to due process and routinization of the process, void of any substance, and ends up being disillusioned with and distrustful of the system.

9.3 Coping with Risk: Conditions for a Rational Discourse

There is a need for a structure or organizational model of risk debates that acknowledges the conditions of the respective risk arena and addresses all three levels of risk conflicts. Most authors agree that such a debate should be organized according to the rules of a rational discourse (see McCarthy, 1975; Habermas, 1984; Bacow and Wheeler, 1984:190–194; Kemp, 1985; Burns and Überhorst, 1988; Fiorino, 1990; Renn, 1992). A rational discourse is defined as a communication process in which all affected parties resolve a conflict or engage in joint problem solving using a specific set of rules. These rules are summarized in *Table 9.1*.

The success or failure of a rational discourse depends on many factors. The following conditions are among the most influential:

(1)   *Time.* A discourse cannot be organized in a week or even a month. It is advisable to allocate sufficient time for a discourse before the actual decision has to be made. This is not always politically feasible, because many decisions have to be made instantaneously. Most siting conflicts, however, have provided evidence that delays in the decision process resulting from insufficient consultations with the affected parties are much longer than the preparation time needed to organize a discourse prior to the decision (Kasperson, 1986).

(2)   *Openness of result.* A discourse will never accomplish its goal if the decision has already been made (officially or secretly) and the purpose of the communication effort is to "sell" this decision to the other parties. Individuals have a good sense of whether a decision maker is really interested in their point of view or if the process is meant to pacify potential protesters (Fiorino, 1989).

(3)   *Equal position of all parties.* A discourse needs the climate of a "powerless" environment (Habermas, 1984). This does not mean that every party has the same right to intervene or claim a legal obligation to be involved in the political decision-making process. However, the internal rules of the discourse have to be strictly egalitarian; every participant must have the same status in the group and the same rights to speak, make proposals, or evaluate options (Kemp, 1985). Two requirements must be met: First, the decision about the procedure and the agenda must rely on consensus; every party needs to agree. Second, the rules adopted for the discourse must be binding for all members, and no party is allowed to claim any privileged status or decision-making power. The external validity of the discourse results are, however, subject to all legal and political rules that are in effect for the topic in question.

(4)   *Willingness to learn.* All parties have to be ready to learn from each other. This does not necessarily imply that they have to be willing to change their preferences or attitudes. Conflicts can be reconciled on the basis that parties accept other parties' positions as a legitimate concern without giving up their own point of view. Learning in this sense entails

- recognition of different forms of rationality in decision making (Perrow, 1984; Habermas, 1984);

- recognition of different forms of knowledge, whether systematic, anecdotal, personal, cultural, or folklore wisdom (Habermas, 1971);
- willingness to subject oneself to the rules of argumentative disputes, that is, to provide factual evidence for claims, to obey the rules of logic for drawing inferences, to disclose one's own values and preferences vis-à-vis potential outcomes of decision options, etc.

(5) *Resolution of allegedly irrational responses.* Discourses in which the public interest groups or affected individuals are represented frequently demonstrate a conflict between two contrasting modes of evidence: the public refers to anecdotal and personal evidence mixed with emotional reactions, whereas the professionals play out their systematic and generalized evidence based on abstract knowledge (Lynn, 1986; Keeney and von Winterfeldt, 1986; Dietz *et al.*, 1989). A dialogue between these two modes is rarely accomplished because experts regard the personal evidence as a typical response of irrationality. The public representatives often view the experts as uncompassionate technocrats who know all the statistics but couldn't care less about a single life lost. This conflict can only be resolved if both parties are willing to accept the rationale of the other party's position and to understand and maybe even empathize with the other party's view (Bacow and Wheeler, 1984:191; Zeiss, 1989). If over the duration of the discourse some familiarity with the process and mutual trust among the participants have been established, role-playing can facilitate that understanding. Resolving alleged irrationalities means discovering the hidden rationality in the argument of the other party.

(6) *De-moralization of positions and parties.* The individuals involved in a discourse should agree in advance to refrain from moralizing about each other or each other's position (Bacow and Wheeler, 1984:191). Moral judgments on positions or persons impede compromise. Something cannot be 30% good and 70% bad; either it is good, bad, or indecisive. As soon as parties start to moralize about positions, they can no longer make trade-offs between their "moral" position and the other parties' "immoral" positions without losing face. A second undesired result of moralizing is the violation of

the equality principle stated above. Nobody can assign equal status to a party that is allegedly morally inferior to the other parties involved. Finally, moralizing masks deficits of knowledge and arguments. Even if somebody knows nothing about a subject or has only weak arguments to support his or her position, assigning blame to other actors and making it a moral issue can help to win points in the public arena (Scheuch, 1980). Many parties in a discourse try this route if they feel they are not being taken seriously or their rationality is not accepted. Given that conditions (1)–(5) are met, there is a good chance that participants will voluntarily agree to refrain from the "unfair" instrument of moralization. The absence of moralizing about other parties or their position does not mean refraining from using ethical arguments, such as "this solution does not seem fair to future generations," or "we should conserve this ecosystem for its own sake." Ethical arguments are essential for resolving environmental disputes.

9.4   Coping with International Constraints: Requirements for Understanding and Performance

When a discourse involves cross-national participation, additional requirements need to be taken into account. Since discourse is based on language, all participants must be able to communicate with each other and to understand subtle differences in wording and phrasing. Furthermore, understanding implies not only the recognition of meaning but also the detection of common metaphors, cultural idioms, and hidden messages. One of the main problems in international negotiations has been the misunderstanding resulting from translations and their interpretations by the various actors.

In addition to language problems, participants in cross-national panels face the difficulty of basing their interpretations and recommendations on the social and political structures that they are familiar with (see Chapter 2 and Chapter 6). For example, in a Canadian–US workshop on coastal management, the US participants from various citizen initiatives took it for granted that they represented the "public," whereas the Canadian participants regarded themselves as members of interested parties. It took quite a while before the two groups of participants agreed on a common role and self-image (Great Lakes, 1987).

A major problem of transboundary participation concerns the cultural, political, and social differences and peculiarities of each country involved in the process. People have different perceptions of the legitimacy of decision-making processes, have different aspirations with respect to the input of experts and stakeholder groups, and differ in their confidence in regulatory agencies. Furthermore, they have different attitudes toward the risk issues or objects in question. Cross-cultural studies on the perception of risk and risk management are rare. Recently, an edited volume containing five empirical studies on risk perception was published, shedding some light on the question of whether risk perception can be traced to universal human traits or to culturally specific factors (Renn and Rohrmann, 2000). The wealth of knowledge gained from the studies in this book and from other recent investigations has demonstrated clearly that neither the claim of irrationality as the main source of intuitive risk perception nor the claim of a deterministic relationship between universal risk characteristics and perceived risk can be sustained in light of the empirical evidence presented. Although risk perceptions differ considerably among social and cultural groups, there also appears to be an agreement about the genuine nature of risk perception. More specifically, the meaning of risk is multifaceted, and beliefs about the causes and circumstances of risk tend to be integrated into a consistent belief system that might guide or even "override" the evaluation of hazard-specific information. Rather than evaluating risk with a single formula, most people use a set of multiple attributes, many of which make normative sense.

This insight into risk perception has major implications for transboundary participation. Although the international scientific communities performing risk analyses may agree that policies should be based on the quantitative assessment of probabilities and harm, people in all cultures use additional criteria for evaluating different options with uncertain impacts, particularly if the risks refer to health or environmental damage. Some of these criteria, such as the capability of individuals or social institutions to control risks, can be found in almost any country in which such research has been conducted. Others are specific to the culture or political system of each participating country. The German Scientific Advisory Council on Global Change (WBGU) recently published a list of evaluative criteria to be used as universal yardsticks for evaluating global transboundary risks (WBGU, 1999). These universal criteria need to be enriched with the specific criteria that each participating country or culture decides to add to the list. It is essential that the relevant attributes and values used by people in each culture (and also each subculture) in appraising various options for risk management are taken into consideration when making judgments about the acceptability of technologies or environmental policies. This is why models of transboundary participation should include an analysis of the values and criteria that each participating group shares with its own people.

Any participation procedure, regardless of whether it applies to national or international issues, must have an addressee to whom recommendations are directed. This is particularly difficult in the case of a transboundary risk issue. In some instances, joint governmental commissions are already in existence and have the power to promulgate new regulations. In other instances it might be necessary to use regional bodies, or to have subnational or national governments set up temporary boards or commissions to act as mediators between the participatory bodies and the legal decision makers. A third possibility would be a direct mandate by each government for the various participatory bodies. The discourse organizers also need to allocate sufficient clout to the recommendations of the discourse participants; although it may not be possible to make the recommendations legally binding, it is essential that all participants and observers gain the impression that the recommendations will be implemented if technically and politically feasible, as has happened in the case of the Black Forest participation (Carius *et al.*, 1997). Ignoring recommendations or changing them without a compelling reason is worse than having no discourse at all.

A discourse among participants from different countries and cultures requires a rather stringent structure with respect to goals, procedures, and nature of recommendations. It needs to address public concerns as they are represented in each participating country, to collect local knowledge from each participant's perspective, to take into account different cultural traditions, and to exchange arguments among the various stakeholder groups. These goals can be achieved only if the following conditions are met:

- A *clear mandate for the discourse participants.* What are the discussion topics? What is the product that they are asked to deliver?
- A *clear understanding of the options and permissible outcomes of such a process.* If, for example, the site for a risk-producing facility has already been chosen, the discourse can only focus on issues such as choice of technology, emission control, and compensation.
- A *predefined time table.* It is necessary to allocate sufficient time for all the deliberations, but a clear schedule including deadlines is required to make the discourse effective and product oriented.
- A *mutual understanding of how the results of the discourse will be integrated into the decision-making process of the regulatory agency.* As a tool in the pre-decisional phase of policy formation, the recommendations cannot serve as binding requests. Rather they should be regarded as consultancy reports similar to reports from the scientific consultants who articulate technical recommendations to the legitimate public authorities. Official decision makers need to acknowledge and to process the reports by the discourse panelists, but they are not obliged to follow their advice. However, the process will fail in its purpose if deviations from the recommendations are neither explained nor justified to the panelists.

The mediator who facilitates such a process should be neutral in his or her position on the siting question and respected by all participants. Any attempt to restrict the maneuverability of the mediator should be strictly avoided.

9.5   A Three-Step Model of Public Involvement

Is there any procedure that would meet the requirements for such a discourse and at the same time ensure the incorporation of expertise, social values, and international experiences? Many models for public participation that promise to facilitate a rational discourse have been suggested in the literature (Crosby *et al.*, 1986; Kraft, 1988; Burns and Überhorst, 1988; Chen and Mathes, 1989; see reviews in: Nelkin and Pollak, 1979; Pollak, 1985; Fiorino, 1990; Renn *et al.*, 1995).

A detailed discussion of these models is beyond the scope of this chapter. Instead, we focus on one hybrid model of citizen participation that we have termed "cooperative discourse." With several modifications,

this model has been applied to studies on energy policies and waste disposal issues in West Germany, waste-disposal facilities in Switzerland,
and sludge-disposal strategies in the United States (Renn *et al.*, 1985,
1989; 1991; 1993). The model entails three consecutive steps:

(1) *Identification and selection of concerns and evaluative criteria.* The
     identification of concerns and objectives is best accomplished by
     asking all relevant interest groups (i.e., socially organized groups
     that are or perceive themselves to be affected by the decision) to re-
     veal their values and criteria for judging different options. It is cru-
     cial that all relevant value groups be represented and that the value
     clusters be comprehensive and include economic, political, social,
     cultural, and religious values. Only by explicit discussion about
     these values can intercultural dialogue work. The value-tree analysis
     technique has proved appropriate for eliciting the values and criteria
     for such a list (von Winterfeldt and Edwards, 1986; von Winterfeldt,
     1987; Keeney *et al.*, 1987). The resulting output of such a value-tree
     process is a list of hierarchically structured values that represent the
     concerns of all affected parties.

(2) *Identification and measurement of impacts and consequences re-
     lated to different policy options.* The evaluative criteria derived from
     the value tree are operationalized and transformed into indicators by
     the research team or an external expert group. These operational def-
     initions and indicators are reviewed by the discourse participants.
     Once approved by all parties, these indicators serve as criteria for
     evaluating the performance of each policy option on all value di-
     mensions. Experts from various academic disciplines with diverse
     perspectives on the topic of the discourse are asked to judge the
     performance of each option on each indicator. For this purpose, a
     modification of the Delphi method has been developed and applied
     (Webler *et al.*, 1991). This method is similar to the original Delphi
     format (Turoff, 1970), but is based on group interactions instead of
     written responses. The objective is to reconcile conflicts about fac-
     tual evidence and reach an expert consensus via direct confrontation
     among a heterogeneous sample of experts. The desired outcome is
     a specification of the range of scientifically legitimate and defensi-
     ble expert judgments and a distribution of these opinions among the

expert community, with verbal justifications for opinions that deviate from the median viewpoint.

(3)   *A rational discourse with randomly selected citizens as jurors and representation of interest groups as witnesses.* The last step is the evaluation of potential solutions by one group or several groups of randomly selected citizens (Dienel, 1978, 1989). These panels are given the opportunity to evaluate and design policy options based on the knowledge of the likely consequences and their own values and preferences. The participants are informed about the options, the evaluative criteria, and the consequence profiles. The representatives of interest groups and the experts take part in the process as witnesses; they provide their arguments and evidence to the panels, who ultimately decide on the various options. This deliberation process takes time: citizen panels are conducted as seminars over three to five consecutive days. All participants are exposed to a standardized program of information, including hearings, lectures, panel discussions, videotapes, and field tours. The process is similar to a jury trial, with experts and stakeholders as witnesses and advisers on procedure as "professional" judges.

Figure 9.2 illustrates the functions and procedure of this model. The figure shows that all three groups (experts, interest groups, and the general public) play a role in each step, but that they are encouraged to impact the decision process with the specific knowledge in which they are most proficient. This division of labor provides a check-and-balance process and a sequential order for multiple actor involvement.

Organizing a cooperative discourse requires careful planning and preparation and relies on the willingness of the communicator to learn from the participants and to adjust his or her preferences if deemed necessary. Several procedures lend themselves to organizing a cooperative discourse. However, it is not so much the structure of the process that determines the success or failure of a risk discourse as the willingness of all participants to meet the conditions outlined above.

9.6   Application to International Risk Conflicts

How can such a discourse be organized if participants from several countries are involved? The first part of the discourse should take place within

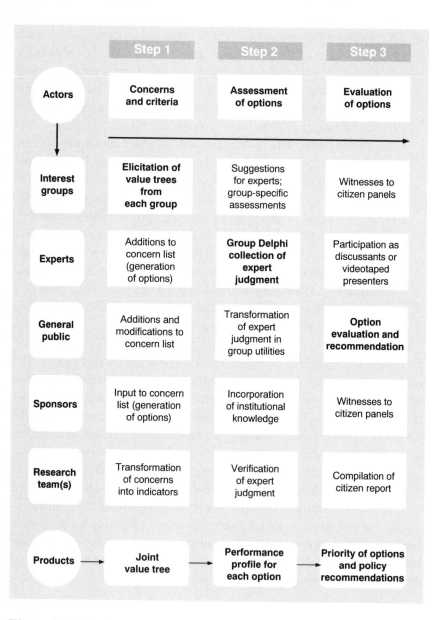

Figure 9.2. Basic concept and elements of the three-step participation model.

each participating country. All relevant stakeholder groups in each country should develop their own value trees and define their concerns for their own country as well as for neighboring countries. Once the groups have solidified their list of concerns, a joint panel of stakeholder group representatives from the different countries should meet and try to adjust their lists of concerns and identify areas of consensus and of dissent. This is an important exercise, because it helps the citizens in the third step of our discourse model to focus on those issues that need to be resolved.

If questions of dissent refer to factual issues, we suggest holding a workshop with experts from all participating countries. This workshop could be organized as a Group Delphi. The main objectives of such a workshop should be to address the factual conflicts, to try to assess the "state of the art," and to define the scope of legitimate interpretations of existing data and models. These are not easy tasks, particularly if scientists and technical experts have different ideas about methodological issues and the appropriateness of models. There is, however, no rational alternative to such a procedure.

Once the main concerns and the factual knowledge are both documented, citizen panels should be organized in each country. Because of language problems and difficulties in intercultural communication, it may be too cumbersome to have mixed panels from the beginning. The task of the panels should be to look at various policy options (from doing nothing to making technical modifications to paying compensation) and evaluate them with respect to (i) factual outcome (in terms of risk reduction or financial distribution) and (ii) main concerns (elicited from the stakeholder groups). As such a task requires careful planning and execution, a time period of six months for biweekly meetings and a final workshop of two to three days seems necessary to reach competent and fair conclusions.

The discourse in each panel should start with an extensive discussion of the agenda and the decision-making procedure. Unless these questions are resolved, any substantial debate is bound to fail. The mediator should make several suggestions, which can be modified by the participants. It is essential that an agreement on agenda and procedure be based on consensus among all participants. In addition to the formal procedure, the mediator should introduce the rules of debate (such as refraining from moralizing). Parties are more inclined to accept these rules if they are made explicit at the beginning of the session.

The substantive debate should start with a comprehensive debate about the risks in general and their distribution over the various regions. In addition, the participants should have knowledge about the responsibilities and legal obligations of government and industry within each national context. Conceptual presentations and discussions about implicit values and goals should prepare the ground for a more formal analysis of the values and evaluative criteria of the participants. Once the value issues are identified, potential conflicts between values can be addressed. If factual knowledge is disputed beyond the results of the expert workshop, the panel should identify additional experts and/or evaluative criteria in order to evaluate the validity of competing claims. The discussion about competence implies an analysis of the past record of the risk generator and the relevant national or regional regulatory agency. The mediator may encourage the participants to suggest modifications or changes that would help them to be more confident about the competence and openness of the respective institutions.

If the issues have been addressed in a satisfactory manner at the first or second level, the mediator may return to the conflicts pertaining to the third level. In separate group sessions with each participating group, the mediator should try to identify value violations and potential value compensations. Based on these group interviews, he or she should design several conflict resolution options and present them to the audience. In negotiations with each group, a consensus may evolve to favor one option over the others.

For a controversial issue such as transboundary risk management, it is not unlikely that all parties will reject all options the mediator proposes. In such a deadlock situation, the mediator can try the following strategies:

- Suggest an arbitration process by which a neutral outside party makes decision on the basis of preferences expressed by each group.
- Suggest the involvement of a neutral jury.
- Suggest replacing the consent principle with some voting rule (such as two-thirds approval).
- Reopen the discussion on issues at the first and second level and hope to facilitate a compromise by clarifying additional factual issues and modifying management practice.

Even if the mediation process does not produce any tangible results in the form of an accepted compromise, the mediator's analysis in terms of value violations and the suggested modifications for risk management are valuable input to making a better and probably more acceptable decision by the legitimate political bodies.

If the panels produce some tangible results, it might be advisable to have each panel designate one or two bi- or multilingual representatives to serve on an international panel. It is important that these representatives identify themselves with the panel from which they originate. This way, each national panel feels truly represented in the international panel. The panelists should be encouraged to report back to their national panel members to avoid any alienation during the process. At the end, the international panel should try to resolve the remaining conflicts between the different national panels.

9.7 Transboundary Conflicts and International Regimes

Organizing participatory processes for transboundary risk management requires more than designing a suitable structure for making public involvement possible. Having an appropriate procedure in place is necessary but not sufficient for international participation. In addition to the organizational task of structuring participatory processes, risk managers need to take into account the legal and political frameworks of each participating country as well as international regimes on which the respective policy-making process is founded. The goal is to use international and transnational participation as a policy tool to enable an individual, group, state, or organization to influence the behavior of the conflicting parties without resorting to physical force or invoking the authority of the law (Kriesberg, 1991:19; Bercovitch, 1992:7).

The history of international participation is largely limited to the application of conflict mediation rather than citizen participation in transnational planning or cooperative political decision making. International mediation, defined as an organized effort to bring conflicting parties together under the supervision of a neutral facilitator, has been used in cases ranging from conflicts about sovereignty and the colonial wars of independence to current conflicts about the use of natural resources (Susskind and Babbitt, 1992:30). Communicative action constitutes the basis for mediation and negotiation. In such situations it is possible for the actors' preferences and identities to be changed by the communication process; that is, the participants have to be willing to change their convictions, preferences, and interests during the mediation process (Risse-Kappen, 1995:178). The study of conflict and peace and the research on international regimes in the past two decades have demonstrated that communicative action as well as strategic action can be a first step toward generating long-term cooperation and lasting peace structures in the sense of "international governance." These peaceful structures of "governance without government" can be set up by international organizations, international conventions, and above all international regimes (Rittberger, 1989; Rosenau and Czempiel, 1992; Kohler-Koch, 1993; Young, 1994). International regimes, in particular, appear to be appropriate institutions for coping with transboundary risks. The research on regime consequences substantiates their problem-solving capacity in that they maintain the idea of a "cooperative discourse" among the disputing parties and institutionalize a just and sustainable conflict regulation (Breitmeier and Wolf, 1993:341).

According to the literature, international conflicts can be classified by their subject and substance, pointing to different management styles and, at the same time, to the appropriate model for problem solving and settlement. So conflicts can be assessed with respect to the probability that participants will agree to cooperate and regulate risk sources voluntarily through permanent institutions.

International and transboundary conflicts can be differentiated by the following criteria: differences in interests, means, and/or values. Whether conflicts are more or less amenable to mediation and regime regulation depends on the substance of the underlying values and interests of the conflict.

- A conflict of interests arises if two or more actors experience a situation of scarcity; each actor places a claim on a specific good (such as a common resource), but not enough of this good is available to satisfy each party's demand.
- A conflict of means arises over dissent about the right way to accomplish a commonly agreed aim.
- A conflict of values relates to dissent about the status or importance of an object or a policy and its link to highly esteemed aspects such as security, power, or territoriality (e.g., spheres of influence, borders, etc.).

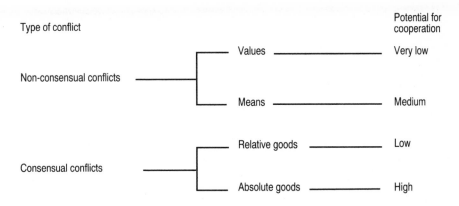

Figure 9.3. Types of conflict and potential for cooperation. Source: Efinger *et al.*, 1988:96.

Additionally, it makes sense to distinguish between absolute and relative goods. Absolute goods convey value to each party regardless of how much value any other party attributes to this good (no exclusive use). Relative goods, on the other hand, increase in value if the other parties have less access to the same good. On the basis of this classification of conflicts, Efinger *et al.* (1988) have developed a schema of potentials for cooperation and regime conduciveness with respect to different types of international and transboundary conflicts (*Figure 9.3*).

Much theoretical and empirical research corroborates the assumption that international conflicts about absolute goods lend themselves to transboundary cooperation, whereas conflicts of means are difficult to reconcile and conflicts of relative goods are even more difficult to resolve. Conflicts about values – such as security, power, spheres of influence, borders, etc. – are the least likely to produce agreement or institutional means for conflict resolution.

Transboundary risks include the whole range of the conflict typology, from the least likely to be resolved conflicts of values to the most likely to be resolved conflicts of absolute goods based on different interests. Therefore, it might be very important to filter out the core element or the main subject of transboundary risk conflicts so that one can assess the likelihood of agreement. Depending on the type of conflict, the most adequate conflict resolution strategy can be selected in order to enhance the prospects of resolving the conflict by peaceful means. If a transboundary risk conflict concerns only a limited resource, then it is very likely that a compromise or even a consensus among the participants will be achieved and that the conflict will be settled cooperatively and durably. If an issue involves a transboundary risk linked to values such as security, the exercise or distribution of power, or political influence, there will be only a limited opportunity for a cooperative and consensual solution.

Kriesberg (1991:22) distinguishes four phases of conflict deescalation that each mediation process must undergo before an institutionalization of the problem-solving activity can take place. In the first phase, the mediator needs to reduce the opponents' willingness to use threats of violence. In the next phase, he or she needs to bring all opponents to the negotiating table. In the third phase, the negotiation process is conducted and chaired by the mediator. In the last phase, a common agreement is reached and subsequently implemented. If the conflicting parties do not willingly engage in a consensual problem-solving effort, international mediation is not feasible. The principle of nation-state sovereignty and noninterference in domestic affairs of states, which is determined in Article 2 Paragraphs 1 and 7 of the United Nations Charter, prohibits direct intervention from the outside (Czempiel, 1994a:139–140).

Although, the likelihood of a successful mediation of conflicts about values is comparatively low, there are some prominent examples of successful mediation and lasting agreements. The Cyprus conflict was at least partially resolved with the help of American mediators (Walker, 1993:103); United Nations Under-Secretary-General for Special Political Affairs Diego Cordovez mediated between the Soviet Union and Afghanistan, leading to the Soviet withdrawal in 1982; the Organization of African Unity (OAU) served as a mediator in the Libya–Chad conflict (Amoo and Zartman, 1992); and at the end of September 1995, US Assistant Secretary of State Richard Holbrooke and European Union arbitrator Arnt Bildt brokered an agreement between Bosnia, Croatia, and Rest-Yugoslavia on basic principles for the republic Bosnia-Herzegovina (NZZ, 1995). US President Bill Clinton was instrumental in negotiating the Dayton Peace Accords, agreed to by Croatians, Serbs, and Bosnians. One of the most remarkable and outstanding examples of external mediation is Washington's long-standing effort to mediate in the Arab–Israeli conflict about security and territory.

These cases demonstrate that even conflicts about security and territory can be successfully settled by outside mediation. Since successful mediations are evident in the most difficult category of conflicts about values, the probability of successful mediation of transboundary risks is relatively high, particularly in cases that do not concern values but absolute goods or means. In spite of the theoretical potential for successful conflict resolution, a great number of mediations have not been successful. According to quantitative surveys from Bercovitch and Regan (1997), 981 violent conflicts worldwide have been approached by means of mediation since World War II. In their survey, there were three categories of success: cease-fire, partial settlement, and full settlement. In 38.5% of the cases the mediation process achieved a success, that is, a cease-fire agreement was attained or the conflict was partially or fully settled. In nearly 20% of the cases the disputes were at least partially settled. Only 5% of the conflicts were completely settled by mediation.

9.8 Managing Transboundary Risks by International Regimes

One essential result of game-theoretical research is that actors with egoistic interests can develop cooperation without referring to a central authority (e.g., Axelrod, 1984). This basic knowledge forms one of the crucial assumptions in the analysis of the formation of international regimes. Regimes constitute an institutionalized, normative framework of cooperation by which actors, because of collective interests and converging expectations, act and behave according to a set of implicit or explicit principles, norms, rules, and decision-making procedures (Krasner, 1983:2). The experiences in international relations have shown that the majority of problems do not represent zero-sum games, where one party's damages or losses imply benefits or advantages for the other parties. Most international and transboundary relations can be characterized as conflicts about controversial interests or controversial means to reach common interests.

Different approaches exist to explain regime evolution, structure, and change on the basis of some fundamental conditions and features (Kohler-Koch, 1989; Efinger *et al.*, 1990; Rittberger, 1993). The relevant prerequisites of regime creation are voluntary participation, a willingness to engage in a compromise or consensus, the prospect of reaching mutual gains, and, if necessary, the acceptance of an autonomous decision-making institution. Cooperation is easier to accomplish if all participants can sustain their nation-state status without establishing a kind of "international government." The procedures suggested above to involve representatives of the affected public in the decision-making process meet the conditions for a successful international regime as long as the cooperation among stakeholders and public groups can be institutionalized as a regular consultation process.

An important advantage concerning transboundary risk management by participatory regimes lies in the reduction of social and transaction costs. Without an agreement, each side will try to maximize its own benefits at the expense of the other side. It can be shown that such a partial maximization effort will lead to high transaction and social costs for all parties involved, provided none of the actors is powerful enough to implement his or her maximizing strategy unchanged by the strategies of all others (in this case we have one winner and several losers). If all actors strive to maximize their own benefits and each strategy impedes the realization of all the other strategies, the overall costs of the combined effects tend to be higher than in the case of a mutual settlement. In addition, transaction costs can be reduced in negotiated agreements by means of centralizing monitoring and control of outcomes. In this sense, regimes can reduce transaction costs for all participants (Keohane, 1984).

The role that members of the public can play within an international regime of cooperation depends first on the interest and potential commitment of the public with respect to the factual issue (Müller and Risse-Kappen, 1990:384). If the public is not interested in the subject, policymakers have the option of utilizing the conventional platforms of international cooperation. If there is public interest in the issue, public participation provides a meaningful contribution to and enhancement of the political decision-making process. Involving the affected populations not only increases the legitimacy of the decision outcome, it can also help to include the anecdotal knowledge about regional conditions and particularities in the deliberation process. Furthermore, public involvement may serve the overarching goal of strengthening ties between neighbors and foster further forms of transboundary cooperation. If foreign-policy action is not reflected in public opinion, public participation can improve the acceptance of the decision-making process in each country. Finally, public participation could be a basic element of a more democratic decision-making style in foreign affairs, particularly if foreign-policy action relates to transboundary risks that affect the public at large.

A recent Delphi inquiry among leading European participation experts concluded that participatory elements are essential for sustaining democratic practices in a globalized world (Allen *et al.*, 1999). The less control national governments seem to have over political and economic development, the more important the inclusion of participatory elements at both the regional and international levels. While the international level requires the involvement of stakeholders such as NGOs (see discussion in Sections 9.6 and 9.7), the regional level demands involvement of citizens affected by the decisions regardless of whether these citizens live within or outside national boundaries. In addition, similar or even identical participatory processes may be introduced for regions with similar social and economic structures throughout Europe, or even the world, as a means of learning from each other and exchanging strategies and experiences. Although these international transboundary experiences may benefit the policy-making process, the experts of the Delphi inquiry strongly recommended that the EU should not develop only one single prototype of public participation or publish something like a cookbook for all participating countries. The issues in question as well as the cultural, political, and social factors that prevail in each region should be the guiding orientations for structuring the participatory process. Models such as cooperative discourse (Renn, *et al.*, 1993) or the Danish consensus conference (Andersen, 1996) were regarded as necessary, useful, and important structuring tools for developing an adequate and case-specific procedure for each participatory project, but not as a recipe for a generalizable procedure of public involvement.

Our model of cooperative discourse developed as a domestic participation procedure could indeed serve as a potential orientation for compensating the democratic deficit in transboundary governance and closing the gap between public opinion in domestic affairs and foreign policy-making. This is of particular relevance if scientific uncertainty prevails in the issue area and the public perceptions of risk assessments diverge nationally, as, for example, in the case of the transboundary harmonization of genetically modified organisms (GMOs) in Europe (see Chapter 3), or if the public perceptions are culturally influenced, as in the case of the BSE problem (see Chapters 4 and 5). Nations with a long-standing tradition of public participation could initiate such transboundary discourses and thus contribute to a further spread of public involvement in neighboring nations. At the same time, however, caution is necessary to demonstrate respect for other political traditions and customs. A first step may be to involve representatives of stakeholder groups, as this type of involvement is almost independent of the national styles of political decision making. Furthermore, corporatist political structures are most conducive to international regimes (Zürn, 1993:283). Starting from corporatist structures, representatives of influential stakeholder groups could agree to start the negotiation among themselves before opening the platform to non-organized citizens. Such a strategy implies that the discourse organizers identify the actors and their interests, determine the political levels that need to be addressed, and create or activate the political arenas in which the mediation procedures can take place. For example, in the issue area of transboundary air pollution the existing international institutions primarily attend to transboundary pollution, but policymakers in areas with high local concentrations of air pollution in Eastern Europe stress the local political arena (see Chapter 4). The international support usually targets transboundary issues over the local problems. This example makes clear how important it is to address the different political levels and to integrate local concerns.

The case of the Slovak nuclear plant Mochovce near the Austrian–Slovak border is an example of an unsuccessful attempt at implementing public participation. Completion of the Soviet-style nuclear plant may endanger the Slovak population, but it also generates transboundary risks for the nearby Austrian residents. The financing of the nuclear plant by the European Bank for Reconstruction and Development (EBRD) was tied to a requirement to organize public hearings in neighboring states. The Slovak government agreed to this condition because completion of the nuclear plant depended on international credit. A public hearing was supposed to take place to enable Austrians to raise their concerns about the plant. The planned public hearing did not take place, however, because the builders refused to communicate with representatives of the general public and were only willing to deal with selected representatives of organized stakeholder groups behind closed doors. When this became public knowledge, the Austrian government canceled the hearing. Austrian Minister for Environment, Youth, and Family Affairs Maria Rauch-Kallat then suggested that the credit from the EBRD be approved despite the deficient participation process. The reason was that she was concerned about the safety of the reactor and wanted to be sure that the money was spent to improve the Slovak energy situation and to facilitate a change to an ecological and sustainable energy policy. With the approval of the credit line, the Austrian and Slovak governments missed the opportunity to initiate a public participation project with respect to transboundary conflicts and to create a regime dealing with transboundary nuclear risks.

In contrast, the agreements on the Great Lakes negotiated between the United States and Canada are an example of a successful and effective settlement of transboundary conflicts and risks. This regime included extended public participation as a means of consensual problem solving and joint decision making (Renn and Finson, 1991; Becker, 1993; WBGU, 1998). In the Great Lakes Water Quality Agreement, both nations have committed themselves to improving and protecting one of the world's largest ecosystems. The regime regulates the common use of the transboundary lakes and rivers, and the monitoring of water pollution in the common river basins and their ecosystems. Since the first treaty was signed in 1909, public input has been collected and integrated into the decision-making process. Over the years, binational institutions were established that helped to prevent conflicts or to resolve them before they grew into serious problems. Conflict resolution was accomplished through negotiations between US federal states and the Canadian provinces and by the creation of an International Joint Commission (IJC). Both countries also created public forums in which citizens were encouraged to participate in regime development, improvement, and implementation. The IJC organized numerous public hearings. Participation and public information programs were set up as regime components in the 1980s. A dispute resolution procedure was established by which technical experts and stakeholder groups gathered to develop commonly derived management options. These options were presented to public forums where residents had the opportunity to voice their opinions. All results were published in proceedings that included the recommendations of all parties. Under the auspices of the IJC, the governmental decision makers in each country or state were then asked to design further policies in line with the recommendations of the public involvement process.

With this brief examination of the potential of public participation within international regimes, one may conclude that international regimes can only benefit from enhanced participation if the political cultures of the affected nations are conducive to such an approach and if the appropriate structures for public input are in place and institutionalized. The example of the Great Lakes demonstrates that a careful planning process and a commitment by existing institutions to take public recommendations seriously were crucial conditions for the success of this regime. If any of the critical decision-making bodies is unwilling to accept public input as a valuable contribution to the decision-making process, transboundary participation is likely to fail. This is a major lesson from the Mochovce case study.

9.9 Conclusions

The objective of this chapter was to review the potential of public participation for resolving transboundary risk conflicts. The procedure of public involvement is as much an issue of dissent as a problem of the subject matter itself. Politicians, stakeholders, experts, and citizens have become aware that they can exercise power in changing or delaying projects. The functioning of public involvement is therefore contingent on the approval of the technique or model of participation by the affected constituencies. Furthermore, whatever model is selected must be compatible with the international regime that constitutes the decision-making framework for collectively binding policies.

In the context of increasing globalization of environmental issues, and considering the fact "that the planet's ecosystem is in danger and that its protection will require modifications in traditional interpretations of state sovereignty" (Keohane *et al.*, 1993:4), countries all over the world must cope with many issues and risks, especially environmental risks, that transcend frontiers or affect people and the environment beyond political capacities of national sovereignty. Accordingly, it is necessary to link procedures of transnational mediation, participation, and cooperation with institutional regimes in order to manage transboundary risks more effectively and democratically. The United Nations has mandated its member states to incorporate citizens and non-state actors into the political process of decision making (UNDP, 1993:Chapter 4), including cases of transboundary decision making. Czempiel (1994b:2) assumes that increased public participation in the political decision-making procedures within existing political systems will spill over into international affairs. Citizens will demand more participatory rights if their livelihood is affected by other nations' actions.

Zürn (1992:509) has argued that the potential for democratic decision making has not yet been transferred to the international policy-making process, despite the fact that legal procedures exist for implementation. In the current research about "world society" (e.g., the World Society Research Group at the Technical University of Darmstadt), the question has been raised whether the "democratic deficit of ... governance structures" (Wolf, 1996:3) can be compensated for by nongovernmental actors. Many approaches focus on NGOs in international cooperation (e.g., Haufler, 1993; Schmidt, 1996; Schmidt and Take, 1997), but the general public as a nongovernmental actor in foreign-policy-making has been rather neglected in theoretical studies on international policy-making as well as in practice. Nevertheless, the demand for increased public involvement in policy-making decisions has grown in recent years, and there have been good examples that show the prospects and opportunities of transboundary participation.

Involving citizens in the decision-making process requires careful planning, thoughtful preparation, and the flexibility to change procedures on the demand of the affected constituencies. This is particularly true for international conflicts or transboundary risk management. One might be tempted to ask, If citizen involvement is so difficult and painful for resolving international conflicts, why should any agency or commission bother to promote participation and go beyond direct government-to-government negotiation? The first response to this question is that social acceptance of any policy is closely linked with the perception of a fair procedure in making the decision (Rayner and Cantor, 1987). The best "technical" solution cannot be implemented if the process of decision making is perceived as unfair or biased. Fairness is already a major issue in national environmental policies; it becomes the main battlefield of debate within an international context. The second response to this challenge is more fundamental: Our experiences from previous projects and the implementation of our cooperative discourse model clearly indicate that the public has something to contribute to the planning process. Experts and regulators are often restricted in their assessment of a project and confine their analysis to the typical risk factors. Local specifics or other dimensions of concerns are often neglected. Public participation helps to include these concerns in the decision-making process and to prevent potential consequences that the experts involved were not aware of (Crosby, 1986; Fiorino, 1989).

The central tenet to keep in mind concerning public participation projects is that the public is in principle capable of making prudent decisions. Public input is not only strategically necessary to gain acceptance, it is essential to making the right decision. However, the rationality of public input depends on the procedure of involvement. Provided citizens are given a conducive and supportive structure for discourse, they are capable of understanding and processing risk-related information and articulating well-balanced recommendations. The discourse models are an attempt to design a procedure that allows citizens to take advantage of their full potential and includes the professional knowledge and expertise necessary to make prudent decisions.

The transfer of the cooperative discourse model to an international audience has not been tested and implies additional problems. Participants speak different languages, they come from different political traditions, and they have different experiences in facing risks. In spite of all these difficulties, it is our conviction that a carefully designed participation program will not only be instrumental in resolving eminent risk conflicts among nations, but will also contribute to a climate of cooperation and mutual understanding.

Note

[1] For more information on the Fourth Ministerial Conference about the Environment for Europe, see http://www.mem.dk/aarhus-conference/index.htm.

References

Allen, P., Büttner, T., Laske, T., Renn, O., Schneider, E., Simosi, M., and Zwetkoff, C., 1999, *The Resolution of Environmental Disputes in Europe*, Final Report for the EC Environmental Research Program, Contract No.: ENV-CT 96-0270, University of Surrey, Guildford, UK.

Amoo, S.G., and Zartman, I.W., 1992, Mediation by regional organizations: The Organization for African Unity (OAU) in Chad, in J. Bercovitch and J. Rubin, eds, *Mediation in International Relations. Multiple Approaches to Conflict Management*, St. Martin's Press, New York, NY, USA, pp. 131–148.

Andersen, S., 1996, Expertenurteil und gesellschaftlicher Konsens: Ethischer Rat und Konsenuskommissionen in Dänemark, in C.F. Gethmann and L. Honnefelder, eds, *Jahrbuch für Wissenschaft und Ethik*, De Gruyter, Berlin, Germany, and New York, NY, USA, pp. 201–208.

Axelrod, R., 1984, *The Evolution of Cooperation*, Basic Books, New York, NY, USA.

Bacow, L.S., and Wheeler, M., 1984, *Environmental Dispute Resolution*, Plenum, New York, NY, USA.

Barber, B., 1983, *The Logic and Limits of Trust*, Rutgers University Press, New Brunswick, NJ, USA.

Becker, M.L., 1993, The International Joint Commission and public participation: Past experiences, present challenges, future tasks, *Natural Resources Journal*, **33**(2):235–274.

Bercovitch, J., 1992, The structure and diversity of mediation in international relations, in J. Bercovitch and J. Rubin, eds, *Mediation in International Relations: Multiple Approaches to Conflict Management*, St. Martin's Press, New York, NY, USA, pp. 1–29.

Bercovitch, J., and Regan, P. M., 1997, Managing Risks in International Relations: The Mediation of Enduring Rivalries, in G. Schneider and P.A. Weitsman, eds, *Enforcing Cooperation: Risky States and the Intergovernmental Management of Conflict*, MacMillan, London, UK, pp. 185–201.

Breitmeier, H., and Wolf, K.D., 1993, Analysing regime consequences: Conceptual outlines and environmental explorations, in V. Rittberger, ed., *Regime Theory and International Relations*, Clarendon Press, Oxford, UK, pp. 339–360.

Burns, T.R., and Überhorst, R., 1988, *Creative Democracy: Systematic Conflict Resolution and Policymaking in a World of High Science and Technology*, Praeger, New York, NY, USA.

Carius, R., Köberle, S., Oppermann, B., Renn, O., Schneider, E., and Schrimpf, M., 1997, Bürger gestalten ihre Region – am Beispiel der Bürgerbeteiligung an der Abfallplanung für die Region Nordschwarzwald, in M. Birzer, P.H. Feindt, and E. Spindler, eds, *Nachhaltige Stadtentwicklung*, Economica Verlag, Bonn, Germany, pp. 73–84

Chen, K., and Mathes, J.C., 1989, Value oriented social decision analysis: A communication tool for public decision making on technological projects, in C. Vlek and G. Cvetkovich, eds, *Social Decision Methodology for Technological Projects*, Kluwer, Dordrecht, Netherlands.

Crosby, N., Kelly, J.M., and Schaefer, P., 1986, Citizen panels: A new approach to citizen participation, *Public Administration Review*, **46**:170–178.

Czempiel, E.-O., 1994a, *Die Reform der UNO. Möglichkeiten und Mißverständnisse*, C.H. Beck, Munich, Germany.

Czempiel, E.-O., 1994b, Vergesellschaftete Außenpolitik, *Merkur*, **48**(1):1–14.

Dienel, P.C., 1978, *Die Planungszelle*, Westdeutscher Verlag, Opladen, Germany.

Dienel, P.C., 1989, Contributing to social decision methodology: Citizen reports on technological projects, in C. Vlek and G. Cvetkovich, eds, *Social Decision Methodology for Technological Projects*, Kluwer Academic Press, Dordrecht, Netherlands, pp. 133–150.

Dietz, T., Stern, P.C., and Rycroft, R.W., 1989, Definitions of Conflict and the Legitimation of Resources: The Case of Environmental Risk, *Sociological Forum*, **4**:47–69.

Efinger, M., Rittberger, V., and Zürn, M., 1988, *Internationale Regime in den Ost-West-Beziehungen. Ein Beitrag zur Erforschung der friedlichen Behandlung internationaler Konflikte*, Haag and Herchen, Frankfurt/M., Germany.

Efinger, M., Rittberger, V., Wolf, K.D., and Zürn, M., 1990, Internationale Regime und internationale Politik, in V. Rittberger, ed., *Theorien der Internationalen Beziehungen: Bestandsaufnahme und Forschungsperspektiven*, Sonderheft der Politischen Vierteljahresschrift No. 21, Westdeutscher Verlag, Opladen, Germany, pp. 263–285.

Fiorino, D.J., 1989, Technical and democratic values in risk analysis, *Risk Analysis*, **9**(3):293–299.

Fiorino, D.J., 1990, Citizen participation and environmental risk: A survey of institutional mechanisms, *Science, Technology, and Human Values*, **15**(2):226–243.

Funtowicz, S.O., and Ravetz, J.R., 1985, Three types of risk assessment: Methodological analysis, in V.T. Covello, J.L. Mumpower, P.J.M. Stallen, and V.R.R. Uppuluri, eds, *Environmental Impact Assessment, Technology Assessment, and Risk Analysis*, Springer, New York, NY, USA, pp. 831–848.

Great Lakes United Water Quality Task Force, 1987, *Unfulfilled Promises: A Citizens' Review of the International Great Lakes Water Quality Agreement*, Chicago, IL, USA, and Toronto, Canada.

Habermas, J., 1971, *Knowledge and Human Interests*, Beacon Press, Boston, MA, USA.

Habermas, J., 1984, *Theory of Communicative Action. Vol. 1: Reason and the Rationalization of Society*, Beacon Press, Boston, MA, USA.

Haufler, V., 1993, Crossing the boundary between public and private: International regimes and non-state actors, in V. Rittberger, ed., *Regime Theory and International Relations*, Clarendon Press, Oxford, UK, pp. 94–111.

Kasperson, R.E., 1986, Six propositions for public participation and their relevance for risk communication, *Risk Analysis*, **6**(3):275–281.

Keeney, R., and von Winterfeldt, D., 1986, Improving risk communication, *Risk Analysis*, **6**(4):417–424.

Keeney, R.L., Renn, O., and von Winterfeldt, D., 1987, Structuring West Germany's energy objectives, *Energy Policy*, **15**(4):352–362.

Kemp, R., 1985, Planning, political hearings, and the politics of discourse, in J. Forester, ed., *Critical Theory and Public Life*, MIT Press, Cambridge, MA, USA.

Keohane, R.O., 1984, *After Hegemony: Cooperation and Discord in the World Political Economy*, Princeton University Press, Princeton, NJ, USA.

Keohane, R.O., Haas, P.M., and Levy, M.A., 1993, The effectiveness of environmental institutions, in P.M. Haas, R.O. Keohane, and M.A. Levy, eds, *Institutions for the Earth: Sources of Effective International Environmental Protection*, MIT Press, Cambridge, MA, USA, and London, UK, pp. 3–24.

Kohler-Koch, B., 1989, Zur Empirie und Theorie internationaler Regime, in B. Kohler-Koch, ed., *Regime in den internationalen Beziehungen*, Nomos Verlagsgesellschaft, Baden-Baden, Germany, pp. 17–85.

Kohler-Koch, B., 1993, Die Welt regieren ohne Weltregierung, in C. Böhret and B. Wewer, eds, *Regieren im 21. Jahrhundert – zwischen Globalisierung und Regionalisierung*, Leske and Budrich, Opladen, Germany, pp. 109–141.

Kraft, M., 1988, Evaluating technology through public participation: The nuclear waste disposal controversy, in M.E. Kraft and N.J. Vig, eds, *Technology and Politics*, Duke University Press, Durham, NC, USA, pp. 253–277.

Krasner, S.D., 1983, Structural causes and regime consequences: Regimes as intervening variables, in S.D. Krasner, ed., *International Regimes*, Cornell University Press, Ithaca, NY, USA, and London, UK, pp. 1–21.

Kriesberg, L., 1991, Formal and quasi-mediators in international disputes: An exploratory analysis, *Journal of Peace Research*, **28**(1):19–27.

Lynn, F.M., 1986, The interplay of science and values in assessing and regulating environmental risks, *Science, Technology and Human Values*, **11**(2): 40–50.

Majone, G., 1979, Process and outcome in regulatory decision-making, *American Behavioral Scientist*, **22**(5):561–583.

McCarthy, T., 1975, Translator's introduction, in J. Habermas, ed., *Legitimation Crisis*, Beacon Press, Boston, MA, USA.

Müller, H., and Risse-Kappen, T., 1990, Internationale Umwelt, gesellschaftliches Umfeld und außenpolitischer Prozeß in liberaldemokratischen Industrienationen, in V. Rittberger, ed., *Theorien der Internationalen Beziehungen: Bestandsaufnahme und Forschungsperspektiven*, Sonderheft der Politischen Vierteljahresschrift No. 21, Westdeutscher Verlag, Opladen, Germany, pp. 375–400.

Nelkin, D., and Pollak, M., 1979, Public participation in technological decisions: Reality or grand illusion, *Technology Review*, **9**:55–64.

NZZ, 1995, *Neue Zürcher Zeitung*, 28 September.

Perrow, C., 1984, *Normal Accidents: Living with High Risk Technologies*, Basic Books, New York, NY, USA.

Pollak, M., 1985, Public Participation, in H. Otway and M. Peltu, eds, *Regulating Industrial Risk*, Butterworths, London, UK, pp. 76–94.

Rayner, S., and Cantor, R., 1987, How fair is safe enough? The cultural approach to societal technology choice, *Risk Analysis*, **7**(1):3–13.

Renn, O., 1986, Decision analytic tools for resolving uncertainty in the energy debate, *Nuclear Engineering and Design*, **93**(2 and 3):167–180.

Renn, O., 1992, Risk communication: Towards a rational dialogue with the public, *Journal of Hazardous Materials*, **29**(3):465–519.

Renn, O., and Finson, R., 1991, The Great Lakes Clean-up Program: A Role Model for International Cooperation?, EUI Working Papers EPU No. 91/7, European University Institute, Florence, Italy.

Renn, O., and Levine, D., 1991, Credibility and trust in risk communication, in R. Kasperson and P.J. Stallen, eds, *Communicating Risk to the Public*, Kluwer Academic Publishers, Dordrecht, Netherlands, pp. 175–218.

Renn, O., and Rohrmann, B., eds, 2000, *Cross-Cultural Risk Perception. A Survey of Empirical Studies*, Kluwer, Dordrecht, Netherlands.

Renn, O., Albrecht, G., Kotte, U., Peters, H.P., and Stegelmann, H.U., 1985, Sozialverträgliche Energiepolitik: Ein Gutachten für die Bundesregierung, HTV Edition *Technik und sozialer Wandel*, Munich, Germany.

Renn, O., Goble, R., Levine, D., Rakel, H., and Webler, T., 1989, *Citizen Participation for Sludge Management*, Final Report to the New Jersey Department of Environmental Protection, CENTED, Clark University, Worcester, NJ, USA.

Renn, O., Webler, T., and Johnson, B., 1991, Citizen participation for hazard management, *Risk – Issues in Health and Safety*, **3**:12–22.

Renn, O., Webler, T., Rakel, H., Dienel, P.C., and Johnson, B., 1993, Public participation in decision making: A three-step-procedure, *Policy Sciences*, **26**:189–214.

Renn, O., Webler, T., and Wiedemann, P., eds, 1995, *Fairness and Competence in Citizen Participation. Evaluating New Models for Environmental Discourse*, Kluwer, Amsterdam, Netherlands, and Boston, MA, USA.

Renn, O., Webler, T., and Kastenholz, H., 1996, Procedural and substantive fairness in landfill siting, *Risk – Health, Safety and Environment*, **7**(2): 145–168.

Risse-Kappen, T., 1995, Reden ist nicht billig. Zur Debatte um Kommunikation und Rationalität, *Zeitschrift für Internationale Beziehungen*, **2**(1): 171–184.

Rittberger, V., 1989, Frieden durch Assoziation und Integration? Anmerkungen zum Stand der Forschung über internationale Organisationen und Regime, in B. Moltmann and E. Senghaas-Knobloch, eds, *Konflikte in der Weltgesellschaft und Friedensstrategien*, Nomos Verlagsgesellschaft, Baden-Baden, Germany, pp. 183–205.

Rittberger, V., ed., 1993, *Regime Theory and International Relations*, Clarendon Press, Oxford, UK.

Rosenau, J. and Czempiel, E.-O., eds, 1992, *Governance without Government. Order and Change in World Politics*, Cambridge University Press, Cambridge, MA, USA.

Rushefsky, M., 1984, Institutional mechanisms for resolving risk controversies, in S.G. Hadden, ed., *Risk Analysis, Institutions, and Public Policy*, Associated Faculty Press, Port Washington, NY, USA, pp. 133-148.

Scheuch, E.K., 1980, Kontroverse um Energie – ein echter oder ein Stellvertreterstreit, in H. Michaelis, ed., *Existenzfrage Energie*, Econ, Düsseldorf, Germany, pp. 279–293.

Schmidt, H., 1996, Problem-solving in World Society. State Responses to Global Environmental Problems, Working Paper No. 4 of the World Society Research Group, Technical University Darmstadt, Darmstadt, Germany.

Schmidt, H., and Take, I., 1997, Demokratischer und besser? Der Beitrag von Nichtregierungsorganisationen zur Demokratisierung internationaler Politik und zur Lösung globaler Probleme, *Aus Politik und Zeitgeschichte*, B 43/97, pp. 12–20.

Slovic, P., Layman, M., and Flynn, J.H., 1993, Perceived risk, trust and nuclear waste: Lessons from Yucca Mountain, in R.E. Dunlap M.E. Kraft, and E. Rosa, eds, *Public Reactions to Nuclear Waste. Citizens' Views of Repository Siting*, Duke University Press, Durham, NC, USA and London, UK, pp. 64–86.

Susskind, L., and Babbitt, E., 1992, Overcoming the obstacles to effective mediation of international disputes, in J. Bercovitch and J. Rubin, eds, *Mediation in International Relations: Multiple Approaches to Conflict Management*, St. Martin's Press, New York, NY, USA, pp. 30–51.

Turoff, M., 1970, The design of a policy Delphi, *Technological Forecasting and Social Change*, 2(2):84–98.

UNDP (United Nations Development Programme), 1993, *Human Development Report 1993*, Oxford University Press, New York, NY, USA, and Oxford, UK.

von Winterfeldt, D., 1987, Value tree analysis: An introduction and an application to offshore oil drilling, in P.R. Kleindorfer and H.C. Kunreuther, eds, *Insuring and Managing Hazardous Risks: From Seveso to Bhopal and Beyond*, Springer-Verlag, Berlin, Germany, pp. 377–439.

von Winterfeldt, D., and Edwards, W., 1986, *Decision Analysis and Behavioral Research*, Cambridge University Press, Cambridge, MA, USA.

Walker, J., 1993, International mediation of ethnic conflicts, *Survival*, **35**(1): 102–117.

WBGU (German Scientific Advisory Council on Global Change), 1998, *Welt im Wandel: Wege zu einem nachhaltigen Umgang mit Süßwasser. Jahresgutachten 1997*, Springer-Verlag, Berlin, Germany.

WBGU (German Scientific Advisory Council on Global Change), 1999, *Welt im Wandel: Umwelt und Ethik*, Metropolis, Marburg, Germany.

Webler, T., Levine, D., Rakel, H., and Renn, O., 1991, The Group Delphi: A novel attempt at reducing uncertainty, *Technological Forecasting and Social Change*, **39**(3):253–263.

Wolf, K.D., 1996, Defending State Autonomy: Intergovernmental Governance in the European Union, Working Paper No. 5 of the World Society Research Group, Technical University Darmstadt, Darmstadt, Germany.

Young, O.R., 1994, *International Governance: Protecting the Environment in a Stateless Society*, Cornell University Press, Ithaca, NY, USA, and London, UK.

Zeiss, C., 1989, Impact management priorities at waste facilities: Differences between host community residents' and technical decision makers' values, *Journal of Environmental Systems*, **19**(1):1–23.

Zürn, M., 1992, Jenseits der Staatlichkeit: Über die Folgen der ungleichzeitigen Denationalisierung, *Leviathan*, 4, Westdeutscher Verlag, Opladen, Germany.

Zürn, M., 1993, Bringing the second image (back) in: About the domestic sources of regime formation, in V. Rittberger, ed., *Regime Theory and International Relations*, Clarendon Press, Oxford, UK, pp. 282–311.

Chapter 10

International Negotiation and the Management of Transboundary Risks

Gunnar Sjöstedt

10.1 Introduction

One objective of this chapter is to assess the special difficulties of dealing with risks that become *agenda items* in international negotiations on transboundary environmental issues. Environmental risks represent possible future ecological deterioration, including reduced health and safety for human beings. This is a neglected research area, although risk taking is a salient element of negotiation and bargaining theory. In this special context of risk management in negotiation, environmental risks as such are drivers of intergovernmental cooperation. But they are also associated with other types of risk pertaining to the construction of negotiated agreements to manage transboundary environmental problems. Such risks of *ineffective abatement* and *implementation failure* may affect the willingness of governments and other actors in international environmental negotiations to commit themselves to allocating scarce resources to cope jointly with an environmental issue. Like environmental risks addressed in a negotiation, risks associated with abatement and implementation may also appear as issues on the negotiating table; in other words, they may manifest as *negotiated risks*.

Another aim of this chapter is to assess possible approaches to managing negotiated risks; that is, the search for an agreement in a negotiation that integrates accords concerning environmental risks as such with accords regarding abatement and implementation risks. Different categories of risk require somewhat different treatment and consensus. Therefore, negotiation strategists need to consider the possibility that an approach that is effective for dealing with one category of negotiated risk may have negative consequences for the management of another kind of risk. For example, a strong emphasis on the management of implementation risks in a negotiation may increase perceived abatement risks in the sense that some negotiating parties may prefer suboptimal technical solutions to a transboundary environmental problem if an optimal solution represents a binding commitment that is too far-reaching from a political point of view. On the other hand, a positive association between the management of different categories of negotiated risk is also conceivable.

The motivation for this study is the observation that international negotiation represents an important instrument for the management of transboundary environmental risks. The management of risk may be facilitated by a greater awareness of the special problems of coping with negotiated risks. In particular, it is important to make a distinction between international interaction regarding transboundary environmental issues in a context of crisis and interaction in a context of risk. Although they often coincide, in principle crisis and risk represent quite different conditions for the achievement of an international agreement.

Transboundary environmental issues are likely to become important in the forthcoming accession negotiations between certain Eastern and Central European (ECE) countries and the European Union (EU) (Grabbe and Hughes, 1997). These issues will probably also prove to be difficult to pursue to a successful outcome. It is entirely possible that environmental problems will turn out to be more demanding in the accession negotiations than is generally expected. A basic explanation is the great disparities with regard to the scale of environmental problems in, on the one hand, the EU and, on the other, the ECE region (Carter and Turnock, 1996). Another reason is the noteworthy cultural differences between "East" and

"West" in Europe, which condition how both the political elite and the general public perceive environmental issues and the risks that they represent. Thus, it is important to clarify how transboundary environmental risks should be approached in international negotiation.

10.2 Negotiation of Transboundary Environmental Issues in the Contexts of Crisis and Risk

Sustainable political solutions to transboundary environmental problems are typically framed as formal international agreements, such as the 1979 Convention on Long-Range Transboundary Air Pollution established to cope with acid rain in Europe (see Chapter 4; Larsson, 1996). International agreement is produced by international decision making, which may take different forms depending on the context, issues, or participants involved (Stine, 1994; Underdal, 1998). Transboundary decisions on environmental risks may, for example, represent a form of crisis management, or they may be routinized and guided by the procedural rules of an international convention or organization. Regardless of their mold, in each particular situation decisions made jointly by several governments typically depend on a process of negotiation to produce a viable agreement. Negotiations are not automatically successful, if by success we mean the achievement of an agreement (Underdal, 1993).[1]

Negotiations may fail for various reasons, notably because of a lack of sufficient political will to accept binding commitments in an agreement. However, negotiation failure may also depend on intervening factors that hinder parties from making collective choices where otherwise they could have produced an agreement. Negotiations involve not only interests, but also emotions, attitudes, and cultural backgrounds. Negotiators do not necessarily conform to the model of a rational actor at the negotiating table. Furthermore, it is debatable whether agreement is always a good measure of negotiation success. An agreement may have only a modest effect on the problem it is designed to cope with. For example, in the negotiation on harmonizing regulations concerning genetically modified food, risk assessment procedures have produced an agreement that is difficult to implement because public values were not taken into account (see Chapter 3).

Transboundary environmental issues have characteristics that may negatively affect an international negotiation. For example, diverging risk perceptions (Drottz-Sjöberg, 1991) or risk constructions among negotiating parties may obstruct a bargaining process. If two parties discern quite dissimilar risks associated with the same issue, they are likely to have difficulties understanding each other, perhaps to such a high degree that an attempt to reach an agreement between them becomes totally thwarted. This was precisely the case in the negotiations between Slovakia and Hungary regarding the Gabcikovo hydropower station on the Danube River. Throughout the debate, authorities on both sides of the river made very different use of expert opinion, with remarkably contrasting constructions of the environmental issues. The Slovak discourse asserted that the diversion of the river would improve the ecology of the region, whereas the Hungarian discourse emphasized medium- and long-term risks to groundwater and other crucial environmental conditions (see Chapter 6).

Thus risk perception has a special and often crucial role in negotiations on transboundary environmental issues, even if its effects are not always obvious.[2] The perception of an environmental risk at stake in a negotiation is often a main motive for entering into an international agreement prescribing costly abatement measures (Sjöstedt, 1993a). For example, the member states of the climate regime have agreed to reduce what they consider to be the cost-effective use of fossil fuels because this is considered a productive strategy for preempting jointly perceived future negative – possibly catastrophic – consequences of climate warming (Kyoto Protocol, 1997). However, some countries have not ratified the Kyoto Protocol; in one of these countries, the United States, it appears that the discourse surrounding the ratification procedure differs markedly from that in countries that have ratified the Protocol (Gelbspan, 1995). Most notably, the costs and benefits of reducing greenhouse gases are perceived and constructed differently (Linnerooth-Bayer, 1999).

Thus, in a functional sense, diverging risk perceptions may be similar to differing party interests in helping to determine how the various actors position themselves vis-à-vis others in the negotiation. If existing perceptional differences regarding risks are blurred or hidden at the outset of a negotiation, they may help give a false impression that the road to an agreement is smooth and without complications. When diverging risk perceptions that are inevitably conditioned by the social and economic context eventually surface later in the process, they may have an unnecessarily destructive impact by causing irritation, frustration, and friction. If party A does not understand that party B has a different appreciation of an environmental risk, A may wrongly consider B's negotiation performance to be irrational, incompetent, or outright obstructive. Once such an assessment has been made, it may have long-term repercussions for party A's relationship with party B.

Improved understanding and communication of risk perceptions and constructions are an important, but still somewhat neglected, approach to the facilitation of negotiation on transboundary environmental issues (Brown, 1995; Johnstone-Bryden, 1995). Risk taking has certainly always been a broad and important theme in the analysis and theory of bargaining and negotiation. The topic that has been overlooked is risks as *items on negotiation agendas*. The problems of coping with environmental issues in international decision making ultimately depend on how those issues are framed and conceived of by the policymakers in the negotiating arena. This arena includes not only those negotiating the issues at the table, but also the authorities and other actors "back home," to whom the negotiators are accountable (Sjöstedt, 1993a).

Issue frames are, in turn, conditioned by context. One important context is that of crisis, and international decision making on important transboundary environmental issues has often contained an element of crisis management. In these cases, decision makers have been called on to cope immediately with an actual environmental disaster, although the issues involved may also represent a longer-term risk (Falloux, 1993). In fact, an element of crisis often has been necessary to launch an environmental negotiation in the first place. In most environmental issue areas, negotiation has not begun until the governments of the countries concerned began to look at the issue at stake (e.g., acid rain or ozone depletion) as an actual – or looming – crisis with immediate or near-term negative consequences (Benedick, 1991; Shaw, 1993). Of course, the 1986 accident at the Chernobyl nuclear power plant is the starkest case illustration (Sjöstedt, 1993b). Prompt abatement measures were considered necessary by many European states in order to neutralize the hazardous effects of observed radioactive downfall resulting from the Chernobyl disaster (Ebel, 1994). The Convention on Early Notification of a Nuclear Accident and the Convention on Assistance in the Case of a Nuclear Accident or Radiological Emergency were responses to the Chernobyl disaster. These two agreements were rapidly negotiated in a few months in 1986. They also spawned a number of bilateral agreements specifying the terms of the Vienna treaties taking local circumstances into account.

The bovine spongiform encephalopathy (BSE) issue also required a climate of acute crisis management to be addressed in earnest in international negotiation. The BSE case is a good illustration of the complicated interaction that often occurs between the management of crisis and the management of risk in international decision making on transboundary environmental issues. Crisis management unfolded in the EU institutions as a direct response to the observed increasing number of infected cattle in several countries, primarily the United Kingdom. Drastic measures were undertaken to wipe out the BSE disease, including the slaughter of whole herds of cattle. This crisis management was concerned with the actual and perceivable problem of "mad cows," but was driven by risk perception that BSE could be transferred to humans (see Chapter 5; Ford, 1996; Lette, 1996).[3]

Risks, as considered here, are "future possible, negative consequences of present choices or events" (Drottz-Sjöberg, 1991). In principle, environmental risks need to be approached differently in a negotiation and in an unfolding environmental crisis. In a crisis, parties must cope with negative effects on the environment that are transpiring "here and now." In addition, an environmental risk can pertain to a future situation in which hazardous repercussions of current and otherwise desirable activities may – or may not – occur. As these future consequences of present choices cannot be observed before they have actually taken place, they need to be assessed in advance. Over the past few decades, there has been a great deal of methodological development and practice with regard to assessing risks – both those with a long statistical history (e.g., car accidents) and more novel risks of technological failure (e.g., nuclear accidents) or insidious risks (e.g., toxic chemicals) – with the help of some sort of forecasting method ranging from pure guesswork to the employment of a scientific model. There is also a great deal of documentation about the inherently subjective nature of the scientific assessment of risk, which means that risk assessments will almost invariably differ between negotiating parties. This variance can stem from the many different ways of framing and structuring the risk assessment problem, which may complicate the negotiation process.

Such complication was clearly illustrated in the EU negotiations to approve the sale of herbicide-tolerant oilseed rape (see Chapter 3). The United Kingdom framed the issue as the assessment of the risk that the glufosinate-tolerance gene would cause environmental harm by spreading to other related species. The authorities eventually pronounced this harm to be negligible, arguing that, even if the gene spread, there were other alternatives for weed control. Thus, the probability of spread, and the uncertainties involved in generating this probability, were not an issue in the United Kingdom. Alternatively, in France the issue was framed as one of great unknowns about the spread of herbicide-resistant genes and the socioeconomic consequences thereof. Nongovernmental organizations (NGOs) throughout Europe framed the issue even more broadly, warning that the alternatives – broad-spectrum herbicides – would damage habitats essential for wildlife, thus threatening biodiversity. Eventually, the United Kingdom also changed its framing of the issue, accepting a looser boundary between genetically modified organism (GMO) legislation and pesticide legislation, although they still accepted intensive agriculture as the normative baseline for risk assessment.

As this case illustrates, one of the most difficult challenges in international negotiations on risk issues is dealing with the different framings of the risk issue during the formal risk assessments. This challenge is, of course, not unique to international negotiations, since differing risk assessments have been a core feature of domestic negotiated policy on risk issues. However, the international setting adds a level of complexity in establishing "consensual science" across sovereign borders.

10.3   Categories of Negotiated Risk: An Overview

Decision makers striving to cope with a transboundary environmental issue may be confronted with a very complex risk situation. A closer look at this problem reveals that it has several dimensions. Three different categories of negotiated risk are discernible. First, as discussed above, transboundary environmental issues can be viewed as risks to what society values, such as ecosystems and human health.[4] Thus, the negotiation must ultimately fashion an agreement on how much to reduce the risks and at what price, and how to share the costs. Second, there is the risk of implementation failure, the prospect that not all parties to an international agreement will honor all their obligations all the time. Third, negotiating parties will have to appraise plausible abatement risks – the likelihood that costly abatement measures will not produce intended results even when there is no compliance failure. Analysts usually have not conceived of abatement and implementation problems. Nor are these problems necessarily considered to be risks by negotiating parties. It is conceivable that all parties to a negotiation are convinced that a negotiated agreement is completely instrumental and cost-effective, and that all parties will – and can – adequately implement their treaty obligations. The point is, however, that if abatement and implementation are problematic, they may be perceived as risks by some or all parties. When abatement and implementation problems are seen as risks, they will be treated as such in the comprehensive assessment that parties make before they decide whether they will accept a proposed agreement to cope with a particular environmental risk. For example, if risks of abatement and/or implementation are perceived to be high, some or all parties may be reluctant to commit scarce resources to cope with a transboundary environmental risk.

The three types of risk identified above are examined here within a negotiation perspective. The basic question is how risk management can be facilitated, considering that each particular kind of risk (environmental, implementation, or abatement) must be handled differently, Thus, a facilitation strategy that proves to be effective with regard to one type of risk may be less useful – or even counterproductive – when other types of risk are addressed.

10.3.1   Transboundary environmental risks

All the cases of transboundary environmental issues discussed in this book have been dealt with in negotiations between two one or more countries and have been at least partly viewed from a risk perspective. Representatives of the EU and individual member states have been talking to Lithuanian authorities about the safety of the Ignalina power plant. A trans-European regime has been negotiated to cope with acid rain and is being developed further in ongoing talks. The problem of the construction – and deconstruction – of the Gabcikovo dam has generated recurrent consultations between Hungary and Slovakia. The "mad cows" of the BSE crisis have led to intensive consultations and international decision making within the EU. Genetically modified food has developed into a sensitive agenda item in the continuing difficult talks between the EU and the United States in the agricultural sector.

Negotiated risks addressed in international talks are rarely constructed identically in neighboring countries. This helps explain why different parties at the negotiating table often perceive the same issue very differently, as did, for instance, the Slovaks and the Hungarians in the case of the Gabcikovo dam, or the Scandinavians and the Lithuanians in discussions about the Ignalina power plant, or the British and the Germans in quarrels over "mad cows" in Brussels.

Paradoxically, perceptional differences push parties to deliberately reconstruct transboundary environmental risks when putting them on the agenda of an international negotiation. This is usually done in the early stages of a negotiation process, when the agenda is set and issues are systematically clarified. To move in the direction of a binding agreement, parties need an explicit accord on how the environmental risk put on the negotiating table is to be specified. Deliberate risk reconstruction is thus a formal part of the negotiation process in which perceptional differences, and diverging interests, are meant to be harmonized into a common understanding of the environmental risk at hand. How transboundary environmental risks are (re)constructed in a negotiation may be critical for its progress and outcome. Issue clarification represents a strategically important element of negotiation.

The negotiated risk is not merely a topic in the negotiation but has other functions as well. Hence, formally harmonized risk perceptions provide a general motivation for negotiation and agreement that may be transformed into clear joint objectives. Parties can lean on these joint objectives when they proceed from agenda setting to ensuing process stages pertaining to negotiation on formula and detail. In successful negotiations, the consensual knowledge used in defining negotiated risks as issues also typically gives an indication of how these risks are to be framed in an agreement. For example, if emissions to the atmosphere of specified substances (e.g., sulfur or carbon dioxide) are defined as the carrier of risk, then the logical solution is the reduction – or elimination – of these hazardous releases. A comparison of two cases reported in this book illustrates the importance of consensual knowledge and the harmonization of risk perceptions in a negotiation. The acid rain regime represents a success story in spite of great political obstacles at the outset of the process. In this negotiation, considerable time and effort were dedicated to the construction of a common understanding of risks associated with acid rain. In this case, the common understanding meant that risks in terms of probability and extent of harm were essentially removed from the agenda. The critical loads approach adopted in the acid rain negotiations represented a strategy of avoiding risk calculations. This is an important reminder that consensual knowledge established during a negotiation framing the understanding of a transboundary environmental risk does not necessarily represent the best platform for the achievement of an efficient negotiated outcome. Like other international accords, consensual knowledge usually reflects constraints of political feasibility. Regardless of the quality of risk assessment with regard to acid rain from a scientific point of view, the approach selected in the negotiations on long-range transboundary air pollution was instrumental in the sense that it cleared the way for an agreement to reduce sulfur emissions. In contrast, when the BSE crisis erupted, decision makers and negotiators were unprepared. There was no time to build consensual knowledge within the EU institutions before draconian decisions had to be made. This situation contributed to a direct confrontation of differing risk perceptions in key countries such as the United Kingdom and Germany.

10.3.2   Risks of noncompliance with international agreements

There is a general consensus among international lawyers that most states implement most international agreements most of the time (Henkin, 1979; Chayes, 1995). This means, of course, that some governments fail to fully implement their international agreements some of the time. Even if governments rarely disregard the commitments instituted in an international treaty altogether, they may try to circumvent some of the stipulations occasionally, or even persistently over time. Compliance failure remains one of the great problems in the practice of international law (Chayes, 1995; Victor *et al.*, 1998). The question of how to avoid compliance failure has been an issue in its own right in many environmental negotiations. For example, supervising sulfur emissions effectively was an important topic in the building of an acid rain regime in Europe. Parties to the negotiations on genetically modified foods were confronted with similar problems, such as how to establish that foodstuffs actually contain genes that have been modified. In the BSE case the difficulties of monitoring international trade in British beef impeded complete implementation of the EU decisions to prohibit meat exports from the United Kingdom. The Gabcikovo dispute illustrates that governments, in this case Hungary, sometimes deliberately break the stipulations of a treaty.

A party to a negotiation trying to calculate, say, the costs and benefits of a proposed environmental agreement must include the possible risk of implementation failure in its appraisal of the pending accord. The expected benefits of an agreement will be devalued if it is foreseen that some countries will not honor their obligations. The reasons for a country's implementation failure may differ from one case to another. Different causes may, in turn, represent dissimilar risk problems. In particular, there is reason to distinguish between *risks concerning trust* and *risks concerning feasibility*.

Trust concerns the direct association between two or more particular parties to a negotiation. As seen from a risk perspective, the key question is whether another party, or a number of parties, are trustworthy: Will they reliably carry out costly abatement measures stipulated in an environmental agreement (Bac, 1995)? Or will they try to avoid implementing their treaty obligations if they feel that they can get away with it (Scheberle, 1997)?

Free riding (obtaining a benefit at another's expense or without the usual expense) is often a response to a particular situation, such as an economic slump, when a government finds it burdensome to comply with a treaty. In this case, free riding is temporary and will be discontinued when the conditions for treaty implementation improve. Sometimes some parties to a treaty are granted the right to free ride in the sense that some exceptions are acknowledged for them with regard to the general provisions of the treaty. Developing countries often have been given such rights of exception in many economic and environmental agreements. Economies in transition have demanded the same privilege. The acid rain regime in Europe arguably has been constructed in such a way that in reality it grants similar exceptional treatment to some Mediterranean and East European countries. These cases indicate that free riding is not necessarily incidental, but may also manifest as a long-term strategy for weaker states.

The theory of collective goods predicts that small countries are likely to be free riders, because their individual performance (e.g., compliance or noncompliance) has little impact on the effectiveness of an international regime containing, for instance, rules about emission reductions. Other states will not be penalized by the free riding of small states (Olson, 1971). Free riding, however, is not necessarily restricted to small states, as predicted by the theory of collective goods. There is also evidence that powerful states have broken or bent those provisions of international treaties that they have considered to be too costly (Ahnlid and Vedovato, 1989). There are at least two reasons why other states would tolerate free riding by such leading nations. First, it is crucial for other states that these leading nations remain parties to the international agreement concerned. Imagine, for instance, if the United States were to leave the World Trade Organization (WTO) or the climate regime: the importance of these two international institutions would become effectively reduced in the eyes of most other member states. It would, for instance, mean harsher conditions for other states if the United States were to leave the WTO and deal with complicated and sensitive issues like, say, genetically modified food bilaterally instead of within the context of a world trade regime. Second, leading nations are usually difficult to punish if they break the rules of a regime, as they are typically relatively invulnerable to sanctions by smaller states and often are in a position to carry out hurting countermeasures.[5]

A country's political will to comply with an agreement is, however, not a sufficient condition for its full implementation. There may also be a lack of feasibility in implementing negotiated solutions to transboundary environmental problems. A government must consider the possibility that other countries involved in the negotiation may lack the necessary competence or resources to live up to the commitments they are expected to make in the proposed international treaty. One reason may be a shortage of technology to cope with a certain environmental problem at the source point. A second explanation may be a lack of know-how and scientific knowledge about environmental problems and appropriate abatement techniques; or it may be a lack of capacity to use available abatement technology optimally. For example, the general ambition of retaining biodiversity requires special competence at several different levels of decision making and implementation in a given country (Swanson, 1997; Hunter, 1999). Hence, the preservation of certain species presupposes difficult decisions in ministries or central agencies about how critical geographical areas should be protected. Environmental laws and governmental regulations concerning biodiversity cannot, however, be properly implemented unless people in the field at "the grassroots level" are fully knowledgeable about the concrete measures needed for the preservation of particular species. Critical decisions may have to be made concerning exactly what trees should be spared in a forest or how much vegetation should be saved along dikes and roads. Unless the necessary knowledge and know-how exist and are distributed properly in a society, a national government may be unable to honor an international agreement even if it is determined to do so and makes a commitment to that effect in a negotiation.

10.3.3   Abatement risks

International abatement action must be driven by an international agreement, which is typically the result of complicated negotiation, trade-offs, and compromises between a great number of countries. The agreement reflects what is politically attainable in terms of binding commitments by the governments concerned. Political feasibility does not, however, guarantee that abatement will be effective. For example, it is quite clear that the commitments made in the 1997 Kyoto Protocol to the UN Framework Convention on Climate Change to reduce greenhouse gases are insufficient to eliminate the global problem of climate warming. Similarly, many observers in Western Europe believe that the security measures undertaken in Ignalina and other nuclear power stations in the former Soviet bloc are insufficient. Thus, parties negotiating an environmental agreement have to consider the possibility that the costs that they are willing to accept to eliminate a transboundary environmental risk may lead to ineffective, or even entirely useless, abatement measures. This is the risk of ineffectiveness.

Abatement measures may also come to represent "opportunity risks" in a party's calculations if decision makers deem that the resources allocated to abatement measures could have been used to cope with the environmental issues at hand more effectively (say, domestically at the local level), or to serve some other important social or economic purpose. For example, in environmental negotiation (notably in the climate talks) one recurrent issue has been whether costly abatement measures should be undertaken immediately or whether they should be postponed until a new and more cost-effective "green" technology has been developed (Jain and Clark, 1989).[6] The BSE crisis in the EU was exacerbated by a dispute about opportunity costs of abatement measures. The British argued that the stringent restrictions of beef exports from the United Kingdom were unnecessary. Similarly, the authorities in Lithuania considered the termination of domestic production of electricity too high a price to pay for the increased environmental and health security that would be attained by the closure of the Ignalina nuclear power station.

10.4   Management of Negotiated Environmental Risks

The parties involved in international environmental negotiation are in principle always confronted with the three categories of negotiated risk described above: risks of noncompliance and insufficient abatement, as well as environmental risks as such. However, usually this risk perspective is not overly stressed by negotiating parties. One important reason for this is that environmental risks are often eclipsed by the crisis that puts the environmental issue on the agenda in the first place. However, it seems that international talks on transboundary environmental problems could in many cases be facilitated if the risk perspective were highlighted more and the significance of the three risk categories were better clarified.

10.4.1   Support approaches

At least four categories of approaches can be employed to support negotiations on transboundary environmental issues: ensuring compliance, financial/technical assistance, negotiation facilitation, and collective learning. These support strategies may be launched by actors involved in the negotiation concerned or by external third parties. Combinations of support approaches, or mixed support strategies, are also conceivable.

There have been calls for ensured compliance in the recent literature on international environmental cooperation and regime building (Chayes, 1995; Brown Weiss and Jacobson, 1999; Varvaele, 1999). A strategy of ensuring compliance aims at improving the prospects of satisfactory treaty implementation. Essentially, this approach rests on two pillars. The first is a system of authorized international sanctions that can be used to penalize signatory parties that refuse to fully implement a treaty. The second is improved transparency, for example, in the form of recurrent reporting by national governments or on-site inspection or monitoring (e.g., by means of satellite pictures). Thus, the primary aims of a strategy of ensuring compliance are, first, to make it more difficult for a government to avoid implementing measures prescribed in a treaty and, second, to make such illegal actions more costly. The involvement of NGOs may enhance a strategy of ensuring compliance in different ways and make it more effective (Alvanak and Cruz, 1997; Corell, 1999; Dunér, 1999).

The essence of financial/technical assistance is subsidization of those countries lacking the necessary competence or resources to negotiate or implement an environmental agreement. In the past decade, such environmental assistance has been used frequently by the EU, as well as by individual EU member states, in order to promote environmental policies in various ECE countries. Environmental aid to other countries has, in fact, been incorporated into national environmental policies. The rationale of such assistance is that "on the margin" it is more cost-effective to reduce hazardous emissions at foreign rather than domestic source points to improve domestic ecological quality. Environmental aid may take different forms. It may, for instance, represent purely economic assistance to cover the expenses for, say, "green" industrial investments aimed at reducing hazardous air pollution. Technical or scientific assistance to cope with environmental problems as such or with abatement measures is another important type of environmental assistance. One example is the technical assistance that the EU and individual member states have offered Lithuania in exchange for closing the Ignalina nuclear power station (Lithuanian Energy Institute, 1997). Aid programs have sometimes been problematic and controversial because donors and recipients have had different objectives and priorities (Löfstedt and Sjöstedt, 1996). Ignalina is a dramatic example: Donors have given technical assistance to support the closure of this nuclear power plant. The recipients – the Lithuanian authorities – have accepted this assistance in order to extend its existence.

Creative mediation is a form of third-party intervention in a negotiation (Stenelo, 1972). The primary aim is to help the parties in a negotiation to cope with a perceived conflict of interest in an imaginative way, particularly if the dissension has led to a stalemate. The case of the Gabcikovo dam is a good illustration of the problems of deadlock. According to Linnerooth-Bayer and Vari (see Chapter 6), a critical obstacle to an agreement in this dispute has been that the parties – Hungary and Slovakia – have framed it as a zero-sum situation. The goal of creative mediation, should it be attempted, would be to reframe the conflict as a non-zero-sum situation.

Framing is hence an important approach to creative mediation; the mediator makes parties perceive the issue(s) causing a deadlock from a new angle. Other typical strategies use compromise, issue linkages, and trade-offs to break a deadlock. The revised issue perceptions open the way for negotiation solutions that to that point have not been feasible. The negotiations concerning the part of the Sinai peninsula that Israel took over from Egypt in 1973 offer a good illustration. These talks started as a zero-sum game ("your gain is my loss") about desert territory reclaimed by Egypt. This negotiation problem was solved only after a third party had reframed territory as sovereignty for Egypt and as security for the Israelis. The disputed territory was formally returned to Egypt (sovereignty), but part of it was also declared a weapon-free zone under the supervision of the United Nations (security for Israel; Rubin, 1981). Perhaps a similarly imaginative negotiation approach may create an opening for an equally constructive solution to the complicated Gabcikovo problem.

Collective learning has been a crucial element of most negotiations on transboundary environmental issues (Corell, 1999). Such international talks tend to unfold according to a recurrent process pattern. In the prenegotiation phase, preparatory consultations among selected countries pave the way for a new negotiation and eventually lead to formal initiation procedures. Agenda setting determines the issues and the organization of the whole negotiation. In negotiation on formula, parties agree on a concrete approach to cope with principal negotiation problems. Subsequent bargaining on detail completes the preparations for an agreement. The final accord is often followed by postnegotiation for interpretating and sometimes further developing what has been achieved. These talks may turn into prenegotiation for a new round of talks.

Transboundary environmental issues typically have been complex and cumbersome for negotiating parties, primarily national governments. Often relatively little has been known about the issues at stake at the outset of the international negotiation – as was the case with the negotiations on acid rain, BSE, and climate warming. Therefore, parties have needed scientific knowledge and information in order to clarify the issues, to identify the stakes involved, and to understand the consequences they precipitate. The input of scientific communities has supported, and sometimes guided, a process of issue clarification in the negotiation, leading to the construction of consensual knowledge pertaining to issues and their consequences, and to abatement possibilities. This process typically has had the character of collective learning, incorporating most of the actors in the negotiation. Such collective learning is especially important when the agenda is being set but may occur during other process stages of the negotiation. For example, scientific knowledge may be useful for sufficiently developing a negotiation formula or for the construction of reliable implementation controls, which may occur in connection with negotiations on formula or on detail.

Negotiation on long-range air pollution in Europe – the problem of acid rain – offers a good illustration of the significance of consensual knowledge and collective learning in a successful negotiation on transboundary environmental problems. The development of the critical loads concept and its application in a Europe-wide effort to map different regions and soil types fostered a continent-wide commitment to a common target of limiting the acidity of soils and lakes. This outcome was the result of collective learning rather than the imposition of a politically motivated goal. It should be acknowledged, however, that collective learning around a commonly defined concept or goal is not always the key to reaching a credible and legitimate outcome to an international negotiation. This is abundantly clear from the failure of the EU member states to harmonize risk assessment procedures and outcomes for genetically modified crops. The 1990 EC Directive, which resulted from an EU-wide negotiation, mandated formal and harmonized risk assessments for releases of genetically modified crops at the national level. It would appear that a process of collective learning around the risk assessment concept would be necessary for implementing this directive and building consensual knowledge. On the contrary, the expert-based technocratic process underlying this harmonization directive has failed because it ignored the obvious: the same risks can be (and usually are) constructed differently by different persons or groups within and across borders. Thus, in order to function effectively, consensual knowledge has to be acknowledged by all the participants of the bargaining process, or at least by a dominant majority.

10.4.2 Support approaches in the management of negotiated environmental risks

The four support approaches described above are not direct strategies for managing negotiated risks in environmental negotiation. However, the application of each particular support approach has interesting implications for risk management in negotiation. The impact of particular approaches differs to such a high degree that the element of risk management is an important consideration when support strategies are compared and evaluated for application purposes.

10.4.3   Ensuring compliance

There is an obvious relationship between a strategy aiming at ensuring compliance with international agreements, on the one hand, and the risk of compliance failure on the other. The main purpose of a strategy of ensuring compliance is to discourage parties from venturing a partial or full policy of noncompliance. This objective may be particularly important given the expected accession of a number of ECE countries to the EU. The problems of policy implementation are likely to worsen with growing membership in the EU.

A strategy aiming at ensuring compliance could generate positive spillover effects to the management of abatement risks. A lack of compliance is likely to amplify abatement risks. A reasonable hypothesis is that parties will be more willing to undertake costly abatement measures if credible measures are planned to secure acceptable compliance discipline than if compliance failures are likely to occur. Otherwise, the total impact on the overall management of negotiated risks is quite limited.

A strategy of ensuring compliance is not, however, a universal instrument for coping with all sorts of implementation problems. It is strongly focused on enhancing trust among the participants in a negotiation and thus presupposes unwilling partners. However, sanctions are a poor instrument for dealing with implementation problems pertaining to the lack of institutional resources. If a government lacks the capability (e.g., the technical know-how) to carry out policy measures required by an international treaty, sanctions are not an effective instrument for achieving an acceptable degree of implementation. A consistent and effective strategy of compliance control will possibly have a general constraining effect on a negotiation on transboundary environmental issues. When the concerns of compliance control guide the negotiation, parties will strongly concentrate on elements of an international agreement that can be implemented with certainty and that can be controlled. Parties will emphasize the search for "the lowest common denominator," which will reduce the level of aspiration with regard to environmental problem solving.

10.4.4   Financial/technical assistance

Aid and assistance may have a much broader impact on overall management of negotiated environmental risks than compliance control. Thus, assistance may help parties to handle all three types of negotiated risk.

Countries may receive financial or technical assistance to implement an agreement (risk of infeasibility) or to participate in an international program of joint compliance control. Economic or technical aid may help governments to cope with abatement risks (risk of ineffectiveness) as well as environmental risks as such. For example, countries lacking sufficient analytical capacity may receive the necessary knowledge and information from other governments or international organizations.

Considering its many beneficial effects, it is not surprising that financial/technical assistance has frequently been used to facilitate international cooperation in Europe, particularly with ECE countries at the receiving end. However, assistance is not a sustainable support strategy for the future (Löfstedt and Sjöstedt, 1996). The political support for environmental aid to ECE nations is likely to weaken in West European donor countries. Those ECE countries that integrate into the EU will likely experience mounting pressure to accept the same commitments and abatement costs as the other EU member states. ECE governments, on their side, are also growing less interested in receiving environmental aid, because they have begun to consider it an unacceptable interference in their domestic policy-making (Löfstedt and Sjöstedt, 1996).

10.4.5 Creative mediation

Creative mediation may be useful for dealing with sticking points in all stages of a negotiation process, from pre- to postnegotiation. In the EU context, external facilitators have often been employed at the European Summits, where heads of government and state deal with each other. Creative mediation does not represent risk management directly, regardless of the risk at hand – implementation failure, abatement risks, or environmental risks as such. However, it may help create favorable conditions for other more conventional approaches to the management of negotiated environmental risks. For example, in the negotiations on acid rain in Europe, the use of the Regional Acidification INformation and Simulation (RAINS) model to suggest and appraise schedules of emission reductions represented a kind of creative mediation that had an important impact on the process. In the BSE case, the construction of more solid consensual issue knowledge with the help of the scientific community could have given a critical boost to the mediation.

10.4.6   Collective learning

Collective learning pertains to the management of transboundary environmental risks in particular, but it has important positive spillover effects on the management of other types of negotiated risk as well. Consensual knowledge of transboundary environmental issues is typically built up in such a way that its problem definition clearly indicates a solution. For example, in the consensual knowledge about long-range air pollution in Europe, reductions of sulfur emissions are allegedly necessary because these releases produce acid rain. Collective learning is of strategic importance not only for agenda setting but for the whole negotiation. Without consensus on how the environmental issues at stake are to be understood, delimited, and eventually framed for negotiation purposes, parties will find it difficult, if not impossible, to reach a meaningful agreement about appropriate abatement measures. This goes for the parties directly engaged in the negotiation, their circle of experts, and NGOs and others who have an indirect influence on negotiated outcomes. Establishing the necessary issue-related consensual knowledge has usually been a cumbersome, and somewhat protracted, process (as, for example, in the case of acid rain or climate warming). It is not sufficient that consensual knowledge represents a general comprehension of the environmental problem(s) that are to be coped with by negotiating parties. On the contrary, parties need to share a very precisely formulated issue interpretation that may serve as a frame of reference in a bargaining process containing increasingly important elements of careful "editing diplomacy" as agenda setting turns into bargaining about formula. The way environmental risks are presented in consensual knowledge will strongly condition how parties perceive the issues, but it will also determine the degree of determination with which they are willing to pursue a costly abatement solution.

Joint learning in a negotiation is significant both because it produces consensual knowledge and because the process of learning is a collective one. When parties construct consensual knowledge together they also build up a commitment to this interpretation, which in itself is an important prerequisite for ensuing effective negotiation. This commitment is shared not only by the delegates at the table but also by several layers of people in national administrations preparing negotiated issues. The buildup of institutions, rules, and policies for coping with many (but not all) environmental and health problems in Western Europe has been accompanied by long-term processes of intensive exchange of issue-specific knowledge and information regarding the risks to ecosystems and human health. This institutional communication and commitment has largely lacked a counterpart in the ECE region. During the Cold War era, there was policy harmonization in the ECE region, but the character of harmonization in the East was fundamentally different from that in the West. In the East, harmonization was essentially a top-down process in which command signals were given to capitals from a central authority. In the West, top-down policy-making and policy implementation were often accompanied by bottom-up processes of collective learning, which unfolded not only in the EU institutions but also elsewhere, notably in the Organisation for Economic Co-operation and Development (OECD). Hence, many EU environmental policies have been founded on solid and comprehensive issue-related consensual knowledge constructed by the complex processes of collective learning.

Collective learning emerges as a natural response to the needs of an unfolding negotiation process. In a facilitation perspective, collective learning may be organized in different ways. For instance, according to one common approach (the WTO "model"), the process of collective learning takes place in a working group, which is guided by a chairperson selected from the group participants and is administratively supported by an international secretariat. However, the arrangements for collective learning have sometimes been much more elaborate than in the WTO model – for example, the use of the RAINS model for issue analysis in the talks on long-range air pollution in Europe. Thus, an important means of facilitating negotiations on transboundary environmental risks is to begin by developing an appropriate organization and plan of action for the production of consensual knowledge. The forthcoming accession negotiations between a number of ECE countries and the EU is an example of a situation where a facilitation strategy to support collective learning needs to be carefully considered. ECE countries will be obliged to accept an EU environmental regime that stands on a groundwork of consensual knowledge that they may not share completely, or may not fully acknowledge because their governments did not participate in its construction. Therefore, special measures may be necessary to integrate ECE countries into the system of shared knowledge before they are requested to pledge their acceptance of the *acquis communautaire* in the environmental area (Johnstone-Bryden, 1995). One approach may be to initiate a substitute process of collective learning. It is important to note that such processes of knowledge building should not be limited to the official national delegates performing at the table. NGOs should be involved, as well as the public concerned with the issues discussed at the table, in line with Renn and Klinke's model of participation (see Chapter 9).

10.5   A Final Observation

Regimes are norms, principles, rules, and procedures pertaining to a particular issue, around which actor expectations converge (Krasner, 1983). The management of negotiated risks is a natural part of international regime building for the purpose of coping with transboundary environmental problems. This chapter has demonstrated the need to make this particular kind of risk management more distinct and has argued that better facilitation measures for this purpose need to be developed. By referring to examples of transboundary environmental risks in the special context of negotiation, we have shown that risk management in terms of support strategies should consider environmental risks as such, as well as risks concerning implementation and abatement. The analysis developed in this chapter demonstrates that the three categories of risk need to treated quite differently in a facilitation program. Sometimes this problem can be avoided entirely because complete priority is given to the management of one category of risk, say that of implementation. Nevertheless, packages of two or more support strategies need to be constructed in order to maximize the positive impact on risk management in negotiation. Such package building is a delicate and complicated operation, as a management approach that is effective with respect to one kind of negotiated risk may be ineffective – or, even worse, counterproductive – with regard to another. For example, there is no guarantee that collective learning will improve compliance discipline. Compliance control will not help parties to understand environmental risks better. Indeed, too strong an emphasis on compliance control will probably impede constructive collective learning. Still, combinations of different strategies of risk management in negotiation must be considered in future complicated environmental negotiations between the EU and various ECE countries.

Acknowledgments

In preparing this chapter I have benefited considerably from the advice of and comments by my coeditors, Joanne Linnerooth-Bayer and Ragnar Löfstedt. I wish to emphasize Joanne's contribution, in particular. Her penetrating and constructive critique improved not only many sections and arguments but the whole structure of the chapter as well.

Notes

[1] Note, however, that agreement is not the only conceivable criterion for a successful negotiation. The process of negotiation may produce values that usually cannot be incorporated into a treaty, for example mutual trust and understanding among the parties involved (or among some of them).

[2] Although it can be argued that one cannot perceive something that will occur in the future because it does not exist, the expression "perception of risk" has become commonly accepted. This convention is accepted in this chapter.

[3] Note that a dispute about the exact meaning of the word "indicating" was at the heart of the conflict concerning mad cows. On the British side the official assessment asserted that the evidence that BSE could be transferred to humans from cattle was much too weak to serve as a basis for political action. In Germany and other continental countries an opposite evaluation was made: the only reasonable evaluation of the available evidence regarding BSE was that there was a genuine health risk to those who had eaten meat infected with BSE, and that therefore political action was mandatory.

[4] Note that risks can also arise when there are no human choices, as in the case of earthquakes. Environmental issues do not represent risks when they pertain to an accident that has occurred, or is happening, which has known consequences.

[5] A common proposition in the literature is that international regimes cannot become fully effective unless they are "policed" by a leading nation, preferably a hegemon.

[6] The issue of climate change is one example. For a long time the United States and some other countries refused to accept a binding commitment to begin reducing greenhouse gas emissions, arguing that new and "greener" abatement technology was being developed and that investments to cope with the greenhouse effect should be delayed until this new technology was available (Gelbspan, 1995).

References

Ahnlid, A., and Vedovato, C., 1989, I morgon regionalism: det nationella handelssystemets framtid, *Världspolitikens dagsfrågor* 1989:5, Utrikespolitiska institutet, Stockholm, Sweden.

Alvanak, L., and Cruz, A., 1997, *Implementing Agenda 21: NGO Experiences from around the World*, NGLS, Geneva, Switzerland.

Bac, M., 1995, Incomplete information and incentives to free ride on international environmental resources, *Beijer Discussion Paper Series*, 60, Stockholm, Sweden.

Benedick, R., 1991, *Ozone Diplomacy: New Directions in Safeguarding the Planet*, Harvard University Press, Cambridge, MA, USA.

Brown, V., 1995, *Risks and Opportunities: Managing Environmental Conflict and Change*, Earthscan, London, UK.

Brown Weiss, E., and Jacobson, H., eds, 1999, *Engaging Countries: Strengthening Compliance with International Accords*, MIT Press, Cambridge, MA, USA.

Carter, F., and Turnock, D., eds, 1996, *Environmental Problems in Eastern Europe*, Routledge, London, UK.

Chayes, A., 1995, *The New Sovereignty: Compliance with International Regulatory Agreements*, Harvard University Press, Cambridge, MA, USA.

Corell, E., 1999, The Negotiable Desert: Expert Knowledge in the Negotiations of the Convention to Combat Desertification, Tema, Universitet, Linköping, Sweden.

Drottz-Sjöberg, B.-M., 1991, *Perceptions of Risk: Studies of Risk Attitudes, Perceptions and Definitions*, Center for Risk Research, Stockholm School of Economics, Stockholm, Sweden.

Dunér, B., 1999, *The Art of NGO-ing*, Swedish Institute of International Affairs, Stockholm, Sweden.

Ebel, R., 1994, *Chernobyl and Its Aftermath: A Chronology of Events*, Center for Strategic and International Studies, Washington, DC, USA.

Falloux, F., 1993, *Crisis and Opportunity: Environment and Development in Africa*, Earthscan, London, UK.

Ford, B., 1996, *BSE: The Facts: Mad Cow Disease and the Risk to Mankind*, Corgi, London, UK.

Gelbspan, R., 1995, *The Heat is On: The Climate Crisis/The Cover-up/The Prescription*, Perseus Books, Reading, MA, USA.

Grabbe, H., and Hughes, K., 1997, *Eastward Enlargement of the European Union*, Royal Institute of International Affairs, London, UK.

Henkin, L., 1979, *How Nations Behave: Law and Foreign Policy*, Columbia University Press, New York, NY, USA.

Hunter, M., ed., 1999, *Maintaining Biodiversity in Forest Ecosystems*, Cambridge University Press, Cambridge, UK.

Jain, R., and Clark, A., eds, 1989, *Environmental Technology, Assessment and Policy*, Horwood, Chichester, UK.

Johnstone-Bryden, I., 1995, *Managing Risk: How to Work Successfully with Risk*, Avebury, Aldershot, UK.

Krasner, S., 1983 (ed.), *International Regimes*, Cornell University Press, Ithaca, NY, USA.

Kyoto Protocol to the United Nations Framework Convention on Climate Change, 1997, UNFCCC Secretariat, FCCC/CP/1997/7/Add.1, http://www.unfccc.de.

Larsson, P., 1996, Regimförhandlingar på miljöområdet. En studie av förhandlingarna om LRTAP-konventionen, Lund Political Studies 93, Lund, Sweden.

Lette, K., 1996, *Mad Cows*, Dove Books, Los Angeles, CA, USA.

Linnerooth-Bayer, J., 1999, Climate change and multiple views on fairness, in F. Toth, ed., *Fair Weather? Equity Concerns in Climate Change*, Earthscan, London, UK.

Lithuanian Energy Institute, 1997, *Handbook about the Ignalina Nuclear Power Plant for the Emergency Preparedness Organizations around the Baltic Sea*, Lithuanian Energy Institute, Kaunas, Lithuania.

Löfstedt, R., and Sjöstedt, G., eds, 1996, *Environmental Aid Programmes to Eastern Europe: Area Studies and Theoretical Application*, Avebury, Aldershot, UK.

Olson, M., 1971, *The Logic of Collective Action: Public Goods and the Theory of Groups*, Shocken Books, New York, NY, USA.

Rubin, J., 1981, *Dynamics of Third Party Intervention: Kissinger in the Middle East*, Praeger, New York, NY, USA.

Scheberle, D., 1997, *Federalism and Environmental Policy: Trust and Politics of Implementation*, Georgetown University Press, Washington, DC, USA.

Sjöstedt, G., ed., 1993a, *International Environmental Negotiation*, SAGE Publications, Newbury Park, CA, USA.

Sjöstedt, G., 1993b, Negotiations on nuclear pollution: The Vienna Conventions on Notification and Assistance in Case of a Nuclear Accident, in G. Sjöstedt (ed.), *International Environmental Negotiation*, SAGE Publications, Newbury Park, CA, USA.

Shaw, R., 1993, Acid-rain negotiations in North America and Europe: A study in contrast, in G. Sjöstedt, ed., *International Environmental Negotiation*, SAGE Publications, Newbury Park, CA, USA.

Stenelo, L.-G., 1972, Mediation in international negotiations, Studentlitteratur, Lund, Sweden.

Stine, D., 1994, *International Environmental Decision Making*, University of Michigan, Ann Arbor, MI, USA.

Swanson, T., 1997, *Global Action for Biodiversity: An International Framework for Implementing the Convention on Biological Diversity*, Earthscan, London, UK.

Underdal, A., 1993, The outcomes of negotiation, in V. Kremenyuk, ed., *International Negotiation: Analysis, Approaches, Issues*, Jossey-Bass Publishers, San Francisco, CA, USA.

Underdal, A., ed., 1998, l*The Politics of International Environmental Management*, Kluwer Academic Publishers, Dordrecht, Netherlands.

Varvaele, J., ed., 1999, *Compliance and Enforcement of European Community Law*, Kluwer, The Hague, Netherlands.

Victor, D., Raustiala, K., and Skolnikoff, E., 1998, *The Implementation and Effectiveness of International Environmental Commitment: Theory and Practice*, MIT Press, Cambridge, MA, USA.

Chapter 11

Transboundary Environmental Risk Management in the New Millennium: Lessons for Theory and Practice

Ragnar E. Löfstedt and Gunnar Sjöstedt

11.1 Introduction

The case studies in this volume present topical and controversial risk issues that cross national political borders on the European continent. These extra-regional risks require political solutions beyond the nation-state and thus raise a set of issues for both the theory of their management and its practical applications. Because of a general lack of research and institution building in this area, transboundary risk management can be considered a new and developing topic for risk researchers and practitioners.

This lack of research and institution building is surprising considering transboundary risks are both prevalent and serious throughout the world –

especially in Europe, where a large percentage of the population is located close to a national border. Scandinavia's largest environmental problem continues to be acid rain, most of which originates in continental Europe (see Chapter 4). Biotechnology and its regulation across European borders and across continents is a transboundary risk issue on both a European and a global scale (see Chapter 3). And decade-long controversies over the risks of border developments – as, for example, in the case of the Gabcikovo dam project – can fuel European ethnic hostilities and greatly complicate European unity (see Chapter 6). Despite the prevalence and seriousness of transboundary risks, most research has focused on local and national environmental risk problems, such as the siting of nuclear waste depositories in Sweden and the United States (e.g., Kunreuther *et al.*, 1990; Drottz-Sjöberg, 1996, 1998), the siting of waste incinerators in Austria and the United Kingdom (Linnerooth-Bayer and Fitzgerald, 1996; Löfstedt, 1997), and the public perceptions of nuclear power (e.g., Sjöberg, 1999).[1] These local and national risks are comparatively well understood. A large body of interdisciplinary research has shown that factors associated with public and policymaker perceptions are important in their management (Slovic, 1987); that deliberation among the various actors is helpful (Renn, 1999; see also Chapter 9); and that communication among the scientific community, policymakers, and the public is essential (NRC, 1989).

There are three types of organizing forces that combine to "manage" transboundary risks. Market-based institutions (e.g., liability for polluting behavior) and governance by treaties and regimes (e.g., in regulating sulfur emissions in Europe) are two of the most discussed institutional forces at the transnational level. In addition, the cases in this book demonstrate the increasingly important role of non-state and non-market actors – including the collective action of millions of consumers and public protestors – constituting a third organizing force that can either complement or compete with market-style institutions and national or international authority (Goldman, 1998). During the public demonstrations against the World Trade Organization in Seattle in 1999, we witnessed the potential of this "third force" in setting limits to markets and international trade, partly (and importantly) as a reaction to transboundary risk issues inherent in the trade of products and resources.

Transboundary environmental risks that cross politically sovereign borders pose new challenges for risk-management theory and practice.

National cultural styles can complicate the management process considerably, a point brought home by the radically opposing constructions of the risks from the Gabcikovo dam project on either side of the Danube River (see Chapter 6). National history and political relations also add to the complexity of transboundary risk management – nations with a history of close cooperation are, generally, more willing to work together to solve transboundary issues than those without such a history (Majone, 1985). While local cultures can differ considerably within nations, an important and obvious differentiating characteristic at the international level is the lack of institutions and procedures for mediating these cultural and historical differences.

11.2   Lessons for the Theory of Transboundary Risk Management

11.2.1   A short review of relevant literature

In sharp contrast to risk issues at the local and national levels, there is little interdisciplinary research that focuses specifically on the assessment and management of environmental and public health risks across borders. However, there is a vast literature on related topics that can serve as a basis for an interdisciplinary approach to the study of transboundary risks. First, there are the social theorists such as Beck (1992) and Giddens (1985) who argue that transboundary risks are all part of the "risk society," where risks can no longer be controlled by human forces as they become uninsurable and global (e.g., the Chernobyl accident; Giddens, 1985; Blowers, 1993; Beck, 1994, 1999; Miller, 1995; Lidskog, 1997). Some of these ideas are explored by Brian Wynne and Kerstin Dressel in Chapter 5, where they argue that the bovine spongiform encephalopathy (BSE) crisis is an example of a risk that is both international (there were BSE cases in several European countries, including France and Switzerland) and not controlled (the scientific community did not correctly access the risks associated with BSE when it was first diagnosed in the 1980s).

A second area of research on transboundary hazards has been developed by researchers involved in the explicit examination of cross-boundary issues, for example, the wide literature on the development and practice of river basin institutions that span national boundaries. These researchers have not focused on transboundary risks *per se*, but have examined boundary regimes more generally – for example, those operating between the United States and Mexico, and the United States and Canada (Linnerooth-Bayer, 1990; Linnerooth-Bayer and Murcott, 1996; Milich and Varady, 1998; see also Chapter 6). The researchers in this area are from various academic backgrounds but are largely dominated by geographers and lawyers.

Political scientists have focused on multicountry brokered environmental treaties and their effectiveness (e.g., Dahl, 1994, 1997; Skjaerth, 1994; Majone, 1996; Salay, 1996; Weiss and Jacobson, 1996; Dua and Esty, 1997; Salay, 1996; van der Heijden, 1997; Esty and Mendelsohn, 1998; Victor *et al.*, 1998; see also Chapter 4). This research extends to examining institutional models of global governance, especially for dealing with externalities in which one nation pollutes another without incurring any associated costs (e.g., UK sulfur and nitrogen oxide emissions affect Scandinavia but pose few environmental problems in the United Kingdom [Milich and Varady, 1998; see also Chapter 4]). One way of dealing with these transnational externalities – one which follows the route of domestic institutional development – is an expansion of the scope and role of the United Nations (UN) or the development of other supranational institutions to manage the transborder risks (e.g., Sjöstedt, 1993; Majone, 1996; Jackson, 1998; Victor *et al.*, 1998). A recent, novel idea in the literature is the development of a new form of supranational democratic organization, where individuals from all over the world are asked to vote for a group of "international leaders," commonly referred to as cosmopolitan democracy (Held, 1995). Some view this and other forms of supranational institutions as being vital for dealing with transboundary problems as they become more pervasive and global, for example, as problems are exported in the name of trade (e.g., the shipping of hazardous waste to Africa from Europe and North America) and as multinational companies use the global market to site plants in countries with lax safety and environmental standards (Beck, 1999; Held *et al.*, 1999).

Another area of research relevant to transboundary risk management is the investigation of international regimes, which have been defined as institutions set up to regulate the behavior of states, companies, and other organizations (Levy *et al.*, 1994; Hasenclaver *et al.*, 1997). While binding rules specified in international treaties represent the hard core of regimes, their existence depends on binding procedures, norms, and principles (Krasner, 1983). Procedures are manifest in organizational, administrative factors. Norms give direction from general and widely accepted propositions like that of the "polluter pays" principle. Principles express consensual knowledge about the issues covered by a regime and often focus on critical causal relationships, such as emissions of sulfur leading to long-range transboundary air pollution that eventually produces acidification problems at the recipient end. The building of international regimes designed to cope with transboundary environmental issues is a complex process involving nation-states, markets, and civil society.

International supranational institutions are therefore not the only form of global governance. Indeed, regime theorists speak of global governance in the absence of global government, and many national governments are moving away from top-down regulatory styles to make more use of market forces and market-style incentives. Thus another line of research is pursuing the legal, institutional, and economic issues of extending personal and national liability for environmental damage across sovereign states. Liability regimes that span national borders are thus "in the making" in Europe and elsewhere. Important European directives now impose transnational liability on exporters of hazardous wastes (Hiltz and Ehrenfeld, 1991), and the International Law Commission is developing rules and procedures for liability regarding international waters (Brubaker, 1993; McHugh, 1994). This "marketization" of transboundary risk management is increasingly embodied in international treaties, for example, the tradable permits idea for regulating greenhouse gas emissions (Jackson, 1998).

As the cases in this book demonstrate, however, neither supranational nor market-style institutions can stand alone in managing transboundary risks (see Chapter 6). Market forms of regulation can be powerful institutions – as has been shown by the radical use of liability regimes in the United States. However, even if international law becomes effective, liability rules cannot fully replace regulatory bodies. Yet, hierarchical regulatory and rule-setting institutions are also limited, especially at the international level. The limits of the European Commission are illustrated in the case study on biotechnology presented in Chapter 3, in which the "top-down" pronouncement of European experts on the risks of genetically modified (GM) crops was categorically rejected by local and national authorities and the public. Market regulatory provisions would probably fare no better, as the limited success of labeling GM foods (and letting the consumers weigh the risks and benefits) in Europe has demonstrated.

The limits of supranational organizations or markets in coping with transboundary risks in Europe are not, however, the focus of this book. Rather, an important message is that the third organizing force – sometimes referred to as civil society – has been neglected and should be studied as a way of complementing both top-down institutions and markets. This third force is the informal and often spontaneous management of transboundary risks through the decentralized decisions and actions of the public and public groups. The influence of this third force has been illustrated throughout the case studies presented in this volume: the European-wide harmonization of biotechnology products has been blocked by public, farmer, and consumer reaction; the population on both sides of the Danube River appeared willing to accept an easily implemented compromise solution to the decades-long Gabcikovo dam controversy; local reactions to the BSE threat – and barriers to a commonly accepted European policy – were distinguished by different constructions of the risk within Europe; and, as was shown in the Ignalina case, the win–win solutions of environmental aid are imperfect solutions when the perceptions and concerns of the public and local policymakers are not considered.

11.2.2   Lessons for theory and research

The neglect of civil society as a third organizing force has important lessons for research in this area. Specifically, it suggests that future research areas might give attention to several issues that may help alleviate conflicts surrounding cross-border issues, namely, understanding public and policymaker concerns about transboundary environmental risks; understanding the environmental policy backgrounds of individual nations and multinational organizations (e.g., the European Union [EU]) where these decisions are made; and designing deliberative transboundary processes that bring the public and nongovernmental organizations (NGOs) more directly into the risk assessment and management process. In the sections that follow we discuss each in turn.

11.2.3 Understanding public and policymaker perceptions and concerns about transboundary risks

Public and policymaker concerns with regard to transboundary hazards vary from country to country and from issue to issue. In some cases these varying concerns are directly related to national interests. For example, Germans and Swedes are more concerned about the environmental problems associated with acid rain than are the British, as they are more affected by these problems (Boehmer-Christiansen and Skea, 1991; Löfstedt, 1995; see also Chapter 4). In other cases different perceptions, although still related rather directly to national interests, are more subtle and not well understood. Regarding Swedish–Finnish conflicts on how best to regulate pulp and paper production using a similar type of base material (long-fiber pulp from spruce and pine forests), Auer (1996) concludes that underlying geographical differences explain why the Swedes are more concerned about chlorinated organic compounds and the Finns are more concerned about regulating organic pollutants. Eighty percent of the Swedish pulp mills are located on the coast, where organic pollutants are less of a problem, while a majority of the Finnish pulp mills are located inland, where organic pollutants of the freshwater river ways are a major concern (Auer, 1996).

Similar types of differing concerns and national interests are apparent in the criteria for environmental aid programs expressed by Sweden and Lithuania. Over the past several years, Sweden has funded East European environmental initiatives, but mainly those that the Swedish policymakers and public have been most concerned about, namely, transboundary radiation from East European nuclear reactors (one of Sweden's largest receivers of aid has been the Ignalina nuclear power station in Lithuania; see Chapter 2); acid rain, particularly from Poland (see Chapter 4); and water pollution (see Salay, 1991; Kristoferson, 1994; Löfstedt, 1995, 1998; Löfstedt and Sjöstedt, 1995, 1996; Sjöberg, 1999). In terms of creating a better environment in the recipient communities, however, it is questionable whether these areas should be given priority for aid. Studies by the World Bank, for example, point out that environmental aid to East European nations should focus on local public health issues, for example, reducing pollution from small district heating plants rather than from large power stations (World Bank, 1993). As one policymaker in

Poland eloquently put it, "The Swedes are more concerned about salmon swimming in the Baltic Sea than the health of our children" (see Löfstedt, 1998).

In yet other cases, the different perceptions and concerns among the parties involved cannot be so directly tied to national interests. For example, both Austria and Norway had similar interests in banning British beef to enhance their local beef markets. Yet, in sharp contrast to Austria, Norway was little concerned about the BSE issue. Similarly, with regard to biotechnology, agricultural lobbies in both Canada and the United States have economic interests in promoting biotechnology products, yet there is a considerable popular movement to ban genetically modified organisms in Canada that is not present in the United States (*Economist*, 2000).

11.2.4 Understanding national policy histories

Studies on national policy histories can also help us to understand disparate perceptions and constructions of risk across national borders, as is illustrated by the response to Sweden's funding of safety improvements at the Ignalina nuclear power station (see Chapter 2). Sweden is financing safety improvements at this plant for two related reasons: First, there is a high degree of Swedish concern regarding transboundary nuclear radiation (Sjöberg, 1999), which should not be surprising considering Sweden was the Western nation worst hit by the 1986 Chernobyl accident (Broadbent, 1986). More importantly, however, policymakers fear that an accident at the Ignalina nuclear power station could jeopardize the future of Sweden's 12 nuclear power plants, which currently produce 50% of the country's electricity.

Another example demonstrating the importance of history in the management of transboundary risks is the long-standing controversy over the Gabcikovo hydropower station. Only by understanding the historical development of this controversy – especially its roots in the socialist systems of Hungary and Czechoslovakia, with their idealistic promotion of large-scale, centralized projects – is it possible to fashion arrangements for resolving the present-day conflict. Similarly, the historical records of relations between the United Kingdom and Germany shed light on the different perceptions of the BSE risks and the conflicts on this issue between these two countries.

11.2.5   Designing deliberative transboundary risk management processes

A great deal of research and experience in managing risks at the local and national levels has shown the limitations of expert-dominated, top-down procedures for resolving controversial environmental risk issues. An alternative approach emphasizes deliberative risk management practices that directly involve the many interested and affected parties, even during the "fact-finding" stages of the risk assessment process. The proponents of this approach argue that credible and legitimate compromises in settling transboundary environmental disputes will necessarily take account of public and stakeholder values (Royal Commission for Environment and Pollution, 1998), especially at the risk characterization stage (NRC, 1996). Of course, deliberative and participatory processes are not suited for all types of risk disputes – certainly not for resolving crisis situations, such as occurred immediately following publication of the scientific evidence on BSE. They might be particularly well suited, however, to managing border risk disputes, as was demonstrated by the public participation process during the Gabcikovo controversy. At the EU level there is increasing interest in involving the public and other stakeholders more directly in issues such as the controversies surrounding GM foods, nuclear power plant safety, and water pollution (see Chapter 9).

As Renn and Klinke point out in Chapter 9, however, a participatory risk management process across national borders presents formidable problems. For example, there can be language barriers as well as cultural differences. But the outcomes of public participation in the policy-making process may well be worth overcoming these obstacles. Involving the interested and affected parties in, for instance, panels or consensus conferences can lead to more rational and credible processes. These processes might be particularly well suited to resolving close-to-home border disputes. For instance, there has been a long-standing dispute between Sweden and Denmark over the Barsebäck nuclear reactor, which is located in Sweden close to the Danish border. An earlier study showed that the Danish public favored a tit-for-tat solution (that is, closing one reactor in Sweden in return for closing an equivalent amount of electric-generating capacity from Danish coal-fired plants), whereas the Danish policymakers viewed the situation as a Swedish rather than a joint Swedish–Danish problem (Löfstedt, 1996a, 1996b). Deliberative procedures have the potential to reveal these different framings and views on fairness at an early stage of the negotiation process. More research, especially documenting experience with deliberative processes at the local level, could aid in the development of such procedures by addressing the formidable challenges discussed in this book.

11.3   Lessons for Practice: Motives and Possibilities

In this developing area of research on transboundary environmental and technological risks, *lessons for theory* are closely associated with *lessons for practice*. Academic analysis can have an impact on the effective practical management of transboundary environmental problems. Management represents both policy measures in the traditional meaning, that is, negotiating and implementing international treaties, putting into place liability and other market mechanisms, harmonizing national regulations, and so forth. But it also includes spontaneous patterns of performance by whole populations or large groups of people in one or more countries (e.g., fear of eating beef in many parts of Europe following the BSE crisis; see Chapter 5). *Lessons for practice* pertain to a discussion of the general advantages and disadvantages of principal approaches to the management of transboundary environmental and technological risks that need to be further developed for policy application. Different situations are likely to require somewhat different responses by government authorities and the general public. Lessons for practice from academic research may contribute to clarifying the obstacles nations have to master when they are developing or implementing individual or joint solutions to transboundary environmental problems.

Environmental policy-making and regime building have proven to be cumbersome in many contexts, at the national as well as the international levels. Environmental issues have typically been technically complex, the scientific knowledge has often been insufficient, and the stakes have been uncertain. Uncertainty can be especially high regarding the positive effects of environmental abatement measures, because they typically accrue in the distant future. For example, it is difficult to show relationships between environmental improvements of Scandinavian lakes and Swedish and Danish investments in sulfur dioxide abatement technologies for Polish coal-burning power plants (Löfstedt, 1998; see also Chapter 4). Although benefits are uncertain in the short term, investments in transboundary abatement technologies can lead to consulting opportunities for the country providing the investment (Löfstedt and Sjöstedt, 1995), to inexpensive investments for purchasing long-term security (Sweden's investments in Ignalina's safety systems have arguably led to a reduction in the possibility of a serious accident at the plant; see Chapter 2), and to learning valuable lessons in risk communication and management techniques that are readily transferable to the national setting (see Chapters 6, 8, and 9).

11.3.1 Facilitation strategies

Voluntary action taken by individuals, businesses, and other organizations may contribute to both generating and solving environmental risk problems (e.g., saving energy to reduce greenhouse gas emissions; see Chapter 4). In this regard, *lifestyle* is an important factor that may change "spontaneously" over time (e.g., rejecting products containing genetically modified organisms; see Chapter 3). Lifestyle changes can be supported and facilitated by national or international institutions. For example, a government may organize effective dissemination of pertinent information or establish forums such as open hearings for the exchange of information between government authorities and the public.

Another important lesson for practice from this project is the importance of understanding how transboundary risk issues are perceived and constructed by the interested and affected parties within and across borders. Worldviews and interests can greatly influence how issues are framed and how risks are perceived. While national interests differ according to the perceptions of risks (e.g., the Slovaks and Hungarians continue to view the risks of the Gabcikovo project quite differently), we find very similar perceptions among like groups across borders (e.g., Hungarian, Austrian, and Slovak environmentalists demonstrated together against the Gabcikovo project). These different perceptions can also influence the response to a crisis situation (see Chapter 10). In Chapter 5, Wynne and Dressel discuss the opposing views of British and German officials during the BSE crisis, views that can only partly be explained by differences in national interests with regard to the ban on British beef. Alternatively, although it was not evident during the BSE crisis, an emergency situation can generate political will and action among countries with otherwise opposing national interests and even ideologies. For example, at the time of the Chernobyl accident, policymakers and regulators in all European nations worked together to ensure that the risks of the Chernobyl accident were properly understood and assessed.

Cases describing aid for improving the Ignalina reactor (see Chapter 2), the European response to the BSE crisis (see Chapter 5), and international policy on the trade of GM foods (see Chapter 3) demonstrate the need to conceive of transboundary environmental risks as *constructions* that typically differ across nations depending on history, cultural worldviews, ideologies, and national interests (Majone, 1985). Without such awareness, the responsible national parties will find it difficult to establish the consensual knowledge necessary for effective joint problem solving.

The experiences from the cases in this book should also function as reminders for practitioners that transboundary environmental issues cannot be adequately understood with only expert assessments of the probabilities and consequences of the risks at issue. As clearly shown in the cases of the Gabcikovo plant, the BSE issue, and biotechnology, as well as with regard to the early Swedish–UK assessments concerning the risks of acid rain (Boehmer-Christiansen and Skea, 1991), experts within and across countries provide remarkably different risk assessments of the same issue. A great deal of research has documented the inherently subjective processes of expert risk assessment and the conflicts and contradictions that arise among the experts. Risk controversies across borders are proving to be no exception to the failure of political risk management processes that are grounded solely in expert assessments; however, cross-border institutions for making decisions in the face of controversial and conflicting risk evidence are lacking. Thus, expert conflicts can easily escalate to international political conflicts, as was evident in both the Gabcikovo controversy between Slovakia and Hungary and in the BSE controversy between Germany and the United Kingdom. There are exceptions, however, as illustrated by the successful negotiations to reduce sulfur emissions in Europe, where expertise and quantified information using the critical loads concept led to a scientific consensus among countries with different national interests. In this case, systematic calculations and a computer model produced a form of consensual knowledge that served as an instrumental basis for bargaining on formula and detail, which eventually led to an agreement.

Hence, an important lesson for practice is that effective transboundary risk management must usually, but not always, proceed in the face of conflicting expert assessments of the risks and widely different perceptions and concerns about the risks on the part of the interested parties. These different perceptions among the experts and the interested and affected parties make adequate communication all the more important. At the EU level, this will mean, at the least, making decision processes open and transparent. For close-to-home border risk issues, instrumental *risk communication* should include all the affected and interested parties on both sides of the border. Without effective communication, we can expect increasing distrust of those responsible for making the decisions, especially in light of widely different risk constructions and expert evidence. Special measures will be necessary to make risk communication comprehensive and effective enough in the dialogue between the older EU member states and the East and Central European countries striving to become formally integrated into the EU.

11.3.2 Developing transborder deliberative processes

An important lesson for practice is the development of transborder deliberative processes, especially to manage bilateral or multilateral border disputes over the imposition of risks by one or more countries. As public distrust of national policymakers continues to increase in Europe and elsewhere (Klingemann and Fuchs, 1995), making national (let alone international) environmental policies will be increasingly more difficult. In such situations, the development of transborder deliberative processes, as advocated by Renn and Klinke (see Chapter 9), should be encouraged. As discussed in the 1996 National Resource Council document *Understanding Risk*, public involvement as early as the risk characterization stage may lead to improved outcomes, since with deliberation the public need not trust their national authorities – they are involved in the policy-making process themselves.

11.4 Concluding Remarks

The present volume offers several important insights into theory and practice with regard to transboundary risk management:

- There is a need to understand public and policymaker perceptions and concerns about transboundary risks. Public and policymaker concerns with regard to transboundary hazards vary from country to country and issue to issue. To help resolve present-day conflicts, it is therefore important to understand why some policymakers and the public in some countries are concerned about certain topics and

issues and why those in other countries are not. A good example
is the case of nuclear power. There is no Europe-wide consensus
regarding how best to deal with the continent's reactors. For example, the Danes, who do not have reactors, are much more concerned
about them than are the French and the Swedes, who do. To make
progress in such a conflict-laden area, studies need to be conducted
on why these differences are present. Such studies would help answer questions such as why the Danes are concerned about nuclear
power. Case studies in this book have looked at such conflict-laden
issues in some detail, specifically with regard to acid rain and East
European nuclear reactors. We hope that this topic area is one that
both researchers and practitioners will explore in the future.

- There is a need to understand national policy histories. Our research
  has shown the need to examine both historical and cultural dimensions in order to understand disparate perceptions and constructions
  of risks across national borders. This was clearly depicted in the Ignalina case, in which the Swedes have decided to fund safety measures at the Ignalina nuclear plant as a form of insurance that will
  allow the continued operation of Sweden's own reactors.

- There is a need for more deliberative processes. Similar to findings
  at both the local and national levels, the existing risk management
  tools used in present-day transboundary risk management will not
  work, as nations in Europe and elsewhere are heading toward an era
  of distrust. What is needed is an alternative approach that directly
  involves many interested and affected parties, even during the "fact-
  finding" stage. This point is elaborated at some length in Chapter 9
  and was demonstrated in the public participation process during the
  Gabcikovo controversy (see Chapter 6).

- There is a need for improved market/liability regimes to ensure that
  individual nations who contribute to transboundary pollution are
  also liable for this pollution, rather than letting it become a so-called
  commons problem. The issue here is revoking the "victim pays principle." As Patt points out in Chapter 4, this is the case with acid rain
  associated with transnational externalities, in which Poland and the
  United Kingdom pollute other nations for free, while Sweden and
  the other Scandinavian victims pay the bills. One way around this is
  via an expansion of the scope and role of the UN or the development

of other supranational institutions charged with managing the transboundary risks (see Majone, 1996; see also Chapter 10).

- There is a need for more effective implementation of environmental agreements to ensure not only that transboundary environmental problems are truly reduced, but also that national policymakers, stakeholders, and the public do not question the whole international agreement process, which could have detrimental effects on policymaking in the long term. At the present time, most national governments feel powerless in the light of international environmental problems, be they the damming of rivers (see Chapter 6) or dealing with acid rain problems (see Chapter 4). One way of handling these issues is to ensure that supranational environmental agreements actually have teeth (see Chapter 8).
- One of the most important lessons arising from this three-year project and the resulting book is that communication is crucial. To solve transboundary environmental issues, policymakers, diplomats, and regulators in both the polluter and victim nations must see and believe that there is a need to communicate about these controversial issues. As discussed throughout this book – in the BSE case (see Chapter 5), the acid rain controversy (see Chapter 4), and the issue of aid to the Ignalina plower plant (see Chapter 2) – this is not always the case.

Acknowledgments

Parts of the work reported in this paper are based on research funded by the Swedish Council for the Planning and Coordination of Research (FRN). We are grateful to Joanne Linnerooth-Bayer for providing us with helpful comments on earlier versions of this manuscript.

Note

[1] An exception to this is the large amount of research conducted on ozone depletion and global warming (e.g., IPCC, 1996).

References

Auer, M.R., 1996, Negotiating toxic risks: A case from the Nordic countries, *Environmental Politics*, **5**(4):687–699.

Beck, U., 1992, *Risk Society*, Sage, London, UK.

Beck, U., 1994, The reinvention of politics: Towards a theory of reflexive modernization, in U. Beck, A. Giddens, and S. Lash, eds, *Reflexive Modernization. Politics, Tradition and Aesthetics in the Modern Social Order*, Polity Press, Cambridge, UK.

Beck, U., 1999, *What is Globalization?*, Polity Press, Cambridge, UK.

Blowers, A., 1993, Environmental policy: The quest for sustainable development, *Urban Studies*, **30**:775–796.

Boehmer-Christiansen, S., and Skea, J., 1991, *Acid Politics: Environmental and Energy Policies in Britain and Germany*, Belhaven Press, London, UK.

Broadbent, N., 1986, Chernobyl radionuclide contamination and reindeer herding in Sweden, *Collegicum Antropologicum*, **10**(2):231–242.

Brubaker, D., 1993, *Marine Pollution and International Law: Principles and Practice*, Belhaven Press, London, UK.

Dahl, A., 1994, *Environmental Actors and European Integration: Attitudes Towards Further Integration*, EED report 6, Fridtjof Nansen Institute, Lysaker, Norway.

Dahl, A., 1997, National freedom of action in EU environmental policy: The cases of Denmark and the Netherlands, *Environmental Politics*, **6**(3):68–98.

Drottz-Sjöberg, B.M., 1996, Stämningar I Storuman efter folkomröstningen om ett djuptförvar, SKB, Stockholm, Sweden.

Drottz-Sjöberg, B.M., 1998, Stämningar I Malå efter folkomröstningen 1997, SKB, Stockholm, Sweden.

Dua, A., and Esty, D.C., 1997, *Sustaining the Asia Pacific Miracle: Environmental Protection and Economic Integration*, Institute for International Economics, Washington, DC, USA.

Economist, 2000, To Plant or Not to Plant, 15 January, pp. 30–31.

Esty, D.C., and Mendelsohn, R., 1998, Moving from national to international policy, *Policy Sciences*, **31**:225–235.

Giddens, A., 1985, *The Nation-State and Violence*, Volume 2 of *A Contemporary Critique of Historical Materialism*, Polity Press, Cambridge, UK.

Hasenclever, A., Mayer, P., and Rittberger, V., 1997, *Theories of International Regimes*, Cambridge University Press, Cambridge, UK.

Held, D., 1995, Democracy and the new international order, in D. Archiburgi and D. Held, eds, *Cosmopolitan Democracy. An Agenda for a New World Order*, Polity Press, Cambridge, UK.

Held, D., McGrew, A., Goldblatt, D., and Perraton, J., 1999, *Global Transformations*, Polity Press, Cambridge, UK.

Hiltz, C., and Ehrenfeld, J.R., 1991, Transboundary movements of hazardous waste: A comparative analysis of policy options to control the international waste trade, *International Environmental Affairs*, **3**(1):23–63.

IPCC (Intergovernmental Panel on Climate Change), 1996, *Climate Change 1995: The Science of Climate Change*, Cambridge University Press, Cambridge, UK.

Jackson, T., 1998, Joint implementation and cost effectiveness under the Framework Convention on Climate Change, *Energy Policy*, **23**(2):117–138.

Klingemann, H.D., and Fuchs, D., 1995, *Citizens and the State*, Oxford University Press, Oxford, UK.

Krasner, S., ed., 1983, *International Regimes*, Cornell University Press, Ithaca, NY, USA.

Kristoferson, L., 1994, *Beauty and the East: An Evaluation of Swedish Environmental Assistance to Eastern Europe*, Stockholm Environment Institute, Stockholm, Sweden.

Kunreuther, H., Easterling, D., Desvousges, W., and Slovic, P., 1990, Public attitudes toward siting a high-level nuclear waste repository in Nevada, *Risk Analysis*, **10**(4):469–484.

Levy, M, Young, O., and Zurn, M., 1994, The Study of International Regimes, WP-94-113, International Institute for Applied Systems Analysis, Laxenburg, Austria.

Lidskog, R., 1997, The reinvention of politics? Science and politics in the development towards sustainability, in *Science Ethics and Sustainability: The Responsibility of Science in Attaining Sustainable Development*, Uppsala University Press, Uppsala, Sweden.

Linnerooth-Bayer, J., 1990, The Danube River basin: Negotiating settlements to transboundary environmental issues, *Natural Resources Journal*, **30**(3):629–660.

Linnerooth-Bayer, J., and Murcott, S., 1996, The Danube River basin: International cooperation on sustainable development, *Natural Resources Journal – International River Basins*, Summer edition, Part 2, **36**(3):631–657.

Linnerooth-Bayer, J., and Fitzgerald, K., 1996, Conflicting views on fair siting processes: Evidence from Austria and the US, IIASA Symposium on Fairness and Siting, Special issue of *RISK: Health, Safety and Environment*, **7**(2):119–134.

Löfstedt, R.E., 1995, What factors determine Sweden's provision of environmental aid to Eastern Europe?, *Global Environmental Change*, **5**(1):41–49.

Löfstedt, R.E., 1996a, Fairness across borders: The Barsebäck nuclear power plant, *RISK: Health, Safety and Environment*, **7**:135–144.

Löfstedt, R.E., 1996b, Risk communication: The Barsebäck nuclear plant case, *Energy Policy*, **24**(8):689–696.

Löfstedt, R.E., 1997, Evaluation of siting strategies: The case of two UK waste tire incinerators, *RISK: Health, Safety and Environment*, **8**:63–77.

Löfstedt, R.E., 1998, Transboundary environmental problems: The case of the burning of coal in Poland for heating and electricity purposes, *Global Environmental Change*, **8**(4):329–340.

Löfstedt, R.E., and Sjöstedt, G., 1995, Environmental aid to Eastern Europe: problems and possible solutions, *Ambio*, **24**(6):366–370.

Löfstedt, R.E. and Sjöstedt, G., eds, 1996, *Environmental Aid Programmes to Eastern Europe: Area Studies and Theoretical Applications*, Avebury, Aldershot, UK.

Majone, G., 1985, The international dimension, in H. Otway and M. Peltu, eds, *Regulating Industrial Risks*, Butterworths, London, UK.

Majone, G., 1996, *Regulating Europe*, Routledge, London, UK.

McHugh, P.D., 1994, The European Community Directive – An alternative environmental impact assessment procedure?, *Natural Resources Journal*, **34**:589–628.

Miller, M., 1995, *The Third World in the Global Environmental Politics*, Open University Press, Buckingham, UK.

Milich, L., and Varady, R.G., 1998, Managing transboundary resources, *Environment*, **40**(8):10–15, 35–41.

NRC (National Research Council), 1989, *Improving Risk Communication*, National Academy Press, Washington, DC, USA.

NRC (National Research Council), 1996, *Understanding Risk*, National Academy Press, Washington, DC, USA.

Renn, O., Webler, T., and Kastenholz, H., 1995, Procedural and substantive fairness in landfill siting, *RISK: Health, Safety and Environment*, **7**(2): 1171–1184.

Royal Commission for Environmental Pollution, 1998, *Setting Environmental Standards*, Her Majesty's Stationery Office, London, UK.

Salay, J., 1991, *Östeuropas miljö Problem och Framtidsutsikter*, Naturia, Stockholm, Sweden.

Salay, J., 1996, *Electricity Production and SO₂ Emissions in Poland's Power Industry*, Department of Environmental and Energy Systems Studies, Lund, Sweden.

Sjöberg, L., 1999, Risk perception in Western Europe, *Ambio*, **28**(6):543–549.

Sjöstedt, G., ed., 1993, *International Environmental Negotiation*, Sage, Beverly Hills, CA, USA.

Skjaerth, J.B., 1994, *Institusjonell effektivitet i internasjonalt versus overnasjonalt miljosamarbeid*, EED Working Paper 3, Fridtjof Nansen Institute, Lysaker, Norway.

Slovic, P., 1987, Risk perception, *Science*, **226**:280–285.

van der Heijden, H-A., 1997, Political opportunity structure and the institutionalisation of the environmental movement, *Environmental Politics*, 6(4):25–50.

Victor, D.G., Raustiala, K., and Skolnikoff, E.B., eds, 1998, *The Implementation and Effectiveness of International Environmental Commitments*, MIT Press, Cambridge, MA, USA.

Weiss, E.B., and Jacobson, H.K., 1996, Why do states comply with international agreements? A tale of five agreements and nine countries, *Human Dimension Quarterly*, 1(1):1–5.

World Bank, 1993, *Environmental Action Programme for Central and Eastern Europe*, World Bank, Washington, DC, USA.

Address by Birgitta Dahl, Speaker of the Swedish Parliament

How Can Transboundary Environmental Risk Studies Contribute to Regional Cooperation to Minimize Threats to Health and the Environment?

Based on my experience in environmental policy as former minister for environment, as a member of the Nordic Council, and as acting chair of the High Level Advisory Board on Sustainable Development to the Secretary-General of the United Nations (UN), I would like to give some views on the contribution of transboundary risk studies, based on advanced scientific verification and agreed methods of measurement, to regional cooperation. I think we can divide the possible contributions into three categories: The first is the value of the process of transboundary studies itself. This process should have the effect of creating networks of experts and of helping to unify data collection and measurement in the participating countries.

The second category is the contribution to the political decision-making process. Clearly, risk studies make no sense unless they lead to concrete policies, and these have to be decided on by the political bodies, often in conflict with partial interests such as those of various branches of industry, etc.

The third category is reaching to the public to create support for necessary measures that may be unpopular in the short run. In one of our Nordic studies – "The Nordic Environment," from 1993 – great efforts were made to present the data in diagrams so that an easily grasped visual presentation could be given to the media and to schools. Public support is necessary in any democratic system, not least to counteract campaigns from various interest groups who see some environmental proposals as a threat to their interests.

A good example of an in-depth study of environmental risks that came to be used extensively in the international field is Professor Bert Bolin's report on acid rain, which was part of the preparatory work for the UN Conference on Environment and Development in Stockholm in 1972. Likewise, the Intergovernmental Panel on Climate Change (IPCC) led by Professor Bolin played a strategic role before and after the Rio Summit in 1992 and in the successful negotiations leading to the UN Framework Convention on Climate Change.

With the signing of the Helsinki Convention in 1974, the work for the protection of the environment of the Baltic Sea Area entered a new stage, and the monitoring work of HELCOM (the Helsinki Commission) has been an essential part of the implementation of its decisions at the ministerial level. This work entered a new, more ambitious stage with the commitments made at the meeting in Ronneby in 1990, leading to the report of the Task Force, which identified more than 100 environment risk zones, so-called hot spots, in the area and suggested how to address them and with what priorities.

Many environmental studies have also been conducted as a part of Nordic cooperation, and we have had some experience of their contribution to relevant measures. For instance, the Nordic conferences on air pollution in 1986 and on pollution of the sea in 1989 were preceded by comprehensive reports to the public.

The Nordic example is valuable from another aspect as well. The Nordic Convention of Environmental Protection establishes that responsibility for the environment does not stop at national borders, but also embraces the other Nordic countries.

The more project-oriented expert cooperation has its framework in the Nordic Council of Ministers' cooperation programs. In 1989 a new program for environmental cooperation was adopted. The actual management of the cooperation program takes place through programs of two to four years' duration within individual sectors. This presumes that joint plans of action are drawn up in areas where measures are likely to support and reinforce each other.

Among these, the Plan of Action for the Control of Marine Pollution has given the reduction of toxic organic matter and nutritive salts the highest priority. It has also implemented strict measures to reduce discharges of toxic metals and oil. The Plan's initial goal is to reduce discharges of nutritive salts and heavy metals to half the 1985 level by 1995. Furthermore, the plan addresses pollution from offshore oil activities, control of pollution from ships, and prohibition of dumping and incineration of waste at sea. The Nordic Council of Ministers have likewise worked out Nordic action plans against air pollution and regarding cleaner technologies, waste, and recycling.

In 1994, the general environment program was replaced by an environmental strategy for the period from April 1994 to March 1996. In this strategy, greater stress was placed on the so-called neighboring regions to promote solutions to environmental problems in the Baltic Sea, Barents Euro-Arctic, and other regions, and to secure international understanding for Nordic environmental and nature conservation policies, especially in relation to the European Union (EU). The strategy also aimed at ensuring that environmental considerations are integrated into other sectors, with a view toward promoting sound development.

In this context, one may ask if such extensive work in the Nordic region, ranging from academic studies to intergovernmental working groups and policy-oriented plans, has really been useful in proportion to the time and effort put into it. To answer such questions, we had the Swedish Agency of Administrative Development (*Statskontoret*) evaluate the Nordic plans of action for air pollution, pollution of the seas, and wastes. The Agency noted that the plans were based on a large number of research and development projects at national and Nordic levels during the 1980s. As to the action plans' relevance to the political decision-making process, it was noted with regret that they had been used only to a very limited extent outside the government offices. The Agency found that the interest in these plans would have been greater had the stated environmental requirements been more specific regarding different sectors. As they were written, the declarations by the Council of Ministers were more relevant for general reference and for defining the moral responsibilities of the governments. These plans of action were best adapted to the political decision-making level, whereas the project activities behind them were of a much more technical nature. A problem of the action plans seems to have been that the goal statements were too fixed to exact numerical values (e.g., percentages, etc.). Yet, environmental goals must be formulated concretely enough to be understood by the general public. It would therefore be better to avoid percentages and concentrate on aims regarding quality that nonetheless express decisions to take ambitious measures.

As to the effects of these action plans on national and international work, the Agency found an obvious interaction between national plans, Nordic plans, and the work within international conventions. Sometimes this has been very useful, such as when we were able to coordinate the emission levels for Sweden's and Finland's pulp industry so that we could avoid distortion of competition. Another example is that sulfur dioxide emissions in Finland have been reduced by 60% till 1990 because this was a Nordic requirement. There have been problems in international cooperation when the Nordic countries have taken different views, and we have found it to be a clear advantage to base our position on a Nordic norm, which creates a common pressure at the international level.

Regarding Eastern Europe in particular, the Agency's evaluation states that much of the long-range air pollution in the Nordic countries originates in Eastern Europe. The establishment of the Nordic Environment Financing Company (NEFCO) has been a constructive way of dealing with these problems. It is of great importance to give the people in these countries an increased consciousness of environmental problems. Otherwise, concrete measures in, for instance, the heavy industrial sector will have only small consequences. There should also be broad cooperation with experts and researchers in Eastern Europe to gain access to their experience and knowledge. It is also essential to examine cost–effectiveness, to work on models for calculating critical load limits, and to include the financing of emission reductions that become necessary in different areas.

Thus it can be noted that the processes of establishing Nordic action plans and creating a common platform for international work have led to a common Nordic view on many environmental questions, which has given us considerable strength in the work with international conventions, such as conventions regarding transboundary air pollution. This Nordic work has also led to a rational distribution of work and resources among those Nordic countries whose resources are always limited.

It is also an advantage in this often slow and laborious process of defining plans of action that one has been forced to reach unified concepts regarding the environment. Ideally, this process would give information about the size of the emission reductions, etc., that would be needed and how they should be distributed among different sources. One tries to do this rationally with both risk evaluation and a view to cost–effectiveness regarding the proposed measures. I have also mentioned the advantage of creating networks in which the interested persons and groups in all the Nordic countries can be involved and can rapidly gain access to all available information. The cooperation and distribution of work in networks of working groups and projects have had a general stimulating effect that may have been more valuable than the actual documents produced.

In conclusion, I should stress that no country can discuss or do anything about its environmental problems in isolation – and this is particularly true for Sweden and the other countries in the Baltic Sea basin. These environmental issues include the problems of the Baltic Sea itself, acid rain, threats from nuclear installations such as Ignalina, Sosnovy Bor, and others, the difficult environmental problems associated with old-fashioned East European industries, and threats from abandoned military installations.

Studying and discussing environmental transboundary threats today is therefore not only interesting but necessary, and it is necessary to do so in an environment of cooperation – between different disciplines and between countries. Environmental problems can only be solved in cooperation and it is important not to stop at the studies, but to go ahead to solutions and to the policies and investments that may be needed.

As a last example of what a study based on solid and convincing evidence can accomplish, I would like to mention that scientific studies by experts from the United Kingdom and the Nordic countries – that is, from countries causing emissions and countries being hit by them – led to a change of opinion on the part of Prime Minister Margaret Thatcher regarding climate change, which she presented at a climate conference in 1990 in what I believe was her last public appearance before her resignation.

Risk analyses, scientific facts, and good measurements are thus very important instruments, but we all know that they cannot give exact estimates and thus liberate decision makers from the responsibility of making decisions. There is almost never an absolute truth. In a democracy, it is the citizens and their elected representative who have the responsibility. Risk analyses and facts are good instruments when we strive to live up to this responsibility, but in the final analysis the responsibility rests with us.

Index